HORACE WHITE, NINETEENTH CENTURY LIBERAL

Joseph Logsdon

CONTRIBUTIONS IN
AMERICAN HISTORY
NUMBER 10

Greenwood Publishing Corporation
Westport, Connecticut

FOR MARY

Library of Congress Catalog Card Number: 77–105982
SBN: 8371–3309–2

Greenwood Publishing Corporation
51 Riverside Avenue, Westport, Connecticut 06880

Printed in the United States of America

Courtesy Chicago Historical Society

Horace White (1834–1916)

As Editor of the *New York Evening Post*

Contents

vii

Acknowledgments

PART of the leisure needed to conduct this study was made possible by grants from the University of Wisconsin and Louisiana State University in New Orleans. Horace White's daughters, Mrs. John Mead Howells of New York and Miss Amelia White of Santa Fe, New Mexico, allowed me to use their father's papers which had remained in their possession. For this generosity and for the complete freedom of their use, I am very grateful. The opinions and suggestions of those who kindly read the manuscript are evident in the biography. Matthew T. Downey, Stanley I. Kutler, Robert H. Irrman, and Helen Richardson provided important information and insights. To Richard N. Current, who suggested this study, I am especially indebted. His criticism, encouragement, and keen judgment were invaluable. My wife's enduring contribution is acknowledged in the dedication. The special role of David Levy, who helped at every point of the project, could perhaps be acknowledged only on the title page itself.

Introduction

In 1912, Horace White, then an old man, finished writing a biography of his contemporary and friend, former Senator Lyman Trumbull of Illinois. The look backward into the previous century had brought him to an unexpected conclusion. In the evening of his life, he felt compelled to admit in the book's preface that Andrew Johnson had charted the proper course for the nation after the Civil War. For most historians in the early twentieth century, this admission posed no difficulty; none of the reviewers, certainly, found any special meaning in his candor. But for Horace White the preface was a confession, a confession which, he explained to a curious friend, was "good for the soul."

In many ways, the preface of White's biography of Lyman Trumbull could serve as an introduction to his own life's history. His reappraisal of Andrew Johnson was more than a casual remark. As editor-in-chief of the *Chicago Tribune* over four decades earlier, White had led the attack on Johnson and unfurled the banners of a radicalism that threatened to make a "frog pond" of Mississippi. The victory over Johnson in 1866 had been the culmination of a dedicated antislavery career. Thus, his confession meant more than historical honesty; it implied a serious reconsideration of his own early life.

White's disillusionment had actually started well before 1912; as early as the 1870s he began to feel that leaders in the United States had gone astray. Together with an important but beleaguered band of nineteenth-century American Liberals, White viewed the postwar nation with growing pessimism and alarm. His feeling of victory after the Civil War was followed by a gnawing sense of defeat. This pattern of elation and discouragement reveals much about American history in the late nineteenth century; for, although White was a relatively obscure figure, he was closer than most men to the public issues and personalities of his day. As a young man he had rubbed shoulders with John Brown and other militant Free-Soilers and had assisted in the rapid rise of Abraham Lincoln and the Republican party. As an older man—living longer than most of his generation of laissez-faire liberals—he remained active in more than a dozen major and minor crusades.

Many nineteenth-century journalists were more than just professional newspapermen. Like White, they were composite creatures—politicians, scholars, public advisers and critics. From the Lincoln-Douglas debates to the anti-imperialist crusade, White not only observed but participated in the major movements of his day. Viewing events from his perspective is revealing, not only because he was frequently an important and active agent, but also because he wrote almost daily commentary and analysis for a half-century. Unlike Congressmen, often removed from their constituencies in the relatively isolated national capital, White watched events from two of the nation's most dynamic cities, and the interaction of social and economic forces on contemporary political questions was often much clearer in Chicago and New

York than it was in Washington, D.C. The rise and fall of Radical Republicanism as well as the disillusionment of nineteenth-century laissez-faire intellectuals may become much more understandable viewed from the world of Horace White than from the worlds of Charles Sumner or Grover Cleveland.

HORACE WHITE,
NINETEENTH CENTURY
LIBERAL

1

A Young Man
and a New Town

HORACE White was a product of New England. He was born in Colebrook, New Hampshire, on August 10, 1834. Yet he knew little of the place of his birth and never considered himself a New Englander, for he was only an infant when his father, Horace White, a twenty-six-year-old Dartmouth physician decided, with a small band of townsmen, to move to the midwestern prairies. But his youth might just as well have been spent in New England, because the men who set out from Colebrook transplanted the Northeast in the Old Northwest. The New Hampshire band followed an oft-repeated pattern of corporate migration. They formed the New England Emigrating Company, pooled their resources, and sent an advance party out to stake a claim and make arrangements for others to follow.[1]

Horace White, Sr., led the advance party. Furnished with necessary funds and the company sleigh, he set out in the winter of 1836 across the northern shore of Lake Erie to Detroit. From there he went on to Chicago and then scouted an area that today includes eastern Iowa, southern Wisconsin,

and northern Illinois. After joining two other members of
the company and inspecting several sites with them, he decided to purchase one-third of the twenty thousand-acre claim
of a shrewd New England speculator, Caleb Blodgett, located
at the convergence of the Rock River and Turtle Creek, just
above the northern border of Illinois. The doctor made a
sound, hard-headed decision. He chose an area that held
groves of solid oak, good soils, a fine gravel quarry, and plenty
of pure fresh water. He must have found, too, that the Rock
River Valley had a New England look that would make his
townsmen feel quite at home. Leaving his two comrades to
prepare the area for cultivation, the young physician returned
to Colebrook in April, 1837, to start the colony westward. On
arrival, he found the awaiting pioneers "in good spunk."[2]

New England came. One by one the members of the company trickled into the new settlement after long, hazardous
trips. The uprooting must have proved difficult for Dr.
White, for he had last minute hesitations. "I find it hard to
resist the various importunities to remain to renew my practice," he wrote.[3] His wife had brought another son into the
world while he was gone. But opportunity lay in the West.
In November he went back to the new settlement and arranged
quarters for his family.

After the spring thaw in 1838, Dr. White, his pregnant wife,
and their two infant sons left New Hampshire. Boats took
them over the longest stretch of the trip (from Albany to Chicago) by way of the Erie Canal and the Great Lakes. A wagon
carried them over the last but most hazardous leg of the
journey. Mud and swamps forced them to walk much of the
distance over a primitive road. The ninety mile journey from
Chicago to the settlement could take more than a week; and
the trek often had to be repeated by members of the colony,
since Chicago for the first years was their depot for eastern
mail and supplies.

The risks and hardships of the frontier did not last long.

Indians were never a problem. They had been driven north by troops several months before the emigrants arrived, and the organized effort of the New Englanders ameliorated the worst features of frontier living. The White family lived in a one-room shanty by the Rock River, but only for a short time. The very first year, the city fathers built a sawmill and the people abandoned their log cabins. Neat white board houses, arranged in carefully laid-out plots, took the place of the ugly log shanties. Mrs. White made her own soap and candles, but the bulk of the family's supplies came to them commercially. Specialization developed quickly: carpenters, innkeepers, merchants, lawyers, mill hands, commercial farmers, real-estate agents, tailors, teachers—all played a part in the first years of town life. Schools were in operation from the start, and the road designated "College Street" suggested even more ambitious plans. The founders of the settlement were realistic, business-minded New Englanders. They never pretended to come West for religious or political reasons; neither were they indigent squatters. They came West for better lands and better living conditions. By 1839, in two short years, they had constructed a thriving village of two hundred people—Beloit.

Dr. Horace White played one of the major roles in the birth of the new town. He handled the company's finances, arranged for the survey of lands, and directed the apportionment of farms and village plots. Later he donated sections of his own large landholdings for village parks and attended to the building of the first schoolhouse. In 1840 he contributed largely to the construction of the first meetinghouse by allowing his patients to convert their medical bills into materials and services for the stone building. He saw the church completed but lived only a few weeks to enjoy it; unfortunately for the town and his family, he died a young man. The rigors of a doctor's life in a frontier region, where he had to drive long distances in all sorts of weather, cut him off at the early age of thirty-three. He was buried on Christmas Day, 1843, nine days before the dedication of the church he had done so much to build. He had received only a small return on his large investment of money and energy in the building of a community. But the investment was not wasted: what he left behind would make a mark on his son.[4]

Horace White, Jr., knew little of his father. He was only nine years old when the doctor died. The father he remembered best was Samuel Hinman, whom his mother married in 1845. Hinman, a widower with four children, took his new wife and her four to his farm at Prairieville, Wisconsin, about twenty miles west of Milwaukee. Deacon Hinman was a stern Puritan, a pillar of several early Presbyterian churches in Wisconsin.[5] The religious atmosphere of his home was new for the White children. Their father had been "sceptically inclined." True, he had "come forward" during the great revival of 1840, and subsequently he had joined and supported the Congregational church.[6] Yet he never had baptized his children. The deacon saw to that in 1846 and thereafter raised the children in a rigorous Calvinistic persuasion. The theater, the circus, dancing, cards, or tenpins he labeled the tools of Satan. Temperance was his rule and pious language his law. The reading of novels was anathema, for it could lead his children to falsehood. Nevertheless, young Horace read *The Arabian Nights* on the sly, as he afterwards confessed. The Episcopalians under the hill, he recalled, were considered "on slippery ground" for reveling in such dangerous things as dancing and fiction. "Unitarians, universalists and free thinkers were classed together as infidels. That the Roman Catholic church was the scarlet woman of Babylon we had no doubt."[7]

Horace White and his new family stayed on the Prairieville farm for only two years. In 1848, Deacon Hinman, who had been a trustee of Beloit College since late 1845, returned to Beloit with his charges to supervise the building of the first college edifice. If Horace White's father and his New Hampshire associates had laid the economic and social foundations of Beloit, his stepfather and a later wave of New Englanders managed the town's religious and cultural life. The professional practitioners of Calvinism usually followed on the heels of the Yankee exodus. They guarded vigorously against "the painful tendency on the part of a great portion of the emigrants from the East, to throw off the restraints of the religion of their fathers." The area around the town, in Wisconsin and Illinois, was a homogeneous Yankee locale. It was "a land which Providence seemed to have reserved to become the New-England of the Northwest." Deacon Hinman and other guardians of an orthodox Puritan faith moved with a firm hand to make the most of such fertile territory. In 1844 a group of local Congregational and Presbyterian leaders met at Beloit and determined to found a college which would strengthen their gains in the surrounding area. Such a college in Beloit, while satisfying the demand of the community for higher education, would also insure its religious tone and supply the churches with needed clergy.[8]

When the New Hampshire founders plotted a "College Street," they probably had Dartmouth in mind. But it was Yale that became the model for higher education in Beloit. A majority of the clerical incorporators, including the major figure, Samuel Peet, had graduated from Yale. After Deacon Hinman supervised the completion of the first building, the two man faculty—Jackson J. Bushnell and Joseph Emerson, both Yale alumni—began their classes. The president of the college, A. L. Chapin, was a Yale alumnus too. Yet if Yale had stamped a certain homogeneity on the new college, it had also lent an unmistakable mark of excellence as well.[9]

Horace White, at the age of fifteen, entered the third class of the college in 1849. Stints in various grammar schools in Beloit provided him with an elementary education. An academy run by a former New England schoolmaster, Sereno

T. Merrill, gave Horace and other fortunate youths the training necessary for college. Merrill grounded them in algebra,
English grammar, and geography, and drilled them in the
basic reading skills of Latin and Greek, languages which were
vital for the classical curriculum of the college. The academy's
program, by design, prepared Mr. Merrill's boys for the college entrance examinations, which Horace White and three
other young men passed in 1849.[10]

After passing the examinations, the four lads signed a simple
covenant with their Puritan college:

> Being admitted a regular Student in Beloit College, I hereby
> acknowledge myself to pursue faithfully the studies and obey the
> laws of the Institution.[11]

Horace was not an exceptional student, but he tried to satisfy
the first pledge of his covenant. By now the faculty had grown
to five, and they offered an education almost unobtainable
elsewhere in the Northwest and comparable to instruction in
the East. Classics formed the core of instruction for literature,
philosophy, and history; there were neither modern languages
nor any elective courses. Mathematics and a smattering of
the natural sciences rounded out the curriculum. President
Chapin, in the senior year, taught the political economy of
Frances Wayland.[12] This pattern of instruction was Yale's
and substantially that given to every gentleman of the age.
The curriculum, in fact, differed only slightly from that taught
to gentlemen for several centuries.

Horace had some difficulties with the second pledge of his
covenant—"to obey the laws" of the college. The Democrats
in the territorial legislature, fearing the Know-Nothing sentiments of some of the founders, had softened the religious
appearance of the college by inserting some non-sectarian
provisos in the charter of 1846.[13] Nevertheless, Beloit remained a Puritan camp. Calvinistic laws, written and un-

written, ruled the college and the town. To students, President A. L. Chapin, as well as many of his faculty, seemed aloof and frequently preoccupied. Once in college and away from home, Horace rebelled against the brittle code of ethics. Precocious enough to maintain satisfactory grades without serious study, he quickly formed a prankish companionship with a fellow student, Jonas Bundy. Another classmate, Asher Curtis, recalled the two as poor scholars but "decided Ladies' men . . . greatly petted in the community."[14] In his second year at college Horace's rebellion took a more serious turn. He refused to keep a tidy room. He took to smoking tobacco and then to drinking liquor in his room and in town hotels. Finally, in the second term, after exercising some patience, the faculty agreed that the recreant, "having been guilty of intemperance, gaming, falsehood and being under the imputation of theft," should be suspended until the spring vacation. One can only imagine the reaction of Horace's stepfather, who was not only a college trustee but a temperance advocate and a model of virtue.[15]

President Chapin resolved to save the stepson of the deacon and the son of the town's founder. To the president it seemed that Beloit, although a small town of only two thousand persons, provided too many temptations for young White. A rural environment would be better. Chapin found a minister in Genesee, Wisconsin, the Reverend Charles W. Camp, who could keep Horace abreast of his class in studies and at the same time keep him out of trouble.

The change of environment wrought no miracles. Horace still smoked and continued to saunter idly about, treading on "the stepping stones to the temple of vice." His guardian treated him gently but viewed the task of redemption pessimistically. After a few weeks he "saw no great hope as yet —save in the converting grace of God." A stay of six months, however, bolstered the weak hope of the Reverend Mr. Camp and bore out the faith of President Chapin. Horace gave up smoking "as something boyish and foolish." His guardian attributed the change to "the influence of the Holy Spirit upon his heart." Although the lad did not "come forward" during any of Camp's frequent revivals, the minister felt that Horace was "not far from the Kingdom of God." When he returned his charge to President Chapin, Camp felt that although the youth still showed an "indolent disposition— a wish to get along superficially," he had nonetheless grown in "manliness and self-respect" and had begun to gain the "power of self-government." The minister was confident that the young man could suppress "those evil habits wh'c have so nearly wrought his ruin."[16]

To insure that Horace had finished sowing wild oats, Deacon Hinman made him live at home while finishing college. The rebellion was over; Horace completed his last two years without incident. The Reverend Mr. Camp had also managed to keep him up in his studies so that his grades did not suffer when he returned to his former class. He graduated with them in 1853.

Horace White had experienced a privileged youth. Few of his generation in the Northwest received the education of a gentleman. The frontier did not produce everywhere an egalitarian society; not all frontiersmen fitted the image of Daniel Boone. Horace White's family could not be considered wealthy, but they lived well. His mother's inheritance of her first husband's land established Deacon Hinman as a leading real estate agent in the region. Deacon Hinman, in turn, shared the bounty with his family. He provided two female Irish servants for his wife and college educations for his five sons. Horace White, a college-educated, New England-bred Protestant, stood apart from a vast majority of people in the Northwest. He was one of the "best people," as he and others often referred to themselves.

Quite naturally, even before he had reached political maturity, he considered himself a Whig. From the very beginning, Beloit proved a stronghold of Whig sentiment in the Democratic Northwest. The New Englanders of Beloit set themselves off from Southern emigrants who settled the mining regions of Wisconsin at the west and from the European emigrants who filled the Wisconsin cities at the east. The embroilment of the college charter in the territorial legislature in 1846 aired the political animosities and antipathies that existed between them and the other settlers of the Northwest. Likewise, when the legislature granted the charter for the University of Wisconsin, the Beloit faculty doubted the wisdom of such secular and egalitarian education as would be provided in a free, state-run university open to all. To the leading citizens of Beloit, Jacksonianism was nonsense.[17] Horace White recalled the bonfire built on the main street of Beloit to celebrate the election of William Henry Harrison in 1840. He grew up with the "clear conviction that Whigs were more respectable than Democrats." "That was the only difference," he reminisced, "that we recognized."[18]

New issues modified this easy political distinction before Horace White was old enough to vote. The year 1848 brought a crisis, particularly for Wisconsin: Congress that year made it a state. The focus of politics, thereafter, shifted from territorial matters to national complexities. For the first time the youth listened to public debates on slavery.[19]

Many of the Beloit settlers looked on slavery as a social and moral evil; some, like Deacon Hinman, were even abolitionists. From his stepfather Horace received abundant antislavery literature, but generally the town fathers purposely played down the issue. They had fostered a delicate balance between Presbyterians and Congregationalists. In 1840, Stephen Peet guided the formation of the Presbyterian and Congregational Convention of Wisconsin. This association was able to heal locally the rupture between the two faiths that had occurred nationally in 1837. Stephen Peet knew better than anyone else that abolition sentiment could throw his fragile coalition apart and wreck any concerted missionary efforts. Although an abolitionist himself, Peet admitted that he could not even hint at his convictions in the lead-mining region of southwestern Wisconsin, where he found many former slave owners from the South. Abolition also opened the door to "Oberlinism," which the minister feared most of all. "Oberlinism was inclined," Peet's biographer wrote, "to emphasize abolition, arminianism and evangelism and would bring discord to the Convention." When Peet and other members of the convention decided to found a college in Beloit, they had the president of Lane College in their midst to remind them of the disruption that could be inspired by antislavery activists. Peet and others were determined that they would not have another Oberlin on their hands. Even with all their care, some people in Beloit still withheld their pledges for the college and stalled its construction, fearing that abolition would take root in the institution. Beloit College, therefore, when finally built, remained conservative on the antislavery issue.[20]

Politics in 1848 took the delicate issue out of the hands of the city fathers; antislavery activity became respectable and widespread in Wisconsin. Speakers flooded into Beloit, many of them maverick Democrats who had never dreamed of setting foot in that Whig town. Fourteen-year-old Horace White and the boys of Mr. Merrill's school joined the processions, lifted banners, and shouted the magic words of "Free Soil, Free Speech, Free Labor, and Free Men."

This first national explosion of antislavery sentiment, White claimed, had made him feel as though he were experiencing a "new birth." At this point, he determined to enter journalism so as to continue the fight. And with this resolution in mind, he entered college the next year. His college life did not demonstrate any continuing zeal, but as soon as he graduated, in 1853, he set out for a journalistic career.[21]

The year of Horace White's graduation was an important year for Beloit: the railroad had finally come. Gone was the dependence on the stagecoach and unreliable roads. In one sense, both of the offspring of Horace White, Sr., had achieved maturity together—the son he never got to know and the town he loved so well. The Galena and Chicago Union Railroad linked Beloit to Chicago and to the world beyond. The railroad was magic; it transformed the future of towns and men. Horace White was one of its first passengers.

NOTES

1. Stewart H. Holbrook, *The Yankee Exodus* (New York, 1950), pp. 112–114. Lois Kimball Mathews, *The Expansion of New England* (Boston, 1909), pp. 240–245. Both books place the New England Emigrating Company within a large setting.

2. Robert P. Crane, "The Early History of Beloit," *Beloit Free Press,* January 3, 10, 1878. Crane was one of the two men who made the first trip to the settlement with Horace White, Sr. Horace White to Alfred Field, May 10, 1837, cited by the *Book of Beloit* (Beloit, 1936), p. 9.

3. Horace White to Alfred Field, May 10, 1837, cited by the *Book of Beloit,* p. 9.

4. Horace White, "The Beginning of Beloit," *Semi-Centennial Anniversary of Beloit College* (Beloit, 1897), pp. 106–107. See also an extended typescript version, "The Founding of Beloit," p. 11, in the Horace White Family Papers and the Beloit College Archives. Robert K. Richardson, *Centenary History, First Congregational Church in Beloit* (Beloit, 1938), p. 12.

5. *Past Made Present, Presbyterians in Wisconsin* (Milwaukee, 1901), pp. 147, 153.

6. Lucian D. Meare, "Historical Address," *Semi-Centennial Anniversary of the First Congregational Church* (Beloit, 1888), p. 35.

7. Baptismal Records of the First Congregational Church of Beloit, July 4, 1846, copied from the notes of Mrs. Robert K. Richardson, Beloit, Wisconsin. White, "Founding of Beloit," pp. 16–17.

8. *First Annual Report of the Trustees of Beloit College,* January, 1849 (Beloit, 1849), pp. 10–11. Robert K. Richardson, "How Beloit Won Its College," *Wisconsin Magazine of History* 26 (March, 1945): 290–306.

9. Edward D. Eaton, *Historical Sketches of Beloit College* (New York, 1928), pp. 31–32. Robert K. Richardson, "The Mindedness of the Early Faculty of Beloit College," *Wisconsin Magazine of History* 19 (September, 1935): 33–34.

10. White, "The Beginnings of Beloit," pp. 108–109. Sereno T. Merrill,

Narrative of Experiences in the Life of Sereno T. Merrill (n.p., 1900), pp. 22–25. See also Horace White to Ellery Crane, May 25, 1897, Ellery Crane MSS, Beloit Historical Society.

11. Matriculation book, Beloit College Archives.

12. Beloit College grade records, Recorder's office, Beloit College. *Catalogue of the Officers and Students of Beloit College* (Beloit: 1850, 1851, 1852, 1853), passim.

13. Robert K. Richardson, "The Non-Sectarian Clause in the Charter of Beloit College," *Wisconsin Magazine of History* 22 (December, 1938): 127–155.

14. Asher Curtis, "Personal," *The Round Table* 38 (September 25, 1891): 12.

15. Beloit College Faculty Minutes (October 15, 25, December 31, 1850; January 2, March 29, September 24, 1851), Archives of Beloit College.

16. Charles W. Camp to A. L. Chapin, October 14, 1851, April 7, 1852, A. L. Chapin MSS, Archives of Beloit College.

17. Richardson, "The Mindedness of the Early Faculty," pp. 32–70. See also in the same journal, Richardson, "The Non-Sectarian Clause," pp. 127–155.

18. Horace White, "An Address," *The Round Table* 50 (February 26, 1904): 171.

19. Ibid.

20. Stephen Peet to Milton Badger, February 24, 1845, Stephen Peet Papers, Archives of Beloit College, copied from the Papers of the American Home Missionary Society, Chicago Theological Seminary. L. E. Murphy, *Religion and Education on the Frontier: A Life of Stephen Peet* (Dubuque, 1942), pp. 57–58, 102. J. Bushnell, "Reminiscences of Early Days and the Financial Affairs of the College," *Quarter-Centennial Anniversary of Beloit College* (Beloit, 1872), pp. 22–24.

21. Horace White, "An Address," p. 171.

2

Armageddon
and El Dorado

ARRIVING in Chicago by rail was an appropriate way for young Horace White to enter the Illinois town. The Galena and Chicago Union Railroad, which brought him there, reached out several months later to the Mississippi, and by 1856 it was joined by four other lines in the race from the lake port to the mighty river. Railroads soon crisscrossed the entire state. Between 1850 and 1856, Illinois built more miles of track than other state in the Union, and most of this construction converged on Chicago.[1] Iron rails stretched out into the hinterland to draw men, money, and material into an explosive, expanding urban complex. Almost any young man in the area with energy and ambition was bound to feel the magnetic draw of the midwestern metropolis.

The railroads had touched off a massive boom. Chicago was growing rapidly. In 1850 not even thirty thousand people lived there,[2] but by 1853 the population had easily doubled and showed no sign of subsiding. Commerce was expanding; real-estate speculation was spurting; and buildings were thrown up to meet the incoming tide of humanity. These were the flush times of Chicago.

Horace White, only nineteen, came to the bustling town with little money and even less experience. But he had a college degree; few others coming to the city could say the same. Little else, apparently, had won him the position that awaited him there. Determined to enter journalism, he had applied for a job to the *Chicago Journal,* the major Whig organ of the region, shortly before his graduation from Beloit College. It was natural that he should look to Chicago, since the weekly newspaper of his home town, the *Beloit News,* presented him with little opportunity for his ambitions. That small operation offered him not much more than his boyhood job of delivering the weekly sheet to homes of its readers. Therefore, when Charles Wilson, owner of the *Chicago Journal,* replied to his letter and gave him a chance to prove his worth, Horace White lost no time in taking up the challenge and opportunity of daily journalism in Chicago.[3]

The easy life and well-planned appearance of Beloit now became a part of Horace White's past. Chaos and confusion ruled Chicago's development. Beneath the new buildings, the sewage system offered little service. Few of the streets were paved, and the wooden sidewalks concealed an expanding population of their own: rats infested the decrepit boardwalks and came out regularly to cavort at night. The appearance of the city amazed and shocked foreign and eastern visitors.[4]

Horace White, nonetheless, did find some congenial surroundings. The family of George Wadsworth, one of his college friends, offered him a place to live, and the Young Men's Christian Society became the center of his social activities. Polite lectures, proper concerts, and popular plays rounded out his entertainment. The particular attraction in 1854 was a dramatic adaptation of Harriet Beecher Stowe's *Uncle Tom's Cabin.* Yet, for all its refinements, Chicago was not Beloit.

True, there were the college-educated and eastern-bred families like the Wadsworths with whom White easily mingled, but the social diversity of the city contrasted sharply with the homogeneity of his hometown. The commercial activity of Chicago had drawn many Irish and German immigrants and attracted American natives from varied areas of the nation. Negroes, although making up less than one percent of the population, dramatized its diversity.[5] In Chicago, the decrepit blighted the new, wealth mocked poverty, and native habits clashed with immigrant folkways. Richard Wilson, the editor of the *Journal,* made this new environment inescapable for Horace White; the editor assigned him to report the daily news of the city.[6]

Sharing his duties with Henry M. Smith, a young man from Massachusetts, White came face to face with the everyday life of Chicago. Each day he listened to the petty crimes brought before the police court, where his knowledge of Latin and Greek did not prepare him for the "several languages" in which the proceedings were sometimes conducted. Fortunately, however, he shared a mother tongue with the McGuires, Reillys, and O'Haras, whose names usually filled the notices of drunken and disorderly behavior. As a reporter, he frequently joined the festivities of St. Patrick's Day parades, fireworks displays, and railroad celebrations. Cholera in 1854 brought some grimness to his task. But most of his reporting consisted of the boring job of collecting the statistics of Chicago's commercial activity. It would have been hard to convince a young reporter that among those numbers of prices and deliveries at the produce markets lay the story of Chicago's fabulous growth.[7]

All of a day's reporting of local affairs seldom exceeded a column or two in the *Journal.* The four-page paper, in fact, was put out by only a three-man editorial staff. Horace White's title of City Editor was somewhat pretentious: the management of the *Chicago Journal* was far more generous with titles than with money. City Editor White received only five dollars a week and that irregularly.[8]

For all the humdrum and unrewarded tasks of early Chicago journalism, occasionally the daily fare was enlivened by a lager beer riot, a barbarous brawl, or a political election. More than likely all three activities occurred together. As there was no registry law in the city, illegal voting could be prevented only by someone challenging a suspicious voter. Since a direct challenge could only be regarded as an insult, and since few Chicagoans of the 1850s felt like ignoring an insult, Horace White witnessed "a good many knockdowns."[9] It was his job to be where trouble was expected and there was plenty of it in Chicago's early political life.

Incidents of fisticuffs at the polling booth usually redounded to the Whig's benefit. At least the Whigs thought so and made the most of each clash. Ignorance and barbarism, the *Journal* frequently lamented, formed the base for Democratic dominance in the city. Charles Wilson, a fanatical Whig of the Thurlow Weed school, ran a highly partisan newspaper. He wrote only occasionally for the paper; but since he owned it, he dictated its editorial policy. "His orders," Horace White recalled, "when he gave any, had to be obeyed."[10] Richard Wilson, the owner's brother, carried the burden of the editorial writing; and he was in full sympathy with his brother's political outlook. Whether White agreed with the proprietor and the editor, he never indicated; but he did pick the *Journal* as the paper with which he wanted to work; and he still considered himself a Whig. Yet his generation of Whig progeny knew little of Henry Clay or Daniel Webster. If the Free-Soil movement had disturbed the workings of the two-party system in his home town of Beloit, Horace White found that it had created chaos in Chicago.[11] Surely the conviction of the *Journal's* editorials belied the confusion of Chicago's politics. Indeed, the *Journal's* peppery partisanship was only a deathbed vigor.

A proliferation of daily newspapers reflected the flux and fragmentation of parties and factions in Chicago. The *Chicago Democrat,* owned and edited by "Long John" Wentworth, vacillated frequently as Wentworth tried to reconnoiter the damaged ranks of the Democratic party before each of his political adventures. Ebenezer Peck, bitter foe of Wentworth, established the *Democratic Argus* in the city "for the sole purpose of making war on his old enemy."[12] The *Democratic Press,* edited by an antislavery pair—William Bross and John Locke Scripps—had difficulty in finding a foothold among the Democrats. Their paper survived the fierce newspaper competition only by publishing the best commercial news in the city. Charles Wilson might scoff at this debacle of the Democratic dailies, but, although no other paper dared lift high the tattered Whig banner, the Know-Nothing *Tribune* of A. J. Stewart won readers away from the *Journal's* following.

The political situation in Chicago must have confused Horace White and most other newcomers to the city. Yet one thing was certain: Stephen A. Douglas was king. He had deservedly won the name "Little Giant" for constructing a formidable power base in the confusion of Chicago politics. Horace White, however, had hardly settled in Chicago long enough to piece together the political puzzle before the whole picture changed. On January 3, 1854, Douglas reported his bill for the organization of the Nebraska Territory.

Announcement of the bill immediately evoked an unprecedented unanimity among Chicago's daily newspapers.[13] On February 8, a mass rally of "Democrats, Whigs and citizens of all shades of politics" met to protest against the breakdown of the Missouri Compromise.[14] The *Journal,* entertaining hopes of a Whig resurgence, pummeled the "Little Giant" daily. A new excitement came to politics in the nation and focused itself on Stephen A. Douglas, the Illinois senator. Though at nineteen still ineligible to vote, Horace White found himself thrust into the center of a political maelstrom.

The Kansas–Nebraska Act caused an astounding outburst of indignation in the North. By allowing settlers in the new territories of Kansas and Nebraska to make the ultimate decision whether they would live in a society of slave or only free labor, Douglas probably hoped to avoid serious Congressional controversy. But he badly miscalculated in judging the public response in the North. The final version of the bill, by expressly repealing the terms of the Missouri Compromise that forbade slavery in the northern region of the Louisiana Territory, broke the bonds of sectional restraint. Douglas may have won some support in the South by giving in to the constitutional doctrine that Congress had no right to keep slavery out of any U.S. territory, but he fatally alienated thousands of former friends in the North. Perhaps nowhere was this condemnation more dramatic than in his own bailiwick of Illinois.[15]

With incredible confidence and daring, Douglas reacted to the criticism in his home state by damning his opponents and initiating a systematic purge of the "abolitionists" from the Democratic party. To counter the cabal of newspaper chieftains aligned against him in Chicago, he helped establish the *Chicago Times* in August, 1854. When he finally returned to Chicago on the evening of September 1—a homeward trip "lighted with his burning effigies"—the senator came face to face with his embittered foes in Cook County. Boldly, he spoke out in defense of the Kansas–Nebraska Act. He bantered with a hostile crowd of ten thousand for over two hours. Finally, after being shouted down whenever he tried to speak, Douglas stormed away from his rostrum, dismissing the debacle as the work of an abolitionist mob bent on spoiling his homecoming.[16] With good reason, he decided not to make another appearance in Chicago. In fact, he made no more speeches in the whole Cook County region during the rest of the 1854 campaign. The Chicago reception was evidently a shock to the Little Giant.

Horace White was a witness to Douglas's embarrassment that evening. Sitting on the platform as a reporter, he had a good vantage point from which to watch the senator's encounter with the hostile audience. Many years later, he recalled that the meeting was "certainly a failure," but insisted that there was no violence and that Douglas's petulance only aggravated an already contentious crowd.[17]

A month later, Horace White met Douglas again, in Springfield, Illinois. The young newspaperman went there to report an expected clash between Douglas and the Whig leader, Abraham Lincoln. Their independently scheduled speeches before the state legislature did not constitute an official debate, but the press had so billed it. In his early dispatches to Chicago, White prepared his upstate Whig readers for coming reports. He pictured the senator as "desponding" and claimed that communities all over the state had turned "the cold shoulder . . . to the small giant." Wherever Douglas went, his presence was "the signal for an upstarting of giants more gigantic than himself, who arm themselves with truth and do fearful battle with Nebraska and its putative father."[18]

White did not allow Douglas to speak for himself; he gave scant attention to his address before the Assembly. Any cheering that the Illinois senator received, White attributed to a "hired gallery of two dozen desperados." The young reporter's particular venom, however, seemed reserved for a "harmless, renegade, doughface Whig, Gen. Singleton," who proclaimed bipartisan support for the Kansas–Nebraska Act. "While eating all the dirt that drops from Douglas," White sneered, "he spreads slime on the name of Henry Clay."[19]

On the following day, Abraham Lincoln answered Douglas's

speech before the same audience. He invited Douglas to attend and reply if he wished. Douglas accepted. Lincoln did not, at first, strike the impetuous Horace White as a giant raised up in the wake of the Kansas bill. In fact, when Lincoln was introduced to White, just before he addressed the Assembly, he left the young reporter totally unimpressed. White recalled the introduction: "I did not expect much of a speech from him."[20]

Before the day was over, however, Horace White had changed his mind. "Lincoln is a mammoth," he wrote back to the *Journal.* "He had this day delivered a speech, the greatest ever listened to in the state of Illinois, unless himself has made a greater. Stephen A. Douglas never in his life received so terrible a back fall. For vigor of thought, strength of expression, comprehensiveness of scope, keenness of argument—extent of research, and candor of presentation, the speech of Mr. Lincoln has rarely been equalled in the annals of American eloquence."[21]

Known as the Peoria speech (Lincoln repeated it there twelve days later), it was one of Lincoln's finest oratorical achievements. His "eloquent arguments on the subject of slavery" and his "stirring appeals" to North and South alike, warning against the further expansion of slavery, overwhelmed the young *Journal* reporter.[22] "The speech of 1854," White recalled late in his life, "made so profound an impression on me that I feel under its spell to this day."[23] White dismissed Douglas's reply with a few sentences: "He immediately launched into a stout Nebraska speech of his own, and left Mr. Lincoln's argument untouched. This was the only course open to him. Lincoln had built a fortress impregnable as Gibraltar. Compared with Abraham Lincoln, Stephen A. Douglas is not discernable with the microscope."[24]

Lincoln left a lasting impression on the *Journal's* neophyte reporter. From that moment, Lincoln became his champion. Not yet a Republican, Lincoln already demonstrated his power to charm the younger generation of antislavery radicals like Horace White and yet hold the allegiance of the more conservative Whigs of his own generation. His success in Illinois politics was, in no small measure, due to this ability. Because of leaders like Lincoln, the Whigs of Illinois retained their deathbed vitality, and with the issue of Kansas, they hoped to rebound to a new life by upsetting the Democrats in the state elections of 1854.

Lincoln, because of his speeches in Springfield and other cities during the campaign, became the overwhelming Whig choice for the Senate seat of Douglas's Democratic colleague, James Shields. White begged Lincoln to come to Chicago to speak in his own behalf for the Senate seat. In his letter, the young journalist expressed the buoyant hopes of the Cook County Whigs for Lincoln's election to the Senate. White must have been very impressed by Lincoln's speech at Springfield. He told Lincoln that if eight to ten thousand other persons in Chicago could hear him speak, "the people will demand of the Representatives to elect a Whig Senator."[25]

Lincoln came to Chicago but coyly calculated his moves for the senatorship. He knew the pitfalls of Illinois politics far better than Horace White. To win behind a coalition of Free-Soilers, anti-Nebraska Democrats, Whigs, Know-Nothings and immigrants was not an easy assignment; but to expect discontented Democrats to vote for an established Whig spokesman was perhaps the most naive of White's assumptions. Nonetheless, Lincoln almost snatched the prize. Teasingly close, the senatorship went instead to Lyman Trumbull, as a handful of insurgent Democrats, led by Norman Judd, stubbornly refused to cast their ballots for Lincoln.

White would remember Lincoln's defeat in the 1854 race as his "first great disappointment in politics."[26] He was slow in forgiving the irreconcilable Democrats—Judd, Palmer, and Cook—for their share in bringing it about. For the Whig party, however, Lincoln's defeat was much more than a disappointment. The loss marked the party's demise. The next statewide election in 1856 found Illinois politics radically changed.

Shortly before Lincoln's defeat in the Legislature, Horace White left the *Journal* to become the General Agent in Chicago for the New York Associated Press.[27] He had abandoned the sinking ship of midwestern Whiggery none too soon; the *Chicago Journal* lost ground steadily in the next few years to antislavery journals which were untrammeled by tattered party traditions. White did not, however, move immediately into the new Republican party. After the November elections of 1854, the excitement of Kansas died down. The lull in 1855 almost seemed to bear out the amoral confidence of Stephen A. Douglas that the country would return its attention from rash antislavery rhetoric to its normal pursuits of speculation and enterprise. The railroad boom continued, indifferent to the turmoil created by the Kansas–Nebraska Act: as the temporary excitement in politics passed, many returned to a full time pursuit of prosperity. Even White left his post at Armageddon, bedazzled by the prospect of bounteous wealth and easy fortune.

White's work for the Associated Press put him in close contact with Circuit Judge John D. Caton, who controlled most of the telegraph lines in Illinois over which White gathered news for the Eastern papers. Overhearing Caton mention that he owned some undeveloped coal lands near LaSalle, Illinois, White proved that those months spent pouring over the commercial prices at the *Journal* office had not been wasted. He tried to interest the wealthy jurist in an ambitious mining operation. Railroad construction promised to open the region to the Chicago market, making the investment a sure thing. White tempted Caton: "I need not tell you there is money in it, with the present everlasting demand and exorbitant price, which will probably not be less, during the lives of either of us."[28]

To reinforce his case with the judge, White called upon his closest friend, Edward Daniels, then the State Geologist for Wisconsin. Daniels, like White, mixed speculative activity with antislavery activism. Daniels was one of the two men who overpowered the guard and released Sherman M. Booth from the Milwaukee Customs House jury room, where Booth was imprisoned for his part in the rescue of a runaway slave named Glover from federal marshals.[29] Daniels received White's call and temporarily resigned his commission in the quest for El Dorado. After making a tentative examination of the bituminous deposits, Daniels excitedly made a joint purchase with White of a quarter section of Judge Caton's coal lands.

Even before the results of the final tests were in, White made use of his newspaper connections to publish an article in the *Journal* hinting at their explorations. "I think this will create a healthy curiosity in the public mind," he wrote to Caton, "and this curiosity can be carried hereafter whenever it may seem expedient." White then spelled it out for the judge in the clearest possible terms: "It may seem best for those who first develop the mine and bring it to market, to dilute the stock to about 10 percent and sell."[30] When Daniels's final report confirmed their hopes for a high-quality coal, White urged the judge to contemplate even greater land purchases. "I tell you there are some great fortunes in that section of the country for those who know how to get at them."[31] The prospects were bright, for demand was high and the judge had railroad friends who could give them good transportation connections to their mine.

Complications, however, ended their hopes for a quick fortune. Another group of enterprising young men held claim to lands that proved the key to any successful mining of the coal deposits in the region. Unsatisfactory negotiations with these men for a consolidation of interests tempered White's initial enthusiasm; mutual distrust between the two parties spoiled his early dreams.[32] By April, 1856, after months of bickering, White thought the whole operation had come out "wrong-side-up," and by May he was ready to give up his plans of cornering the coal market in Chicago.[33]

He turned his attention instead to a swift speculative scheme. He tried to convince Caton that they should organize a watered stock company, sell out quickly, and reap a handsome profit on their first investment. Any attempt to begin actual mining, White felt, would prove "disastrous."[34] Lest the judge feel uneasy about such a scheme, White carefully explained the ethics involved:

> The moral bearings of the question as I understand it to be about as follows: If we put the thing on a paying basis on which it would pay with careful and efficient management we are bound to represent all the facts to whomsoever become the purchasers of the stock we have disposed of and that is all. If they cannot go on and manage the thing as judiciously as we did, they will suffer the consequences of their own stupidity or perverseness just as they suffer it in all other cases. In short the morals of the case do not differ in the least from the morals of the simple transaction of selling out land at LaSalle to anybody who thought he could make money out of it.[35]

White had hardly laid his pen down that day in May, 1856, when the sound of trumpets from Kansas called him back to his post at Armageddon. Fortune would have to wait; the free-state men of Kansas were imperiled. The lull in politics was over. Unlike his forebears, White could not concentrate on frontier wealth and fortune. Word exploded into Chicago that on the evening of May 21 barbarous brigands from across the Missouri border had sacked and pillaged Lawrence, Kansas, center of free-state sentiment in the Territory. However exaggerated the accounts were that reached the North,[36] the Lawrence disaster marked the climax of a series of clashes between the opposing camps in Kansas. Free-Soilers in the North viewed it as the worst indignity suffered by the free-state men. Fraudulent voting by Missourians had forced the free-staters to set up a rival government in Topeka, which President Franklin Pierce refused to recognize. The Topeka band stood helpless as their foes silenced their newspapers, jailed or forced their leaders into exile, and finally left their citadel of Lawrence in ruins.

Edward Daniels, White's friend, had toured Kansas in April, shortly before the Lawrence disaster. Witnessing the increasing violence in the Territory, he warned the readers of the *Chicago Tribune:* "Kansas will never be enslaved, but hundreds of its brave and noble may yet fall before the blast which is preparing on the frontier. Secure some system of organized action."[37] Daniels heard the news of Lawrence back in Wisconsin, and he followed his own earlier advice by helping organize a convention in Madison to secure aid for the free-state men in Kansas. All over the North similiar relief agencies were springing up to meet the call for weapons and supplies.[38] In Illinois, the antislavery men established their group on May 29. White wrote to Daniels that the Illinois band planned to "fit up a military organization in Chicago, and march to Kansas immediately and if we are successful I am going straight."[39] White hoped to join his stepbrother, Moses Hinman, who had been present at the destruction and pillaging of Lawrence.[40] Their father, Samuel Hinman, had sent Moses off to Kansas earlier in the year, outfitting him with a Bible and a Sharps rifle—a combination made famous by the Kansas conflict. On the leaf of the Bible, Deacon Hinman penned his advice: "The Bible for constant use, the Rifle for stern necessity only."[41]

White, along with many other northerners, felt that the condition of Kansas was exactly the kind of "stern necessity" Deacon Hinman had in mind. They demanded armed action and blood if necessary. At a meeting held in Chicago on May

31, to hear free-state leader James Lane, five hundred men and a large sum of money were pledged for the relief of Kansas. A few weeks later, under the auspices of a committee created at that meeting, Horace White left for Kansas among a party of seventy-five armed men from Chicago. Flamboyant reports, which proceeded their journey up the Missouri river, alarmed the proslavery ranks. At Lexington, Missouri, a vigilante band boarded their boat, disarmed them, turned them around, and forced their retreat to Alton, Illinois.[42]

Frustrated and embarrassed by this rebuff and checked by the virtual blockade of the river, the free-state protagonists in the North called for even greater effort. At an executive meeting of the New England Emigrant Aid Company, Andrew Reeder, a former territorial governor of Kansas, proposed the formation of a national organization to coordinate relief measures for free Kansas. This organization, he felt, should raise two million dollars and send five thousand armed settlers into the territory. To carry out Reeder's ambitious proposals, a convention of delegates from the local relief societies met in Buffalo on July 9, 1856.[43]

Abolitionist Gerrit Smith, in a keynote address to the convention, urged the delegates to shed blood if necessary to insure the safety of the "brethren in Kansas." The convention agreed that armed action was necessary and accordingly established the National Kansas Committee, with headquarters in Chicago, to coordinate the activities of the scattered relief societies already in existence. To head the committee, the convention chose Thaddeus Hyatt of New York and selected an executive committee of Chicago residents (J. D. Webster, chairman; H. B. Hurd, secretary; and George Dole, treasurer) to man the central office.[44]

When the Chicago committee returned from Buffalo, they named Horace White to serve as the assistant secretary. He threw himself into the job with enthusiasm. Actually a large part of the Chicago office fell on his shoulders, as the other men of the committee had to watch over their own businesses in Chicago.[45] Unsettled, impetuous, and independent, White had plenty of freedom and energy to give to the job.

His restlessness had just caused the delay of his plans to marry Martha Root, a childhood sweetheart, because her father frowned on their marriage. White's outspoken antislavery opinions probably had little to do with the decision by the Reverend David Root, for the minister was a former agent of the Massachusetts Antislavery Society, and as a patron of Beloit College had tied strong abolitionist provisos to his large contributions. White's failings were of another sort; Root questioned the young man's "religious character and want of regular profession." Yet even this disappointment apparently could not change White's mind; he was determined to throw himself into the free-state cause.[46]

Since Missourians had blockaded the river against free-state arms shipments, the main task of the Committee was to open a land route through Iowa. As the railroads in Iowa extended only a few miles beyond the Mississippi River, the Committee had to buy horses, wagons, and gear. They also had to find stopping places along the way for their projected expeditions. By late August, the Committee finally began to send small shipments of clothes, guns, and provisions to relieve the free-state settlers. White handled the bulk of the correspondence, shipping arrangements, and book work involved in the ambitious project.[47]

The climax of the Committee's operations came in September, when they armed and sent off a semimilitary detachment of about three hundred men to defend the Topeka government. They took this desperate measure only after they had ascertained from a direct interview with President Pierce that he would not change his policy toward Kansas.[48] White's friend Edward Daniels went along with a part of the expedition as one of the commanders. On September 26, Daniels described the entourage to his mother and sister:

I write from my tent 10 o'clock at night. We are in the midst of Iowa pushing rapidly towards Kansas. . . . We march about 25 miles per day and will be in Kansas if we have good success in about 12 days. We have good news from there of peace and quiet. We are very much disposed to rejoice at this for although prepared to fight we do not at all crave the opportunity. We have three artillery and rifle companies and will be joined by other parties till our number reaches 500. . . . The people are very kind here, as we pass they bring us many little luxuries and bid us God speed. . . . Today as I stood addressing the men from the top of a cannon which I had mounted as a rostrum a man came up and addressed me whom I used to know at Oberlin, a very strange meeting that. . . . I am sitting upon the ground writing upon a cartridge box and leaning against a stock of guns. Write me to Lawrence, Kansas, where I hope to be next week.[49]

Fortunately, Daniels and the army never reached Lawrence. Already armed to the teeth with cannon and Sharps rifles obtained in Chicago, the force was bolstered by the generosity of Governor James Grimes, who provided hundreds of muskets from the arsenals of the Iowa militia.[50] The presence of such armaments in the Territory could have seriously aggravated the bloody crisis. Before the army entered Kansas, Governor John W. Geary, only recently appointed, intercepted the force with federal troops and disarmed them.

When word of the capture reached Chicago a few days later, White impetuously condemned Geary's interference as another demonstration of the Federal Government's support of the proslavery forces in the Territory. Receiving this news on the heels of Democratic victories in Pennsylvania, he felt despondent but hoped that the Republicans could redress their losses in Pennsylvania by making some political capital of Geary's capture of the free-state army.[51] White and the Chicago Committee accordingly diverted their attention from Kansas to the national elections. White even planned to "go out on the stump" himself. "There are two or three things," he wrote to the Committee's president, "that I wish to tell the 'Sovereigns' of Illinois before they vote for President."[52]

White saw the whole future of the nation wrapped up in the campaign. A defeat of Fremont he found "in some degree frightful to contemplate."[53] The intensity with which he had thrown himself into the antislavery conflict caused him to espouse a radicalism foreign to his fathers. He belonged to a unique generation of violent middle-class Americans who were willing to use force even against the Federal Government if it remained unsympathetic to their cause.

Although he never shouldered a gun in actual combat, he found vicarious heroes in men like John Brown. He met Brown frequently at the committee offices in Chicago and personally provided him and his sons with Sharps rifles and Navy revolvers.[54] White once boasted to a compatriot that "if Kansas were made of heroes as John Brown, Missouri and the Gen. Government combined would have existed in Kansas at our pleasure. Along the border east of Ossawattomie John Brown is a synonym for all the devils."[55]

White's conclusion that the Federal Government had allied itself with the proslavery forces in Kansas was far too simple. Unenviable as his task was, Governor Geary actually labored hard to avert bloodshed. He slowly neutralized the conflict by an impartial use of federal troops, and with the help of Governor Sterling of Missouri eventually secured free passage of the Missouri River. Four months of open warfare in Kansas thus came to an end; and White's hope to make political capital of Geary's intervention had backfired. The energetic efforts of Geary, which brought pacification of Kansas, undoubtedly aided in Buchanan's victory in November.

Horace White and the National Kansas Committee viewed the turn of events with mixed feelings of relief and frustration. The war had ceased. Yet the money and effort which they had put into military operations and the construction of an

Iowa passage had vanished like smoke.[56] And the failure of the expedition did not rebound to Fremont's election, as they had hoped it would. Their efforts seemed wasted. Even the free-state men had been critical of the committee in Kansas, as the money (more than $100,000) and the clothes and provisions gathered by the National Kansas Committee did little to meet the needs of the actual settlers in the Territory. In letters to the northern press the settlers frequently grumbled over the committee's inefficiency. Their barbs rankled Horace White. Finally he wrote the committee's president in New York, Thaddeus Hyatt, asking to have friendly editors "prevent the people of Kansas from settling their quarrels with each other and our committee in the columns of the New York daily press."

At the same time, White tried to defend himself by explaining the expense and delays involved in opening a land route to Kansas after the proslavery forces made the Missouri River "a highway to sure d——nation." He admitted that his office had, until recently, shipped little clothing and provisions to the settlers but insisted that costly armaments were a much greater priority for the free-state cause in the early months of their operation.[57]

Unless the committee could persuade itself that the dispatch of their military expedition had forced Geary's hand to open Missouri River traffic and neutralize the conflict, there was truth in the charge that the National Kansas Committee accomplished little during its brief existence.[58] After their lavish preparations for the expedition and their excited effort in the presidential contest, the committee was unable to do much more. The fears that brought money and material to their coffers were stilled by Geary's actions.

With the cessation of hostilities, free-state protagonists once more engaged in a race to beat the proslavery forces in sending settlers to Kansas. The Topeka government, counting on a substantial free-state majority, helped insure the peace by devising a strategy of temporary accommodation with the "bogus government" in Lecompton. Horace White explained their general plan to a curious Greeley: "It is proposed to make the 'Constitutional Convention' entirely harmonious . . . and the present plan is to let these gentlemen play out their game in their own way; adopt their Constitution and get it through Mr. Buchanan's Congress if they can; cut loose from the General Government and then break their whole assortment of crockery when we get able. At the present rate of Free State Emigration we shall not have to wait long."[89]

Both Horace White and Edward Daniels turned their energy to this altered phase of the Kansas battle. Their motives consisted of a curious blend of politics, philanthropy, and profit. They no longer had to choose between Armageddon and El Dorado. Daniels, in his new capacity of Agent of Emigration for the National Kansas Committee, arranged group fares for prospective free-state settlers on the railroads and steamships leading to the territory. He also made regular reports of territorial conditions in northern newspapers. His reports were glowing. Kansas, he wrote, offered "magnificient physical resources" and with its central position and vigorous population would soon become a "model commonwealth." "There, if anywhere in the West," he concluded, "life will be surrounded with fine conditions, and enterprise and industry will reap a sure harvest of competence and wealth."[60] Daniels had reason to paint a glowing picture. With White, he planned to purchase a quarter section of Carbondale, Kansas, from Dr. Charles Robinson, who also mixed politics with business.[61] Their hopes must have been running high as property in Kansas reached "fictitious prices."[62]

After filing a claim in Kansas for one hundred sixty acres of the Carbondale townsite and making a preliminary agreement with Robinson in early May, 1857, White returned to Chicago to try once more to unload his coal lands on an unsuspecting buyer.[63] Expecting capital from a quick sale, he got a "cargo of lumber selected and ready for shipment—consisting of flooring, siding, shingles, doors and sash."[64] But tight money in Chicago thwarted his plans; no one wanted his coal lands even at reduced prices. He could not raise the necessary capital for his Kansas adventure. The panic of 1857 was under way. White and Daniels were lucky to be merely inconvenienced by it; in a few months the Kansas bubble burst, ruining hundreds of eager speculators.

White had actually seen for himself the early signs of calamity in Kansas but did not properly interpret their meaning. He reported to the *Chicago Tribune* in May that the early spring had been "a disastrous one for Kansas," as crops contended against the double blows of frost and drought. "No month of March or April," he wrote, "had been so 'boistrous rough.' "[65] The summer brought no relief to Kansas, for the whole nation slumped under a severe economic depression. The crisis ended many a Kansas adventure.

A few months earlier, White might have extended the pattern of his family's westward movement; he might have founded another city like his father before him. But the depression halted his pioneering plans. When Charles H. Ray, editor of the *Chicago Tribune,* asked him to join the editorial staff, the young man was in no position to refuse the offer. Once again his dreams of fortune had faded. He would have to stay in Chicago for awhile. Although he did not know it, he had made a very lucky decision. The real fortunes were to be made in American cities.

NOTES

1. "Illinois in 1856," *Chicago History* 4 (Summer, 1956): 227.
2. Bessie Louise Pierce, *A History of Chicago*, 2:3 (New York, 1940).
3. From an autobiographical typescript of White's first years in Chicago,

p. 1. The sketch is in the Horace White Family Papers (hereafter cited as White, "Arrival in Chicago").

4. Bessie Louise Pierce, *As Others See Chicago* (Chicago, 1933), pp. 141–147, 154–165, 166–170. See also "Chicago in 1856," *Chicago History* 4 (Fall, 1956): 266–274, 276.

5. Pierce, *A History of Chicago*, 2:3, 11.

6. White, "Arrival in Chicago," pp. 1–2.

7. White, "Arrival in Chicago." *Chicago Journal*, January 7, 9, 1854. See also undated autobiographical typescript, Horace White MSS, Illinois State Historical Library.

8. White, "Arrival in Chicago," p. 4.

9. Ibid., p. 9. See also *Chicago Journal*, March 8, 1854, for an example of a report of one such political fracas.

10. White, "Arrival in Chicago," p. 3.

11. Don E. Fehrenbacher, *Chicago Giant* (Madison, Wis., 1957), pp. 102–103, 117–118.

12. Ibid., pp. 117–119.

13. Ibid., pp. 127–128.

14. *Chicago Journal*, February 6, 9, 1854.

15. Ibid., May 26, 1854.

16. The best and certainly the most accurate account of this gathering can be found in Granville Davis, "Douglas and the Mob," *American Historical Review* 54 (April, 1949): 553–556.

17. White, "Abraham Lincoln in 1854," a published address, delivered before the Illinois State Historical Society, January 30, 1908, p. 9. No copies of the *Chicago Journal* for September, 1854, exist today. White's reporting, however, must have particularly irritated Douglas. The angry senator wrote to the editor of the newly formed *Chicago Times:* "Trust the Tribune, Dem. Press, & Chicago Democrats as allies & organ of the great abolition Party. Make no distinction between as respects their politics. This is the course I take in all my speeches. Mr. White is getting more subscribers for you than any other Paper Bus." Stephen A. Douglas to James W. Sheahan, September 14, 1854, as cited in *The Letters of Stephen A. Douglas*, ed. Robert W. Johannsen (Urbana, Ill., 1961), p. 330.

18. *Chicago Journal*, October 5, 1854. White's letter to the *Journal* was dated October 3, 1854.

19. Ibid.

20. White, "Recollection of Abraham Lincoln," *New York Evening Post*, February 12, 1905.

21. *Chicago Journal*, October 9, 1854. White's letter was dated October 4, 1854.

22. Ibid.

23. White, "Lincoln in 1854," p. 11.

24. *Chicago Journal*, October 9, 1854. *Illinois State Register*, October 6, 1854.

25. Horace White to Abraham Lincoln, October 25, 1854, Robert Todd Lincoln Collection, Library of Congress.

26. White, "Lincoln in 1854," p. 19.

27. White, "Arrival in Chicago," p. 4.

28. White to John D. Caton, June 19, 1855, John D. Caton MSS, Library of Congress.

29. Manuscript biographical sketch in the Edward Daniels MSS, State Historical Society of Wisconsin.

30. White to John D. Caton, July 6, 1855, Caton MSS.

31. Ibid., July 31, 1855, Caton MSS.

32. Ibid., November 29, 1855, December 26, 1855, February 19, 1856, April 3, 1856, April 12, 1856, Caton MSS. See also White to John A. Rockwell, January 18, 1856, Rockwell Papers, Henry Huntington Library.

33. White to John D. Caton, April 18, 1856, Caton MSS.

34. Ibid., May 23, 1856, Caton MSS.

35. Ibid.

36. Bernard Weisberger, "The Newspaper Reporter and the Kansas Imbroglio," *Mississippi Valley Historical Review* 36 (March, 1950): 644-646. Weisberger suggests that "it was made to appear that the 'ravagers' of Lawrence left Genghis Khan looking like a new minister," p. 644.

37. *Chicago Tribune,* April 18, 1856. Daniels' letter from Topeka, Kansas, was dated April 8, 1856.

38. Ralph V. Harlow, "The Rise and Fall of the Kansas Aid Movement," *American Historical Review* 41 (October, 1935): 1-25. See also Samuel A. Johnson, "The New England Emigrant Aid Company" (Ph.D. dissertation, University of Wisconsin, 1935), pp. 292-293. Many of the conclusions of this dissertation can be found in an article by Johnson, "The Emigrant Aid Company in Kansas," *Kansas Historical Quarterly* 1 (November, 1932): 429-441.

39. White to Edward Daniels, May 31, 1856, Daniels MSS.

40. *Chicago Tribune,* May 31, 1856.

41. William Smith Hinman to Ellery Crane, December 3, 1910, Crane MSS. William, Moses's brother, copied the inscription from Moses's Bible in this letter to Crane. The combination of a Bible and a Sharps rifle came to be known as a Beecher's Bible, named after Henry Ward Beecher, who was reported as saying in the *New York Tribune,* February 8, 1856, that "the Sharps rifle was a truly *moral* agency, and that there was more moral power in one of those instruments, so far as the slaveholders of Kansas were concerned, than in a hundred Bibles." Cited by W. H. Isley, "The Sharps Rifle Episode in Kansas History," *American Historical Review* 12 (April, 1907): 548.

42. Johnson, "N. E. Emigrant Aid Co.," pp. 259-260.

43. Harlow, "Kansas Aid Movement," p. 15.

44. Ibid., pp. 15-16.

45. White, from an undated autobiographical sketch in the Horace White MSS. He also recalled his assignment to the National Kansas Com-

mittee in a letter to W. H. Isley, June 11, 1906, W. H. Isley MSS, Kansas State Historical Society.

46. White to Edward Daniels, May 31, 1856, Daniels MSS.

47. White to William Barnes, August 25, 1856, September 26, 1856, William Barnes MSS, Kansas State Historical Society. White to Thaddeus Hyatt, November 13, 1856, November 24, 1856, Thaddeus Hyatt MSS, Kansas State Historical Society. White to C. P. Williams, December 8, 1856, Eli Thayer MSS, Brown University. White to Bronson Murray, August 31, 1856, Bronson Murray MSS, New York Historical Society. The records of the National Kansas Committee, like many other documents, were destroyed by the Chicago fire in 1871.

48. Edward Daniels, who with Thaddeus Hyatt and William Arny interviewed Pierce on August 30, 1856, wrote a letter to the National Kansas Committee on September 1. It was published in the *Chicago Tribune,* September 5, 1856. To the question "whether any change in the policy of the Administration is to be expected," Pierce replied: "No Sirs! THERE WILL BE NONE."

49. Edward Daniels to "Mother and Sister," September 26, 1856, Daniels MSS. The expedition has also been described by Robert Morrow, another member, but many years later. See Robert Morrow, "Emigration to Kansas in 1856," *Transactions of the Kansas State Historical Society* 8:302–315.

50. Morrow, "Emigration to Kansas in 1856," p. 305. Richard J. Hinton, *John Brown and His Men* (New York, 1894), p. 56.

51. White to Thaddeus Hyatt, October 20, 1856, October 26, 1856, Hyatt MSS.

52. Ibid., October 24, 1856, Hyatt MSS.

53. Ibid., October 20, 1856, Hyatt MSS.

54. White, undated autobiographical sketch, Horace White MSS. See also White's letters to Brown, January 27, 1857, February 18, 1857, March 21, 1857, in F. B. Sanborn, *The Life and Letters of John Brown* (Boston, 1885), pp. 360–362. In May, 1857, White urged that a brass cannon be delivered to Brown. Horace White to Jonas Jones, May 5, 1857, Horace White MSS. The issue of guns to Brown and his sons is referred to in White's testimony before the Mason Committee in 1860, *Harpers Ferry Invasion* (published by congressional resolution, June 15, 1860), p. 248.

55. White to Thaddeus Hyatt, October 26, 1856, Hyatt MSS.

56. The National Kansas Aid Committee collected over $120,000 in cash and 763 packages of food, according to White in an undated autobiographical sketch in the Horace White MSS. The totals as of January, 1857, were accounted for by White at a convention in New York City and reported in the *New York Tribune* on January 26, 1857. Neither total, however, accounted for the direct shipments of guns that were received. White wrote many years later to W. H. Isley that there were "other expenditures which it was deemed not advisable to publish at that time." White to W. H. Isley, June 11, 1906, Isley MSS.

57. White to Thaddeus Hyatt, October 24, 1856, Hyatt MSS.

58. Harlow, "Kansas Aid Movement," pp. 17–18. Johnson, "N. E. Emigrant Aid Co.," pp. 299–300.

59. White to Horace Greeley, March 31, 1857, Horace Greeley Collection, New York Public Library.

60. *Chicago Tribune,* February 17, 1857. Daniels's letter was dated February 16, 1857.

61. White, undated autobiographical sketch, Horace White MSS. White to Edward Daniels, May 12, 1857, Daniels MSS. White to Charles Robinson, May 15, 1857, Robinson MSS, Kansas State Historical Society. For an account of Robinson's speculations see Johnson, "N. E. Emigrant Aid Co.," pp. 340–341.

62. *Chicago Tribune,* April 23, 1857.

63. White to John D. Caton, May 30, 1857, and June 13, 1857; Caton MSS.

64. White to Charles Robinson, May 15, 1857, Robinson MSS.

65. *Chicago Tribune,* May 20, 1857. White's letter is dated May 11, 1857.

3

The Rise of a Party
and a Paper

THE "WORLD'S Greatest Newspaper," as it proclaimed itself in later years, had humble origins. Under the direction of A. J. Stewart, the *Chicago Tribune* was originally a Whig morning paper with decided Know-Nothing prejudices. After a checkered and unsuccessful run under Stewart, it changed hands and began a long career of joint ownership and direction. In 1855, Charles H. Ray, Joseph Medill, and Charles Vaughn purchased a controlling interest in it. Largely because of Joseph Medill's superlative business sense—particularly his insistence on large capital investments—the *Chicago Tribune* began to show immediate profits. Casting away the anchors of Whig allegiance and Know-Nothing sympathies, the ambitious editors steered their new enterprise into the mainstream of the antislavery movement. Circulation increased; advertising expanded; profits rose. The *Tribune* began to challenge the *Democrat* and the *Times,* then the leading daily papers in the city.[1]

Horace White knew well the potential of the new *Chicago Tribune.* He and his Free-Soil compatriots in Chicago looked upon it as the organ for their sentiments. The National Kansas Committee printed their notices and circulars in the *Tribune* and found easy access in its columns for letters and dispatches from the Kansas Territory. The editor-in-chief, Charles Ray, had tied the success of his paper to the Republican party and was eager to take advantage of each and every disturbance in Kansas. Although Buchanan defeated Fremont in 1856, the *Tribune* won a voice of importance as the Republicans made a thumping statewide victory in Illinois. The young party seemed destined for greater victories; and the *Tribune,* as Chicago's leading Republican newspaper, was prepared to ride on the coattails of its political patron to even greater profits and prosperity.[2]

Horace White must have joined the newspaper with high hopes. Even Charles Wilson's offer of the editorship of the *Chicago Journal* could not induce him to abandon his subordinate role on the *Tribune* editorial staff.[3] He was now connected with a speculation that promised great future rewards as well as a regular and handsome present salary. He found the proprietors, moreover, compatible in outlook and ideas. Charles Ray and Joseph Medill were members of a confident and buoyant business class bent on an expanding economic and ideological empire. They envisioned Republicanism as a solvent for all the ills of the day. Free Soil, Free Labor, and Free Men was the cry of their imperial designs. White shared the editors' confident expectation of victorious Yankee civilization:

> Eli Thayer is the apostle of a new social movement; and we are among his disciples. Organized emigration in the hands of the resolute, shrewd, energetic, hardworking, money loving, and God fearing Yankee race, will prove the social and political regeneration of the Continent. . . . Troops of Yankee men . . . will be the heralds of a higher civilization—the civilization of labor—in Guata-

mala, Honduras, Yucatan, and Nicaragua, as well as in Kansas [,] Missouri, Virginia, and Tennessee.[4]

However high Horace White's dream may have been for his new attachments to the paper and the party, they were quickly shattered by the double blows of economic disaster and political duplicity.

The depression of 1857 hit the *Tribune* hard. Gambling on preeminence among Republican journals in Illinois, the editors had invested heavily in a new Hoe press and the first copper-faced type in the city.[5] The technology of journalism in the past decade had become more efficient but also much more expensive. The economic battle between city newspapers in the nineteenth century, moreover, was particularly fierce. "The over-competition of all the rivals," the *Tribune* bewailed before the depression, "starves and cripples all. The whole pathway of newspaperdom is strewn on either side with the bleaching bones of defunct concerns."[6] Publishing a newspaper, therefore, was precarious business even in prosperous times. The depression doubled the natural hazards; it almost smashed the *Chicago Tribune* completely. Having pulled their way to the top, Ray and Medill suddenly found themselves in a desperate struggle for survival in a panic-struck city.

The early months of 1858 almost stilled the whirling presses of the *Tribune*. As mortgages fell due, creditors cast a foreboding eye towards the paper's predicament. Each day was bringing news of business failures in Chicago. The *Tribune,* a major manufacturer, was by no means immune from the cyclic hazards of American finance. As with most companies, the employees felt the blows of the depression first. Horace White lost his job at the beginning of 1858; the *Tribune* could no longer afford his salary. As there was nowhere else for the young man to turn for employment, he continued to work in the editorial rooms for six months without pay. By living on savings and loans, he hoped to weather the economic crisis.[7] Others in the city, without savings and without sources of credit, were less fortunate. "The number of poor people," the *Tribune* reported, "who throng the Relief Society's rooms for help, continues unabated. We paid a visit yesterday morning and found the room crowded with men, women and children of all ages and conditions."[8]

If the economic disaster were not enough, a political crisis arose which beclouded the future of partisan journalism in Chicago. In the fall of 1857, Douglas staged a party revolt which threatened to crush the *Tribune*'s hopes of gaining financial recovery during the Congressional elections of 1858. Breaking with the administration, Douglas refused to support the Lecompton constitution, which the "bogus" government in Kansas had formed to meet the requirements for statehood. He took a determined stand against the fraudulent methods by which the constitution had been passed. Patronage reprisals by Buchanan only increased his anger and determination. Douglas's bold maneuvering put the *Chicago Tribune* and the Illinois Republicans in a most awkward position.

The *Tribune* editors had aggressively and irreversibly tied the future of their paper to the fortunes of the Republican party in Illinois. They had focused their attacks on the Little Giant. Retreat was impossible; surrender unthinkable. With consternation they watched Eastern Republicans, with Horace Greeley in the lead, soliciting an alliance with Douglas and offering him a haven within the Republican party. The editors were infuriated when Douglas sent feelers for a reconciliation with their paper.[9] Editor-in-chief Ray warned his readers: "He kisses to betray."[10] But other Republicans in Illinois hesitated. They were forced to admire Douglas' heroic posture and admit his new popularity.[11] Even Ray himself finally admitted to being a bit bewildered by it all. In writing to Trumbull, he confessed: "We are almost confounded by his anomalous position and know not how to treat him and his overtures to the Republican party. Personally I am inclined to give him the lash; but I want to do nothing that will damage our cause or hinder the emancipation of Kansas. . . . We are in the dark and need light."[12]

In March, 1858, James N. Sheahan, a Douglas spokesman on the staff of the *Chicago Times,* came to Ray and complicated matters even further. Having just returned from conversations with Douglas in Washington, Sheahan spelled out a surprising proposal. Douglas, he claimed, was willing to step down from the Senate and concede the office to the Republicans, if the Republicans would, in turn, cooperate with anti-Lecompton Democrats "to break the back of Buchanan in every county in Illinois." A Democrat would run for Congress in each of the nine congressional districts, but they expected that the Republicans would win all four northern districts as well as a majority of seats in the state legislature.

With cautious enthusiasm, Ray spread the word of his conversation with Sheahan among Republican leaders in Illinois.[13] The decision on how to react finally rested with Abraham Lincoln. No Republican leader in Illinois, it appears, ever discussed a bargain with Douglas himself; his own views on this matter remain unclear. But Lincoln wasted no time in making up his mind on how to react. "My judgment," he wrote in reply to Ray's letter, "is that we must never sell old friends to buy old enemies. Let us have a state convention," he continued, "in which we can have a full consultation; and till which, let us all stand firm, making no committals as to strange and new combinations. This is the sum of all the counsel I could give."[14]

The Illinois Republicans followed Lincoln's advice. They met in convention on June 16, 1858, at Springfield and prepared to meet the formidable problems which lay before them. Reporting the arrival of delegates to the state capital, Horace White portrayed a mood of urgency in the convention. Republicans had "come up in their might" not only to defeat the local Democrats but also to put "out of joint every meddlesome bone thrust into their dish from abroad."[15]

To accept Douglas into the fold would have ruined the fortune and fame of many Illinois Republicans. The convention instead threw down the gauntlet to the insurgent Democrats led by Douglas and to his pragmatic Republican allies led by Horace Greeley. Without precedent, the convention nominated Abraham Lincoln by acclamation as their choice for the Senate. Never before had a party assembled in Illinois to bind their legislators' selection of a senatorial candidate.[16] But the Republicans felt that this show of unanimity was necessary in the face of outside pressure.

Lincoln, who had urged his fellow Republicans to stay clear of Douglas, keynoted the convention with one of his most famous declarations, the House Divided speech. After he finished the short oration, he went to the editorial rooms of the *Illinois State Journal* to supervise the printing of his speech. There he found Horace White. Lincoln had encountered the young reporter on the speaker's platform and asked him to take the manuscript of his speech over to the *Journal* office in order to proofread the printed copy.

Many years later Horace White would claim that Lincoln told him then that his Springfield friends had urged him not to use the words "this government cannot endure permanently half slave and half free," since the sentence might be misunderstood and misrepresented by conservatives during the campaign.[17] Lincoln felt, however, that his first concern was to undermine the anti-Lecompton glamour of his daring opponent. He was forced by Douglas's action in Congress to take this advanced antislavery posture. In his convention speech, Lincoln accordingly spelled out the Republican design for the eventual extinction of slavery. He knew that Douglas could not stand on this ground, since the Little Giant's doctrine of popular sovereignty floated on an amoral assumption that it mattered little whether slavery was voted up or voted down.

Thus Lincoln with a single bold stroke pointed out that there was something at stake in the senatorial contest.

Lincoln's position, however, would not be easy to defend in the crucial Whig counties in central Illinois where abolitionist sentiments and radical notions were frowned upon. The tension between the importance of Whiggish moderation and the necessity of an advanced antislavery posture would haunt Lincoln throughout the fall campaign. Nonetheless, Lincoln's forceful speech and the convention's unprecedented resolution gave the Illinois Republicans and Lincoln a firm base of action against Stephen A. Douglas. Lincoln and his party had girded themselves for battle as undefiled Republicans.

After the convention, the *Chicago Tribune* met its own problems by a comparably bold maneuver. It merged its staff and equipment with the *Chicago Democratic Press*. With this action, the owners calculated that their combined resources and circulations would enable them to survive the depression and eventually raise their new paper to a prominent position in Chicago journalism.[18] The *Tribune* did not simply swallow up the *Press*. Indeed the *Press* brought a formidable editorial staff, led by William Bross and John Locke Scripps, into the new arrangement and supplied the new concern, the *Chicago Press and Tribune,* with the greater part of its equipment.[19] Though the *Press and Tribune* seemed a promising venture, much still depended on the future of the Republican party in the state. The unity and enthusiasm of the Springfield convention may have raised the editors' hopes; but the battle would still be difficult, and their personal fortunes would remain insecure.

Douglas's warm homecoming on July 9 revealed the precariousness of their position. His trip home in 1858 was far different from his chilling journey to Chicago in 1854. Torchlight parades now replaced the burning effigies of 1854. In Chicago, Douglas received a tumultuous ovation from a gathering quite the opposite from that hostile crowd that White had seen four years earlier. The work of the Republicans and the *Press and Tribune* was cut out for them. It would be an uphill fight.

Lincoln's nomination by the Republican convention enabled his supporters to concentrate their attention exclusively on the two men in the battle for the Senate. Since state legislatures still selected U.S. Senators, party conventions had seldom picked a nominee. The polarity posed by the Republican action made possible the famous debates. On the first day of the appearance of the *Press and Tribune,* an editorial reviewed the "debate" between the two men in 1854 at Springfield and taunted, "if Mr. Douglas cares about repeating the experiment of 1854 . . . we have reason to believe he can be accommodated."[20] Later in the month the challenge was repeated and Douglas's grounds for refusal ascribed to simple cowardice.[21] Since Lincoln had already begun a procedure of following in Douglas's path and refuting the Little Giant's positions, Douglas in early August accepted a limited schedule of seven joint engagements throughout the state.

The newly formed *Chicago Press and Tribune* put White back on a salary and assigned him the task of reporting the campaign. The full resources of the paper were thrown into the fray. Besides hiring White, the editors also engaged Robert Hitt, a shorthand reporter, to give them verbatim transcriptions of the major campaign speeches. In July their investment paid off with a minor victory, as White and Hitt scooped the *Times* with a word for word copy of the early orations by Lincoln, Douglas, and other speakers. After the debates were arranged, the *Press and Tribune* editors had their reporting team cover the seven joint engagements. They also directed White to travel around the state with Lincoln to the single engagements which had been arranged by the Republican state committee. The *Times* matched the *Press and Tribune* reporting contingent of White and Hitt with two shorthand reporters, Henry Binmore and James Sheridan.[22] No state election had ever received such coverage. Particularly at the joint debates, correspondents of dozens of papers, including eastern journals, gathered to broadcast the speeches across the land.

For Horace White the opportunity to accompany Lincoln was one of the most memorable occasions of his life. He met Republican politicians from all over the state who were eager to have their own campaigns written up in his reports to the *Chicago Press and Tribune.* The contacts he made during this campaign and the experience he gained strengthened his footholds on the paper and in the party. His most significant experience, however, was the close friendship which he developed with Abraham Lincoln. Although many years his senior, Lincoln treated White with deference and sincerity, and the conditions of travel brought the two men close together. White came to know Lincoln during the campaign as a profound conversationalist, an absorbing storyteller, and an emotional orator.

Perhaps the most humorous of White's experiences was an incident that occurred on the way to an engagement at Clinton. Traveling by rail from Springfield during the evening, the two men had to change trains at Decatur for Clinton. White fell asleep, having asked Lincoln to wake him at the transfer point. Lincoln himself, however, dozed off and awoke barely in time to get off the train. White, awakened by daylight the next morning, found himself at the Indiana state line. He hurried back to Clinton, but arrived in the evening after Lincoln had delivered his speech. When White found Lincoln, the Republican leader laughed raucously. After he became President, he told the tale whenever he encountered White in company with others.[23]

The relationship that White formed with Lincoln during the 1858 campaign remained a bond between them. Lincoln treated the young man with good humor and respect. Yet there was always "an implacable garment of dignity" about Lincoln that caused White in his later years to doubt as apocryphal anecdotes in which authors boasted of an undue familiarity with the Republican leader. White insisted, for example, that no one called him "Abe," not even his law partner and confidant William Herndon.[24]

Hearing Lincoln speak day after day, White became deeply impressed with the candidate's moral conviction. He did not overlook Lincoln's ability as a politician or doubt his desire for official advancement. Yet White never questioned Lincoln's antislavery commitment; he always felt that the Republican leader's antislavery position was a genuine expression of profound feeling. Douglas would time after time throw Lincoln off guard while Douglas adroitly pulled himself out of difficult situations, but White felt that Lincoln made up for his lack of "mental agility" by his "moral superiority and blazing earnestness."[25]

Lincoln, like most other Republicans, did not subscribe openly to any theory of racial equality. Unlike Douglas, however, he never conceded that there was an inherent inferiority of Negroes and could never agree to the right of one group of people to enslave another. Lincoln found justification for his views in the Declaration of Independence, particularly in the line "all men are created equal."[26] He would not exclude Negroes from the natural rights made explicit in this document, even though it might cost him votes in areas where negrophobia ran high. Douglas, on the other hand, never lost an opportunity to appeal to racial antipathies. This difference in moral conviction caused White to admire Lincoln and despise Douglas. White became so emotionally involved in the campaign that he refused to meet Douglas on the invitation of one of the *Chicago Times* reporters, James Sheridan. A more mellow Horace White later recalled: "I took my politics very seriously. I thought that all the work of saving the country had to be done then and there."[27] Perhaps nothing so attests to Lincoln's personal indignation with slavery as the rapture with which White, an abolitionist, idealized the Republican candidate. White had come to know Lincoln well.

At the official opening of his canvass at Beardstown on August 12, Lincoln gave one of his most famous declamations on the Declaration of Independence. White was so impressed that he insisted on sending a "verbatim" copy of Lincoln's words to the *Press and Tribune*. Since White was not a shorthand reporter, and since Robert Hitt accompanied the entourage only to the later joint debates, White wrote out the passage from memory, showed it to Lincoln for his approval, and sent it to Chicago as part of his report of Lincoln's Lewistown speech on August 17.[28] White may have added some flourish to Lincoln's words but they still remain impressive:

Representatives in old Independence Hall, said to the whole world of men: "We hold these truths to be self evident: that all men are created equal; that they are endowed by their Creator with certain unalienable rights; that among these are life, liberty and the pursuit of happiness." This was their majestic interpretation of the economy of the Universe. This was their lofty, and wise, and noble understanding of the justice of the Creator to His creatures. [Applause.] Yes, gentlemen, to *all* His creatures, to the whole great family of man. In their enlightened belief, nothing stamped with the divine image and likeness was sent into the world to be trodden on, and degraded, and imbruted by its fellows. They grasped not only the whole race of men then living, but they reached forward and seized upon the farthest posterity. They erected a beacon to guide their children and their children's children, and the countless myriads who should inhabit the earth in other ages. . . .

Now, my countrymen (Mr. Lincoln continued with great earnestness,) if you have been taught doctrines conflicting with the great landmarks of the Declaration of Independence; if you have listened to suggestions which would take away from its grandeur, and mutilate the fair symmetry of its proportions; if you have been inclined to believe that all men are *not* created equal in these inalienable rights enumerated by our chart of liberty, let me entreat you to come back. Return to the fountain whose waters spring close by the blood of the Revolution. Think nothing of me—take no thought for the political fate of any man whomsoever—but come back to the truths that are in the Declaration of Independence. You may do anything with me you choose, if you will heed these sacred principles. You may not only defeat me for the Senate, but you may take me and put me to death. While pretending no indifference to earthly honors, I *do claim* to be actuated in this contest by something higher than an anxiety for office. I charge you to drop every paltry and insignificant thought for any man's success. It is nothing; I am nothing; Judge Douglas is nothing. But do not destroy that immortal emblem of humanity—the Declaration of American Independence.[29]

On August 21, Lincoln met Douglas for the first joint debate at Ottawa. Robert Hitt came down from Chicago to transcribe the contest word for word. He was joined by thousands of others who came to hear the well-advertised oratorical contest.

At Ottawa, Douglas spoke first and took the initiative. He taunted Lincoln with several difficult questions on the anti-slavery issues of the day. He also presented a radical platform which he claimed the Republicans had written and Lincoln had endorsed in 1854. Lincoln denied the charge, but Douglas won temporary advantage; he had caught Lincoln off guard. Though neither could claim a clearcut victory, many Republican leaders, particularly the editors of the *Press and Tribune,* felt discouraged at Lincoln's defensive posture.

Horace White and Robert Hitt normally had little time to concentrate on the content of the debates. White focused his attention on the crowds and settings in order to prepare colorful descriptions which would introduce the verbatim copy of the debates. Hitt riveted his attention on the words of the debaters, not on the progression of their thoughts. Indeed it was a relief for him, in that first debate at Ottawa, when Douglas began to read from the 1854 platform. He could relax for a moment and copy that document from the files when he got back to Chicago. In doing this, he discovered that Douglas had read from an incorrect and considerably more radical version of the platform than had been printed in the *Democratic State Register*. Overjoyed at finding something with which to offset Douglas's advantage at Ottawa, the editors of the *Press and Tribune* hammered for weeks at Douglas's duplicity and deliberate use of a forgery.[30]

Even with this unexpected advantage, Republicans were restive. Lincoln had not responded immediately or forcefully to Douglas's charges and questions at Ottawa. Their candidate was deliberate, cautious, and ever judging the total impact of his words. He was not concerned with gaining temporary advantage. Instead, he waited to confer with Republican leaders and listen to their advice on possible answers to Douglas's questions. Almost everyone whom he consulted urged him to go to the offensive at Freeport, the site of the next debate.

Joseph Medill, after conferring with Norman Judd, Ebenezer Peck, and several other Republican politicians, forwarded the group's advice to Lincoln.[31] The answers he sent were more radical than those Lincoln actually used. But one of the "ugly questions" which Medill urged Lincoln, in turn, to put to Douglas was remarkably similar to the famous question which Lincoln used in the debate. The purpose of the question was to point out the apparent contradiction between the doctrine of popular sovereignty (which ostensibly gave residents in a territory the right to decide the slavery question) and the recent Dred Scott decision (which seemed to forbid the exclusion of slavery from any federal territory). Medill's version read: "What becomes of your vaunted popular sovereignty in Territories since the Dred Scott decision?" Medill obviously felt no apprehension about Lincoln's use of such a question. Whether others did, historians will probably never fully ascertain.

Horace White was actually responsible for starting the historical dispute. He brought up the whole matter in a chapter which he prepared for John L. Scripps's official campaign biography of Lincoln in 1860. In that chapter on the 1858 elections, White wrote: "Two prominent facts of the campaign, in Mr. Lincoln's view, were 'Popular Sovereignty,' so called, and the Dred Scott decision—each a sham and a fraud, yet directly antagonistic. Mr. Lincoln therefore resolved to present them to Mr. Douglas in the form of a brief interrogatory, so worded, that even the latter could find no avenue for escaping or dodging the contradiction. He mentioned to some of his friends at Freeport that such was his purpose. They unanimously counseled him to let that topic alone, 'for,' said they, 'if you put that question to him, he will perceive that an answer giving practical force and effect to the Dred Scott decision in the Territories inevitably loses him the battle, and he will therefore reply by affirming the decision as an abstract principle, but denying its practical application.' 'But' said Mr. Lincoln, 'if he does that, he can never be President.' His friends replied, with one voice, 'That's not your lookout; you are after the *Senatorship*.' 'No, gentlemen,' rejoined Mr. Lincoln. '*I am killing larger game. The battle of 1860 is worth a hundred of this.*' "[32]

In the 1890s, White repeated substantially this same story in his memoirs of the debates in William Herndon's expanded biography of Abraham Lincoln. In this account, however, White added that the council of critical advisers took place at Dixon, Illinois, not Freeport. Joseph Medill further complicated the plot by adding a third version in the *Chicago Tribune* on May 19, 1895. Medill claimed to have accompanied Lincoln on the train to the Freeport debate. While en route, Lincoln supposedly showed Medill his draft of the famous question. Medill criticized it and upon disembarking in Freeport urged others to warn Lincoln of the perils of using such a question. Medill later gave still another version to Jesse Weik, Herndon's associate, backing up White's tale of a conference at Dixon.[33]

A recent historian, Don E. Fehrenbacher, has brought the controversial Freeport story under critical analysis. He has thoroughly discredited Medill's reminiscences by comparing them with the editor's letter to Lincoln on the morning of the debates. Not only was Medill in Chicago but more importantly, he urged Lincoln to use the "Freeport Question" or a version very similar to it. Fehrenbacher also discredited White's version of a Dixon conference, since Charles Ray, who claimed to be there and later told White about it, actually was out of Illinois on a business trip.[34]

The matter, unfortunately, does not die so easily. Fehrenbacher does not consider, for example, that the original account in 1860 was written by Horace White, and that account is not marred by White's later tale of a Dixon conference. Henry C. Whitney, moreover, provided another version which Fehrenbacher did not consider and which is very close to Horace White's original account: "At the Brewster House in Freeport, just before the second debate, Lincoln read to Washburne, Uncle Sam Hitt, Tom Turner, Judd and two or three others, the questions he was going to spring on Douglas. Washburne advised against it." Thus, it may have been Elihu Washburne who criticized the question, not Medill or Judd. Fehrenbacher has unquestionably removed much of the rubbish connected with the "Freeport Question," particularly the notion that Lincoln was ignoring the Senatorship race and viewing "the bigger game" of the presidency in 1860. But there still seems evidence enough to continue, unsettled, the controversial story that Republican advisers warned Lincoln against his using the question at Freeport.[35]

When Lincoln posed his question to Douglas, the Little Giant exceeded his former boldness by taking an advanced post-Dred Scott version of his doctrine of popular sovereignty. Douglas maintained that the Dred Scott decision was irrelevant, since no slaveholder would bring his chattels into Kansas knowing the unwillingness of the majority of the settlers to protect his human property. The free-soilers could, moreover, pass "unfriendly legislation" to discourage the introduction of slaves into the territory. Douglas's suggestion that Lincoln had heard his reply "a hundred times from every stump in Illinois" only masked its novelty. True, Lincoln had heard Douglas hint at this position on July 16 at Bloomington and may also have read reports of Douglas's speech the next day at Springfield when he said, "Slavery cannot exist a day in the midst of an unfriendly people with unfriendly laws." But Lincoln had never heard Douglas say what he heard at Freeport, that "the people of a territory can by lawful means, exclude slavery from their limits prior to the formation of a state constitution . . . ," that "if the people are opposed to slavery they will elect representatives to that body who will by unfriendly legislation effectually prevent the introduction of it into their midst."[36]

Lincoln found that response new and quite unexpected. Indeed only several weeks before, on July 31, when a friend asked Lincoln how he felt Douglas would respond to a similar question, Lincoln demonstrated that he did not anticipate Douglas's answer at Freeport: "You shall have hard work to get him directly to the point whether a territorial Legislature has or has not the power to exclude slavery. But if you succeed in bringing him to it, though he will be compelled to say it possesses no such power, he will instantly take ground that slavery can not actually exist in the territories, unless the people desire it, and so give it protective territorial legislation."[37]

Whatever Lincoln's motives or expectations may have been in using the question, Horace White and the editors of the *Press and Tribune* felt that Douglas's ability to maintain his free-soil posture by the use of the Freeport doctrine was crucial in winning the election. They likewise had not anticipated such a forceful response, and their enthusiasm apparently lagged in the weeks after Freeport. John Locke Scripps, senior editor of the paper, even considered discontinuing coverage of the debates.[38]

Coverage did not end; wiser minds must have prevailed. Horace White continued to travel with Lincoln on an exhausting tour of Illinois. Most of their energies were spent on the Whig counties in the middle of the state. Lincoln made more than sixty speeches, many of which were over two hours in length. Douglas, likewise concentrating his energies in the central counties, made over a hundred. At the last joint debate at Alton on October 15, Douglas's voice was so worn that he could hardly whisper.

Both candidates had extended themselves to the breaking point. Never before had a senatorial election focused so sharply on the contestants. On the eve of the election, the *Chicago Press and Tribune* even felt obliged to remind the voters "how to vote in the election." They were to vote for legislators pledged to the men and not for the men themselves. It also pleaded with them to go to the polls, as the result would probably be close.

It was. The Republican legislators won a majority of the votes cast, but they did not form a majority of the legislature which would elect a senator. When Horace White saw the inevitable defeat for Lincoln, he was despondent. Yet he was left with an undiluted admiration for the Republican candidate, who had refused to give in to a pragmatic alliance with Stephen A. Douglas. On November 5, 1858, the day after the election, Horace White addressed a letter to Lincoln as "My Dear friend." He tried to encourage the defeated leader but expressed his own glum mood: "I don't think it possible for you to feel more disappointed than I do, with this defeat, but your popular majority in the state will give us the privilege of naming our man on the national ticket in 1860—either President or Vice Prest. *Then,* let me assure you, Abe Lincoln shall be an honored man before the American people. I am going to write an article for the Atlantic Monthly to further that object." Signing "your friend in distress," White added another word of praise: "I believe you have risen to a national reputation and position more rapidly than any man who ever rose at all."[39]

Horace White never wrote that article for the *Atlantic Monthly,* but he continued to fight the battles which his champion had waged throughout the summer and fall of 1858. First, he wrote a detailed critique of Lincoln's failure, blaming the weather, unfair apportionment of the legislative districts, and the duplicity of Seward, Greeley, and Crittenden for giving undue advantage to a Democratic candidate. He noted honestly, however, that it was primarily Douglas' free-soil posture, fortified by the Freeport doctrine, that had won him the victory.[40]

For months after the election White also staged a running battle with Horace Greeley. Denying Greeley's protestations of neutrality in the contest, White showed that, although the New York editor may have made some favorable comments on Lincoln in the daily edition of his paper, he omitted them in the weekly edition which circulated widely in Illinois. From the editorial exchange, White gained the satisfaction that he had settled part of Lincoln's "score" with Horace Greeley.[41] But the battle with Greeley, however bitter it may have been, was only secondary. White concentrated his energies on settling Lincoln's larger quarrel with Douglas.

Before he took up that larger assignment, however, White spent several weeks resting in the East. It was more than a vacation; he finally married Martha Root, whose father apparently had become reconciled to the inevitability of their marriage. White's return to full-time, paid employment on the *Tribune* as their chief reporter and occasional editorial

writer probably helped assuage the abolitionist minister.
There is no evidence that White's "religious character" under-
went any remarkable change but there is no doubt that he
had gained considerable maturity and status in the past several years. His association with the *Chicago Tribune* and the
Republican party had begun to pay dividends.

Not even a honeymoon could keep White's mind off politics
and his nemesis—Stephen A. Douglas. Noting local sentiment
in Connecticut, he reported Douglas's popularity very strong
there—stronger "than was at all pleasant to an Illinois Republican." He concluded that "hardly anything short of an
interposition of Providence would prevent Douglas's nomination by the Charleston Convention and his election by the
people. . . ." To avert this calamity, he thought that he might
be able to induce his former comrades in Kansas to concoct
some "unfriendly legislation" that would unsettle Douglas.
He thought that measures abolishing slavery and nullifying
the Fugitive Slave Law—"argued from texts in Douglas's Freeport speech" would "hit the Charleston target nearly in the
centre of the bull's eye." He speculated that, even if neither
of the measures passed, Republicans "could make a devil of
a blow with it—fill the newspapers North and South; and perhaps this broad suggestion of what fiends are lurking in the
Freeport dogma, will do more Douglas business at Charleston
without any positive enactments." Conferring with Norman
Judd, White received approval of his scheme, though Judd
thought the legislation should be limited to the abolition of
slavery. White recognized that the plan held dangers; for, if
Douglas should win the nomination despite the territorial
action, the Little Giant would then be irresistible in the
North.[42] White thus faced a dilemma similar to the one
Lincoln and his advisers supposedly had faced at Freeport.

White ultimately made the same sort of decision as Lincoln's
supposed gamble at Freeport. In an editorial in the *Press and
Tribune* he urged the Kansas legislators to abolish slavery.

Appealing to his former antislavery associates, he wrote: "Without it [abolition of slavery] Kansas must rest under the imputation of flagrant dishonesty to her political action, and those who fought her battles in the older states, and sent her men, money, clothing and the implements of defence and industry will be left with . . . sour reflections on their greenness." " 'Unfriendly legislation' towards slavery in the territories," White made clear to the legislators, "was Douglas's right bower in the late contest in this State. . . . Let him by all means have the chance to vindicate his position."[43]

White sent the article out to all the members of the territorial legislature whose names he could find.[44] His action apparently helped the passage of a law abolishing slavery in the territory. When this happened, the *Press and Tribune* gloated: "We shall now have a case of Unfriendly Legislation in point, and Mr. Douglas can shoulder his 'great principle' in favor of the Charleston Convention if he chooses."[45] Ultimately, the act did not get through the governor's council,[46] but the reverberations were felt in the United States Senate, as White had hoped, causing one of the bitterest exchanges up until that time between Douglas and Jefferson Davis.[47] The Freeport Doctrine had indeed backfired upon Douglas as Lincoln supposedly suggested it would.

Douglas did not remain long in the sectional spotlight. If some of White's former Kansas associates had helped put Douglas on the defensive, another Kansas friend soon caused the tables to be turned on the gloating Republicans. John Brown's raid on Harper's Ferry dealt the Republican party in Illinois and throughout the nation a nearly fatal body blow.[48]

The Republicans tried desperately to disassociate themselves from the "irresponsible madman," while the Democrats tried their utmost to identify their opponents with the objectives of the executed revolutionary.[49] Shortly after Brown's trial, an investigating body was called to search into Brown's erstwhile associations. Horace White, along with many of the leaders of the Kansas aid movement, was summoned to testify before the Mason Committee. White went to Washington in a cocksure mood. His testimony contained no apology for his actions.[50] After his hearing, he also let it be known that he did not subscribe to the notion that Brown was a madman. He wrote back to the *Press and Tribune* that Brown might have been successful if only he had gained more time to prepare his insurrection.[51] The Mason Committee, however, found it impossible to implicate White or any prominent member of the Republican party in Brown's activities. Indeed, the investigation probably did the Republicans a favor by exculpating them from any responsibility in the Virginia raid.

Brown's invasion, nevertheless, chilled the Republican leaders and forced them into a conservative mood. This sudden shift of sentiment proved a boon for the Illinois Republicans, as bewildered politicians in the party looked about for more moderate men like Abraham Lincoln to head the national ticket in the 1860 elections. On February 10, 1860, just before he left to testify in Washington, Horace White urged Lincoln to get himself in "training for the Presidency." He informed Lincoln that the *Press and Tribune* was about to espouse his candidacy for that office.[52] Lincoln, however, had already gauged the trend of opinion himself. On the very day that Horace White faced the Mason Committee, Lincoln addressed an audience at the Cooper Union Institute in New York City. There Lincoln presented a conservative ideology that interested Eastern leaders and enhanced his availability. His hat was now officially in the ring, and the Illinois Republicans rallied behind him.

There was little division in their ranks. Few of those Illinois voters who had once supported William H. Seward looked upon him with much favor after his flirtation with Douglas in 1858. Bargaining, planning, and conniving, the Illinois Republicans put across Lincoln's nomination in Chicago.[53] To

White, a delegate at the Chicago convention, it seemed that the nomination was only a step to national victory. When the convention verdict was announced, he hastily telegraphed Lincoln in Springfield. He forgot to add his congratulations: "I shall probably be appointed your Biographer in behalf of Follet Foster and Co. Columbus the matter is under consultation among your friends if so I shall go immediately to Springfield."[54]

As it turned out, White wrote only one chapter of the biography, the section on the 1858 campaign. Before settling down to such tasks, he first took another trip to the East. He returned to Illinois in early June with renewed enthusiasm to continue his post as secretary of the Republican State Central Committee.[55] His optimism had been bolstered in the East by his eavesdropping among laborers in Connecticut and New York. He wrote to Lincoln that the nomination was being "received with a genuine bellow of satisfaction among the operatives."[56] To Lyman Trumbull he added that "nothing less than *inspiration* could have guided the Convention to a happier choice, so far as that class of votes are concerned."[57]

Not all was so rosy within the Republican machine in Illinois. Former antipathies between Norman Judd and John Wentworth complicated relations in the state. White encountered some of this friction over the makeup of the State Central Committee, which had fallen under the control of Judd. As a firm ally of Judd, he dismissed all complaints as the resentment of Wentworth's "croakers."[58] White, for many years, would look upon Wentworth as a sinister and untrustworthy Republican. Skirmishes between the two factions almost broke into open warfare; but the Illinois Republicans, faced with depleted campaign funds,[59] managed to sit tight and let the tide of northern resentment against the South carry Lincoln to victory on November 6.

That was a happy day for Horace White. After two disappointments in backing Lincoln for the Senate, he finally witnessed his champion capture the chief office of the land. The years which culminated in the election of Abraham Lincoln had been busy and productive for Horace White. Though only in his middle twenties, he had participated in some of the most momentous events of his times. His short but stormy political career had been intimately intertwined with the growth and success of the Republican party. His boyhood dreams of a career in journalism had become more than fulfilled; he was now connected with one of the nation's most powerful dailies. Yes, it was a happy day. But the exaltation proved short-lived.

NOTES

1. Jay Monaghan, *The Man Who Elected Lincoln* (Indianapolis, 1956), pp. 38–52. This is a biography of Charles Ray, one of the *Tribune* proprietors.
2. Ibid., pp. 53–65.
3. From an autobiographical typescript of White's first years in Chicago. Sketches in the Horace White Family Papers (hereafter cited as White, "Arrival in Chicago").
4. *Chicago Tribune,* January 15, 1858.
5. Don E. Fehrenbacher, "Political Attitudes in Illinois, 1854–1860" (Ph.D. dissertation, University of Chicago, 1951), pp. 69–70.
6. *Chicago Tribune,* March 31, 1857.
7. White, "Arrival in Chicago."
8. *Chicago Tribune,* January 6, 1858.
9. Charles Ray to Lyman Trumbull, November 24, 1857, Trumbull MSS.
10. *Chicago Tribune,* November 26, 1857.
11. Charles Wilson to Lyman Trumbull, December 14, 1857; W. H. Herndon to Trumbull, December 16, 1857; Ebenezer Peck to Trumbull, December 2, 1857; Trumbull MSS.
12. Charles Ray to Lyman Trumbull, December 18, 1857, Trumbull MSS.
13. Charles Ray to O. M. Hatch, March 20, 1858, cited by Ralph G. Newman, "The Douglas 'Deal' Lincoln Spurned," *Chicago Tribune Magazine,* October 4, 1964.
14. Abraham Lincoln to O. M. Hatch, March 24, 1858, cited by Newman, "The Douglas 'Deal' Lincoln Spurned." Hatch, the Illinois secretary of

state, had relayed Ray's letter to Lincoln. See Hatch's letter to Lincoln, March 23, 1858, also cited by Newman, Ibid. For further discussion of the rumored Douglas overture, see Richard A. Heckman, *Lincoln vs Douglas* (Washington, D.C., 1967).

15. *Chicago Tribune,* June 18, 1858.

16. Ibid. Senators at this time were nominated and elected by the state legislatures. The legislature's prerogative of nomination had never before been invaded in Illinois.

17. William Herndon and Jesse Weik, *Abraham Lincoln: The Story of a Great Life* (New York, 1892), 2:92 (hereafter cited as Herndon, *Lincoln*). This edition contained an added chapter written by White on his experiences during the senatorial campaign of 1858. For a recent interpretation of this speech, see Don E. Fehrenbacher, "The Origins and Purpose of Lincoln's 'House Divided' Speech," *Mississippi Valley Historical Review* 47 (March, 1960): 615–643.

18. Monaghan, *Man Who Elected Lincoln,* pp. 107–108.

19. *Chicago Tribune,* March 17, 1899. See also Fehrenbacher, "Political Attitudes," pp. 69–70. Scripps actually became the senior editor of the *Press and Tribune,* although the lines of authority on the paper had not been clearly laid out by the proprietors. His paper, the *Press,* had much more equipment than the *Tribune.* It owned seventeen steampowered presses, employed eighty persons, and published many of the daily and weekly newspapers of Chicago on a contract basis. See the letterhead of a note from William Bross to Lincoln, September 6, 1858, Robert Todd Lincoln Coll.

20. *Chicago Press and Tribune,* July 1, 1858.

21. Ibid., July 28, 1858.

22. Herndon, *Lincoln,* 2:88–89.

23. Ibid., pp. 111–112.

24. Horace White, *The Lincoln and Douglas Debates* (Chicago, 1914), p. 30. This pamphlet was originally an address delivered before the Chicago Historical Society on February 17, 1914 (hereafter cited as White, *Debates*).

25. Ibid., p. 21.

26. An excellent critique of the debates, emphasizing the difference between the combatants, can be found in Harry V. Jaffa, *Crisis of the House Divided* (New York, 1959).

27. Herndon, *Lincoln,* 2:95.

28. White explained the incident to William Herndon in 1865. White to Herndon, May 17, 1865, Herndon-Weik MSS.

29. *Chicago Press and Tribune,* August 21, 1858. The full passage of the apostrophe to the Declaration of Independence may be found in Paul Angle's splendid edition of the Lincoln-Douglas debates. Paul Angle, *Created Equal* (Chicago, 1958), pp. 100–101. The editors of the *Collected Works of Lincoln* (New Brunswick, N.J., 1953–1955 [2: 544]), Roy Basler et al., have cast some doubt on Horace White's 1865 explanation to

William Herndon of the Beardstown location of the famous declaration.

30. Monaghan, *Man Who Elected Lincoln*, pp. 114–115. White claimed that the debates passed directly through Hitt's and his hands to the printer. Although there is a greater variance between the transcriptions of the *Times* and the transcriptions of the *Tribune* than historians have recognized, there is no reason to suspect any undue chicanery. White admitted only to italicizing certain passages. The *Times* charged him with editing Lincoln's speeches, but such charges were written for partisan purposes. See Herndon, *Lincoln*, 2:89. See also *Chicago Times*, October 12, 24, 1858.

31. Joseph Medill to Lincoln, Friday morning [August 27, 1858], Robert Todd Lincoln Coll.

32. John Locke Scripps, *Life of Abraham Lincoln*, ed. Roy P. Basler and Lloyd A. Dunlap (Bloomington, Ind., 1961), p. 147.

33. Herndon, *Lincoln*, 2:109. Horace White to Jesse Weik, August 26, 1908, Herndon-Weik MSS.

34. Don E. Fehrenbacher, "Lincoln, Douglas and the 'Freeport Question.'" *American Historical Review* 66 (April, 1961):599–617.

35. Henry C. Whitney, *Life of Lincoln* (New York, 1908), 1:276. Washburne did not mention the incident in his very short sketch of Lincoln's Illinois years in 1885, but his silence is not enough to settle the controversy. Elihu Washburne, "Abraham Lincoln in Illinois," *North American Review* 141:318–319.

36. Although Douglas had earlier pointed out that the people of a territory could exclude slavery by failing to give it security through legal protection, he took an advanced position at Freeport in insisting that the legislature could also *legally block the introduction* of slavery into the territory by passing "unfriendly legislation." Both the *Chicago Press and Tribune* and the *Illinois State Journal* claimed that the Freeport Doctrine was a new position never preached before by Douglas in Illinois. *Chicago Press and Tribune*, August 30, 1858. *Illinois State Journal*, September 8, 1858 (weekly edition).

37. Lincoln to Henry Asbury, July 31, 1858, in *Collected Works of Lincoln*, ed. Basler, 2:530. Lincoln discussed the unique qualities of the Freeport Doctrine a year later in an Ohio speech. See Ibid., 3:449.

38. Henry C. Whitney to Lincoln, September 23, 1858, Robert Todd Lincoln Coll.

39. White to Lincoln, November 5, 1858, Robert Todd Lincoln Coll.

40. *Chicago Press and Tribune*, November 5, 1858.

41. White to Lincoln, February 2, 1859, Robert Todd Lincoln Coll. See also *Chicago Press and Tribune*, February 2, 16, March 8, 1859.

42. White to Trumbull, December 8, 1858, Trumbull MSS. Fehrenbacher in his study of the Freeport episode underestimates the impact and the importance which contemporaries thought the Freeport doctrine had in the election. It is demonstrably untrue that "nobody at the time ventured to add the Freeport question to the list of causes" determining

the election. Don E. Fehrenbacher, *Prelude to Greatness* (Stanford, Cal., 1962), p. 128. See also *Chicago Press and Tribune,* December 24, 1858.

43. *Chicago Press and Tribune,* December 24, 1858.

44. White to Trumbull, January 10, 1859, Trumbull MSS.

45. *Chicago Press and Tribune,* February 15, 1859.

46. "I did all in my power to secure the enactment of a proper law by our late Legislature against slavery in Kansas; but the Council, a body elected at a time when only the 'loaves and fishes free State men' would accept a Territorial office, defeated it." Martin F. Conway to White, February 18, 1859, Robert Todd Lincoln Coll.

47. *Congressional Globe,* 35th Cong., 2d sess. [February 23, 1859], p. 1255.

48. Charles Ray quickly perceived the import of the invasion on the "moral health of the Republican party." He felt that the quicker Brown would be hanged, the better. Joseph Medill thought it would take two years for the Republican party to make up the damage to its reputation. Ray to Lincoln, n.d. [October 31, 1859], Robert Todd Lincoln Coll. Joseph Medill to Trumbull, April 16, 1860, Trumbull MSS.

49. Oswald Garrison Villard, *John Brown* (New York, 1943), pp. 565–568, 580–584.

50. U. S., Congress, Senate, Select Committee on the Harper's Ferry Invasion, 36th Cong. 1st sess., 1860, Committee Rept. 278. White's testimony given on February 27, 1860, can be found on pp. 245–250.

51. *Chicago Press and Tribune,* March 2, 1858.

52. White to Lincoln, February 10, 1860, Robert Todd Lincoln Coll.

53. See Monaghan, *Man Who Elected Lincoln.* Monaghan goes over the familiar story of the Chicago convention but emphasizes the role of the *Press and Tribune* editors.

54. White to Lincoln, May 18, 1860, Robert Todd Lincoln Coll.

55. White, through his friendship with Lincoln and his service for Norman Judd, won this important position in the Republican machine in Illinois. White to Lincoln, March 31, 1859, Robert Todd Lincoln Coll.

56. Ibid., June 4, 1860, Robert Todd Lincoln Coll.

57. White to Trumbull, June 5, 1860, Trumbull MSS.

58. White to O. M. Hatch, June 28, 1860, O. M. Hatch MSS. See also White to Baker and Bailhache, September 29, 1860, Robert Todd Lincoln Coll. For an elaboration of the feud see Don E. Fehrenbacher, "The Judd-Wentworth Feud," *Journal of the Illinois State Historical Society* 45 (Autumn, 1952):211.

59. White to Trumbull, November 2, 1860, Horace White MSS.

4

"God Bless the Revolution"

WHATEVER rejoicing there may have been in Illinois over Lincoln's election, the exuberance of victory quickly turned into serious thought about the national implications of a Republican President. Although Lincoln had won a majority in the Electoral College, he obtained only two-fifths of the total popular vote. And his vote in the South was practically nil. The news of Lincoln's triumph, moreover, had prompted the legislature of South Carolina to issue its famous call for a state convention. If there were any doubts about what they were to consider, reports from the South soon made it clear that the politicians from Dixie were contemplating secession. As President Buchanan refused to act, and since a policy of deliberate silence veiled Lincoln's ultimate intentions, panic seized the nation.

Southern threats caused many in Congress to search desperately for one more scheme to conciliate the country by compromising sectional differences. John J. Crittenden, Henry Clay's successor in the Senate, offered the most popular proposal. But Republicans held firm; they knew that the very survival of the Republican party demanded such intransigence. The party's resistance to slavery's expansion was its sole cohesive force.

Few Republicans held to this position more tenaciously than Horace White. Southern "bluster" only increased his conviction that Lincoln must hold firm. The *Tribune* urged the country to "settle it now."[1] White's colleague, Joseph Medill, gave a refrain to the staff's opinion when he reviled the "class of d—d fools or knaves who want him [Lincoln] to make a 'union saving speech'—in other words to *let down* to conciliate the disunionists and fire-eaters."[2]

White got a personal report of southern reactions when the president of his old Fremont Club, J. M. Richards, told him about the "pure frenzy" that he had encountered on a trip to Louisiana and Mississippi. White now admitted that war was a "probable event." Richards' recount of a plot (which he had overheard in a New Orleans hotel) to assassinate Lincoln made White bristle with anger. He wrote Lincoln to warn him and to tell him of the growing resentment of people "in this latitude."[3] Lincoln kept his thoughts to himself.

White must have felt uneasy at Lincoln's public silence. He did not know that Lincoln had already urged selected members of Congress to resist any compromise with slavery and to hold firm, "as with a chain of steel."[4] When rumor circulated that Thurlow Weed was on his way to Springfield to advocate conciliation, White dashed off a frantic note to his champion:

> Those who believe they know you fear nothing from such an errand. I have only to say that there are a multitude here who will plunge into blood to the horse's bridles to defend your newly acquired prerogatives, but who will writhe in the bitterness of grief, if the man whom they have almost worshipped, falters in the first hour of danger.
>
> Let me repeat that I have no doubts—no fears—no misgivings.

None of your acquaintances, so far as I know, allow themselves to be troubled in spirit or broken in their rest on your account. But allow me to strengthen your upright purposes to this extent: that among the masses and especially the young men who I meet there is a rising spirit of fierce rebellion against any *compromise* of the principles upon which you were elected—not so much because you were elected upon them as because they are right, because they hold on the conscience and hearts of men.[5]

White must have received some answer to calm his fears, for Republican co-worker Herman Kreismann wrote shortly thereafter to Elihu Washburne that White seemed reassured. The young reporter had been informed through reliable sources that Lincoln would not "leave this question to be settled by prosperity." He also heard to his delight that "Weed came away with an extra large flea in his ear."[6]

Behaving like a Northern counterpart to the Southern fire-eaters, White urged Illinois Congressmen not simply to resist Southern demands but also to mount an offensive. His impetuosity filled a short note to Representative Washburne: "Why in the devil's name don't you present articles of impeachment against Buchanan and Floyd? People here are becoming frantic—absolutely frantic with rage at the treason. If old Buck should show his carcass in these parts he would be hung so quick that Satan would not know where to look for his traitorous soul."[7] On the same day, he told Senator Trumbull that everyone whom he met was "cheered with the prospect of a hearty fight on or about the 4th of March—a square knock-down and drag out." He warned Trumbull that unless Congress quickly checked the chicanery of the Buchanan administration, there would be "thunder from the Northwest." Convinced of the righteousness of the cause, White assured Trumbull that the nation would mount a crusade against the forces of evil. Men were already joining the militia in Illinois and were raising companies to protect their native son during the inauguration ceremonies. "We live in revolutionary times," White told Trumbull, "and I say God bless the Revolution."[8]

White's confidence, at this point, was apparently boundless. Once assured that Lincoln would not compromise with southern demands, he was certain that Lincoln, backed by the bold and fearless Northwest, would slap down southern secession after inauguration day. His confidence in the President-elect, however, was seriously weakened as the new year began.

Manning the editorial helm in the first days of January, 1861, White received a gloomy letter from Joseph Medill, who was then acting as the Washington correspondent for the paper. Word that Lincoln was about to appoint Simon Cameron as his Secretary of the Treasury had reached the excited Capitol. Medill considered the appointment of the wily Pennsylvania politician "a fearful blow at the conscience" of the Republican party. He lamented, "We got Lincoln nominated on the *idea* of his honesty and elected him by endorsing him as *honest Abe*. His first act is, to select, among all the public men in party, the one having the *worst* reputation for honesty." Medill concluded in desperation, "White, by God! We are sold to the Philistines."[9]

The *Tribune* editors had been put on the spot. Their campaign propaganda had demanded as much a crusade against bureaucratic immorality as it had against slavery. Perhaps more so. When Lincoln was nominated, the *Tribune,* for example, confidently predicted that "the age of purity" had returned. The editors assured their readers that Lincoln —the "very soul of integrity"—would bring back the "sterling honesty and Democratic simplicity which marked the administrations of Jefferson, Madison, Adams, and Jackson."[10]

Of course, the editors saw more than political immorality in the appointment. They detected the long crooked fingers of Thurlow Weed. Already anticipating Seward's nomination, they feared that their own influence in Lincoln's councils was dissipating rapidly. Medill complained to White that Lincoln "never could have been heard of except as a retired, played out country politician but for the favors of the *Tribune* and its friends."[11] Medill expressed his frustration more explicitly to his colleagues Ray and Scripps when he warned them of the possibility that "there will not be one *original Lincoln* man in the Cabinet." Medill also struck the first note of the *Tribune*'s wartime independence: "Thank heaven we own and control the *Trib*. We made Abe and by G—— we can un-make him if he "Forneyizes' us."[12]

Medill's announcement of the Cameron appointment stunned Horace White. After reading the news he forwarded his letter to Charles Ray in Springfield, Illinois. With a typical and almost instinctively snap reaction, he proclaimed: "If Cameron goes into the Cabinet I go out of the party. I can stand a good deal of 'pizen' in a political way but I can't stand that."[13]

Along with the editors of the *Tribune*, White tried to force Lincoln to hold back on Cameron's appointment. He could not believe that Lincoln would appoint a man of such charac-ter—a man accused of defrauding the Winnebago Indians of $66,000 in 1832. He reiterated to Lyman Trumbull that he could not belong to a party "which places thieves in charge of the most important public interests." To Trumbull, White frankly admitted that he was "thunderstruck in view of the development in the character of our new President."[14]

White's letter to Trumbull was just one of the score of letters which censured Lincoln's contemplated action. When Lincoln learned of the serious reaction, he hesitated, but only for a moment. He finally appointed Cameron to the Cabinet, although placing him in charge of the War Department rather than the Treasury. This "demotion" helped quiet the critics, especially since it coincided with the appointment of their favorite, Salmon P. Chase, to watch over the nation's finances. Nonetheless, by tapping Cameron for the Cabinet, Lincoln declared his independence from his Illinois friends. Abraham Lincoln now belonged to the nation—never again would his Illinois associates know him as intimately as they had before the election. Even Lyman Trumbull, the state's senior senator, found himself outside of Lincoln's inner circle during the Civil War.[15]

Cameron's appointment also caused the editors of the *Chicago Tribune* to declare their independence from Lincoln. Medill marked out this course to his associate Charles Ray. "Our office is out of debt, and making money. We are independent of him and can afford to be free men—to help or *strike* as seemeth to us best." Medill's reaction set the tone for *Tribune* as it mobilized to cover the activities of the new administration. But it was tempered by several other factors. First, at a crucial moment, Lincoln stepped into a controversy among Chicago Republicans over the postmastership of Chicago. He gave the patronage plum to John Scripps, the senior editor of the *Tribune*. With Scripps heading the major distribution center for newspapers in the Midwest, the *Tribune* was bound to strengthen its predominant role among the journals in the area. However important this consideration may have been in softening the ill feeling of the editors, another consideration far outweighed patronage in bolstering their loyalty to Lincoln. A terrible national crisis faced them; it was no time for division. Medill clearly established this point when he modified his cry of independence to Ray:

> The country is in the jaws of civil war and the throes of dissolution. Our allegiance to principle may render it obligatory upon us to support him to a certain degree after he has turned his back on us and knifed our friends. It is too soon to take ground in the paper against him, or in relation to our future course.[16]

For all White's threats to bolt the party he, too, soon looked at Cameron's appointment in a larger perspective. His faith in Lincoln's political conscience may have been shaken; yet he still saw Lincoln as the bulwark against sectional compromise. In the midst of the Cameron imbroglio, he defended Lincoln's forthright position to an eastern abolitionist. White noted that despite enormous pressure on Lincoln, "his uniform reply has been—'Compromise is the end of Government. If we yield now slavery sweeps the continent.' " "The eagerness for a fight," White added, "has amounted to an agony."[17]

White did not falter in his effort to uphold Lincoln in the crisis. In an attempt to mobilize the young men, eager like himself for a fight, he issued a call for all those under thirty "who are opposed to all concessions and compromises of Freedom to Slavery," to meet at the Metropolitan Hall on January 25 "for the purpose of inaugurating a movement . . . in defence of the Constitution and the Union."[18] From a stage draped with the stars and stripes, White read a series of radical resolutions for the young men to second and approve. Since his first pronouncements on the crisis were too extreme for the bipartisan audience, he was forced to revise them for consideration at the group's next meeting.[19] Nonetheless, even his revised resolutions held an ominous tone. "He will not do posterity the injustice," the young men of the Northwest agreed, "of thrusting upon them the quarrel which belongs to us."[20]

When the cannons aimed at Fort Sumter boomed out the start of war, White remembered his promise to Father Abraham. He reaffirmed his commitment to John Nicolay: "I wrote the President sometime in January that the young men of Chicago would be in at the death to defend his prerogatives *if he would refuse to compromise.* He has kept his promise, and now we are keeping ours. We are drilling every night—over two thousand on the muster rolls—and only eager to hear the second call for troops, which we hope will be for 500,000 men."[21]

With his customary haste, White joined a volunteer company drawn up in Chicago by George Forsyth. He was one of over twenty of the *Tribune* employees who joined the unit in the excitement. White, however, did not march off with the Chicago volunteers. When his new wife heard of his hasty enlistment, she hysterically begged him to resign. Since he had not been mustered into the service by the government, he withdrew easily in the confused and disorganized rush of the North to form an army.[22] White did not, however, withdraw from active participation in the war. He joined the Bohemian Brigade—the corps of newspapermen who reported the war for the Union.[23]

The *Chicago Tribune* quickly girded itself for the demands placed upon it by the war. Gambling again in the midst of another depression, the editors invested heavily in new capital equipment, particularly in a four cylinder Hoe press. They further demonstrated their confidence in the future by buying out John Wentworth's *Chicago Democrat*. Through a state charter, they consolidated their empire by forming the Tribune Corporation. Scripps became the president and Alfred Cowles the secretary-treasurer. Scripps, Bross, Medill, and Ray manned the editorial staff, each with a vote on the paper's policy. Ray, by the force of his ability, managed the day-by-day editorial line. Horace White continued to write editorials and to head the *Tribune* reporting staff.[24]

One of White's first assignments after the start of hostilities was to report Stephen A. Douglas's speech against secession before the Illinois State Assembly. He found the effect of the speech "electrical." "The whole house rose to their feet and gave cheer for Douglas, for the Union and for the Stars and Stripes."[25] Never before had White cheered a Douglas speech; and never again would he have the opportunity, because the Little Giant died five weeks later. For this last patriotic act, White absolved Douglas of all his former sins. When the Democratic chief died, the *Tribune,* which had opposed his career so bitterly, echoed White's judgment: "His last public speech is the standard by which his life is to be measured."[26]

The summer was full of disappointments for men like White who thought simple Jacksonian firmness would quickly quash the rebellion. Because he had expected a quick and decisive encounter, White gave little thought to the objectives of a long, drawn-out battle with the South. He had demanded only that Lincoln refuse to compromise over slavery expansion. Beyond this he had urged little more. When General John Fremont, however, extended the objectives of the war on August 30, 1861, by freeing the slaves of rebels, a new issue confronted the President and his former friends on the *Chicago Tribune.*

The *Tribune* greeted Fremont's proclamation with cheers. The editors felt the radical general had reached the bedrock of the rebellion. They confidently expected that the war would now be extended to include the destruction of slavery, and they freely scoffed at rumors that the President would countermand Fremont's order.[27] When the revocation finally came through, the *Tribune* reported that Chicagoans had read the President's order with "blank astonishment and dismay" and even with "indignation and rage."[28]

Horace White belonged in this category. He responded by dashing off another characteristically hotheaded response, this time to Lincoln's former law partner, David Davis. "Our President has broken his own neck if he has not destroyed his country. The public rage here, caused by his order countermanding Fremont's proclamation, *is fearful,* and my own indignation, I confess, is too deep for words. Accursed be the day that I ever voted for such cowards and blacklegs." White was not close to this cautious old Whig. He admitted that he could not explain why he wrote to Davis but concluded, "the spirit moves me, and this must be my excuse." White probably wrote the hasty note in hopes that Davis would send the message to the President. The note, however, never reached Lincoln's hands.[29]

This emotional reaction against the President by the *Tribune* men was caused by something far more serious than any patronage squabble. Lincoln's unexpected order left them confused and floundering. The *Tribune* editors found themselves forced to criticize their own champion. They appealed to Congress and to the "masses, who furnished the muscle and money for the war." They urged that the popular voice be heard "in tones of thunder."[30]

The struggle did not prove so simple. Reverses suffered by Fremont in the field and rumors of corruption within his armies quickly placed the *Tribune* editors in a very awkward position. Could they support a corrupt and inept antislavery champion? The dilemma was painful, and they began to argue among themselves. William Bross and Joseph Medill went to Missouri to investigate the charges of incompetency against Fremont. They both returned to Chicago thoroughly disillusioned. Ray at first refused to condemn Fremont and started quarreling with Medill. But after another trip to Missouri with John Scripps, Ray returned in agreement with Medill. By a unanimous vote, the editors quickly realigned their paper behind the President and supported the ouster of Fremont from his command.[31]

Bickering persisted on the *Tribune* staff. The polling of peers proved a difficult way to run a newspaper. William Bross supposedly remarked once that the paper "was the result of the matured opinions of four independent thinkers and hence it was always right."[32] Charles Ray, however, felt differently; he was unwilling to continue his management of the editorial department in this fashion. He therefore offered his shares in the Tribune Corporation to Horace White. White received Ray's overture in Cheshire, Connecticut, where he was staying with Reverend Root, his wife's widowed father. White and Ray had both hoped that Root, a wealthy man, would put up the money for the purchase of Ray's *Tribune* stock. After considering the sale, White's father-in-law backed down; the business-minded cleric refused to put up the necessary funds without Ray at the editorial helm. White acquiesced in the decision; he would have even less voice than Ray and apparently also shared little faith in Medill or Bross.[33]

When White returned to Chicago late in October, he purchased several shares in the Tribune company from Ray; but without Root's help, he could buy no more. By means of this small purchase of stock, however, White gained a greater influence on the paper, enabling him to draw the important assignment of reporting the Washington scene during the sessions of Congress. To help cover his expenses in Washington, White got a patronage position in the Treasury Department through the exertions of Elihu Washburne. Washburne also helped him get a seat in the reporter's gallery in both the House and the Senate.[34] After setting his affairs in order in the next few weeks, White left Chicago and embarked upon a new phase of his journalistic career.

NOTES

1. *Chicago Tribune*, December 12, 22, 1860. White may have written these two editorials, as they were recopied later as notes for his projected autobiography. See the Horace White MSS.

2. Joseph Medill to Oziah M. Hatch, November 16, 1860, Oziah M. Hatch MSS, Illinois State Historical Library.

3. White to Lincoln, December 11, 1860, Robert Todd Lincoln Coll. The plot was related in detail in the *Chicago Tribune*, December 10, 1860.

4. Lincoln to Elihu Washburne, December 13, 1860, in *The Collected Works of Abraham Lincoln*, ed. Roy Basler et al., 4:151.

5. White to Lincoln, December 22, 1860, Robert Todd Lincoln Coll.

6. Herman Kreismann to Elihu Washburne, December 27, 1860, Elihu Washburne MSS, Library of Congress.

7. White to Elihu Washburne, December 30, 1860, Washburne MSS.

8. White to Lyman Trumbull, December 30, 1860, Trumbull MSS.

9. Medill to White, January 4, 1861, Charles Ray MSS, Henry Huntington Library.

10. *Chicago Tribune,* May 19, 1860.

11. Medill to White, January 4, 1861, Ray MSS.

12. Medill to Charles Ray and John Scripps, January 6, 1861, Ray MSS. Medill was undoubtedly referring to John W. Forney, a Philadelphia journalist–politician, who had developed a notorious reputation before the Civil War for moving from faction to faction as political expediency dictated.

13. White to Charles Ray, n.d. [Jaunary 7, 1861], Ray MSS. White had told Elihu Washburne shortly before he received Medill's letter that he would despair for the Republic if Cameron was appointed. White to Elihu Washburne, January 5, 1861, Washburne MSS.

14. White to Lyman Trumbull, January 10, 1860 [1861], Trumbull MSS.

15. Ralph Roske, "Lincoln and Lyman Trumbull" in *Lincoln Images,* ed. O. Fritiof Ander (Rock Island, Ill., 1960), pp. 73–74.

16. Medill to Charles Ray, January 18, 1861, Ray MSS.

17. White to Edward L. Pierce, Jaunary 18, 1861, Edward L. Pierce MSS, Harvard University.

18. *Chicago Tribune,* January 22, 1861.

19. Ibid., January 26, 1861.

20. Ibid., January 30, 1861.

21. White to John Nicolay, April 19, 1861, Robert Todd Lincoln Coll.

22. An undated note in White's handwriting, probably written for his projected autobiography, Horace White MSS. See also *Chicago Tribune,* March 17, 1899.

23. The work of war correspondents during the Civil War has been thoroughly covered by several monographs: Bernard Weisberger, *Reporters for the Union* (Boston, 1953); Louis M. Starr, *Bohemian Brigade* (New York, 1954); and J. Cutler Andrews, *The North Reports the War* (Pittsburgh, 1955). All three give attention to White's activities.

24. Phillip Kinsley, *The Chicago Tribune* I (New York, 1943), 145–146. Jay Monaghan, *The Man Who Elected Lincoln,* p. 246. Don E. Fehrenbacher, *Chicago Giant,* pp. 188–189. Franklin W. Scott, "Newspapers and Periodicals of Illinois 1814–1879," *Collections of the Illinois State Historical Library,* 6: 80–81. *Chicago Tribune,* March 17, 1899.

25. *Chicago Tribune,* April 26, 1861.

26. Ibid., June 4, 1861.

27. Ibid., September 4, 7, 1861.

28. Ibid., September 9, 1861.

29. White to David Davis, September 14, 1861, David Davis MSS, Illinois State Historical Library.

30. *Chicago Tribune,* September 14, 1861.

31. Monaghan, *Man Who Elected Lincoln,* pp. 251–260. William Bross, *The History of Chicago* (Chicago, 1888), p. 86.

32. Elmer Gertz, "Joe Medill's War," *Lincoln Herald* 48 (October, 1945):2.

33. White to Charles Ray, October 10, 1861, Ray MSS. Root, who owned sizable land holdings in the West, was a patron of Beloit College.

34. White to Elihu Washburne, November 13, 1861, Washburne MSS. The *Congressional Directory* (1862) lists White among the reporters officially admitted to the Senate and House.

5

Washington
Correspondent

WHEN WHITE arrived in Washington with his young and beautiful wife, he found quarters at Mrs. Chipman's boarding house on Seventh Street, midway between the White House and the Capitol. Their fellow boarders constituted an illustrious delegation of Republican legislators: Senators James W. Grimes of Iowa and William Pitt Fessenden of Maine together with Representatives Justin Morrill of Maine and Elihu Washburne of Illinois.[1] White's wife, Martha, immediately became a favorite of the widower, Senator Fessenden, at Mrs. Chipman's dinner table, and she also became a close friend of the wife of Senator Grimes. Largely through the attractions of his charming wife, White became an intimate associate of these two influential senators. They soon formed what Fessenden thought was a "pleasant family."[2] Their small social circle continued throughout the Civil War, regrouping at the beginning of each congressional session. Letters and visits kept them in touch during adjournments. The close personal friendships which Horace White and his wife made with Fessenden and Grimes established a bond among them that continued for the rest of their lives.

For White, the friendships meant a great deal in his attempt to report the Washington scene. He soon came to be known as a correspondent with "very valuable sources of information."[3] For Senator Grimes of Iowa, the relationship with White was mutually beneficial. Since the Senator's district was in the growing sphere of the *Chicago Tribune*'s influence, Grimes happily took the paper's fledgling reporter under his wing. When Joseph Medill demanded that White give up his year-round job in the Treasury Department so that he could return to Chicago after Congress adjourned, Grimes made White the clerk of his Senate Committee on the District of Columbia.[4] White returned this generosity by placing complimentary notices of the Senator's legislative actions in the *Tribune*. No Senator, not even Trumbull of Illinois, received such favorable coverage in the paper's Washington dispatches.

White's letters to the *Tribune* gave the young man a powerful vehicle. The *Tribune* rightly warned its readers, when his first letter appeared, that their correspondent was no "trimmer or compromiser, but one who believes that to go straight forward in the path of duty is always politic; that right is ever expedient."[5] White lived up to his billing; he wrote boldly. As a result, he frequently drew the ire and attention of Congressmen, generals, and government officials. He was damned, threatened, and accused in both Houses of Congress and many a private office as well.

White found a lot to complain about. He was shocked by the pervasive spirit of corruption and speculation that followed the advent of Republicans to power: Lincoln did not bring back the "age of purity." White frankly admitted that the "tone of morality" was "considerably lower" than it had ever been before. For all their faults, the southern politicians had "a very nice sense of honor so far as the public treasury was concerned." When they left, "the frauds and attempted frauds in the treasury . . . came so fast and from such unexpected quarters, that one is bewildered in contemplating them."[6]

Unfortunately these frauds could have tragic results when men risked their lives on battlefronts with shoddy equipment purchased from speculating contractors. Snooping around Washington, White uncovered one such fraud when he learned that an expedition of General Burnside failed because of useless transports sold to the War Department. His account of Burnside's anger over the incident made a sensational news item.[7]

White's major concern in his letters to the *Chicago Tribune* was not the exposure of wartime frauds. Although he could never stomach corruption, he found this defect in Republican ranks overshadowed by the need for a broad coalition to defeat the slavocracy. As soon as he set foot in Washington, White urged a radical solution to the problem of slavery. He acknowledged the failures and moral obtuseness of John C. Fremont, but he did not let the Missouri exposures end his frantic desire for the North to strike a direct blow at slavery. His first letter from Washington proclaimed that "there is a just God, before whom slavery stands a stupendous crime." "Does any one," he asked, "say that slavery is not the cause the very *sole* cause, of the war?" Anyone doubting that slavery and slavery alone was responsible for the bloodshed, must be "a secessionist at heart" or a plain "lunatic."[8]

A few weeks in Washington, however, convinced White that not everyone shared his point of view. On a tour of the Washington jail with Senator Grimes, he discovered dozens of imprisoned fugitive slaves before he and the Senator had to flee the stinking dungeon with handkerchiefs to their noses. Horror at the official degradation of these fugitives did much to undermine the investigators' faith in the administration, especially since one of Lincoln's favorites, Ward Lamon, the marshal of the District of Columbia, refused to alter the conditions in the jail which White labeled a "Black Hole of Calcutta." Lamon, to make matters worse, humiliated Grimes by barring him from the jail without a pass signed by himself. At this affront Grimes went directly to the White House, but Lincoln's servants refused even to take Grimes's name to the President. Grimes never forgave Lincoln for this insult.[9]

White had already suspected that Lincoln had feet of clay. The Cameron appointment had stunned him and the Fremont imbroglio left him bewildered. The Lamon incident only further shook his faith in Lincoln's moral integrity. He could never understand Lincoln's loyalty to the flamboyant Ward Lamon after the frequent disclosures of the marshal's cupidity and negligence.

The disappointments did not end with Lamon. When White arrived in Washington, rumors circulated that a "serious, if not fatal disagreement on the slavery question" threatened to disrupt Lincoln's cabinet.[10] Ironically, White found that Simon Cameron took the lead of the antislavery faction in the Cabinet by issuing an order that allowed confiscation of fugitive slaves. Again, as in the Fremont case, White had to face the awkward dilemma of defending a man of dubious personal and public character. Bumping into Cameron in the Senate Chamber, White confirmed for himself that the Cabinet dissension was about to break into the open.[11] He doubted that Lincoln would again defy popular sentiment by expelling Cameron. But he discovered in listening to Lincoln's annual message to Congress on December 4, 1861, that the President was not prepared to advance the antislavery cause by advocating emancipation.[12]

Charles Ray, still editor of the *Chicago Tribune,* became so alarmed at the news forwarded by White from Washington that he wrote a frantic letter to Charles Sumner. He accused the President of becoming "reactionary and feeble," and urged the Senator to "carry our principles out to their logical conclusion, and trust God for the consequences." Admitting the embarrassment of having to back Cameron after challenging his nomination to the Cabinet only several months earlier, Ray insisted, nonetheless, that the Radicals had to "accept the issues and the men raised up for the crisis."[13]

White proved more cautious. In a rare exhibition of patience and restraint, he refused to ally himself with the more radical sentiment in Congress. Although he supported Cameron's "just and wise inclinations," he seemed unable to bring himself into open conflict with the President. His letters to the *Tribune* ridiculed those radicals who still made apologies for Fremont. When White singled out Schuyler Colfax for particularly cutting barbs of criticism, Colfax defended himself against the *Tribune*'s "racy correspondent" in a letter to that paper.[14] The Radical Republicans were a divided group.

White looked hopefully for any sign that Lincoln had not abandoned the antislavery cause. No longer privy to Lincoln's inner thoughts, he reflected the confusion in Washington created by Lincoln's reticence and ambiguity. When Lincoln intimated to certain Congressmen that he generally approved of their efforts to confiscate the slaves of rebels, White seized at the information to "correct the painful impression" he had given to his readers regarding the President's conservative policies. Still, he wished that Lincoln would become "the leader of the inspiring cause, rather than its rearguard."[15]

Only a few days later, White began to qualify even this mild praise. The reasons for a sudden halt in Congress's effort to pass a confiscation act seemed to point accusingly down Pennsylvania Avenue to the White House. A confused Horace White confessed that he may have misled the readers of the *Tribune* once again about the President. Still he refused to condemn Lincoln:

> I would do no injustice to the President of the United States, nor say ought which should abate the confidence of the people in him. for upon his shoulders is an awful responsibility. If, with the means

placed at his disposal, he shall fail, his own reflections will be more than he can bear; and let it not be said that my indiscretion placed any straws in the way by which the country might have been saved.[16]

Whatever may have been White's personal opinions of Lincoln during the war, he avoided outright censure of the President in his letters from Washington. Instead, whenever he was displeased, White accused Lincoln's advisers of deceiving the President. His chief villain was Secretary of State William H. Seward, who was consistently blamed for forcing a limited set of objectives upon the Administration.[17]

When Cameron resigned from the Cabinet, White even defended Lincoln's letting Cameron go. He found that Cameron's case "was very similar to Fremont's." Both held the right doctrines on the slavery questions, but "either of them would have bankrupted old Midas himself. . . . The parallel might be carried farther, to the incompetency of the twain."[18]

If White, like the editors of the *Tribune,* held back from criticizing Lincoln, he castigated other civil and military leaders. Soon after he arrived in Washington, White crossed the Potomac to look over the armies in their winter quarters in Virginia. Standing on a hill overlooking a plain, he saw "as far as the eye could reach, the white tents and curling smoke of the camps" which stretched away in the "soft haze of Indian summer." The panorama of the thousands of soldiers struck him with awe.[19] Making occasional trips to the headquarters of the army and gathering military news where he could, White found more than a placid and picturesque scene across the Potomac.

From unnamed army officers White learned that a certain General Lockwood, while on a minor expedition along the Potomac, had captured, flogged, and returned runaway slaves to Confederate lines. Insisting that the "proslavery commander" had forced the "brave lads" of the Fourth Wisconsin and the Sixth Michigan regiments to lay on the lash, White appealed to the soldiers' relatives to call an end to the army's "puerile and proslavery policy."[20] His disclosure of this incident in the *Chicago Tribune* echoed eastward and gained nationwide publicity. He got his first taste of the power that newspaper correspondents held during the war.

White's muckraking drew so much attention that Lockwood's commanding officer, General John A. Dix, called the reporter to a private meeting at Willard's Hotel. Dix denied that Lockwood had flogged any Negroes. But Dix could not answer a corroborative story that Congressman John F. Potter of Wisconsin had received and handed to White before his meeting with the general. White smugly announced his victory to *Tribune* readers: "I am of the same opinion still."[21]

White continued to attack the commanders of the Virginia army relentlessly. Drawing the epithet of the "On to Richmond" correspondent, he wrote that the army needed only the order "Forward, march."[22] With little respect for George McClellan and absolute disdain for the "dyspeptic and laggard" William T. Sherman, he urged that Generals David Hunter and James Lane replace them. The responsibility for initiating this change, White left to Lincoln. Quoting the rumors that Lincoln was as "much annoyed and vexed at the evidence of the army as anybody else," White felt that annoyance and vexation were insufficient. He retorted, "Well, it happens to be *his* prerogative to inaugurate a different system, or to find out satisfactory reasons for the indolence of the army—and his alone. . . . He alone, of all complainers, has no excuse for complaining."[23]

White admitted, however, that Edwin Stanton's appointment to fill Cameron's post could prove the catalyst for a revitalization of the army. He felt encouraged that Lincoln had chosen a man of antislavery convictions to run the War Department, and his friends Fessenden and Grimes were likewise satisfied with the choice after their interviews with Stanton.[24] White was particularly delighted with Stanton's Assistant Secretary, Peter Watson, who had become his close friend after taking up quarters at Mrs. Chipman's boarding house. White introduced the Assistant Secretary to his *Tribune* readers as "a man of unspotted character, great energy, and decided antislavery opinions."[25] He also found his new friend a good source for War Department information.[26]

After a few weeks of waiting for Stanton to effect some startling transformation, White grew impatient. More would be needed, he declared, than Stanton's "mouthfuls of wind," which he and Grimes felt were only showy substitutes for action. There was no reason, White insisted, why the North "should not in sixty days have the rebels encircled in fire."[27] His frustration and restlessness mounted. Indeed, he concluded that the lethargy of the executive department was even beginning to affect Congress. He accused the legislators of "timidity and servility" in handling "finance, foreign relations, military affairs, or executive corruption." Even more importantly they, too, refused to deal head on with slavery; they had no excuse, White insisted, for not having abolished slavery in the District of Columbia.[28]

Almost before he had finished his indictment of civil and military inaction, news of victories by federal gunboats on western rivers caused the emotional young reporter to cover his rash pessimism with an equally hasty optimism. He found it "easy now to conceive that the military power of the rebellion is in a fair way of being broken." It was high time to think about what the nation's objectives were to be after the rebel armies were crushed. To insure peace, White felt that the victors had to abolish slavery. From this, he assured his readers, would proceed myriad national blessings. He urged Congress once again to begin the work in the District of Columbia.[29]

The jubilant mood of victory, however, did not stir Congress from its conservative mood. Nor did the first major victories of the federal armies rejuvenate the nation's finances. Caught now in an almost daily cycle of elation and despair, White again lost hope. He said: "That slavery should be stronger the day after the rebel armies are destroyed than it ever was before, and that the universal bankruptcy and public repudiation should be the reward of the loyal States, is hardly a pleasant banquet for this generation."[30]

The victories in Tennessee and Kentucky also failed to spur the armies of George McClellan on to Richmond as White had hoped. Instead, the eastern army almost suffered another disaster. Preparations to cross the Potomac by means of a pontoon bridge went awry as the floating supports built in the canal between Cumberland and Washington proved too large to get through the locks. General Banks, who had crossed by other means with the expectation of joining the main force in Virginia, found himself in a precarious position. Fortunately, he was able to scurry back to Union quarters unscathed.

Although appalled by the fiasco, White and his associates in Washington were "on the grin" over the "Harper's Ferry fizzle." They were filled with "inextinguishable laughter" and hoped that McClellan would now fall from Lincoln's favor. Reports that "Lincoln acted like a Philistine when he heard the upshot of the affair" increased White's expectation that McClellan's head was about to roll. His friend Grimes jokingly observed that "there were unoccupied rooms in Fremont's house."[31]

When Lincoln presented his special message to Congress on March 6, 1862, calling for compensated emancipation, White grasped at it enthusiastically as a sign that Lincoln was at last ready to take up the antislavery cause. To his editor, White concluded that Lincoln had "broken with the Border States and determined to cultivate our side a while."[32] To *Tribune* readers, White confided that the message, mild as it was, had "excited the warm hopes" of Lincoln's friends—and "of none more than myself."[33] White desperately wanted to have Lincoln take the lead. However much he may have criticized Lincoln, there always remained in his mind an anxious hope than Lincoln was merely playing politics and would eventually come forward as the antislavery champion he had been in Illinois. Mulling over Lincoln's message to Congress for a few more days, White was convinced.

> I am of the opinion that Mr. Lincoln has determined to shake off the Kentucky nightmare and be himself again. Let us recall the speech with which he commenced the memorable campaign of 1858: "A house divided against itself cannot stand. This country cannot exist half slave and half free. Either the opponents of slavery will arrest the further spread of it, *and place it where the public mind shall rest in the belief that it is in the course of ultimate extinction. . . ."* Interpreted by this declaration, as it should be, the special message to Congress can only mean that the President has determined to place slavery where the public mind shall rest in the belief that it is in the course of ultimate extinction, and have visible grounds for the belief. It should be observed that, in point of view, the message came immediately after the clearing out of rebellion from Kentucky and Missouri. . . . It is thought by many that the President has been reserving this shot for the contingency which has now been brought about, and that it was his intention from the beginning, after securing so much ground, to put his views of the incompatibility of slavery and freedom into practical operation.[34]

White speculated that Lincoln would now sign the bill abolishing slavery in the District of Columbia. Elated once again, he looked for and found additional signs of progress in the antislavery cause. He noted the recent assignments of the radical Generals Wadsworth, Hunter, and Ben Butler, and the reassignment of General Fremont which he felt "whatever else may be said of it, is an antislavery fact." Negro catching and whipping had stopped. "Congress after a pretty tough struggle with Marshal Lamon has got the Washington jail purified of its worst elements." "These are gratifying indications of progress," White concluded, "and I for one am disposed to make the most of them, for which 'Old Abe' is entitled to the credit."[35]

White, with his hopes thus buoyed, expectantly turned his attention to the Union armies on the Potomac, where McClellan was about to begin his cautious peninsular campaign. Although military censorship handicapped White's reports of McClellan's preparations, the authorities did not prevent him from telling his editors about the important tidbits of information that he was able to gather from friends or careless officials.[36]

The ease with which he gathered this confidential material illustrates the security problems that federal forces had faced. For example, White gave Charles Ray advance notice of the excursion of the *Monitor,* pointing out that its movements were only a feint for larger operations.[37] He also passed on to Ray the informed surmise that the federal armies would initiate an oblique attack toward Norfolk. He obtained this information from a Lieutenant Wise of the Navy ordinance department, who inferred the strike from the overt attention officers were giving to charts of the Nansemond River and other approaches to Suffolk, Virginia.[38]

Confederates did undoubtedly gather much military intelligence from the reports of northern war correspondents. This was a constant danger. Charles Ray, therefore, placed certain limitations on his own correspondents. White, however, with his eyes centered on exposure, chafed under this restriction, for he hated to "sacrifice so many good things because they happen to be true."[39]

Obliged to equivocate with the news of McClellan's campaign, White turned his attention instead to the actions of Congress. Here he used the power of exposure with daring, particularly in the case of Republican Congressmen who were vacillating or weakening on the issue of slavery in Washington.

When Senator Doolittle of Wisconsin softened the impact of the District of Columbia abolition bill by providing for compensation and colonization, White accused the senator of opposing emancipation. Doolittle quickly turned on him in a pointed speech before the Senate. The senator accused White of holding a sinecure as clerk of the Senate Committee on the District of Columbia and protested that he was unable to "pension correspondents" in order to get the "purchased encomiums so unworthily bestowed, by which great men and heroes are manufactured here." Extremely irritated by White's journalistic barbs, Doolittle branded all his newspaper critics "foolish creatures."[40] To his wife, the senator confidently asserted that his amendment saved the bill from being vetoed.[41]

Although White was disappointed with the moderate provisions of the District bill, he rejoiced that the capital was about to be "purged of the high disgrace and most hateful sin of slavery." He thought, moreover, that the bill would only be the beginning of an antislavery reaction which he boasted had already set in.[42]

His anticipations were shattered when, several weeks later, the confiscation bill of Lyman Trumbull stalled in Congress. White blamed the predominance of lawyers in the Senate for the delay. "It would be strange," he wrote, "if a measure so bedeviled with eminent jurists and constitutional scruples should ever be enacted into a law."[43] The majority of the members of the Confiscation Committee were, in the young reporter's mind, "either too eminent in the legal profession, or too decidedly opposed to radical measures against the rebellion, to afford much ground for hope."[44]

By the end of May, 1862, White's latest fit of despair degenerated into a hopeless despondency. First, Lincoln countermanded the emancipation order of another general—this time that of General David Hunter, one of White's favorites. Then, when the cautious federal offensive into Virginia came to a halt at the second battle at Bull Run, a daring counteroffensive by Lee and Jackson threw Washington into a panic. On May 25, the capital had a big scare. White called it the "craziest panic gotten up. . . . The aggregate result was a city half frantic with terror."[45]

The humiliation of defeat and the failure of Congress to act forcefully against slavery, White maintained, occasioned "gloomy forebodings on the subject of foreign intervention." Loyal senators for the first time, he remarked, began to speak of recognizing the Confederacy. "Naught but a prompt and crushing blow, directed straight at the head of the monster can save us from this galling, ruinous conclusion of all our efforts."[46] But White really expected no such offensive; privately he indicated that he had lost faith in a President who was "irresolute" and a "coward."[47]

Events only increased the gloom. Back home, the Democrats won important victories in Chicago and Illinois; in Washington, Congress emasculated the confiscation bill. To compound White's depression, the Confederates won another series of victories, this time on the Chicahominy. "It has seemed at times," White groaned, "as though the last day had come and found the world plunged in wickedness and sin." The news of the latest Union defeats reached Washington on a dismal, rain-drenched day. "The day after Bull Run," White told his readers, "was not half so melancholy."[48]

The cruelest blow for White came when Lincoln intimated to several members of Congress that he would veto the already weakened confiscation bill which they were about to send to him for approval. White recorded the indignation of his friend Senator Fessenden. Even a "crabbed conservative" like the Senator from Maine, White complained, was "particularly savage on this back-kitchen style of veto."[49] Lincoln, however, had his way: Congress amended the bill and the President approved it. The last minute modification ended the session.

White returned to Illinois in a pessimistic mood. He and the *Tribune* editors had hoped to enter the fall elections on an advanced platform of emancipation and confiscation. They felt they could win on those issues and therefore scolded the President for doubting that the "great body of loyal men" were ready. "The people are already there," they proclaimed.[50]

Still, the editors held back in their criticism of the President; they muted their personal thoughts in the paper. In order to defeat the "copperheads" and "secesh," they had to defend the President's actions. For the rest of the summer, they justified his "despotic power" and held him up as a "clear light even in the foul atmosphere of the Capitol."[51] Only later in September did Lincoln give them a chance to take the offensive they wanted.

Shortly after the Union armies won an expensive victory at Antietam on September 17, Lincoln issued a preliminary edict of emancipation. The *Tribune* editors cheerfully publicized the announcement but privately considered the action insufficient to turn back the tide of popular resentment against the Administration. Others, like Senator Browning of Illinois, thought that the insertion of emancipation into the campaign had insured the Democratic victory.[52] Whatever the cause, the Democrats won major victories in Illinois and elsewhere in the nation.

Horace White, continuing in his position as secretary of the Republican state central committee, was active in the Illinois campaign. After the election he analyzed the result for William Butler, the committee treasurer. Evidently White and others had been bitter that Lincoln did not participate more energetically in the midterm elections. But the President had already smoothed the Radicals' ruffled feathers; immediately after the election he dismissed George B. Mc-Clellan from the command of the Union armies. White felt that the removal of the "moral and military incubus" made up for the defeat. In any case, he did not blame Lincoln for the loss; candidly he admitted, "the people were against us this time. No amount of work could have brought about a different result."[53]

The Whites did not depart for Washington until the middle of December. Since Martha fell sick in Illinois, they could not join their accustomed social circle at the beginning of the congressional session.[54] White arrived at the capital later, during the war's darkest hour. On December 13, General Burnside led the Union forces into the terrible disaster at Fredericksburg. White's first letter to the *Tribune* expressed his despair. "Nearly six months ago," he wrote, "I left Washington enshrouded in gloom on account of the Chicahominy reverses. . . . I return to find it plunged into deeper gloom, occasioned by another disaster, the product of more deplorable blundering than ever before overtook the brave army of the Potomac."[55]

Instinctively White looked about for a scapegoat. He first pointed the finger of blame at General Halleck, then at Burnside, but finally at Secretary Seward, who, White claimed, had "not given up the idea of putting down the rebellion by witchcraft." White cried for Seward's scalp and urged that Lincoln "summarily dismiss and depose every incapable."[56]

Radicals and moderates alike in Congress joined the call for a reorganization of the Cabinet; a caucus of thirty Republican Senators demanded Seward's resignation. White assured his readers that the Senate was a "cowardly body" and only "an overwhelming public opinion could have driven them to this action."[57] He despaired that "from the 4th of March, 1861, to this hour, the government has failed to trust the people." The President had been too much under the influence of the Secretary of State.[58]

By finding a villain in Seward, White could continue to hold back any direct criticism of the President. Even at this point he steadfastly refused to alienate himself publicly from

Lincoln. Getting a report of the senators' interview with Lincoln, White was quick to praise the President:

> Think what a *world of perplexity* hedges the footsteps of Abraham Lincoln at every turn; I believe there was not one of the nine Senators but returned from the interview with higher opinions of the President and better hopes for the country than he felt before.[59]

But Lincoln ignored the senators' demands and Seward withdrew his proffered resignation. White thought this unexpected rebuff by Lincoln would lead to a conflict, which he had "hoped not to see sprung upon the country in a time like this—a conflict between the President and those who are required, by terms of the Constitution, to 'advise and consent' to all his elective appointments." White denied Lincoln's assertion that harmony existed within the Cabinet. "I can affirm of my own knowledge," he wrote, "that it does not exist—that on the contrary there exists the widest possible divergence on the most important subjects of national concern."[60]

Even if White wanted to break with Lincoln, he no longer had an opportunity to mount any kind of offensive. Lincoln's promised Emancipation Proclamation came as scheduled on January 1, 1863. This was no time for a feud. "The Proclamation," White announced, "is received with unmixed satisfaction by loyal men at the Capitol." The reservations in the edict, White further asserted, did not abate anything "from the general joy over the greatest event since crucifixion. . . . A people have been born in a day."[61]

Notwithstanding his elation, White recognized northern opposition to the proclamation and therefore urged Congress to pass "legislation of the most effective sort" which would make emancipation "an accomplished fact before Fernando Wood or Clement Vallandigham run for the Presidency."[62] White realistically faced the struggle that lay before the radical Republicans. "It has cost us twenty months of anguish to get Buell and McClellan removed, and freedom proclaimed to the slaves of rebels. It may cost us more to get rid of other encumbrances, and to put the proclamation in working order."[63]

Whatever role White saw for himself in the new stage of the antislavery battle, he soon had to conduct it outside of the columns of the *Chicago Tribune*. Even before the last session of the Thirty-seventh Congress came to a close on March 14, 1863, White quit sending his regular letter to the *Tribune*. The management of the paper had in recent months fallen to Joseph Medill. Charles Ray, to whom White was allied, finally sold out his interest in the *Tribune,* thereby enabling Medill to take over the editorial lead.[64] Having good reason to suspect that Medill would dispense with his services, White left the *Tribune* to take a position as a clerk in the War Department.[65] His close friend Peter Watson, the Assistant Secretary of War, had undoubtedly arranged the job for him.

Working for the administration was something new for Horace White. No longer obliged to expose inefficiency, fraud, or error in a daily newspaper, he assumed a friendlier posture toward the executive branch. Indeed he became one of Stanton's favorites in the Department.[66] Holding an administrative appointment, however, was not the only reason for his new attitude. Lincoln had committed the government to an antislavery program and had begun a more vigorous prosecution of the war.[67]

Military victories did not immediately follow emancipation as White had predicted. Nor was there a wave of slave insurrections as he had warned the South. Instead the war continued as a dirty, bloody series of battles which only slowly turned the Confederate tide. Lee won another battle with the federal armies at Chancellorville at a very heavy cost of southern lives. White, however, thought only of Lee's victory; he was moved to despair when he wrote to Senator Fessenden in Portland, Maine, about the humiliation of another defeat. Since he was now privy to the exertions of the War Department, he did not castigate the administration. He hoped only that Lee would "get severely punished" before he got back to his own territory.[68] Victories did finally come but at a terrible price—first at Vicksburg and then at Gettysburg, Chickamauga, and Chattanooga. It was no triumphant crusade.

Although White became officially connected with the executive department, he did not cease pushing for antislavery action. True, the administration had become firmly committed to emancipation, but White urged Lincoln to be more forceful. That he was optimistic about Lincoln he indicated when he agreed with Senator Fessenden that the President would "distance his Secretaries" in the battle against the rebellion. He regretted only that Lincoln had become needlessly obsessed with the notion that Radicals intended to substitute someone else for him in 1864.[69]

He was much more critical of Congress. He felt they should take up the emancipation question more boldly and pass a constitutional amendment which would "kill all the heads of the hydra at the same killing." "We have had enough slavery. It has left its ineffaceable marks upon us. We are striving to get rid of it, and we intend to get rid of it. Let us then bury it under a massive constitutional prohibition. Let us 'throw millions of acres on it' that its sepulchre may be at once a wonder and a warning to all future generations."[70]

Two long years in Washington may have sobered the brash young man who came there to cover the activities of that first wartime Congress for the *Chicago Tribune*. Certainly his sojourn in the capital during the darkest hours of the war had matured his judgment. Yet he did not yield an inch to his principles. Time, he felt, had vindicated his earlier demands and justified his strained but continued faith in the President. In a special dispatch to the *Tribune*, he expressed his pleasure as the new year approached.

A more striking contrast can hardly be found in history than that presented by a glance at the circumstances and spirit attending the assembling of the American Congress two years ago, and those which we witness today. . . . The changes wrought by the two years which have intervened may be comprehended in a sentence. We have learned to disregard the feelings of the enemy on the battlefield, and we have been taught to strike down slavery, both as a means of saving the Republic, and as an act of justice to a down trodden race. The statue of Freedom crowns the Capitol at a fitting time. The rising sun may now gild her countenance with true glory, for the President of the United States, in declaring that a revocation of his Proclamation would be "a cruel and astounding breach of faith," has uttered a moral sentiment, by the side of which all his former acts of expediency shrink to their proper significance.[71]

Seeing his words in print again in the *Chicago Tribune* apparently made White anxious to return to his journalistic haunts and activities. When his old friends Grimes and Fessenden returned with the Thirty-eighth Congress, White left the War Department and joined his normal social circle once again.[72] Washington came alive, and the country focused its attention on the Capitol as the rebellion drew to a climax. The newspapers could hardly meet the demand in the nation for the news of the war.

Together with Henry Villard and Adams S. Hill, White decided to capitalize on the demand for information by establishing the Independent News Room service in Washington. Villard and Hill, who had both left the *New York Tribune* after arguments with Horace Greeley, were two of the best members of the news corps covering the war. Taking advantage of a quarrel between the Western Associated Press and the New York Associated Press, the three young men began supplying several major western papers and a few eastern journals with special dispatches and features.[73] Although handicapped in competing with the Associated Press, which held a monopolistic contract with the nation's major telegraph companies, White and his friends proved resourceful enough to earn a "pleasant, lucrative and independent" living from their new business.[74]

White finally gained the wealth he had sought when he left Beloit in 1853. Even during the war, he did not let his antislavery activity interfere with good business. His income in 1864 was over $15,000. Only a few hundred men in Chicago made that much money. Not all of this income, however, came from the newspaper syndicate. Learning of certain proposed taxes on whiskey manufacturers and gambling on higher future prices for liquor, White and several of his friends bought large quantities before the levy was announced and sold their stock at a profit when the new taxes raised the price.[75] To this rather large windfall White added the salary he obtained as clerk of the Senate Military Affairs Committee. Like his previous position on the Senate Committee on the District of Columbia, the job paid him six dollars a day while Congress was in session.[76] But more importantly, the job gave him a good source of information for his news bureau.

The Independent News Room drew attention to itself by making several notable scoops of army news.[77] It drew so much attention, in fact, that officials blamed it for the publication in May, 1864, of a bogus proclamation announcing a significant increase in the draft. The proclamation (actually forged by a rogue in the news corps named Joseph Howard) created a panic among Washington officials who well remembered the draft riots in New York and other cities only a short time before. The North was weary of the decimation of Grant's forces in the wilderness; this was certainly no time for any announcement of a call for three hundred thousand more men.

The General Agent of the Associated Press, D. H. Craig, sensing an opportunity to ruin his young competitor, blamed the big lie on White's concern. Stanton picked up the accusation quickly and threw Villard into custody. He kept Hill under surveillance and brought White into his office for a personal grilling. When officials found the real culprit, Stanton released Villard, apologized to White, and leaked some important news to their syndicate in order to soothe the righteous anger of the young newsmen.[78]

In return for such favors, White came to the defense of the administration when northern papers criticized the government for overestimating the forces with which Jubal Early overran the Shenandoah Valley in July, 1864, and threatened Washington itself. White denounced the War Department's critics in a fashion ironic for one who had savagely criticized the military in the earlier years of the war.[79]

Criticism of the Lincoln administration was reaching its crest. White and his associates had long been radical in their views of the war and slavery, but they did not associate themselves with the Republicans who wished to replace Lincoln as the party's candidate for the presidency in 1864. Fessenden and Grimes, White's closest friends in Congress, were bitterly critical of Lincoln, but they held aloof from the more extreme radicals such as Ben Wade and Thad Stevens. Grimes and Fessenden hated Sumner, looked with scorn on Fremont, and had little respect for Chase. Fessenden's resistance to Lincoln broke down entirely when he accepted the Treasury post in the Cabinet, and Grimes decided he would merely sit out the election. White, for the most part, followed the lead of Fessenden and Grimes but drew closer to the administration as he became more intimate with it. The *Chicago Tribune,* though maintaining its independence, likewise supported Lincoln. When Ben Wade and Henry Davis, for example, published their manifesto in retaliation against Lincoln's pocket veto of their reconstruction plan, the *Tribune* rose to Lincoln's defense even though it had previously supported the Wade-Davis bill in Congress.[80] All of White's closest associates refused to take part in any attempt to dump Lincoln or to mount a third party movement. White himself rejoiced at Lincoln's nomination at Baltimore; in fact, his telegram was the first to break the news of the nomination to the President.[81] The radicals were a divided group; Lincoln retained the support of many throughout the political crisis in 1864.[82]

When White returned to Chicago to help the *Tribune* pump for Lincoln's reelection, he found the paper divided into two new warring factions. Ray's departure evidently had not brought unity to the staff. No particular issue seemed prominent. But since it still took more than two of the major owners to fix editorial policy, Medill was unable to keep the peace. His two year stint as editor-in-chief had witnessed constant bickering. White, only a minor stockholder, threw his weight to the dissidents aligned against Medill. William Bross, who was leading this faction, proposed that the stockholders invite Charles Ray to resume the chief editorship. Medill threatened to leave the paper, but the stockholders held firm and, through White, made Ray an offer of a one year appointment. White had tried to manage the *Tribune* as the paper floundered without editorial leadership. But he quickly stepped down. "The experiment has satisfied me," he wrote to Ray; "I think I know what it is to be in Tophet without claws."[83] White's reference to the ancient valley of human sacrifice probably did not offer Ray much encouragement.

When the governor of Illinois, Richard Oglesby, heard of the proposed shift in the editorial management of the *Tribune,* he hastily wrote to Lincoln to urge him to intervene. Republicans could not afford such divisiveness on the staff of their major newspaper in Illinois. Knowing that Ray had applied to Lincoln for authority to engage in some speculative trade with the Confederacy, Oglesby begged Lincoln to give Ray the necessary permission and thus remove him from consideration as editor of the *Tribune.* Lincoln promptly gave Ray a generous commission to trade with the enemy, and

Ray happily gave up the $3,000 salary offer from the *Tribune* owners in order to travel South in search of his fortune.[84]

The *Tribune* management continued uneasily under the direction of Medill but supported Lincoln vigorously. Fear obviously helped to keep them together, for the prospect of victory looked slim until late August. White's friend Grimes, for example, pessimistically predicted Lincoln's defeat.[85] But the spectacular victories of Sherman in Georgia saved the presidency for Lincoln.

After the election, Grant and Sherman caught the Confederate armies in a slow but steadily tightening viselike grip that crushed the Confederacy. The objectives set by the *Tribune*—an unconditional surrender brought about by a crushing military defeat of the rebellion and the abolition of slavery carried out by a constitutional amendment—were achieved shortly after Lincoln's inauguration in March. When the announcement of Lee's surrender at Appomattox reached Chicago, the people of the city flooded the streets to "shout, sing, laugh, dance and cry for very gladness." In the midst of this jubilation, the *Tribune* editors proudly proclaimed their own personal triumph: "The radical doctrines taught by the Tribune long in advance of their acceptance have been fully endorsed and adopted by the government, and what was at first pronounced impractical radicalism is now revealed as practical statesmanship."[86]

NOTES

1. Charles Jellison, *Fessenden of Maine* (Syracuse, N. Y., 1962), p. 140.

2. Fessenden to Elizabeth Wariner, December 1, 1861, Fessenden Family Papers, Bowdoin College. Fessenden's weekly letters to his cousin, Elizabeth Wariner, frequently mention Martha White. The hardworking widower found young Martha White his closest female companion while in Washington; he enjoyed the diversion of her light talk while on strolls through the city or during evening games of euchre. See, for example, December 1, 1861; May 17, November 30, 1862; March 14, December 6, December 13,

1863; January 10, January 23, February 20, February 27, March 13, March 19, May 7, June 11, July 24, August 27, 1864.

3. Adams S. Hill to Sydney Gay, November 25, 1863, Gay Family MSS, Columbia University. Hill, one of the *New York Tribune's* best reporters, told Gay, his managing editor, that White often shared his scoops with him.

4. White became clerk of the Senate Committee on the District of Columbia in March, 1862. He held this position until the end of the session in July, 1862. When he returned to report the next session in December, he took up his sinecure again and retained it until March 14, 1863, when he became a clerk in the War Department. His salary in the Senate was six dollars a day. See the salary records in the Office of the Clerk of the Senate in the U. S. Capitol.

5. *Chicago Tribune,* December 5, 1861.

6. Ibid., April 1, 1862. Southern newspapers embarrassed White by picking up his comments and using them as propaganda. See his letter, ibid., May 7, 1862.

7. J. Cutler Andrews, *The North Reports the Civil War* (Pittsburgh, 1955), pp. 220-221. *Chicago Tribune,* January 31, 1862. White to the editors of the *Tribune,* January 31, 1862, Ray MSS.

8. *Chicago Tribune,* December 5, 1861.

9. Ibid., December 5, 1861, January 4, January 17, January 20, January 22, 1862. See also *Congressional Globe,* 37th Cong., 2d sess. (1861-1862), pp. 310-311. White to Jesse Weik, August 12, 1914, Weik-Herndon MSS. "The point in the case," White wrote to Weik, "is that Lincoln never took notice of this glaring infraction of law and morals. His obtuseness on this occasion was the cause of coolness that existed between Grimes and Lincoln during all the remainder of L's life."

10. *Chicago Tribune,* December 7, 1861.

11. Ibid., December 8, 1861.

12. Ibid., December 9, 1861.

13. Ray to Sumner, December 6, 1861, Sumner MSS, Harvard University. Ray repeated the same thoughts, though more moderately, to Elihu Washburne and Lyman Trumbull. Ray to Washburne, December 6, 1861, Washburne MSS. Ray to Trumbull, December 6, 1861, Trumbull MSS.

14. *Chicago Tribune,* December 14, 1861, December 28, 1861, January 8, 1861.

15. Ibid., December 19, 1861.

16. Ibid., December 23, 1861.

17. Ibid., December 30, 1861, January 1, 1862.

18. Ibid., January 20, 1862.

19. Ibid., December 18, 1861.

20. Ibid., December 30, 1861. See also January 9, 1862.

21. Ibid., January 14, 1862.

22. Ibid., January 22, 1862.

23. Ibid., January 23, 1862.

24. Ibid., February 1, 1862.

25. Ibid., January 31, 1862.

26. Other reporters likewise found Watson a splendid "leak" for army news. See Adams S. Hill to Sydney Gay, July 14, 1862, Gay Family MSS. Hill, White, and Watson were all close friends.

27. *Chicago Tribune*, February 14, 1862. On White's view of Stanton during the early part of the war, see his autobiographical notes in the Horace White MSS, Illinois State Historical Library.

28. *Chicago Tribune*, February 14, 1862.

29. Ibid., February 18, 1862.

30. Ibid., February 20, 1862.

31. White to Joseph Medill, March 3, 1862, and White to Charles Ray, March 3, 1862: Ray MSS.

32. White to Charles Ray, March 7, n.y. [1862], Ray MSS.

33. *Chicago Tribune*, March 3, 1862.

34. Ibid., March 12, 1862.

35. Ibid., March 17, 1862.

36. Stanton, who initiated strict censorship, created resentment among newspapermen. White called the Secretary "a kind of Mephistopheles" but admitted that Stanton's hatred of McClellan covered a multitude of sins. White to Ray, March 26, 1862, Ray MSS.

37. Ibid., March 7 [1862], in the Ray MSS.

38. Ibid., March 26, 1862, Ray MSS.

39. Ibid.

40. *Congressional Globe*, 37th Cong., 2d sess., Appendix, p. 94. See also White's letter in the *Chicago Tribune*, April 19, 1862, explaining that Doolittle had the remarks directly aimed at White removed from the record. White apparently did not ease up on his criticism of Doolittle, as the senator's son, Henry, pleaded with his father in July, "Can't you shut up that White at Washington? He seems to be the 'head of the pack.'" Henry Doolittle to James Doolittle, July 8, 1862, Doolittle MSS, State Historical Society of Wisconsin.

41. Doolittle to Mary Doolittle, April 29, 1862, Doolittle MSS.

42. *Chicago Tribune*, April 19, 1862.

43. Ibid., May 10, 1862.

44. Ibid., May 15, 1862.

45. Ibid., May 31, 1862.

46. Ibid.

47. White to Charles Ray, May 28, 1862, Ray MSS.

48. *Chicago Tribune*, July 9, 1862.

49. Ibid., July 9, 17, 1862.

50. Joseph Medill to Lyman Trumbull, June 5, July 4, 1862, Trumbull MSS. *Chicago Tribune*, July 28, 1862.

51. *Chicago Tribune*, August 25, 1862. For an examination of *Tribune* editorial policy during the election, see Tracy E. Strevey, "Joseph Medill and the Chicago Tribune during the Civil War Period" (Ph.D. dissertation, University of Chicago, 1930), pp. 138–142.

52. Maurice Baxter, *Orville H. Browning* (Bloomington, Ind., 1957), pp. 144–148.

53. White to William Butler, November 11, 1862, Butler MSS, Chicago Historical Society. Lincoln had dismissed McClellan from his post the day after the elections.

54. William P. Fessenden to Elizabeth Wariner, November 30, 1862, Fessenden Family Papers.

55. *Chicago Tribune,* December 22, 1862.

56. Ibid.

57. Ibid., December 25, 1862.

58. Ibid., December 23, 1862.

59. Ibid., December 24, 1862. White undoubtedly got his report from Grimes or Fessenden, who were members of the delegation which took the caucus resolution to the White House.

60. Ibid., December 25, 1862.

61. Ibid., January 6, 1863.

62. Ibid.

63. Ibid., January 20, 1863.

64. Jay Monaghan, *The Man Who Elected Lincoln,* pp. 286–287. See also *Chicago Tribune,* November 26, 1863. White's position in the dispute is explained in White to Charles Ray, May 28, 1862, Ray MSS.

65. White was a clerk, class four; he served in that office from March 1 to December 15, 1863. See his letters to Stanton, April 3, 1863 (vol. 114: W 359), and November 30, 1863 (vol. 114: W 476), War Department, Letters Received, Main Series, National Archives.

66. David H. Bates, *Lincoln in the Telegraph Office* (New York, 1907), p. 242.

67. White also began to go to Lincoln directly when problems arose. Medill to White, March 5, 1863, in the Robert Todd Lincoln Coll. See also White to Stanton, March 15, 1866, in the Stanton MSS, Library of Congress.

68. White to William P. Fessenden, June 30, 1863, Fessenden MSS, Library of Congress. See also White to Elihu Washburne, April 5, 1863, Washburne MSS.

69. White to William P. Fessenden, November 2, 7, 1863, Fessenden Family Papers.

70. *Chicago Tribune,* November 20, 1863. White no longer wrote the *Tribune*'s regular Washington report; his letter—the first since February, 1863—was labeled as special correspondence.

71. Ibid., December 31, 1863.

72. William P. Fessenden to Elizabeth Wariner, December 6, 13, 1863, Fessenden Family Papers.

73. Henry Villard, *Memoirs of Henry Villard,* 2 (New York, 1904), p. 267. See also Louis M. Starr, *Bohemian Brigade* (New York, 1954), p. 317.

74. Henry Villard to Francis J. Garrison, April 5, 1864, Henry Villard MSS, Harvard University.

75. White's income after deductions in 1864 was $15,442. *Chicago Tribune,* July 18, 1865. There is substantial evidence that a good share of his income came from the whiskey speculations. Medill wrote Elihu Washburne: "As to the whisky business neither Scripps, Bross or myself ever had a cents interest in it. We were not able to keep White or our bookkeeper Cowles out of it." Medill to Washburne, November 21, 1864, Washburne MSS. The charge of wartime speculation was brought against White several times later in his life by political foes. When he countered the charges he did not deny that he made money by speculating on whiskey but only denied that he misused any official position in order to gain inside information on the taxes that would have enabled him to make opportune purchases. See Ward Lamon, "Ward Lamon and the Chicago Tribune" (n.p., 1866), p.63. (A privately published pamphlet which reprinted a letter from Lamon to General Asahel Cridley, n.d.) See also White to Whitelaw Reid, May 12, 1884, Whitelaw Reid MSS, Library of Congress.

76. Records in the office of the Clerk of the Senate, Capitol, Washington, D.C.

77. Bates, *Lincoln,* p. 242.

78. Ibid., pp., 242–243. *Chicago Tribune,* May 22, 1864.

79. *Chicago Tribune,* July 27, 1864.

80. Ibid., August 11, 1864.

81. Bates, *Lincoln,* p. 291.

82. Two important studies of Lincoln and the Radical Republicans fail to give much evidence of the division among the Radicals or, more importantly, the support that many of them gave Lincoln at various times. Arthur C. Cole, "President Lincoln and the Illinois Radical Republicans," *Mississippi Valley Historical Review* 4 (March, 1918): 417–436. T. Harry Williams, *Lincoln and the Radicals* (Madison, Wis., 1941). Two more recent studies have given necessary balance to the political relationship between the President and Radical Republicans: David Donald, "Devils Facing Zionwards," in Grady McWhinney, ed., *Grant, Lee, Lincoln and the Radicals* (Evanston, Ill., 1964), and Hans L. Trefousse, *The Radical Republicans* (New York, 1969).

83. White to Charles Ray, September 29, 1864, Ray MSS.

84. Oglesby to Lincoln, January 17, 1865, and Lincoln to Ray, February 15, 1865, in *The Collected Works of Abraham Lincoln,* ed. Roy Basler et al., 8:289n, 299.

85. James W. Grimes to William P. Fessenden, August 3, 1864, Fessenden Family Papers.

86. *Chicago Tribune,* April 12, 1865.

6

Editor-in-Chief

IN THE *Tribune* office in Chicago, the editors composed their first issues since Sumter without including news of the war. They had not prepared for peace. With their paper swollen in size and circulation by the people's hunger for war news, the editors suddenly faced serious problems of overexpansion. There was no longer a need for the far flung network of reporters and correspondents. No urgency now seemed to require that huge eight-cylinder Hoe press which they had purchased nine months earlier to hurl out hundreds of extra copies of their paper.[1] True, the heavy expenses of telegraphic dispatches, maps, cuts, and correspondence had ended, too, but what could replace the war in creating a demand for news? The editors admitted that military victory signaled a triumph of their own goals in the war. On what new object could they now fix the popular mind that would sustain their vast following?

Although the forced prosperity of the war had placed the major owners of the *Tribune* among the fifty wealthiest men in Chicago,[2] at least one of the owners felt unsure that his inflated income would continue. On April 14, the eve of an ominous day, John Locke Scripps sold his share of the *Tribune* to Horace White.[3] He made a mistake.

The next issue of the *Tribune*, under its reorganized ownership, regretfully found the startling issue which delayed any decline in the paper's circulation. Thousands of people bought copies of the *Tribune* to read the dreadful news of the President's assassination. The huge Hoe press continued to whirl during the next month, as *Tribune* circulation averaged over 45,000 copies. Only the *New York Herald* could claim a wider audience.[4] Buoyed up by this sign of continued prosperity and even more by advertising receipts which topped those of any paper in the West, the *Tribune* owners expanded their eight-column newspaper to ten columns on May 22, 1865, to accommodate the increased advertising.[5] Horace White had made a bargain.

However bright the picture of prosperity may have been to the reading public, the internal workings of the paper were fraught with dissension and frustration. White's purchase of *Tribune* stock led to a shift in the management of the paper. White joined hands with Alfred Cowles, the paper's largest stockholder, to depose Joseph Medill from control of the *Tribune* corporation. White and Cowles remained very close friends and associates; they managed the paper until November, 1874.[6]

As Cowles never entered the editorial offices, and as White had little reputation as an editor, the two asked Charles Ray to return. Finished with his speculative expeditions into the South, Ray once again took the chief editorship from his erstwhile opponent, Joseph Medill.

Personal character and editorial competence, however, were not enough to sustain Charles Ray in his return to the paper. As the *Tribune* editors grew suspicious that Andrew Johnson would not be the heir of Lincoln, the "Joshua" they had hoped would lead them into a prosperous and peaceful postwar land,

dissension returned to the staff.[7] The editors had not anticipated this crisis.

The columns of the *Tribune* gave little indication that the
editors had ever devoted much thought to the postwar society
and the South's place in it. When victory had seemed only a
matter of time, the editors—including White—set their minds
once again on accumulating fortunes by exploiting the country's resources or sharing in the bounty of the commercial and
financial activity of the nation. Slavery and slavocracy no
longer stood as a barrier to free labor and free enterprise.
White's old friend Edward Daniels optimistically reactivated
their coal mines at LaSalle, Illinois, for neither of the men
had taken any time during the war to become involved with
coal digging.[8]

What attention the editors did give to the problem of the
reorganization of the South produced only a sketchy formula.
They were never dogmatic. Very early, however, they did
support limited Negro suffrage—but then only halfheartedly.
More than the fear of their readers' prejudices prompted their
caution. Perhaps one of the most ironic features of Reconstruction politics was that men like White and the other
Whiggish editors of the *Tribune,* who had long fought against
the Democratic party's concepts of a rapidly expanding electorate, had now to defend an expansion of the suffrage to
southern Negroes. The tension in the minds of the editors
manifested itself in the editorials of the *Tribune.* As early as
January 7, 1865, in response to a speech by Wendell Phillips
in Chicago calling for universal suffrage for freedmen in the
South, the *Tribune* replied that "no honest and intelligent
white man will see any danger in permitting an honest and
intelligent black man to vote." At the same time the *Tribune*
editors could not go along with Phillips's advanced radicalism.
They had fought too many battles with the Douglas Democracy in Chicago to accept easily the implications of universal
suffrage for the emancipated slaves.

If the ignorance of a large portion of our foreign vote has been dangerous can Mr. Phillips see no dangers in the votes of the freed slaves, far more generally ignorant, servile and capable of being wrought upon by the arts of demagogues?[9]

Thus the *Tribune* had formed no cabal with Radicals across the nation to reconstruct southern society. The editors had demanded only an unconditional surrender by the South; they had hardly contemplated the terms of peace.[10] In fact, on the eve of Lincoln's assassination, the *Tribune* came out in favor of his plan to reconstruct Louisiana. They agreed with his undoctrinaire position on the status of the Southern states and supported his lenient proposals for temporary governments. They had, as Horace White and Alfred Cowles took control of the paper, pulled the journal up sharply behind Lincoln on the issues of the postwar nation.[11]

Lincoln's assassination, however, set a new tone in their declarations on reconstruction. Edward Daniels, who was in close contact with White and the other editors of the paper, expressed the shock in Chicago caused by Booth's fatal shot: "The blow is dreadful but it has created a healthy indignation. Men's veins which held only milk and water are filled with honest Saxon blood."[12] The *Tribune* screamed out the editors' change of heart:

The chief sentiment we desire to inspire in the breast of a rebel is fear. Yesterday we were, with the late President, for lenity; he had been so often right and wise; he had won upon our confidence that we were preparing to follow and support him in a policy of conciliatory kindness; today we are with the people for Justice. Henceforth, let us treat this hellborn outbreak of slaveholding fiends as a rebellion. We ask not vengeance, but the justice which Abraham Lincoln's clemency would have withheld. They have slain their mediators, their best friends; now let them feel the force of righteousness, retributive justice.[13]

Although a new tone pervaded the *Tribune*'s pronouncements against the South, the paper did not substantially alter its program of Reconstruction. The editors demanded, as they always had, unconditional unionism in the South based not on the Negro vote but on the white Union vote. They still insisted on strict qualifications for Negro suffrage which would have enabled only a handful of freedmen to participate.[14] But the editors now left the specter of the Negro hanging over the white South. They warned that the freedmen constituted "an element of power in the very heart of the rebellion sufficient to meet all the requirements of the problem of reconstruction." "How important it shall be," threatened the editors, "the white people of the South can determine in some measure for themselves."[15] Whatever the occasion demanded to ensure southern loyalty, the *Tribune* claimed itself ready to support—whether that meant universal Negro suffrage or the disfranchisement of white rebels.[16]

To bring about a proper reorganization of the South, the *Tribune* had announced its faith in Andrew Johnson. The editors were convinced by his well-advertised hatred of plantation aristocracy and abhorrence of slavery that he would carry out any measures necessary to effect a new South. Thus when Horace White and Alfred Cowles handed the editorship to Charles Ray in late May, 1865, there was no reason for them to ascertain Ray's commitment to various Reconstruction proposals. On the necessity of making treason odious, on the advisability of limited Negro suffrage, and on the efficiency of governing the South temporarily through military force, the reorganized *Tribune* editorial staff, headed by Dr. Ray, could all agree. On the Reconstruction issue, there was no division among the men who edited the *Tribune*. But Andrew Johnson changed all that.

On May 29, 1865, Andrew Johnson issued his first detailed program for reconstruction. On that day, by proclamation, he set down the conditions for the reorganization of North Carolina. The wording of the document clearly excluded all Negroes from the ballot box. This exclusion placed the *Tribune* editors in an awkward position. Ray demanded extreme caution in dealing with the President. Moreover, he had serious doubts about the advanced positions on suffrage and Reconstruction that a break with Johnson would force the *Tribune* to occupy.[17] Holding the lead in editorial councils, Ray pulled the *Tribune* back from its commitment to limited Negro suffrage and kept it in line with the new President. The editor-in-chief speculated that perhaps Andrew Johnson had a "full and accurate knowledge of the black man in the South, including his fitness or unfitness to be suddenly after a life of bondage, invested with the rights and privileges . . . of citizenship."[18]

Ray's conservatism held the *Tribune* temporarily in check. When a few with greater independence challenged the President in the next week, the *Tribune* came to his defense. Its editorials blasted Wendell Phillips for recommending repudiation of the Union war debt if Negro suffrage were not granted.[19] But Ray could not long maintain his influence.

Early in June, the *Tribune* urged the Administration, "Don't be in haste," and came out strongly against those who wished to demonstrate magnanimity to the South by pardoning Jefferson Davis. Horace White began to exercise his authority in the editorial columns when he criticized Gerrit Smith, who led the group recommending pardon for the former president of the Confederacy. "We have only to say," wrote White, "that men of sterner stuff are required to deal with the practical affairs of life of war and of government. . . . To hang Jefferson Davis as a traitor is to *make* it [rebellion] a crime, and to *give* the protection we have been promised."[20]

White discarded Ray's conservative editorial line completely when Johnson followed the North Carolina proclamation by a similar proposal for Mississippi on June 13. This time the *Tribune* rebuked Johnson. On June 15, the paper challenged his proposal and warned that his policy ran counter to the opinions of a majority in the party.[21]

With Ray's influence pushed aside, Joseph Medill helped to close ranks among the *Tribune* proprietors. The paper once again pushed forward and took the lead in the ideological battle which threatened to reopen within the Republican party. Although the *Tribune* held back from an open split with the President, Medill sent the June 15 editorial to Hugh McCulloch, Johnson's Secretary of the Treasury. He explained the editors' concern:

> We regret exceedingly to be obliged to take issue with him on so grave a subject. But we would be untrue to our great constituency of readers in half a dozen powerful Western states, and untrue to the character and antecedents of the Tribune if we should falter in our duty at this moment.
>
> Our loyal people in the West are becoming nervous and alarmed at the President's evident intention to crowd the loyal colored men of the south away from the polls. . . . The President seems to have stepped out of his way to insert a disqualifying clause excluding the colored men. . . .
>
> The God's truth is there is [*sic*] not 3,000 loyal white men in that State. The mass of white population are just as loyal as Jeff Davis and no more. If Judge Sharkey lived in Illinois or New York he would vote with the copperheads. The government that he will institute will be composed in the main of ex-rebels, the President's proclamation to the contrary. . . . The North must either maintain a large standing army at a heavy cost in that country in order to enforce the laws and support the feeble loyal whites, or it must allow the blacks to support them with their votes. . . . *It is a great blunder,* and the mischievous fruits will be held to our lips hereafter.[22]

Medill asked McCulloch to send the editorial and his long letter to the President, as he did not know Johnson. McCulloch apparently did not honor Medill's request; instead, he wrote a rebuke of the *Tribune's* position. Medill replied angrily that he could not understand why Johnson was "in such a desperate, break neck hurry to foist those rebels into power and place." He concluded by expressing his fear that the nation was "entering on evil days."[23] This inability of the *Tribune* editors to receive a favorable hearing from the Administration no doubt played a part in their suspicion of Johnson's actions. If Lincoln had continued in his office, it is unlikely that he would have so lightly disregarded the opinions expressed by the *Tribune.* Any hypothetical suggestions of Lincoln's handling of Reconstruction would certainly have to consider the reservoir of trust that existed for him among such Radical Republicans in the Northwest as Horace White. That trust had been built up carefully by Lincoln both before and during the war. True, Lincoln had fought his battles with midwestern Radicals. Still, he knew how to make his peace. Historians, unfortunately, have concentrated on Lincoln's differences with Radical Republicans. Most have ignored, however, Lincoln's words and gestures of support for their position.[24]

When the *Tribune* came out so quickly and boldly against Johnson, it was at first in very limited company. The other Republican journals of the city and the nation maintained their support of the titular head of the party. To magnify the isolation of the *Tribune,* a new paper, the *Chicago Republican,* edited by Charles A. Dana, backed Johnson strongly and hoped to win *Tribune* subscribers who might be disturbed by the *Tribune's* threatened treason to the Party.[25]

The *Tribune* editors did not pull back from their position. They held to their own convictions on Negro suffrage. Indeed they advanced their position. "If . . . color alone is made the basis of exclusion from what justice concedes," the *Tribune* pronounced, "the lesser evil is to agitate for the right of franchise for all of the negro race, and to that we shall come." The editors drew the line with South Carolina; surely Johnson would allow "the proper classes of that State to vote."[26]

Indications that the *Tribune* was prepared to defend universal Negro suffrage drew an outcry from some of its readers. Negrophobia, after all, was not solely a southern sentiment. Awkwardly, the editors replied that they did not propose suffrage for all Negroes in the North but rather only for self-supporting and literate Negroes or black veterans of the war. Anyway the issue was not a "question of personal consistency," the *Tribune* editors retorted, for there was in the North no "necessity for extending the suffrage to the blacks in order to secure loyal voters."[27]

However the editors may have hedged their views of Negro suffrage, they had taken a courageous stand on an issue that was potentially explosive in the anti-Negro climate of the North. Their views have to be measured against this background. When Henry Winter Davis came to Chicago to deliver an oration for the Fourth of July celebration, the editors held their ground and commended his radical views of Negro suffrage and his dire warnings against Johnson's course. They hoped that Davis's "noble words" would "prove to be seed sown in good ground." They maintained, moreover, that it was "humanity to place the ballot in the hand of the blackman."[28]

Having established their position, the *Tribune* editors waited for Johnson's next move. That came when the President intervened in favor of William Sharkey, the provisional governor of Mississippi, in his quarrel with Major General H. W. Slocum, the commander of federal forces in the area, over the raising of a civilian militia to keep the peace. Since the militia was made up of Confederate veterans, many in the North feared that the state army would prove a reactionary force. When Johnson's action became known, the *Tribune* announced that the Rubicon had been reached and that the salvation of the Union party depended on itself.[29]

Step by step, Johnson thus forced the *Tribune* into increasingly hostile and more radical opposition to his leadership in the South. Even after the militia controversy in Mississippi, however, not many Republican leaders were ready to match the pace of the *Tribune*'s apostasy. Charles Ray, having departed from the *Tribune,* made it clear, for example, that he disagreed with White's criticism of the President's policies. Writing to Lyman Trumbull, Ray questioned, "What do his assailants expect—to carry the country on the Massachusetts idea of negro suffrage, confiscation and hanging? If so, they will drive all moderate men out of the party." Ray concluded by advising Trumbull to "stand aloof."[30] Trumbull did just that.

Charles Sumner and Thaddeus Stevens led the cry against Johnson. But many of the giants in the House and Senate refused to take a stand. Since Congress was not in session, few were willing to risk an independent stricture against the leader of their party. Still others, like Trumbull, Fessenden, and Grimes, were not willing or prepared to accept the line of battle already marked out by less cautious Republicans, namely Negro suffrage.[31] Horace White had moved his paper out ahead of his old friends in Washington. Taking advantage of some private social correspondence with his close friend Senator Fessenden, White clarified his reasoning in the struggle and his disagreement with Republican moderates:

I wish I could be as well satisfied with the President as you seem to be. I am alarmed at the spirit which seems to animate him. I frequently meet gentlemen of sound Republican principles, who have had interviews with Mr. Johnson, and who have come away from those interviews entirely satisfied with his professions. Then the next we hear is that he has done some outrageous thing, like sanctioning the organization of the Mississippi militia (for attempting which in substance Sherman was denounced and disgraced). I hear now he intends to disband the colored troops because the secesh don't like to see them around. I fear that he will shortly break up the Freedmen's Bureau, or so cripple it that it might as well be broken up. His course seems to be backward. All the copperheads in the land are delighted with him.

I presume you have seen some articles copied in your Eastern papers from the Chicago Tribune somewhat warmly objecting to this backward movement. My idea is that it is best to warn the party in time, so that if Mr. Johnson does intend to go over to the copperheads he shall not take us there with him. If he does not go over to them there is no harm done. I do not regard the danger of driving *him* over there any more imminent than the danger of his taking *us* there. I perceive that it is useless for us to hope for negro suffrage now. It might have been gained in the beginning, but power was ranged against justice, and dragged prejudice along with it and the twain are too strong to be successfully resisted. But then there is one thing we can do and must do and that is to insist on an amendment to the constitution to make representation depend upon voters and not population. We can make our people see the justice of this and we can make them see that it is for their interest to have the law so fixed that a Northern Union voter shall be the equal of a Southern ex-rebel at the ballot box instead of being his inferior. In this way we shall hold out to the Southern States a constant inducement and invitation to enlarge the suffrage, in other words to make their States republican in fact as well as in name. The three fifths rule was one of the compromises of slavery. Now that slavery is dead let us sweep away its consequences. I regard the danger of letting these rebels back into Congress with the political power given them by counting the negroes at five fifths instead of three fifths and aided by the copperheads of the North, as very great. And it especially behooves those intrusted with the National debt to look to it.

My wife said before she went away "tell Mr. Fessenden I am sorry he allowed the President to deceive him." I told her she had better modify the phrase a little bit but she would not.[32]

For the next few months, Johnson did nothing further to accelerate the *Tribune*'s radical course. Indeed the President even hinted that he favored limited Negro suffrage. When Johnson indicated that he intended to keep a "taunt rein" on the South by backing up his demand that they repudiate the Confederate debt, annul the secession ordinances, and pass the Thirteenth Amendment, the *Tribune* announced that northern doubts had been "partially allayed and confidence improved."[33]

This lull demonstrated the unity that Johnson's pronouncements on Reconstruction had been giving to the demands of the Radical Republicans.[34] When he temporarily retreated from his determined stand, the fragile coalition in the Union party threatened to disband. Only the antislavery issue had held the party together. When Congress reassembled in December, 1865, cracks in the antislavery alliance began to appear. The issues of the tariff, the national debt, monetary policy, and transportation began to reassert themselves with an old vigor.

The *Tribune* editorial staff was a microcosm of the national party. The same divisive trend that threatened the deliberations of the Republicans in Congress appeared in the *Tribune* editorial offices in Chicago. White, who held the controlling interest of the paper with Alfred Cowles, supported lower tariffs and Negro suffrage. On one hand, he agreed with Joseph Medill's views on Negro suffrage but disagreed with him on the tariff. On the other hand, he agreed with Charles Ray on the tariff but disagreed with him on Negro suffrage. While Johnson threatened to subvert the antislavery objectives of the *Tribune*, White and Ray could not agree; but when Johnson seemed to be carrying out those objectives, White and Medill argued over other issues which then asserted themselves.

The *Tribune* had avoided much comment on the tariff until the winter of 1865. White believed that tariffs on certain consumer goods had climbed too high. The rhetoric which the *Tribune* developed under White's direction helped to promote a growing economic discontent in the Northwest. A prohibitory duty, the editors proclaimed, was "sheer robbery of the poor for the rich, making the poor poorer, and the rich richer, every day that it continues." Brushing aside the charge of party treason, the *Tribune* announced that the West would not "quietly acquiesce in such nonsense." For political considerations, White denied that his paper was espousing free trade and maintained that it was supporting a pragmatic policy of arriving at an equitable revenue system. Nonetheless he had begun a Republican attack on the protectionist citadel constructed for a variety of reasons during the Civil War.[35]

Capitalizing on the farmers' discontent with the tariff, the *Tribune* also took up their battle with the managers of grain elevators and railroads. The *Tribune* urged the governor of Illinois to convene the legislature "to pass laws to protect the interests of the farmer and the merchants, and to punish both the railroads and elevators for their conspiracy against the welfare of the State."[36] White had his reporters carefully cover the antimonopoly conventions that were then popping up all over Illinois, and he personally assured Elihu Washburne that his paper would "go any length in fighting all these extortionists."[37]

Although capturing a wider audience for the *Tribune* among the rural centers of the state was one consideration in White's decision to fight the "interests," much more lay behind his attack. The *Tribune* had long been a willing spokesman for Chicago's mercantile community, and its editors had played a large role in making Chicago the major entrepôt of the Middle West. The merchants and bankers of that community had a large stake in the farmers' battles against the railroads and grain elevators. If they did not know it, the *Tribune* made it clear to them. "At present," one editorial warned, Chicago is in danger of losing not only the grain trade of the vast region of the country . . . but also the large mercantile traffic which flows thence."[38] The *Tribune* accordingly urged the Board of Trade and the Mercantile Association to use their economic muscle and political influence to end this threat to Chicago's position. When the legislature finally acted by passing laws which regulated railroads and grain elevators in the state, it was the businessmen of Chicago who played the crucial role in effecting the legislation.[39]

Joseph Medill was not at odds with all the crusades that White led as editor-in-chief of the *Chicago Tribune*. Medill had too large a stake and too many friends in the mercantile community of the city to alienate himself from its demands. Nor did he mind the increased circulation and revenue that the *Tribune* gained by supporting the farmers' antimonopoly conventions, for he still had a large share of *Tribune* stock. Indeed, Medill himself was an aggressive champion of the forces that wanted to contain the irresponsible power of the warehouses and railroads. But he did not see the struggle for lower tariffs as part of the antimonopoly crusade. He had long been a promoter of Chicago's industrial community as well as a close friend of Colonel Ward, the northwestern iron magnate. With biting sarcasm he mocked the free traders in Chicago who attempted to link the tariff on iron to the high costs of railroad transportation. He asked them: "If the tariff is the cause of the onerous railroad charges, how happens it that it only affects the freight on roads running west from Chicago?"[40] Neither White nor any of his associates ever answered that question.

When White opened the battle against the tariff in the editorial columns of the *Tribune,* Medill replied critically to the arguments through letters to the editor over the thinly disguised pseudonym, "Protection."[41] When White and Ray and members of Chicago's Board of Trade formed a Free Trade League in Chicago on January 9, 1866, Medill ridiculed White's proposed constitution and urged "the friends of the

'American System' to organize also, and meet sophistry with facts. . . ."[42] Medill got such a group together and took on all comers in a raging battle in letters to the *Tribune*.[43]

The battle in Chicago had serious implications, for a larger contest over the same subject was occurring in Congress. Divisions on the tariff threatened to throw the wartime coalition asunder and there was no greater threat to Republican unity than the vigor with which the northwestern free traders in the party took up the cause of revenue reform. These men had for a decade been some of the most fiercely loyal proponents of Republican goals. But now, under the lead of the *Tribune,* they threatened the very survival of the party. With his old boldness, White demanded to know from Elihu Washburne, "Have we killed King Cotton to set up King Sheeting?"[44] To Justin Morrill, chairman of the House Ways and Means Committee, White issued a threat:

> What we want and are determined to have is access to the markets of the world. It is evident that the committee had no conception of the feeling which exists here on this subject. I tell you now in sober earnest what will be the result of the smothering policy. The South cannot be kept out of Congress forever. When the south does come back the south and west will join hands and rule this country. Despairing of any hope from the East we shall form alliances to secure justice for ourselves. I am not telling what I shall do. I am pointing to an inevitable consequence of a certain line of policy.[45]

White's ominous forecast of a coalition of the West and South on economic questions did not mean that he had, at this time, grown cool to the Reconstruction battle.[46] Johnson would have received no support for his Reconstruction measures from the *Tribune* by advocating lower tariffs. While challenging the protectionist sentiments of eastern Radicals, White's paper continued to promote an advanced radicalism in Congress. In fact, the Black Codes, which southern legislatures passed to restrict Negro freedoms, caused the *Tribune* at this time to issue its classic threat to Mississippi: "We tell the white men of Mississippi that men of the North will convert the State of Mississippi into a frog pond before they will allow such laws to disgrace one foot of soil in which the bones of our soldiers sleep and over which the flag of freedom waves."[47]

Southern action also pushed the *Tribune* to the full radical measure as it endorsed Senator Richard Yates's bill calling for universal suffrage; the *Tribune* pronounced that such a proposal would "fulfill" the requirements of that "wise radicalism which the inexorable logic of events so much demands." The bill would cut off "the last excrescence and extracts—the last throbbing fibre of the cancer of slavery. . . ." "Oppression," the *Tribune* proclaimed, "has never outlived Universal Suffrage."[48]

Despite these radical pronouncements around the turn of the year, the *Tribune*'s tariff crusade had temporarily overshadowed its concern with the problems of Reconstruction. When Lyman Trumbull complained that the *Tribune* had failed to publish one of his major speeches on the Freedmen's Bureau bill, then before Congress, White explained that "with Anti-Monopoly Conventions, Revenue reports, etc." he had been "unable to do so."[49]

But once more President Johnson stepped in and changed everything. Well before other newspapers knew of the President's intentions concerning the Freedmen's Bureau bill, White unequivocally separated his paper from support of Andrew Johnson. Relying on an intimation from Congressman Cook of Illinois that Johnson would veto the bill, White set a rigid editorial line for his paper on February 6, 1866. The long front page editorial allowed the President no excuse or escape this time. It noted that Johnson "had been sweet to both sides" for the past several months but predicted that the President had reached a point of decision. Several bills were about to come before him for signature: the Civil Rights Bill to provide basic legal rights to southern blacks and the bill to enlarge the powers of the Freedmen's Bureau. "The President," White wrote, "cannot sign any one of these bills without abandoning the expectations of being supported by the late rebel element for the next presidency." White was now convinced that the President had committed himself to a new "Reactionary party" hatched in New York "since he issued his first Reconstruction Proclamation."[50] "The people are not blind," the *Tribune* continued:

> They understand that the Southern States, as at present reconstructed would vote solid for Andrew Johnson for the next Presidency. They see his overwhelming interest therefore in having them immediately admitted to Congress, and in securing their votes in the Electoral College. They see his deep interest in gratifying them without stint. It is impossible not to connect his interest with his course, as cause without effect. The simple question is therefore whether the Union shall be reconstructed for the profit of Andrew Johnson or the American People. On this issue we believe that Congress will be firm, they will be backed by the people, and before them the new party of Reaction and Corruption must go down.[51]

White had taken a tremendous gamble in jumping out against Johnson before any overt act by the President. Charles Ray, alarmed by the "savage attack," went to see White immediately. He wrote to Trumbull and warned the senator to avoid any similarly rash action: "You all in Washington must remember that the excitement of the great contest is dying out, and that commercial and industrial enterprises and pursuits are engaging in a large share of public attention. . . . people are more mindful of themselves than of any of the fine philanthropic schemes that look to making Sambo a voter, juror and office holder."[52] Ray was wrong, and so were many others.

The competing Republican papers in Chicago scorned White's attack. The *Republican,* which had been picking up *Tribune* subscribers alienated by White's tariff stand, gloated that the *Tribune,* this time, had gone too far. Charles Dana, the editor, ridiculed White's charges and cautioned Chicagoans that the "bull excommunicating Andrew Johnson" came from a "quarter which in times gone by was equally virulent in its abuse of Mr. Lincoln."[53] The *Journal* joined Dana's condemnation. The only reason the *Tribune* sought a quarrel with the President, it claimed, was "because Johnson refuses to abandon the wise, just and patriotic spirit and policy of his 'illustrious predecessor' and become the mere creature of passion, self-will and radicalism."[54] Both of the *Tribune*'s critics had supported Johnson firmly in his Reconstruction policy and now saw a chance to discredit their rival.

"We are Radicals," shouted the *Tribune* defiantly, "and we don't quarrel with the name. One must be something less than a man, who would not be radical now."[55] On February 13, the *Tribune* announced its support of "universal suffrage for the negro race, perpetual disenfranchisement of all inveterably disloyal citizens, and the immediate trial and punishment of Davis."[56] Having moved the *Tribune* into the waters of an advanced radicalism and drawn conservative criticism from his rival editors in Chicago, White won an unassailable position for his paper as Johnson vetoed the Freedmen's Bureau Bill on February 20. The *Republican* and *Journal* were left in a floundering state as the tide of Republican reaction redounded to the benefit of the *Tribune.* The *Republican* could not reply for a day, and the *Journal* weakly withheld its judgment; neither was able to defend the President's action, which left the freedmen to the "tender mercies of the Southern States."[57] The *Tribune,* on the other hand, claimed a clear vindication of its earlier charges against Johnson and urged that "the forces of freedom be so marshaled that the first move of the enemy shall be the last."[58] Horace White was out in front leading another crusade.

White had angered Charles Ray but found himself back in the good graces of Joseph Medill. Together, White and Medill mobilized popular indignation against the President's veto. They held a mass meeting in Chicago on February 26. Medill, in the midst of this new fight, called an end to his running controversy with White over the tariff. His swan song in the debate was abrupt and dramatic: "Since the announcement of Johnson's veto of the Freedman's Bureau bill and the perusal of his maudlin, disgraceful harangue to the copperheads and rebels of Washington, the readers of the *Tribune* have lost nearly all interest in the Free Trade vs. Protection controversy carried on through its columns."[59] White was only too happy to call a truce. He explained to Elihu Washburne that "the tariff question will not and cannot become a vital one while the reconstruction question remains unsettled."[60]

With Medill now back in the editorial rooms of the *Tribune,* the paper took on a rancor it had seldom exhibited since Lincoln's assassination. It scorned Henry Ward Beecher's plea for magnanimity to the South and reminded its readers that southerners had "maimed, tortured, starved and killed" Union heroes. Patriots, the *Tribune* proclaimed, must "scatter to the winds all these platitudes about magnanimity."[61]

Other Republicans in Illinois, however, still urged Congress to search for some accommodation with Johnson; they did not want Reconstruction policy-making to fall into the hands of Charles Sumner and Thaddeus Stevens. White, however, completely abandoned his earlier fears of the enfranchisement of an untutored mass of black voters and confessed his belief in unrestricted republicanism. "Universal suffrage," White, wrote to Senator Richard Yates, "is the only solution of existing evils, and to that we must come sooner or later. The agitation will never cease till every man has his rights, and it never ought to cease till then." On the same day, the *Tribune* pronounced "that the denial of negro suffrage is the restoration of negro slavery."[62]

White could not understand how any of his antislavery associates in the war could sustain the President's veto of the Freedmen's Bureau bill. Alarmed when he heard that his old employer, Edwin Stanton, had acquiesced in Johnson's actions, White pleaded with the Secretary of War:

> I think that Andrew Johnson is wrong in arresting to the extent of his ability, the onward movement of the country to a perfect consumation [*sic*] of the victory which we achieved in the field. Among the things necessary to be done, and which I think the country will insist upon, are *first,* the protection of the freedmen in absolute freedom and subsequently or ultimately their enfranchisement; and *second* "making treason odious." Whatever may be the real facts it does not *appear* that Mr. Johnson is pursuing a course to accomplish either of these ends, but it does appear that he is pursuing the opposite course. If he shall follow a policy which is fast ruining his own fame, I trust that no acquiescence in such a policy may be found to tarnish the higher fame of the radical Secretary of War, Edwin M. Stanton.[63]

When Johnson followed his veto of the Freedmen's Bureau bill with a veto of Senator Trumbull's other measure, the Civil Rights bill, most of the reluctant moderates in the Republican party joined White in denouncing the President. The *Tribune* on March 31, 1866, grew bold enough now to broach the subject of impeaching Andrew Johnson.[64]

The confrontation had begun. Even the most reluctant moderates in the party ended their long and precarious alliance with the President. Lyman Trumbull, a leader of this faction, had held conferences with Johnson and felt that the President would sign his two measures into law. Hurt and insulted by the vetoes, Trumbull delivered a bitter critique of Johnson's constitutional arguments. But, even then, Trumbull and many moderates were not prepared for Negro suffrage as an alternative. The *Tribune* noted this hesitation and scolded Trumbull. "His constituents," the *Tribune* emphasized, "do not endorse this doctrine that suffrage is no more necessary to the liberty of a freedman than of a non-voting white."[65]

Not many in Congress were prepared to assume the grounds that the *Tribune* demanded. White himself soon recognized that the Reconstruction Committee, headed by his friend Senator Fessenden, was not a radical body but "only fairly representative of Congress and the loyal people."[66] Yet the *Tribune* acquiesced to the Committee's report, which failed to recommend the principle of universal manhood suffrage.[67] White and his colleagues preferred either the plan of Senator Stewart or that of Representative Owen, both of which provided for Negro suffrage. But expediency was the guide. "We will accept now," the *Tribune* announced, "whatever the majority of the people deem reasonable, and labor for the rest in the future."[68] Medill made it clear to Trumbull that the *Tribune* staff made a reluctant compromise:

> The reconstruction plan is received coldly. It elicits no enthusiasm from anyone. . . . I regard it as the offspring of cowardice— want of faith in the people. . . . I can assure you that not one Republican in a thousand and no decent democrat really objects to letting those colored men vote who can read and write. If Congress shall finally adopt the Committee's weak botchery we will give it such support as we can conscientiously, but would a thousand times prefer a plan more nearly based on right, one that is bolder and squarer.[69]

White developed a romantic faith in the power of the ballot. "A freedman without a vote, is not a freedman," his
paper proclaimed. He urged the Republicans to take up
"the inspiring ideas of the Declaration of Independence as
their platform in the coming campaign."[70] Even after he heard
of the Memphis race riot, White urged Congress not to allow
anyone to be disfranchised—white or black, even the ex-rebels.
The *Tribune* accordingly condemned Thad Stevens's suggestion that it was more important to give southern Negroes land
than it was to give them a vote. "Give him his rights, Mr.
Stevens, and he will ask no land," the *Tribune* confidently
retorted.[71] The ballot, White felt, was a cure-all for all the
difficulties facing southern Negroes; he searched no further
into their problems.

For all its remonstrance, the *Tribune* still approved the
compromise measures which eventually took the form of the
Fourteenth Amendment. The editors were frankly worried
over Johnson's patronage power and his appeals to negrophobia; they could not yet judge his strength.[72] Therefore
they sought as large a coalition as the Republicans could
assemble. The election was the important thing. Even though
White knew that the Congressional proposal was "a politician's
dodge rather than the work of statesmen," he agreed that
it had "considerable merit" and that it would enable the
Republicans to carry Illinois and the nation.[73]

After holding back on their demands, the *Tribune* editors
were shocked when they found that others in the party were
not so willing to compromise personal desires for the sake
of unity: protectionists in the House of Representatives passed
legislation which promised to raise tariffs considerably. Even
Medill could not support such a measure; he drew a line
between the protection of American industry and the prohibition of imports. "The *Tribune*," he announced to Senator
Trumbull, "is a unit in its hostility to the ill advised, unnecessary, and mischievous bill."[74] A few days later, White gave

Trumbull the same information: "There is absolutely no difference of opinion about it here—protectionists and free traders both agreeing in considering it a bill of abominations."[75]

The *Tribune* editors screamed out against the eastern Republicans for "introducing such an element of discord into our ranks on the eve of an election."[76] Once again, they warned that such a move could throw the Northwest back into its old alliance with the South. White joined Medill in a letter writing campaign to Congressmen; he urged Trumbull, Fessenden, and Henry Wilson of Massachusetts to postpone or kill the bill in the Senate.[77] Something had to be done to save the party in its struggle with Johnson. By threatening Congressmen in the Northwest and pleading with key senators in the East, the *Tribune* editors played a major part in causing the Senate to table the tariff measure. They gave the credit, however, to the New England Senators Wilson, Sumner, and Foster for their crucial votes. "By their statesmanlike action they have removed from the field of politics an irritating issue, which has no fit place in the great contest now waging."[78]

With the tariff imbroglio out of the way, White turned his attention to another difficulty in the path of Republican victory. This difficulty lay at the heart of what he felt was the fundamental issue of the midterm elections. He explained it to Senator Fessenden:

Seward's letter has opened my eyes to an enormous gap in our platform for the fall campaign. He says that no plan of Reconstruction has been proposed except the President's. This is unfortunately true. If Congress adjourns without passing an enabling act as proposed in the report of your committee a trap will be left open through which every doubtful district in the Union may fall out of our hands. Let us see how it will work. A member of Congress goes before his constituents, and the first question asked him is "what is your plan of Reconstruction"? He reads to them the proposed constitutional Amendment. "Well, if the Southern States ratify, do you proposed to let them in?" "I suppose so" is the answer, *"but I don't know"!* I can conceive of nothing more foolish than the picture of an M.C. sucking his finger before his audience, unable to answer the question whether he proposes ever to readmit the South on any terms. Now anything will beat nothing, and unless Congress passes an act of admission conditional upon the ratification of the Amendment, we shall have exactly nothing to oppose to Johnson's something. Perhaps he would veto such an act. Let him do it and take the odium of obstruction upon himself instead of putting it upon us. Probably it could be passed over his veto. If not a concurrent resolution could be passed expressive of the intention of Congress in that behalf.[79]

If Congress could not agree on such a procedure, the next best thing to do, White felt, was to admit Tennessee (then awaiting admission) on the basis of the Fourteenth Amendment.[80] Republicans could point to this move as an indication of their intentions regarding the South. In the eyes of White, however, this move was merely a matter of expediency. His paper continued to appeal for a "bold positive policy" which would extend the suffrage to "all intelligent loyal people irrespective of color."[81] Johnson's stirring of the muddy waters of racism had caused the *Tribune* to back away temporarily from universal Negro suffrage, but it had not stilled the editors' demand for some Negro suffrage as a symbol of Southern loyalty. To be sure, the *Tribune* editors at no time accepted the Fourteenth Amendment as the final Republican proposal for the reorganization of Dixie.

The main task of this campaign was to discredit Johnson's Reconstruction plans. The President had become the personification of evil. The *Tribune* editors were therefore prepared to use any tools at hand to defeat candidates who backed his proposals, whether they were Democrats or National Union party nominees. The editors blamed the July race riot in New Orleans on Johnson's policies; they associated him both with repudiation-minded Democrats and with bond-bloated New York capitalists; and they labeled him as the heir of Jefferson Davis.[82] When he went out on an ambitious personal campaign tour, they attacked him bitterly. Horace White and his colleagues were certain that this man was plotting to "overthrow and destroy the labor of the nation wrought in the blood of half a million patriots."[83] They pointed out to their readers that every vote for a Republican in the election was "as good as a bullet in the war."[84] That Horace White believed his own propaganda, there is no reason to doubt. Johnson stood, in his mind, as the antithesis of all that he had struggled for, of all that he thought had been won when Lee surrendered at Appomattox.

The *Tribune* described election day, November 6, 1866, as the Gettysburg of the war—the turning point of the rebellion.[85] The overwhelming returns, the *Tribune* happily announced the next day, "proclaim with vehement force and indignation of a free and intelligent people against a faithless Executive." "There never was a popular verdict more overwhelming, more conclusive, more annihilating. The American people have arisen once more in their power and strength, to save the Republic from the second peril with which it was threatened."[86]

Horace White and his colleagues saw the 1866 election as the capstone of the nation's antislavery struggle, as "the grandest popular decision in history." The overwhelming victory, coming as it did upon the heels of the wartime triumph of the antislavery movement, conferred unprecedented prestige upon the principles of men like Horace White. The victory also strengthened their faith in the virtue of "the people" and in the righteousness of unabashed republicanism. Reform, it appeared, had a promising future.

NOTES

1. *Chicago Tribune*, August 21, 1864.

2. The federal income tax list gave the following incomes, after deductions, for the *Tribune* proprietors in 1863: William Bross, $25,957; Alfred Cowles, $26,073; Joseph Medill, $26,790; and John Scripps, $23,856. *Chicago Tribune*, January 7, 1865. In 1864 the figures stood: Bross, $22,472; Cowles $36,180; and Medill, $24,480. *Chicago Tribune*, July 18, 1865.

3. *Chicago Tribune*, April 14, 1865.

4. Ibid., May 16, 1865.

5. Ibid., May 22, 1865, August 20, 1866.

6. The two men held 101 shares of the company, a bare majority of the 200 shares. White held 30 shares.

7. *Chicago Tribune*, April 18, 1865.

8. Edward Daniels's MS diary, January 24, 30, 31, February 3, 8, 18, 22, March 1, 2, 7, 8, 16, 20, 29, 1865, Daniels MSS.

9. *Chicago Tribune*, January 7, 1865.

10. Ibid., April 8, 1865.

11. Ibid., April 14, 1865.

12. Edward Daniels's MS diary, April 16, 1865, Daniels MSS.

13. *Chicago Tribune*, April 17, 1865.

14. Ibid., April 18, 1865.

15. Ibid., April 26, 1865.

16. Ibid., April 27, 1865.

17. *The National Cyclopedia of American Biography*, 39: 327.

18. *Chicago Tribune*, May 31, 1865.

19. Ibid., June 6, 1865.

20. Ibid., June 7, 1865, June 13, 1865. White went beyond the matter of Jefferson Davis in criticizing Gerrit Smith. He accused Smith of aiding John Brown's invasion of the South and then fleeing to an insane asylum to escape prosecution. Smith then sued the *Tribune* for libel. Although the case was settled out of court, White managed to get a statement from one of Brown's sons which implicated Smith in the Harpers Ferry incident. For a discussion of the libel suit, see Ralph V. Harlow, *Gerrit Smith* (New York, 1939), pp. 450–454.

21. *Chicago Tribune*, June 15, 1865.

22. Joseph Medill to Hugh McCulloch, June 16, 1865, McCulloch MSS, Library of Congress.

23. Ibid., June 23, 1865.

24. A recent work has attempted to demonstrate the common bonds on Reconstruction between Lincoln and the Radicals in his party. See Hans Trefousse, *The Radical Republicans*, pp. 266–304.

25. *Chicago Journal*, June 20, 21, 22, 1865. The June 22, 1865, issue of the *Journal* quotes the opinion of the *Republican*.

26. *Chicago Tribune,* June 23, 1865.

27. Ibid., June 30, 1865.

28. Ibid., July 6, 1865.

29. Ibid., September 5, 13, 14, 23, 1865.

30. Charles Ray to Lyman Trumbull, September 29, 1865, Trumbull MSS.

31. Grimes had been growing restive during the summer and wrote to his friend, Fessenden, halfway across the country in Maine: "What do you think of Andy's reconstruction schemes? It strikes me that matters are getting complicated, and that the rebels are having it all their own way." James W. Grimes to William P. Fessenden, July 14, 1865, Fessenden Family Papers. Grimes, however, could not accept the grounds on which his friend, Horace White, had chosen to criticize Johnson. He made this clear to Ray, who had already broken with White over this issue. "I am sorry to learn that you have left the Tribune. . . . As to the negro I have not changed my opinions from the beginning. I think I shall come pretty nearly up to the measure of my duty when I secure to him his rights as a party in the courts, as a witness on the stand, as a scholar in the school and as a christian in the church . . . but I am under the impression that he can live some years and so can we, without bestowing upon him the elective franchise." Grimes to Ray, October 28, 1865, Ray MSS.

32. White to Fessenden, October 9, 1865, Horace White Collection, Beloit College Archives.

33. *Chicago Tribune,* November 16, 21, 1865.

34. For a detailed discussion of Johnson's responsibility in forcing moderate Republicans, a majority of the party, into an espousal of radical measures, see Eric McKitrick, *Andrew Johnson and Reconstruction* (Chicago, 1960), pp. 76–84, 274–325. McKitrick has, however, overestimated the "moderation" of the *Chicago Tribune.* Ibid., pp. 170–171.

35. *Chicago Tribune,* October 9, 16, 1865. For a provocative discussion of northwestern economic radicalism and the *Tribune's* role in it, see Chester M. Destler, *American Radicalism* (New London, Conn., 1946), pp. 50–60.

36. *Chicago Tribune,* November 17, 1865. See also November 21, 28, 1865.

37. White to Washburne, November 18, 1865, Washburne MSS.

38. *Chicago Tribune,* November 24, 1865.

39. Harold D. Woodman, "Chicago Businessmen and the 'Granger' Laws," *Agricultural History* 36 (January, 1962): 16–24.

40. *Chicago Tribune,* January 27, 1866. Medill's remarks were made in a letter to the editor over the pseudonym, "Protection."

41. Medill admitted to the pseudonym in the *Tribune* on February 10, 1866.

42. *Chicago Tribune,* January 10, 11, 1866.

43. The letters appeared almost daily in the *Tribune* during January and February, 1866.

44. White to Washburne, January 30, 1866, Washburne MSS.

45. White to Justin S. Morrill, February 15, 1866, Justin Morrill MSS, Cornell University. Morrill, a former boardinghouse companion of White's in Washington during the Civil War, quickly replied to White's letter. He accused White of making hasty judgments and oversimplifications of sectional interests. He also offered White some advice: "I fear however the new Free-trade dogma of the Tribune (Chicago) is warming your temperament more than you may be aware of." Morrill to White, February 20, 1866, Justin Morrill MSS.

46. Among the three Chicago Republican papers—the *Journal,* the *Republican,* and the *Tribune*—enthusiasm for high tariffs and radical reconstruction ran in an inverse ratio. By espousing lower tariffs, Johnson would have run counter to the papers that supported him in Chicago on Reconstruction. The editors of the *Journal* and the *Republican,* Charles Wilson and Charles A. Dana, respectively, both supported Medill's Industrial Union of Chicago which had been set up in opposition to the Free Trade League which Horace White helped to organize. *Chicago Tribune,* February 22, 1866.

47. Ibid., December 1, 1865.

48. Ibid., February 1, 1866.

49. White to Trumbull, February 2, 1866, Trumbull MSS.

50. Recent scholarship has given some foundation to the *Tribune's* charges. See LaWanda Cox and John H. Cox, *Politics, Principles, and Prejudice* (Glencoe, Ill., 1963), pp. viii, 107–128, 179–180.

51. *Chicago Tribune,* February 6, 1866.

52. Ray to Trumbull, February 7, 1866, Trumbull MSS. Ray became increasingly conservative on Reconstruction and even flirted with members of Johnson's National Union party. Ray to James A. Doolittle, May 24, 1866, Ray Collection, Chicago Historical Society. Ray to Montgomery Blair, April 10, 1866, Andrew Johnson MSS, Library of Congress.

53. *Chicago Republican,* February 7, 1866.

54. *Chicago Journal,* February 7, 1866.

55. *Chicago Tribune,* February 10, 1866.

56. Ibid., February 13, 1866.

57. *Chicago Republican,* February 22, 1866. *Chicago Journal,* February 20, 22, 1866.

58. *Chicago Tribune,* February 21, 22, 1866.

59. Ibid., March 1, 1866.

60. White to Washburne, March 12, 1866, Washburne MSS. McKitrick in *Andrew Johnson,* pp. 367–377, is undoubtedly correct in his criticism of Howard K. Beale's assumption that Johnson could have mobilized support for his reconstruction plans by taking up the issues of lower tariffs and currency inflation. In Chicago, at least, Johnson may have strengthened his hold on the Democrats by supporting lower tariffs, but he would have alienated the support of conservative Republicans who were high-tariff proponents. To be sure, he could not have picked up support of the

low-tariff Republicans like White who were also Radical Republicans. Johnson's association with the Democrats ended any possibility of his splitting the radicals on economic issues, and actually even the Democrats were divided on those economic questions. See Harris L. Dante, "Reconstruction Politics in Illinois, 1860–1872" (Ph.D. dissertation, University of Chicago, 1950), p. 162. For Beale's views see his book, *The Critical Year* (New York, 1930), pp. 225–299.

61. *Chicago Tribune*, March 1, 1866.

62. White to Richard Yates, March 8, 1866, Richard Yates MSS, Illinois State Historical Library. *Chicago Tribune*, March 8, 1866. For the reactions of leading moderate editors in Illinois to the veto see J. L. Wilson to Trumbull, March 6, 1866; D. L. Phillips (editor of the *Illinois State Journal*) to Trumbull, March 5, 1866, Trumbull MSS. The *Chicago Journal*, even after the veto, urged Republicans to stay any open warfare with Johnson, February 26, March 2, 16, 1866.

63. White to Stanton, March 15, 1866, Stanton MSS.

64. *Chicago Tribune*, March 31, 1866. This was apparently the first mention of impeachment by a major Republican journal. The *New York World* picked up the statement and claimed that it was a "leak" of the Radicals' plans in Congress. The *Tribune* labeled the assertion absurd. Ibid., April 10, 1866.

65. Ibid., April 7, 1866.

66. Ibid., April 22, 1866.

67. Ibid., April 30, 1866.

68. Ibid., May 1, 1866.

69. Medill to Trumbull, May 2, 1866, Trumbull MSS.

70. *Chicago Tribune*, May 5, 1866.

71. Ibid., May 10, 1866. Miffed by this criticism, Stevens wrote a letter to the *Tribune*. He felt that the paper had distorted his stand. "I do not often notice mistakes in reports of what I say, but your paper of the 10th instant contains one which I do not choose to let pass uncorrected. . . . I said forty acres of land and a hut are of more importance than the immediate right to vote—both are their due." Ibid., May 16, 1866.

72. White's frantic letters to Trumbull reflected his anxiety that Johnson was about to make drastic changes in the federal patronage. White to Trumbull, May 16, 31, 1866, Trumbull MSS. See also White to Trumbull, June 21, 1866, Trumbull Family Papers, Illinois State Historical Library.

73. White to Trumbull, May 31, 1866, Trumbull MSS.

74. Medill to Trumbull, July 1, 1866, Trumbull MSS.

75. White to Trumbull, July 5, 1866, Trumbull MSS.

76. *Chicago Tribune*, July 3, 1866.

77. White to Trumbull, July 5, 1866, Trumbull MSS.

78. *Chicago Tribune*, July 14, 1866.

79. White to Fessenden, July 17, 1866. Fessenden's personal papers unfortunately have been scattered by bookdealers. This letter has been dipped

into an embellished version of Horace White's biography of Lyman Trumbull, now in the possession of Robert Irrmann, professor and archivist at Beloit College.

Medill agreed with White's observations about the absence of an enabling act and wrote almost the same thing to Elihu Washburne and Lyman Trumbull. "I hope you do not suppose that we can sustain ourselves on the policy of *exclusion*. As the matter now stands we have offered the South *nothing*—no terms whatever." Medill to Trumbull, July 7, 1866, Trumbull MSS. See also Medill to Washburne, July 17, 1866, Washburne MSS.

80. White and Medill to Schuyler Colfax, July 20, 1866, Trumbull MSS.
81. *Chicago Tribune,* July 20, 1866. See also August 6, 1866.
82. Ibid., July 4, August 4, 6, 22, 27, 1866.
83. Ibid., September 10, 1866.
84. Ibid., October 6, 1866.
85. Ibid., November 6, 1866.
86. Ibid., November 7, 9, 1866. See also January 1, 1867.

7

Triumphant Radical

THE RADICAL triumph in the election of 1866 brought Horace White national recognition. Only thirty-two years old, he was the editor-in-chief of the leading Radical newspaper in the West, and his paper's position in that Republican stronghold was virtually unrivaled. Johnson's open challenge of Congress had vindicated White's early forceful warnings against the President's wayward course. As a result, the *Tribune* became the oracle of triumphant Radicalism in the old Northwest.

The bold maneuvers of the *Tribune*'s young editor sustained the immense authority that the paper had won during the Civil War. To meet this continuing challenge of journalistic leadership, White and his colleagues kept the *Tribune* apace with the eastern metropolitan dailies by maintaining large capital investments in their growing enterprise.[1] They fought for and won almost every technical advantage that had once been the monopoly of the great New York journals.[2] The pronouncements of the *Tribune* gained a national audience. White joined a daily editorial forum which included such prominent journalists as Samuel Bowles, Horace Greeley, Edwin L. Godkin, Manton Marble, and John W. Forney.

The emotional surge of the 1866 contest held further importance for the *Tribune* editor-in-chief. Not only did the campaign win him and his paper new laurels, but it also carried him to advanced ideological positions. The elections, White felt, had "wonderfully cleared the political air." He demanded that Congress set aside the Johnsonian governments in the South and thoroughly reconstruct the whole region. White insisted that the southern states, "by persistent rebellion," had forfeited their rights under the Constitution. Once he had agreed with Lincoln that any precise constitutional definition of the status of the ex-Confederate states was a "pernicious abstraction"; now he maintained that those states should be thought of as territories and readmitted to the Union accordingly. All efforts to rejoin the Union, moreover, had to be approved by "all men of lawful age, white or black . . . and their right to participate should be maintained by force if necessary."[3] No longer should the South be allowed to fling back "magnanimous propositions . . . in our faces with scorn."[4]

The intransigence of the South which Andrew Johnson fostered compelled Horace White to advocate measures for which his own education and earlier assumptions had not prepared him. Andrew Johnson had a way of pushing many men into uncomfortable positions. Step by step, moderate Republicans, many with Whiggish notions of society and laissez-faire concepts of government, were set off on a forced march to far extended ideological positions. Horace White was among that beleaguered band.

The Reconstruction imbroglio, for example, forced White to accept the new nationalism implicit in the Civil War. Johnson played a major role in this conversion by permitting almost no diminution of the doctrine of states' rights. White scoffed at Johnson's alarm cry of centralization. Those who raised it, White felt, intended only "to save the Confederate section against the just punishment for their crimes. . . .

Consolidation, or centralization to this extent is a necessity; and so far from being an evil to be condemned or deplored, it is an indispensible blessing."[5]

The Reconstruction experience also forced Horace White to a radical attitude toward the Supreme Court. When the Court threatened in the Milligan case, for example, to undermine Congressional plans for a military reorganization of the South, White demanded that Congress pack the Court. "Unless a remedy is applied," he warned, "the people of this country will cease to be their own rulers . . . and the rebellion will become as victorious as though Grant and Sherman had surrendered to Lee and Johnston, and Jeff Davis himself were in power at the Capitol."[6]

Perhaps the most precarious position that White came to hold in the struggle over Reconstruction was that of universal manhood suffrage. He found himself forced to defend the enfranchisement of a large untutored body of former slaves. Nothing in his education had equipped him for this battle. His schooling at the Whiggish redoubt of Beloit was certainly no preparation; his battles with the Douglas Democracy in Illinois found him among those who had warned against any rapid expansion of the electorate. White frankly admitted his intellectual dilemma in the *Tribune*.

The claim that the right to vote was the natural right of every citizen, without any restriction, "not even that of intelligence and virtue . . . was the doctrine of the old Democratic party." This doctrine, White noted, had led to the inclusion of "not only men of no education, or intelligence, but shoals of emigrants from the Old World." In large cities the results of this course, he maintained, had "awakened grave doubts whether such a policy will not lead to great manifold evil and wrong, and whether it should not be abolished at once." He surmounted his hesitation about universal manhood suffrage in the South by finding the evils limited to large cities, "where the circumstances are peculiar." "In the country everywhere there is no complaint made that men are allowed to vote who should not."[7] Refusing to assume the Democratic ground of natural rights, White did nonetheless come to defend universal manhood suffrage vigorously. But his assumptions were never clearly stated; his reasons were usually pragmatic; and tension was always apparent in his thinking. In the South, the purpose was to reorder society; universal manhood suffrage there was an expedient and little more. More generally, White saw universal suffrage as the best outlet for social strife. The ballot in the hands of the "lower and feebler classes . . . was the only sure defense against collision, violence and bloodshed."[8]

In less than a year White had moved from espousing a limited expansion of the franchise to demanding universal manhood suffrage. Without the political impasse raised by Andrew Johnson, White would surely never have assumed this new ground. He had, long before the Civil War, considered personal freedom and basic legal guarantees as the right of every man, black or white. But to him voting had been a privilege and not a natural right. Race was never in his mind a valid determinant of voting citizenship. But his antislavery idealism never ignored intelligence, virtue, or social class as prerequisites for political power. Andrew Johnson had placed White in a most uncomfortable position. Where he had once criticized Wendell Phillips for reckless proposals, White now found accord with that bold Boston Brahmin. Indeed, White came up to what he felt was the full measure of Republican Radicalism. In January, 1867, he demanded that Congress pass a Constitutional amendment establishing universal manhood suffrage. "Let that amendment be submitted within the next three weeks," he insisted, "and it will be ratified . . . before the Fourth of July next."[9]

Universal manhood suffrage, in White's mind, came to be the balm for all Southern ills. "To establish universal suffrage, is to settle all questions at one blow," he announced. "The moment the ruling faction in the South consents to the rule of all the people, the controversy is at an end."[10] In his editorials he espoused the doctrine with the zeal typical of a new convert. "Universal suffrage," the *Tribune* assured its readers, "is in accordance with the genius of our institutions as remoulded by the war. It is the destiny of this nation, as inevitable as the war itself."[11]

White drew some balm for his ideological discomfort by looking at the international scene. Other liberal theorists, particularly those in England, were also compromising their positions on the extension of the franchise to lower classes. White frequently drew parallels between the suffrage battles in England and those in the United States. He did not consider the English liberals as leaders; in fact, he thought their enthusiasm for electoral reform subjected "them to the charge of being 'Americanized.' " Yet White saw the American Radicals and English liberals engaged in a joint crusade. Universal manhood suffrage, the *Tribune* declared, was the destiny of western civilization. Indeed it was "the great question of the world."[12]

The dramatic Republican victory in the 1866 elections may have excited White's idealism, but it failed to bring immediate action in Congress. The deliberations of that body soon made it evident to White that not all Republicans held the same set of priorities or solutions as he did for the postwar age. With Johnson apparently defeated, the old tensions within the anti-slavery coalition asserted themselves once again.

When the Republican-controlled Congress turned itself to a discussion of the tariff, the *Tribune* grew restive. The editors accused Congress of neglecting the solemn mandate of the people, of failing to "go about the only work for which it was expressly elected." This unforgivable hesitation, the editors charged, was merely Congressional pandering to the interests of "Eastern capitalists."[13]

When the Reconstruction Committee finally broke its silence and issued a report, the *Tribune* condemned almost every one of its recommendations. The report was an attempted compromise between Republican moderates and radicals.[14] Radicals, however, spurned the proposal, since it provided simply for the extension of military rule throughout the South, while ignoring such delicate problems as the legality of the Johnsonian governments and the question of Negro suffrage. In rejecting the committee's "retrograde" formulations, the *Tribune* called for "legislation that will put all other questions at rest by securing universal suffrage."[15]

Universal manhood suffrage continued to be the mark of Horace White's radicalism. All other proposals in his mind simply avoided the bedrock of the Reconstruction problem. When James G. Blaine offered an amendment to the Committee's military bill on February 12, allowing the former Confederate states to regain their Congressional representation after they had ratified the Fourteenth Amendment and guaranteed general Negro suffrage, the *Tribune* applauded loudly for the Maine Congressman. White could not understand, however, why George Julian and other Radicals followed Thaddeus Stevens's lead in opposing the amendment.[16]

White soon found out that Blaine's amendment was defeated not because it was too radical but because it was too moderate. Stevens and others felt that more than Negro suffrage was needed to ensure any reordering of southern society. They were demanding such things as disenfranchisement of former Confederate leaders and confiscation of rebel property. White looked up to discover that Negro suffrage was no longer the advanced position of Radical Republicanism. At this moment, White had passed the climax of his radicalism. Suddenly he found himself in a new role; he began to plead for moderation. Like Blaine, White now viewed Negro suffrage not only as a complete simple solution to Reconstruction but also as a way of avoiding more radical, enduring national involvement in the South.[17] He saw no need for any special protection or relief for the freedmen. Voting rights ended the national obligation to the former slaves.

When Wendell Phillips came to Chicago on the evening of February 21 and pronounced the position of the Stevens-led radicals, White responded quickly to this challenge in his own backyard:

> We beg to assure Mr. Stevens that the people of the North care nothing about the subject of confiscation, so long as the subject of reconstruction is unsettled. The North is impelled by no motives of revenge, and seeks the establishment of loyal Governments in the South on the basis of equal rights. . . . Give the country reconstruction on the basis of universal suffrage, and it will require but a few years to change the whole structure of society in the South, without confiscation, without vindictive measures of any kind, and without even the disfranchisement of the rebel population.[18]

The reconstruction bill that finally passed Congress was a compromise of various moderate and radical proposals. The Republican majority near the end of the session agreed upon Negro suffrage and disregarded confiscation. But they demanded disenfranchisement of certain Confederate leaders. The *Tribune* therefore labeled the bill "imperfect" yet expressed its gratitude that some measure had finally been passed. White's praise was faint: "It is a peace and Union measure. It is a law that will put an end to anarchy and restore constitutional Union and freedom to the people of the rebel States."[18] White was disappointed with the bill; it went too far. True, he accepted the compromise, but—in doing so—he made it clear that he expected no more requirements of the South. Reconstruction, he solemnly announced, was "an accomplished fact."[20]

Radicalism had taken on a new meaning for Horace White,

since universal manhood suffrage was no longer the banner of the vanguard. Furthermore, other forces in the society were beginning to use the rhetoric of Radicalism in ways that White had not intended. Supporters of the eight-hour movement in Chicago, for example, began to probe the meaning of the maxims which White had used in the antislavery crusade. A reader who signed himself "Mechanic" tested the quality of the editor's radicalism:

> Now as none rendered more efficient service in breaking up the old order of things, and freeing the many millions of laboring poor from their few hundred masters than the *Tribune,* why does it turn its back on these many thousands of its friends who so much need its valuable assistance just now, in helping along with this most salutary reform?[21]

The *Tribune* answered this letter in an editorial: "The course of the *Tribune* has not changed; it is the enemy of oppression and wrong everywhere; but it does not believe eight is the same as ten. . . ."[22] In the *Tribune's* opinion, a law requiring employers to employ men for only eight hours and still pay them what they had received in ten amounted to robbery.

The debate did not end. Another labor leader questioned the *Tribune's* stand: "While this war for equality was confined to Southern soil, you had no undue regard for rights of property, as opposed to the rights of manhood." The writer continued with an expression which the *Tribune's* editor well remembered. "That society cannot exist half slave and half free is beginning to have a far greater significance than when Lincoln first made the assertion. Law and custom must give to all persons approximately the value of their earnings, or the name of freedom is a mockery, and incipient republics a failure."[23]

White, a major employer himself and one of the wealthiest men in Chicago, would not tolerate this plagiarizing of antislavery slogans. His editorials labeled the workers' demands as "agrarianism" and damned their arguments as "incendiary."[24] When the labor leaders called for the general strike in Chicago on May 1 that brought out over five thousand workers to march in the streets, the *Tribune* became increasingly alarmed. When the demonstrations turned into riots after the employers refused to meet with the workers, the *Tribune* demanded that the strikers be "reduced to obedience by the bayonet."[25] Fortunately the city authorities did not act so forcibly. Nonetheless, the strike collapsed within a month, after the employers agreed to make no concessions and counterattacked with lockouts. At the end of the confrontation, the *Tribune* blandly urged the workers to forget the episode as one of the "follies of the past."[26]

With such social unrest in Chicago encouraged by men who were adding new meaning to radicalism, it is no wonder that Horace White and his colleagues were hopeful that the southern problem had finally been settled by Congressional action. Such men as White never seriously considered confiscation and redistribution of southern land as a solution to the problems of the former slaves. Whenever a handful of Radicals broached the subject, the *Tribune* had ordinarily given the matter little discussion. When it was pushed with greater insistence in 1867, labor demands in northern cities only further strengthened the *Tribune* editor's attachment to the sanctity of property. In such a setting, White was unwilling to tamper with property rights. Instead, *Tribune* editorials pointed happily to signs which appeared to prove that universal manhood suffrage would settle all difficulties in Dixie "at one blow." Early in April, the paper announced that "the South has finally acquiesced in Negro suffrage . . . and has renounced all scruples and prejudices against meeting the black man on terms of political equality."[27] "Victory at Last" sighed another *Tribune* editorial. "We rejoice with exceeding joy at the near prospect of the restoration of the South to the

Union, and at our approaching rest from the strife and turmoil of the Negro Question."[28] Throughout the spring, White accumulated optimistic omens. He used them all to make his point again that no further Congressional measures were needed.[29] He had almost forgotten about the President of the United States.

Suddenly, indeed overnight, the *Tribune* changed its stance. Andrew Johnson had reentered the scene. On June 16, in a lead editorial, White dramatically altered the position of his paper. He called for Congress to return to session on July to "save the country from impending perils." "We believe," the editorial proclaimed, "that a conspiracy, of which Andrew Johnson is the head, exists to thwart the will of the people."[30]

Up until this time White obviously believed that Johnson had given up the fight. But a "leak" from Washington convinced him that Johnson had all along been fashioning a plot. The tip-off from an unidentified source gave White the gist of an unreleased report of Johnson's Attorney General, Henry Stanberry, which declared unconstitutional the temporary military jurisdiction outlined by the Reconstruction Act. Johnson, White was convinced, had delayed in showing the "cloven hoof of the conspiracy," because he was waiting until after the third of July deadline for Congress to reconvene in a special session. Johnson supposedly would then have a free hand until December to sabotage the Congressional operation in the South. Johnson had been the fox, and "all his recent decency of demeanor" had been feigned, White felt, in order to lull Congress into "the belief that all is fair ahead."[31] Once again Johnson drove Horace White to demand further action on Reconstruction. Johnson had accomplished what Thaddeus Stevens and Charles Sumner could not.

White's warnings once again proved correct, for on June 20 Johnson issued a set of orders which contradicted the Congressional formula for the reorganization of the South. The *Tribune*, in response, once more urged impeachment, a device which it had relinquished to the "extreme wing" of the party.[32] "The people demand that this Copperhead plot shall be effectually exploded, even if impeachment be necessary to accomplish it."[33]

Radicalism, however, could no longer be advocated with abandon. The apex of his radical ideology had already been reached months earlier. White now found himself in the uncomfortable position of a moderate in a revolutionary era. With one hand he had to fight a conspiracy which he considered reactionary; with the other he had to beat down a movement which he considered ultra-radical. Impeachment intensified his dilemma, for it was a two-edged sword. It might be the only way to crush the power of Johnson. Hastily done, however, impeachment could lead to the dominance of the ultra-radicals. The first possibility White admitted openly; the second, he shared for the time being only with his intimate friends.

If Johnson were impeached, Senator Wade of Ohio was next in line for the presidency, and he belonged to the ultra-radical wing of the party. Wade was also in favor of higher tariffs and, of all things, the eight-hour day! As Congress prepared to reconvene, the editor-in-chief of the *Tribune* grew cautious and began to urge careful consideration of any impeachment scheme. He urged Congress not to be swayed by "temporary passion." He must have sighed with relief when the emergency session of Congress ended without taking a vote on impeachment. White advertised his fears only after Congress adjourned. He labeled the aborted attempt at impeachment as a "low and unworthy" scheme "by which parties wanted to get Mr. Wade into the Presidential chair during the unexpired term of Andrew Johnson, in order to forestall the next Presidential election and defeat the nomination of any other candidate next year."[34]

White did not have long to savor his respite after the July session. On August 5, 1867, Johnson once more reawakened political animosities by suspending his Secretary of War, Edwin Stanton, and appointing General Grant to succeed him. Once again White found himself in a similar dilemma. His response was the same. In the *Tribune,* he threatened the "base recreant" with impeachment.[35] But, in his private correspondence, he recognized the hazards of such a move. Johnson had complicated White's response even more this time by giving Stanton's post to General U. S. Grant, the journalist's favorite for the Republican presidential nomination in 1868. This was indeed a crisis. Anxious and indecisive, White wrote to Congressman Elihu Washburne, who was recovering from an illness in Paris:

> Apart from the warm personal interest which I feel for your welfare it has seemed to me most important that you should be at home this year in view of the approaching Presidential election, for reasons which I need not explain. Just now a new fact has been accomplished *viz* the suspension of Stanton and the appointment of Grant to succeed him. I fear that this will have a changing effect upon the General in two ways. It will confirm the impression which many people have that he is in some sense tainted with Johnsonianism, *which I do not believe*. Second, it will give a new impetus to the impeachment movement, the object being to get Wade into the Presidency long enough to give him prestige and patronage to control the next National election.[36]

White thought Grant could have avoided this problem by refusing to take Stanton's post. Why Grant accepted, he did not know; but he did know that the affair had "an unfavorable and unpromising aspect."[37]

White found no easy solution. Still he had to grind out a daily newspaper that had to say something relevant on the major issues of the day. He took an awkward stance in his editorials; defending Grant while criticizing Johnson was no easy task. He resorted to sarcasm and name calling to meet ultra-radical criticism, and he urged that the Republican party move cautiously in their assault on Johnson.[38] "We are not in the midst of a French revolution," he insisted, "where the legislature is governed by a Jacobin club."[39]

White's former Radical friends took full advantage of the occasion. Zach Chandler, a leader of the ultra-radical forces, wrote to White, taking care to point out the error of not having impeached Johnson in the previous session of Congress.[40] In his response to Chandler, White revealed his growing dissatisfaction with radical demands. Although he still considered himself a "Radical," White confessed that he felt "more in harmony" with the men whom Chandler labeled "Conservatives than with any other branch of the party." While avoiding the real issues that divided them, White recognized that Johnson presented the ultra-radicals with the best of the argument. He refused to grant to Chandler that Johnson should have been impeached earlier, but insisted that after the President's removal of Stanton the time had come for that drastic measure. "I am for impeaching him," White admitted.[41]

Writing an editorial that same evening, White finally joined the public demand for Johnson's impeachment.[42] He had no choice if he expected his paper to retain a position of Republican leadership. The demand for impeachment had become too intense. Awkwardly, White climbed on the bandwagon. He made the decision, painfully aware that the crisis had provided "temporary resuscitation of the Dogberries, who dub themselves Radicals, and all other persons Conservatives." "We desire to keep peace with them," the *Tribune* editor warned, "But we shall not allow them to institute a course against wiser and honester Republicans than themselves, with impunity."[43]

White's position in the crisis became a little easier when Grant began to disagree publicly with the President, particularly over Johnson's dismissal of General Sheridan from a post in the South. White gave prominent and consistent publicity to the increasingly petulant exchange between the President and his Secretary of War.[44] Meanwhile, the *Tribune* also gave every assurance that it could of the General's "radicalism." White's appeal to Elihu Washburne seemed to bring results. The Congressman rushed home and issued a statement revealing Grant's agreement with the principle of universal manhood suffrage. The *Tribune* no doubt expressed White's relief in being able to reprimand the "doubting Thomases" who claimed that Grant was "not a reliable, straightforward, Radical Republican."[45] Two weeks later, the *Tribune* came out openly for Grant as President in 1868.[46]

While White and other Republicans jockeyed for power during the impeachment crisis in the fall of 1867, the Democrats won several significant victories in key states. In Ohio, they won control of the state legislature and promised the end of Ben Wade's tenure in the Senate. There were some Republicans who shed no tears. The *Tribune* editor was among those who saw some good in the defeat; his remarks portray the intensity of the fight within the Republican party:

> Doubtless, the political atmosphere will be greatly purified by what happened; heresies that have been crowded into the Republican platform will be eliminated, many unsafe men will be laid on the shelf; the financial legislation of Congress will be more prudent and conservative; the ardor of zealots will be restrained, and the efforts of the real patriots will be redoubled.[47]

If Congress had held a session shortly after Johnson's provocations in August, he probably would have been impeached. But time and intervening events cooled Republican tempers and allowed the moderates to exert greater influence. By the time Congress assembled in late November, many had quietly stepped down from the summer's impeachment bandwagon.

Horace White was among them. Thurlow Weed did not have to remind Washburne and other Grant supporters of their best course: "If the question of impeachment comes to you in the form of Duty, I know that you will discharge your duty. But if it takes the form of Policy or Expediency, it seems to me that the Grant interest which you represent is against it."[48]

White went to Washington himself in order to watch the ominous and delicate proceedings firsthand. He stayed with Elihu Washburne. Before he departed for Washington, he gave careful instructions to his subordinates on the impeachment question.[49] The *Tribune* had remained strangely silent on the issue for several weeks. But it made its new position clear as Congress met: it no longer supported impeachment. Indeed, it labeled the charges against Johnson "strained and threadbare." More important questions faced the party, it insisted, such as the debt, the tariff, and the currency.[50]

When impeachment came before the House in early December, 1867, the Congressmen voted overwhelmingly against it. White's friends in Washington were pleased.[51] The *Tribune* concluded that the "mischief" of impeachment would prove "to be troublesome and distracting no more." The Radical journal was happy to take "not a little credit" for its defeat.[52] Later that month, Chicago received word that it was to be the site of the Republican national convention in 1868. Horace White and his associates had every reason to be pleased. The impeachment crisis seemed behind them. Grant appeared to be the leading candidate. The joy of Christmas was upon the land.

But it did not last long. The political struggle initiated by Johnson within the Republican party had hardly been stilled before the determined President initiated another, this time far more serious. After Congress refused to impeach Johnson and then recessed for the Christmas holidays, Johnson proceeded to fire two more generals who were supervising the reorganization of the South.

White grew understandably desperate. A *Tribune* editorial pleaded: "Cannot Congress devise some means of checkmating the villanious conspiracy of Johnson and Co. to defeat the restoration of the Southern States to the Union?"[53] Frustrated by constant resistance from Johnson and pushed already to the limits of his ideological boldness, White initially was unable to respond. The *Tribune* remained mute on possible retaliation for several weeks. Possessed by what he himself described as a "gloomy feeling," White concluded that Congress had to meet Johnson "on the same ground and be as audacious and obstinate as he is."[54] Finally editorials boomed out a demand for the ultimate weapon: "There is no second choice left to Congress. *It must assert its supremacy as the exclusive law-making power of the nation,* or it must perish beneath the heel of the dictator. If Andrew Johnson steps beyond the line of his sworn duty of obedience to law, let him be impeached and deposed, and let rebellion, treason, Copperheadism or slavery rise up to prevent that action if it dare."[55] Once more, Andrew Johnson pushed Horace White further than the editor of the *Tribune* would have wanted to go.

The expectation of an Armageddon continued. On February 19, 1868, White delineated the crisis: "The conflict is now narrowed down to a question of nerve and a question of force. There is no backward step possible for either party."[56]

The stalemate ended on February 21, when General Lorenzo H. Thomas laid claim to Secretary Stanton's office on the authority of President Johnson. On February 24, the *Tribune* recommended impeachment: "We believe that it is equally the duty and the policy of Congress to impeach Andrew Johnson of high crimes and misdemeanors."[57] Medill, who was hurriedly sent to Washington, reported to *Tribune* readers that men who had "most strongly opposed impeachment are

now the strongest advocates of it." "Fort Sumter and the flag
have been fired upon."[58] Action could not come quickly
enough for the *Tribune* managers. Medill expressed their
anxiety: "We are all nervous about delay in the impeachment
case. That is the overshadowing, all absorbing quest on with
the country just now. Like an aching tooth everyone is impatient to have the old villain out."[59] White sustained this
urgent demand for impeachment in the *Tribune* until late
April. Up to that time he showed no doubts or hesitation.
"The only opposition to impeachment," he insisted, "comes
from the faction calling themselves 'Democrats.' "[60]

Then like a pendulum, White's view of impeachment began
to change. In each impeachment crisis his reaction had been
the same: initial anger with Johnson; then, consideration of
the costs of impeachment; and finally, opposition to such a
move. The *Tribune,* in this final impeachment crisis, did not
reflect White's hesitation until the last moment. On April 21,
White copied into his editorial columns a paragraph from
the *Iron Age* which called for a meeting of protectionists in
New York City on April 28 to "take advantage of the brief
administration of Mr. Wade" in order to pass an "adequate
and well adjusted Tariff Bill." "There is no need of con-
cealing from the public the fact," White remarked, "that one
of the chief obstacles to the impeachment of Andrew Johnson
is the belief which many Senators entertain that Mr. Wade
would seize the occasion of his *ad interim* Presidency to crowd
upon Congress a bill to plunder the public anew under the
miserable pretence of protecting the home industry."[61]

Despite his anxiety over the tariff, White temporarily held
the *Tribune* firm. In fact, in the same editorial, he urged
senators to disregard the threat of Wade's possible accession.
"A new tariff bill is simply impracticable," he explained.
"There is no time now to prepare such a measure—much less
to pass it." Yet the news evidently upset White; his editorials

in the next few days, while still supporting impeachment, defended senators who wished to act independently and in accord with legal sanctions.[62] Only when he received confirmation of a tariff conspiracy did White demonstrate serious reconsideration about the advisability of impeachment.

The first proof of a plot came from the protectionist convention in New York. The ironmaker Peter Cooper stated that he had "reason to *know*" that Wade, as President, would give his immediate attention to higher tariffs. Whatever doubts remained in White's mind about Wade's intentions were removed by the senator in an interview he gave to a reporter for the Cincinnati *Gazette:* Wade announced that he would push aside all other matters as interim president and "concentrate on an adequate tariff."[63]

These revelations threw the *Tribune* office into a frenzy. Medill viewed the protectionist program as "a damnable plot." He labelled the high tariff advocates "cormorants" seized by "the maddness [*sic*] of greed." The *Tribune* editorials shrieked that the "insatiable lobby" could easily bring about the "calamity" of Johnson's acquittal. In support of this argument, White published a Washington dispatch from Murat Halstead. It stated emphatically what few historians have taken seriously: "This contest is a part of impeachment."[64]

Most standard accounts of the impeachment trial do not deal with the possible impact of issues such as the tariff on the eventual acquittal. The rumors that Wade, as Johnson's successor, would appoint ultra-radical Cabinet officers, push for high tariff and soft money schemes, and foist his Cabinet upon Grant frightened many Republicans besides White. Hans L. Trefousse, both in his biography of Ben Wade and in a larger study of the Radical Republicans, has given considerable insight into these fears. George F. Edmunds, who participated in the impeachment proceedings as a senator from Vermont, also corrected subsequent legalistic versions of the trial:

I did know from intimate (and often confidential), personal intercourse with several Senators, including Mr. Fessenden, Mr. Grimes, and Mr. Trumbull, that, to state it mildly, a deep solicitude existed as to the fitness of the President pro tempore of the Senate, Mr. Wade, to act as President if Mr. Johnson should be removed. . . . I have since believed, as strongly as one can believe something that cannot be definitely proved, that had Mr. Frelinghuysen or Mr. Harlan, for instance, been the President of the Senate, Mr. Johnson would have been removed.[65]

White's own actions seem to bear out Edmunds's view. When the intentions of Wade appeared certain, White began to consider the wider political repercussions of his accession to the presidency. Both he and Medill felt certain that the passage of a tariff bill would defeat Grant and the Republican party in the approaching national elections. That prospect was so ominous for White that he dashed off to Washington to see what was happening for himself. Before he left, he revealed his concern in a quick note to Elihu Washburne: "I don't know how it may look to you, but the gathering of evil birds around Wade, (I refer to the tariff robbers), leads me to think that a worse calamity might befall the Republican party than the acquittal of Johnson. Yes, and that worse might befall Grant!"[66]

When White arrived in Washington, he noticed the changed mood for himself. The fear of Wade's accession apparently had frightened moderates once more. White's closest friends in the Senate—Fessenden, Grimes, and Trumbull—had decided against impeachment well before the tariff question blurred the latest outburst against Johnson. Fessenden, however, had been pessimistic before the tariff crisis and viewed impeachment as certain. But by May he spoke of an additional "seven or eight who say they find great difficulties in their way."[67]

White felt certain at this point of the imminent failure of impeachment; he later boasted of his discernment to Washburne.[68] Doubtless this knowledge proved no solace, however, since White faced a painful dilemma as editor of the *Chicago Tribune*. While he was gone, the editorial page had remained silent, but eventually he would have to speak out. Republicans whom he had helped whip into a frenzy over impeachment would obviously condemn any support of acquittal. Yet he felt obliged to defend his close friends in the Senate who would be held responsible for undermining Johnson's impeachment. His initial response, therefore, was very cautious. In a lead editorial on May 6, the *Tribune* announced "the unwelcome intelligence" that impeachment might fail. The editorial explained that "two or three Republican Senators of ability and high standing" would oppose Johnson's conviction on legal grounds and that fear of Wade's tariff plans would probably drive others to vote for acquittal. To protect the *Tribune*'s reputation, the editorial concluded: "Still, we shall hope for the conviction of the wretched apostate, notwithstanding the alleged defection of Fessenden and others."[69]

The equivocation continued until May 12. While still expressing "profound regret" over the inevitable failure of impeachment, White declared: "Better the acquittal of Johnson, than his conviction upon grounds that would not endure scrutiny in the coming Presidential election."[70] White followed this editorial with others that prepared a defense for his friends Trumbull, Fessenden, and Grimes. "We protest," White declared, "against any warfare by the party or any portion of it against any Senator who may, upon the final vote, feel constrained to vote against conviction."[71]

White must have anticipated the reaction; it came fast and heavy. Subscribers responded angrily to his editorials; and Republican newspapers both in Chicago and around the country excoriated his position. When virtual acquittal came on a test vote on May 16, the *Tribune* tried to justify its backsliding by claiming that it had "earlier news than other journals of what was coming." Its subsequent position, White explained, was taken to "prepare . . . the minds of the people for what was inevitable" and also to show "that the failure of impeachment could not affect the duties and the prospect of the Republican party."[72]

After impeachment had failed and Congress had adjourned, the national focus shifted swiftly to Chicago, where Republicans opened their national convention. As a defender of Trumbull, Grimes, and Fessenden, White found himself in the midst of a maelstrom. An exuberant "Soldiers and Sailors" convention met before the Republicans convened. In resolutions and public demonstrations the group reviled the Republican senators who voted to acquit Andrew Johnson. But the moderate Grant forces controlled the major convention. White and his friends dominated the resolutions committee and carefully headed off any rash action against the notorious Seven. White described the holding action to an anxious Charles Eliot Norton:

> It has been a rough fight for us—much worse I imagine than it would have been if the Convention had been held in another city. The mob which drifted into Chicago were perfectly crazy on Sunday, Monday, and Tuesday, but we should have quieted them easily but for the hateful influences of the Congressional impeachers who came here in a state of absolute frenzy, telling the most preposterous falsehoods concerning Trumbull, Grimes and Fessenden.[73]

Holding back the impeachers was no simple task. Angry Republicans throughout the nation expressed their scorn for the recreant senators and their defenders. Nevertheless, White kept the *Tribune* firmly behind his old Senate friends. Fessenden only wished that he had such support closer to home. He envied Trumbull and Grimes. What White's bold defense of his senatorial friends meant to the *Tribune,* on the other hand, is not easy to measure. Fessenden claimed that

White's action meant a subscription increase for the paper. Joseph Medill, however, who dissented strenuously from White's action, said just the opposite. Explaining the rift within the editorial staff to Elihu Washburne, Medill wrote: "Horace continues to blaze away against the impeachers. The paper has lost many subscribers and worse still has lost a great degree of its influence with the radical masses who are deeply offended at White's course; but I am unable to do anything. Trumbull and Grimes are of more importance in W's eyes than the power and friendship of the Republican patrons of the paper. It is a deplorable blunder."[74]

Whatever White's decision may have meant for his paper, it did not immediately harm his position among Republican party leaders. He continued as an insider in the Grant campaign machine. Indeed, moderates such as White had gained firm control of the party before the impeachment crisis; and they retained it after the acquittal. The waning of Reconstruction radicalism was not so much a psychological response to the failure of impeachment as it was a seizure of party control by Republican moderates. Their worst enemies within the Republican party were almost completely isolated from the Grant leaders.[75] White felt so sure of himself and his position that he treated the impeachment question lightly. He wrote to Washburne in that frame of mind: "I think that the Republican party is far stronger than it would have been if impeachment had been successful, and that as soon as we can get people to forget that it was ever attempted we shall march onto certain and overwhelming victory."[76]

Grant's managers could not afford to indulge in recriminations against anyone in the party. The services of all Republicans were needed in the presidential campaign that fall. Internecine warfare would have been disastrous, for the opposition had opened a vigorous canvass appealing to class and racial passions. The Democrats were promising that they would overthrow "Negro domination" in the South and pay off Civil War bondholders in depreciated greenbacks rather than gold.

Horace White had always met anti-Negro sentiment boldly in his paper. Treatment of the currency question in the Midwest, on the other hand, had demanded delicate decisions by the *Tribune* managers. During the war, White had declared himself a bullionist and, accordingly, had condemned the greenback issue when it passed in 1862. But, after the war, he came to recognize the potential economic and political hazards of rapid withdrawal of greenbacks from circulation.[77] His editorials had frequently damned the deflationist schemes of the Johnson administration with a fervor equaled only by his feelings about the President's reconstruction efforts. In attacking the policies of Johnson's Secretary of the Treasury, Hugh McCulloch, the *Tribune* played to anti-eastern and anticreditor sentiments.[78] Some of the *Tribune* owners, bank directors themselves, did not agree with White's policy on this issue.[79] But antideflation sentiment was strong in the Midwest, among businessmen as well as farmers. White, in compromising his own views, apparently felt that it was necessary to make concessions to this sentiment in the West.[80]

As in Reconstruction matters, others went beyond the *Tribune* currency position. Democrats led by George Pendleton and Republicans led by Ben Butler began calling for a repudiation of gold payments for the interest on U. S. Civil War bonds. Joseph Medill felt that the *Tribune* would have to conciliate this repudiation sentiment in order to win in the 1868 campaign.[81] But White refused to compromise any further. Serving on a special subcommittee with his laissez-faire minded compatriot Charles Ray and with Stephen A. Hurlbut, White had drawn up the Republican platform plank and firmly committed the *Tribune* to its defense. "All forms of repudiation" were denounced as "a national crime" by the convention and White urged the party to support the plank "not faltering, not with backward looks at the brazen serpent of repudiation—which some of us, alas! once fell down before—but with our whole hearts."[82]

Such firmness proved to be unnecessary. The Democrats avoided a pitched battle over repudiation. In nominating Horatio Seymour, a spokesman of the New York business community, as their presidential candidate, the Democrats blunted the impact of the financial question in the campaign. Horace White was almost gleeful; he was happy to share the burden of Wall Street. "The 'bloated bondholders' have triumphed in Tammany Hall. The nomination is a deathblow, not only to Pendleton, but also to Pendletonism in every one of its Protean forms."[83] To make White's task even easier, the Democrats nominated Frank Blair for Vice-President. "He is committed to nothing" the *Tribune* declared, "but Civil War."[84] A fugitive letter of Blair's documented the *Tribune*'s declaration. "It is idle," Blair wrote, "to talk of greenbacks, gold, the public faith and public credit. We must restore the constitution before we can restore the finances and to do this we must have a President who will execute the will of the people by trampling into the dust the usurpation of Congress, known as the Reconstruction acts."[85]

This rash letter allowed White to continue the duel with Andrew Johnson. The Democrats had conveniently supplied a second, Frank Blair. In this battle, White could join hands not only with Joseph Medill, who gave up his plans to leave the *Tribune* staff, but also with Ben Butler, Charles Sumner, Horace Greeley, and Ben Wade. Only the Democrats could have cemented that wartime coalition once more. Fully realizing the implication of the Democratic action, the *Tribune* appealed to all Republicans: "The only safety of the nation is in treating the entire Democratic movement as a revival of the rebellion."[86] Armed with the morality of the war, the Republicans won the election with unexpected ease.

For Horace White, Grant's victory seemed to be the long-awaited vindication of his goals. Impeachers, protectionists, repudiators, rebels, and copperheads—all seemed to have been defeated. The Republican triumph, White promised his readers, also meant an "end of the Negro Question." It was in this light that the *Tribune*'s editor-in-chief interpreted Grant's famous campaign appeal: "Let us have peace." Horace White was more than ready for a little "peace"; he was more than ready to retire from the antislavery crusade that had dominated so much of his early life.

NOTES

1. Although 1866 was a big year for the paper, the *Tribune* Company paid no dividends because of large capital expenditures. See Horace White to Charles Ray, December 6, 1866, Ray MSS.

2. White enjoyed flexing his journalistic muscles, particularly under the nose of his old foe, Horace Greeley. "With a field one-tenth as large as that of our New York rival, we have a vastly better newspaper in every department, we make more money, and today our establishment is worth more, and will sell for more on the open market, than that of the N. Y. *Tribune*. We . . . stand . . . as compared with that of our rival, the foremost Republican paper in this country." *Chicago Tribune*, July 13, 1866.

Immediately after the 1866 elections, White, representing the Western Associated Press, demanded that the New York Associated Press treat his group as an equal in the gathering and transmitting of news. After a three month battle, White's original demands were met by the New Yorkers. The battle was won after the *New York World* joined White's association in the revolt. Together they negotiated a contract with the Western Union Telegraph Company that broke the New York Associated Press' monopoly of discounted telegraphic service. *Chicago Tribune*, December 5, 13, 1866, January 11, 1867. See also White to Manton Marble, December 11, 14, 17, 18, 19, 1866; White to D. H. Craig, December 7, 1866; Joseph Medill to Manton Marble, January 13, 1867: Manton Marble MSS, Library of Congress.

The deal which the Western Associated Press made with the Western Union Telegraph Co. proved to be an embarrassment for Horace White. When Elihu Washburne later pleaded with White to back his plan of a government owned telegraph service, White had to confess his impotence: "The fact is that the Western Associated Press, ourselves included, are bound by a written contract with the Western Union Telegraph Co. *til Jan. 1, 1869*, not to advocate said measures hostile to the interests of said telegraph company. This was a part of the machinery by which we were emancipated from the New York press monopoly. Whether right or wrong in principle (and I do not defend the principle), it seemed then to be necessary to enable us to secure independence of the New York ring, who are in my judgement more unprincipled than the telegraph monopolists. Of course we cannot violate the contract while it exists." White to Elihu Washburne, June 4, 1868, Washburne MSS.

3. *Chicago Tribune,* November 11, 1866.

4. Ibid., November 20, 1866.

5. Ibid., November 25, 1866.

6. Ibid., January 15, 17, 1867.

7. Ibid., November 11, 1866.

8. Ibid.

9. Ibid., January 26, 1867.

10. Ibid., February 17, 1867.

11. Ibid., February 21, 1867.

12. Ibid., September 15, 1865, February 21, July 12, 1867.

13. Ibid., January 23, February 7, 1867. In sharp contrast to the *Tribune's* anxious editorials at this time, the *Republican,* the major Republican rival of the *Tribune* in Chicago, remained calm. "The Republican party of the Northwest is no different in its views on the tariff question from the Republican party in the East. It will heartily sustain the policies of Congress upon the tariff question, the reconstruction question, and the currency question; and it will give Congress the time it needs in which to decide upon them all." *Chicago Republican,* February 11, 1867.

14. Eric McKitrick, *Andrew Johnson and Reconstruction,* pp. 478–479.

15. *Chicago Tribune,* February 8, 1867.

16. Ibid., February 15, 1867.

17. W. R. Brock, *An American Crisis* (New York, 1963), p. 297. See also pp. 290–301 for a provocative analysis of Radical ideology on Negro suffrage.

18. *Chicago Tribune,* February 23, 1867.

19. Ibid., February 22, March 9, 1867.

20. Ibid., March 11, 1867.

21. Ibid., March 26, 1867.

22. Ibid.

23. Ibid., May 2, 1867.

24. Ibid.

25. Ibid., May 4, 1867.

26. Ibid., June 13, 1867. See also May 14, 23, June 4, 1867.

27. Ibid., April 11, 1867.

28. Ibid., April 21, 1867. See also April 24, 1867. White's reaction accords with the interpretation of David Montgomery in his book, *Beyond Equality, Labor and the Radical Republicans 1862–1872* (New York, 1967). The labor unrest in Chicago in 1867 surely caused White to stand firm on the ground of equality before the law; he would go no further in dealing

with the problems of the freedmen or urban workers. For a discussion of
the Chicago disorders in Montgomery's book, see pp. 306–310.

29. *Chicago Tribune,* May 18, 1867.

30. Ibid., June 16, 1867.

31. Ibid., June 18, 1867.

33. Ibid., June 21, 1867.

34. Ibid., July 25, 1867. Very little of the correspondence between Horace
White and his close friends, Senators Fessenden and Grimes, has survived.
It is evident, however, that he shared with them the view that impeachment served the interests of men whom they feared and detested in the
party. Fessenden called the advocates of impeachment "animals." Fessenden
to Grimes, May 2, 1867, Fessenden Family Papers. When Johnson created
a new stir in mid-June, Fessenden recognized the dangerous political situation. "Shall you go? It is all nonsense in my judgment, and old Stevens
and others are jumping at a pretence. I am disgusted with Johnson for
giving them such a pretence. God only knows what mischief will be done
if we get together. . . . Besides, we shall be weak—the Pacific Coast is not
to be counted on and Morrill of Vt and Sherman, with many of the House
are in Europe." Fessenden to Grimes, June 18, 1867, Fessenden Family
Papers.

35. *Chicago Tribune,* August 10, 1867.

36. White to Elihu Washburne, August 13, 1867, Washburne MSS.

37. Ibid.

38. The *New York Tribune* directed embarrassing inquiries concerning
Grant to his supporters. To meet this innuendo about Grant's sympathy
with Johnson, White dredged up his detailed store of Greeley dirt. He
reminded his readers of "Greeley's renown as a negotiator" and "his consistency and usefulness as a vegetarian." *Chicago Tribune,* August 17, 18,
1867.

39. Ibid., August 20, 1867.

40. In the previous impeachment crisis, White had listed Chandler as one
who was using impeachment to boost Wade into the presidency. See Ibid.,
July 25, 1867.

41. White to Zach Chandler, August 20, 1867, Zach Chandler MSS,
Library of Congress. Compare White's letter with Greeley's response to
Chandler: "All that is fishy and mercenary in the Republican ranks com-
bines with everything copperhead to escort Grant as the man destined to
curb Radicalism and restore conservatives to power." Horace Greeley to
Zach Chandler, August 25, 1867, Zach Chandler MSS. It is interesting to
note how men used "Radicalism" at different times to serve their own
interests. Once White had accused Greeley of being soft on Johnson and
copperheads. Now the tables were turned.

42. *Chicago Tribune,* August 21, 1867.

43. Ibid., September 6, 1867. White once more became peeved with
Wendell Phillips, labeling him a "fault-finder," the "Great American

Scold," who was "always prognosticating evils that never occur." Ibid., September 14, 1867.

44. Ibid., August 21, 22, 23, 27, 28, 29, 1867.

45. Ibid., October 7, 1867.

46. Ibid., October 24, 1867.

47. Ibid., November 10, 1867. Fessenden exchanged congratulations with Grimes after Wade's defeat in Ohio in October. "If Chandler is saved, however, perhaps the country can stand the loss of Wade." Fessenden to Grimes, October 20, 1867, and Grimes to Fessenden, October 24, 1867: Fessenden Family Papers.

48. Thurlow Weed to Elihu Washburne, November 22, 1867, Washburne MSS.

49. White to Elihu Washburne, November 27, 1867, Washburne MSS.

50. *Chicago Tribune,* November 27, 1867. The *Tribune's* Democratic rival in Chicago, the *Times,* sarcastically reminded the *Tribune* of its demand for impeachment in August. As an explanation the *Tribune* replied that Grant, while Secretary of War, had arrested Johnson's designs in the South, and, as a result, Johnson was no longer a hindrance to Reconstruction. Ibid., December 3, 1867.

51. Although Eric McKitrick in his work, *Andrew Johnson and Reconstruction,* made a major contribution in demonstrating the tensions between the radicals and moderates in the framing of Reconstruction legislation, he does not show how much this tension also affected the impeachment crisis. More than recognition "that they did not have a case" caused moderate Republicans to back away from impeachment. The strong biases of men who supposedly acted on the legal nature of the case must certainly be taken into consideration. Fessenden in his private correspondence after the impeachment crisis in the winter 1867 demonstrates the passionate prejudices that he felt at the time. "We have done much in the time by getting rid of the impeachment folly, and leaving the road open for travel. The impeachment gentlemen in and out of congress are in a great rage. It extinguishes the assinuations [*sic*] of the Radical Radicals. Mr. Wade's visions of being President pro-tem have faded. For once, Mr. Sumner cannot boast of the fulfilment of his prophesy, and his bitterness bests 'wormwood and gall.' It is of no use, however. They are in minority of their own party—and must stay there." William P. Fessenden to Elizabeth Wariner, December 15, 1867, Fessenden Family Papers.

52. *Chicago Tribune,* December 8, 1867. The editorial concluded: "As it led the van during the war, so it now is foremost in those great measures which will restore the country to prosperity and peace."

53. Ibid., December 30, 1867.

54. White to Elihu Washburne, January 16, 1868, Washburne MSS.

55. *Chicago Tribune,* January 14, 1868.

56. Ibid., February 19, 1868.

57. Ibid., February 24, 1868.

58. Ibid., February 28, 1868.

59. Joseph Medill to John Logan, March 18, 1868, John A. Logan MSS, Library of Congress.

60. *Chicago Tribune,* April 8, 1868.

61. Ibid., April 21, 1868.

62. Ibid., April 22, 25, 1868.

63. Ibid., May 1, 2, 1868.

64. Joseph Medill to Elihu Washburne, May 1, 1868, Washburne MSS. *Chicago Tribune,* May 2, 1868.

65. Hans L. Trefousse, *Benjamin Franklin Wade* (New York, 1963), pp. 305–310, and *The Radical Republicans,* pp. 396–398. For earlier treatments of the trial see David M. DeWitt, *The Impeachment and Trial of Andrew Johnson* (New York, 1903); Milton Lomask, *Andrew Johnson: President on Trial* (New York, 1960); Edmund G. Ross, *History of the Impeachment of Andrew Johnson* (Santa Fe, N. M., 1896); and J. B. Henderson, "Emancipation and Impeachment," *Century* 85 (January, 1913):192–211. Edmunds wrote in response to Henderson's article. See George F. Edmunds to the Editor of the *Century Magazine,* January 30, 1913, *Century* 85 (April, 1913):863–865.

66. Horace White to Elihu Washburne, May 1, 1868, Washburne MSS.

67. William P. Fessenden to William H. Fessenden, May 3, 1868, Fessenden Family Papers. Only several weeks earlier, Fessenden wrote to his cousin: "The impeachment drags itself along slowly. . . . The probabilities are now that the President will be convicted." Fessenden to Elizabeth Wariner, April 12, 1868, Fessenden Family Papers.

68. Horace White to Elihu Washburne, May 11, 1868, Washburne MSS.

69. *Chicago Tribune,* May 6, 1868.

70. Ibid., May 12, 1868.

71. Ibid., May 14, 1868. See also May 13, 15, 1868.

72. Ibid., May 18, 1868.

73. Horace White to Charles Eliot Norton, May 20, 1868, Charles Eliot Norton MSS, Harvard University.

74. William P. Fessenden to Frances Fessenden, May 23, 1868, Fessenden Family Papers. For an appraisal of the value of the *Tribune*'s support for Trumbull, see Mark Krug, *Lyman Trumbull: Conservative Radical* (New York, 1965), pp. 267–270.

75. William D. Mallam, "The Grant-Butler Relationship," *Mississippi Valley Historical Review* 41 (September, 1954):259–276.

76. White to Elihu Washburne, June 4, 1868, Washburne MSS.

77. For White's wartime reactions to greenbacks, see his letters in the *Chicago Tribune,* January 20, February 14, 1862. After the war, White clarified his personal attitude concerning the greenbacks to Edward Atkinson, one of the leading proponents of rapid specie resumption: "I imagine that there is not much difference between us on the currency question. I am more nearly a bullionist in principle than anything else. Perhaps I would go farther in that direction than you are willing to go. The thing that puzzles me is how to get back to the bullion without smashing every-

body in the country except—no, I will except nobody. . . . It seems to me that this can be best done by reducing the national debt as fast as practicable and allowing the country to grow up to the volume of the existing currency, rather than shrinking the currency to the actual size of the country—a process which involves panic and bankruptcy, and which is sure to encounter fierce resistence. . . . I think they are the opinions of a large majority of the people in the West. . . . you will readily perceive that the debtor class are not going to be convinced by any mere disquisition on political economy." White to Edward Atkinson, September 25, 1867, Edward Atkinson MSS, Massachusetts Historical Society.

78. *Chicago Tribune,* March 26, 1866, January 20, 1867, February 12, 26, 1867.

79. William Bross, director of the Manufacturers National Bank of Chicago as well as a major proprietor of the *Tribune,* took issue with White's compromising of the financial issues of the day. When the *Tribune* first came out against McCulloch's deflationary schemes, Bross apologized to the Secretary of the Treasury for the position of the paper. He explained that the decision was made against his will. He concluded: "The rapid fall in gold at the time, as much as anything for the time being determines the policy of the paper, frightening my associates for the time being." William Bross to Hugh McCulloch, March 31, 1866, Hugh McCulloch MSS.

80. Recent students of the financial problems of postwar America have noted the difference between an inflationist sentiment and an anticontractionist sentiment. Men of either persuasion, however, could unite against schemes of rapid specie resumption. Robert Sharkey, *Money, Class and Party* (Baltimore, 1959), pp. 81–134. See also Irwin Unger, *The Greenback Era* (Princeton, N. J., 1964), pp. 41–162. For the anticontractionist attitude of Chicago businessmen see Unger, pp. 155–158. Edward Atkinson after a visit to Chicago and the West reported the attitude of White and his colleagues to Hugh McCulloch. "The editors of the Chicago Tribune are alarmed, have pronounced against paper money but have their own method of cure and think the prejudice against the Banks must be yielded to." Edward Atkinson to Hugh McCulloch, November 7, 1867, Hugh McCulloch MSS.

81. Joseph Medill grew alarmed at the political advantage he felt the Democrats gained because of the Republican platform position on repudiation: "we have no issue that we can make against the Dems. Andy Johnson is played out. . . . We must stand on the defensive and defend Shylock and his pound of flesh—high taxes, high interest, gold for the bondholders, not for the people." Joseph Medill to Elihu Washburne, June 25, 1868, Washburne MSS. Medill urged Republicans to give some ground on the repudiationist sentiment in order to avoid defeat. See Joseph Medill to John Sherman, June 25, 1868, John Sherman MSS, Library of Congress.

82. Adams Sherman Hill, "The Chicago Convention," *North American Review* 107 (July, 1868):173, 177. Hill, who stayed at White's home during the convention, undoubtedly received the inside information about the

resolutions from White, his close friend ever since their joint work as Civil War correspondents. See also the *Chicago Tribune*, July 3, 1868. White's decision on the financial question, coming as it did shortly after the impeachment imbroglio, caused Medill to express exasperation with his editor in-chief: "I am done playing second fiddle to W. I must either write and print my own notions of party policy or not write at all. W. and I differ on many things, and in the management of a paper we would differ daily. He is a cautious, timid conservative. *I ain't.* I believe in 'striking from the shoulder,' at the enemy or at false friends. I am no man's man. He *is.* So we must separate. Sorry, very sorry but no help for it." Joseph Medill to Elihu Washburne, June 28, 1868, Washburne MSS.

83. *Chicago Tribune*, July 10, 1868.

84. Ibid.

85. Ibid. The Blair letter continued: "There is but one way to restore the government and the constitution, and that is for the President elect to declare the Reconstruction acts null and void; compell the army to undo its usurpations at the South; disperse the carpetbag State governments; allow the white people to recognize their own government and elect Senators and Representatives." The letter appeared many times in the *Tribune* during the campaign. See Ibid., July 11, 13, 23, August 3, 10, 13, 1868.

86. Ibid., September 3, 1868.

8

Let Us Have Peace— and Free Trade Too

Horace White was anxious to end the Civil War. Several times before he had prematurely announced the coming of peace, but each time he was disappointed. Nevertheless, Election Day, 1868, found him optimistic again. All his country's enemies were defeated; all his party's heretics were expunged. "There need be no division in its ranks of Radicals and Conservatives," White declared. "Andrew Johnson is now impeached most effectually. . . . This is emphatically an era of unity and good feeling in the Republican party, and it can be made the harbinger of future triumphs if those who are entrusted with power use the victory of Tuesday with discretion and moderation."[1]

Events quickly dispelled such optimism. Then as before, when an end to the issues of the war seemed imminent, the Republican wartime coalition threatened to become a shambles. Only the constant harassment of Andrew Johnson had held the Republican alliance together after Appomattox. Grant's victory in 1868 did nothing to heal the latent disagreements within the party. On the contrary, it finally uncovered the fragile construction of the Civil War coalition. During the interim between the election in November, 1868, and Grant's inauguration in March, 1869, Republican factions fought ferociously in Congress. Three sensitive issues caused the trouble: reconstruction, the currency, and the tariff. The debate over each made it painfully obvious to Horace White that the Republicans were not entering an "era of good feelings."

Immediately after the Civil War, White had been anxious to take up and settle various economic questions. In 1865, he had presented a constitution for a Free Trade society in Chicago and opened a vigorous discussion of economic issues in the *Tribune.* The actions of Andrew Johnson, however, caused him to postpone or subordinate that effort. The prerequisite for a consideration of economic questions, he always acknowledged, was an end to the debate over Reconstruction. "So potent are the issues growing out of the existence of slavery," White reiterated in 1868, "that it is futile to attempt to fix the public attention upon any others, however momentous."[2] White had hoped, however, that Grant's defeat of the Democrats would shelve the issue of national reunion once and for all. For him November 5, 1868, was to have been the last day of the rebellion.

The Georgia legislature quickly precluded that hope. During the 1868 campaign, the white majority of that body expelled the black legislators and prohibited Negroes from serving thereafter in the Georgia House and Senate. At the time, White used the incident to indict Grant's opposition. "The Democracy have begun a little too soon to carry into practice the recommendations of Frank Blair and the New York Convention."[3] The *Tribune* issued a testy threat: "If it becomes necessary to send Sherman's army into Georgia again, to re-establish the supremacy of law, they will go with alacrity, and it will not be required of them to visit the State a third time for the same purpose."[4] After Grant's election, however, White took a different view of the situation. When a bill was introduced in Congress to set aside the Georgia state government until the constitution was amended to make Negroes eligible for office, the *Tribune* objected: "We hope that Congress will not entertain or pass a measure of this kind."[5] White blasted the proposal as the work of the "screeching wing" of the Senate. "It is not a measure conceived in the interest of peace, but in favor of renewed strife, discord and contention."[6]

The reason for White's change of opinion is not hard to find. In the midst of the renewed argument over reconstruction, Republican protectionists had reopened another quarrel by passing a tariff proposal. White found the two questions forebodingly intertwined: "The Moorhead Tariff bill, which is now being rushed through Congress by the representatives of special interests, aided by the bulk of the Southern carpet-baggers, is a diabolical outrage on thirty millions of people."[7] Ironically, White praised Andrew Johnson for utilizing his final veto against the measure. "The last act of Mr. Johnson's career as President, we are glad to say, is an act to protect the people against flagrant robbery."[8] White expressed no joy when Congress concluded its long conflict with the President by overriding his last executive protest.[9]

The vote of the Moorhead Tariff was important, for it demonstrated the economic views of the Congressmen recently selected in the reconstructed states. From this point on, the *Tribune* and Horace White used the term "carpetbagger" only as a term of derision. During the campaign the *Tribune* had blasted the derogatory use of the word as a revival of nativism. Pointing to men like Andrew Johnson, Daniel Webster, and Abraham Lincoln, the *Tribune* had insisted that "the right of citizens of one state to migrate and become office holders in other states is part of our political system. . . . The real objection to these Northern men is that they have no sympathy with the rebellion." As proof the *Tribune* pointed to men from Illinois who moved South after the war, became Democrats, and were fully accepted. But after the bulk of the carpetbaggers voted for higher tariffs and stiffer reconstruction measures, the *Tribune* editors changed their views about the new governments in the South.[10]

The election was not over long before the *Tribune* also began to show its discomfort within the antirepudiation alliance. White himself was committed to eventual specie payment of the greenbacks, but he continued to insist upon a very gradual program. He berated "all the various mixtures of the Greeley-Morton-McCulloch devices" that called for rapid deflation.[11] To the "whole active business public" in the West, rapid deflation "would be in effect a confiscation."[12] If anything, the West needed more currency through a better share of the distribution of national bank notes. "It is simply preposterous," the *Tribune* declared, "for the Eastern States to suppose this condition of things will be tolerated much longer."[13]

Grant's election thus did not bring to Republicans the harmony which White had glibly predicted in November. Indeed, by defeating the opposition which had held the party together in fear, Grant's victory signaled a renewal of the East-West, debtor-creditor, high tariff-low tariff, Radical-Conservative bickerings within the party's ranks. What side Grant would take in these disputes was still unclear, but Horace White had his hopes.

Several years before Grant's election White had carefully laid some plans for such an eventuality. He tried to educate the general in the problems of political economy. In 1866 White had written to Elihu Washburne, "I am persuaded that Grant is to be the next President if he gives *us* half a chance to nominate him. Before *his* term is over the question of high protective tariffs is going to be an overmastering one in our politics." To introduce Grant to the subject, White sent him a copy of the *Catechism on the Corn Laws.* As the volume had been written by a major general in the British army, White considered the book an elegant choice. He hoped that U. S. Grant would "read up a little on the question, beforehand."[14] Grant's modern biographer was perhaps correct when he surmised that White's enclosure was shelved among the military volumes in the new library just given to the general by wealthy northern businessmen.[15]

White was rather confident that Grant would be on his side in any major conflict within the party. He almost relished a fight as he chuckled to Washburne after the election: ". . . within one year the Butlers, Sumners, Chandlers, Tiltons, *et al* will be full mouthed against the Administration: Let 'em come on, I say. They will have a good time."[16]

The first important encounter between Republican factions took place over the makeup of Grant's cabinet. White used all of his influence to get David A. Wells appointed as Secretary of the Treasury, since that officer would say the most about the tariff and currency questions.[17] Wells, acting as Special Commissioner of the Revenue in Washington, had fully identified himself with the low-tariff persuasion that winter when he issued a report condemning the Moorhead tariff.[18] White also hoped that Washburne would take the Interior Department and Fessenden the State Department. Condescendingly, he offered a sop to others in the party. "I suppose the 'Radicals,' as they style themselves, must have a representative in the Cabinet. Why not take Wade, and make him Postmaster General? The screechers all went for 'old Ben' first for President and next for Vice President."[19]

When Grant finally announced his Cabinet, none of White's favorites were among the appointed. Still, the *Tribune* approved the President's selections. White was particularly delighted with the choice for the Secretary of the Treasury— A. T. Stewart, New York's wealthiest merchant. True, Grant had not chosen Wells. Nevertheless, White interpreted Stewart's appointment as a slap at the "high tariff fanatics and plunderers." Thinking over the matter, he dubbed Stewart as the "best selection" for the post.[20]

Unfortunately Grant had blundered. As a merchant, Stewart was an ineligible candidate under the original provisions for the Treasury post. White was disappointed, for Stewart was a personal friend as well as a sympathetic free trader.[21] White urged Washburne to search for some accommodation by which Stewart could stay in the Cabinet.[22] But pleading did not help as Congress refused to accept the wealthy importer. To make matters worse, Grant followed Stewart's resignation with the nomination of George Boutwell, whose appointment the *Tribune* editor feared more than any other. "He is one of those conscientious fanatics," White had once remarked, "who are more dangerous to a party than a score of irresponsible 'critters' like Wade, Chandler, and Butler."[23]

Grant's handling of the Cabinet appointments discouraged and confused White.[24] The Treasury was taken over by a dangerous radical, yet the contradictory nominations for that position gave no clear indication of Grant's own view of economic questions. Recovering quickly from his apprehensions concerning the Cabinet imbroglio, White confessed his hope to Washburne that they might "take a fresh start with a good chance of success." He concluded his letter to the Congressman with a series of his own recommendations for other appointments.[25] White was still optimistic that an era of retrenchment, economy, and reform was about to begin. To that end he urged that the reins of power be fully committed to the President's hands.

After the Cabinet crisis a calm settled over the country. The focus of attention turned away from Washington and the unsettled issues of the war. The subsequent months of 1869 seemed to confirm Grant's promise of a national peace.

Those were important months for Horace White. In April, the *Tribune* moved into a new building. The establishment had outgrown its old quarters. Since the beginning of the

Civil War the paper had grown steadily. Only twelve years before, White had been a part-time reporter. Now he was editor-in-chief. Only twelve years before, he and others had to work without salaries; now the owners were paying $800 a week to their employees and almost $5,000 a month for wire services and special dispatches. The market value of the paper had risen from $200,000 at the beginning of the war to well over $1 million in 1869.[26] Circulation for the daily continued to hover near the wartime high of 50,000 copies while advertising profits kept mounting.[27] The *Chicago Tribune* had become a massive concern. To house the enterprise, White and his associate, Alfred Cowles, financed a $250,000, four-story, "fire proof" stone building, filled with $100,000 worth of furnishings. White himself sank nearly $100,000 into the new construction.[28]

It was a year for building. Shortly after the *Tribune* moved into its new facilities, White joined a celebration in Chicago for the completion of the Union Pacific Railroad. Along with other Midwestern businessmen he also took one of the first journeys across the West by rail.[29] His paper speculated that the road was the long sought passage to the East. The new *Tribune* building was in the center of Chicago and Chicago seemed to have become the center of the universe. Congress, the editor contended quite seriously, should consider moving the nation's capital into the booming heartlands of the Midwest.[30]

During this calm in old Civil War contentions, White turned once more to the development of the coal mines which he had purchased as a young man.[31] The slavery turmoil had frequently interrupted his development of those mines. He hoped there would now be enough relaxation of the old issues that he could turn his attention again to economic interests of his own, his city, and his nation. *Tribune* editorials expressed his mood: "It is needless to disguise the fact that the old things are passing away, and all things become new. Old issues are fading from sight. Slavery is abolished and impartial suffrage established, or so nearly so that there is scarcely enough difference of opinion to make a political campaign upon. The right of every man to exchange the products of his labor freely," the argument proceeded, "is as sacred as any right that God has given him. The political party which shall affirm and maintain this right will surely triumph in the end."[32]

White was sure that the Republican party under Grant's leadership would take the lead in espousing his new set of political priorities. The new President was justifying "the most ardent hopes of those who elected him," the *Tribune* remarked on July 1, 1869. According to White, retrenchment, economy, and reform had rightfully become the motto of the administration. Grant's first months in office had given America "a more perfect peace and a more certain and enlarged prosperity than the country has known for many years."[33] Actually Grant had done very little during those first few months in office. He had utilized neither White's nor anyone else's program for economic progress and domestic peace. He simply postponed decisions, and, in doing so, he maintained relative harmony within the party in 1869.

White's set of prescriptions would certainly have shattered the Republican party, for the *Tribune* editor was advocating a rigorous formula of laissez-faire remedies for the nation's economic ills. Shortly after the Civil War, White had plunged into a study of classical economics—in response, no doubt, to the heated debate over the tariff. To share his new knowledge with *Tribune* readers, he regularly reprinted long selections from the works of European theoreticians. The French free-trader, M. Frédéric Bastiat, was his favorite.[34] The seriousness of White's studies was attested to by his editing a new translation of Bastiat's *Sophisms of Protectionism* in 1869. His preface to the book indicated a wide reading in classical economic theory. Under the auspices of the Free Trade League, the work was republished in 1870 and distributed widely. White was evidently very proud of the new edition. When the protectionist Horace Greeley published a book on political economy about the same time, the *Chicago Tribune* predicted that "the two treatises, being on the opposite sides of the great political question of the day (or that which will soon be the great question), will undoubtedly become the manuals of opposing clubs and speakers, to a large extent, throughout the country."[35]

For White, these new concerns formed a logical extension of his reform ideology. He simply added Free Trade to the earlier antislavery slogan of Free Soil, Free Labor, and Free Speech. And he fully expected most of the former abolitionists and the bulk of Republican intellectuals to follow the new banner. Again, White worked within an international liberal framework. Joining a dialogue with English sympathizers, he gained confidence from their sanctions of intellectual respectability. He exchanged letters with John Stuart Mill and John Bright and printed several in the *Chicago Tribune*. Eventually he also joined the Cobden Club of London and threw his energies into the British inspired Free Trade League in the United States. Increasingly, the doctrines of European laissez-faire economists began to influence White's public pronouncements. One editorial, for example, pleaded for the introduction of ten thousand Chinese to work in local textile mills, since "the cheap labor of the Chinese has precisely the same effect on the labor market as the still cheaper labor of the horse, the steam engine, and of all machinery." The *Tribune* urged Chicago to "steal a march on other communities . . . in obtaining the earliest and largest supply of Chinese labor."[36] To invigorate business, taxes also had to be reduced by local and national authorities. Public employment had to be cut back and brought under an efficient program of civil-service reform. Monopolies that restricted trade had to be broken. Finally, tariffs had to be reduced in order to stimulate national and international trade.

White knew that each of these moves would entail serious repercussions in politics at every level. But he coldly anticipated that "parties will soon be dividing on new questions." Reconstruction and the Civil War were over, White chanted in frequent editorials. "We have other business before us —business of taxation, of finance, questions of internal communication and transportation, questions of labor and production, of capital and monopolies, and to act upon these important subjects we want quite another . . . class of representatives than those whose sturdy patriotism supplied the lack of general information during the dark days of the rebellion."[37] "It is time for a 'new deal,' " White declared on another occasion, "and we have not the smallest doubt that it will be made."[38]

White began to abet such a revolution in politics on a local level, in Chicago. Boldly challenging the loyalties of his readers, he demanded that the corrupt and extravagant Republican rule in the city come to an end.[39] "The whole establishment needs to be cleaned out."[40] Volunteers heeded White's call; on September 25, 1869, they announced a Citizens' Ticket. The slate was a bipartisan group of candidates, containing eight Republicans and seven Democrats. The platform of the movement took no position on national affairs; it simply echoed a taxpayers' revolt. "It is time," the document read, "for all citizens to look after their immediate interests and property."[41] The next day the *Tribune* gave the group its blessing: "All is quiet at last on the Potomac, where for ten years all had been stormy. Now is the season for reform at home—in our city of Chicago. Let the deadbeats go out. Their Augean stables want cleaning. None but new brooms can do it."[42]

The Democratic party could never have won the sympathy of White and other Republicans; the independent stance of the Citizens' Ticket was a political necessity. But not all the brooms were new. The old politico John Wentworth, for example, headed the campaign committee to elect the bipartisan slate, and the other leaders were seasoned politicians and hard-headed businessmen. They were not novices. They went about their work systematically: political organizations were established in every ward, and young men's clubs were added where it proved necessary. White, in addition to his daily editorial support of the movement, pitched in himself on the grass roots level by joining the Second Ward campaign committee.[43]

This local political episode was very important in White's career, for it anticipated arguments and appeals that he would soon be making on the national level. As Republicans in the city, for example, pleaded for solidarity in order to meet future Democratic threats on national issues, White answered: "Reconstruction is done. Our financial honor is assured beyond cavil or reproach. There is no single national question at issue between the Republican and Democratic parties. They are both living upon the memories of the past."[44]

It was a strange sight indeed to see the *Chicago Tribune* and the *Chicago Times* cooperating in a political struggle.[45] But concurrent, nonpartisan taxpayers' revolts in San Francisco and Cincinnati encouraged White's independent mood.[46] The calm on the national scene confirmed it. "Vote for the citizens' ticket," White urged Chicago voters, "on the platform of Grant, retrenchment, economy, and reform."[47] Chicagoans listened to the appeal. The Citizens' Ticket swept into office. Horace White was triumphant.

Grant took no part in the local elections of 1869. Indeed, he still had taken no action on any major issue. U. S. Grant remained the stolid Sphinx. White therefore continued to define his formula for national action without reference to any real knowledge of Grant's own thinking. Emboldened by the reformers' victory in Chicago, White presented a prospectus for his paper which explicitly proclaimed an end to war issues and demanded that the nation debate the financial questions at hand.[48] The editor moved out ahead of his party, gambling once more on political trends. He evidently anticipated Grant's concurrence.

The climax approached as Grant prepared to deliver his first annual message to Congress in December, 1869. Grant did dwell on the delicate economic issues of the day, as did his fiscal officers who delivered concurrent communications to Congress. Boutwell, the Secretary of the Treasury, explained his policies to reduce the debt by buying bonds and hoarding gold. Grant, in his speech, gave a free hand to Boutwell by agreeing to no reductions in taxation or the tariff until the interest rate on the debt was reduced from 7 to 4½ percent.

The reports crippled White's high expectations for the administration. He leveled his first public rebuke at Grant's presidential performance. White challenged the President's commitment to Boutwell's plans, for they implied a postponement in any war on protectionism by the administration. For the next several weeks White hammered away at the Secretary's fiscal policies.[49] Before the year's end, he received new ammunition for his attack from a report by David A. Wells, who had continued in his role as Special Commissioner of the Revenue. Wells, at variance with Boutwell, recommended sharp reductions in tariffs and taxation in order to stimulate the nation's economic growth. White was delighted; he printed Wells's report in full.[50] Privately, he informed Wells that his report was "the most important and valuable state paper ever produced in this country on any financial or economical subject. The high tariff gentry will never get over it."[51] Making the most of Wells's report, White mobilized his staff in order to "blaze away" at protection in the columns of the *Tribune*.[52] Although neither Grant nor Boutwell had defended protectionism, they did not join a crusade against high tariffs. White decided to begin the struggle without the President's help. He had led vanguards before.

White had allies—important allies. Many, like him, were devotees of classical economics, but not all of them were motivated by ideology. Among the men who reinvigorated the moribund free-trade organization in Chicago were prominent businessmen who had a stake in the decrease of tariff rates.[53] In his inaugural address in the spring of 1869, J. M. Richard, president of the Chicago Board of Trade, clarified the mercantile community's vital interest in lower tariffs. Richard insisted that protection did not benefit international grain traders. Those traders, he proclaimed, could not wait for a fulfillment of the protectionist promise of an internal market large enough for their produce while they paid higher costs on manufactured goods.[54] Chicago was not unique in this regard: all around the country free traders drew funds and support from significant sectors of the business community.[55] Even in the West, the antiprotectionist battle was never simply an agrarian protest. The *Chicago Tribune* was always more an organ of the city's Board of Trade than a spokesman for the neighboring agricultural community.

The timing for an all-out attack on high tariffs seemed propitious. Early in February, 1870, Georgia added the final vote needed to ratify the Fifteenth Amendment. This amendment gave White still another reason to hammer home the refrain that Reconstruction should no longer stand in the way of natural economic alignments in American politics. "The negro, by being merged politically with the rest of the people, ceases to be an object for special attack or special defence, and thus drops out of general politics."[56] Universal suffrage had been written into the Constitution. White's Radicalism never insisted on anything more for the Negro.

Tariff reduction rather than universal suffrage had for more than a year been the watchword of Horace White's political concern. When Congressman John A. Logan sought a *Tribune* endorsement in his bid for the Senate, White presented his new test for all national candidates: "I shall not knowingly support any man in national politics who votes taxes upon A & B to enable C to carry on his private business.

. . ." Stating the same thought positively, White concluded: "I shall use my influence to secure the election of somebody who is opposed to the arrant heresy of Protection."[57] White had postponed such a requirement in 1866 and again in 1868; he would delay no longer. His letter to Logan signaled his determination to wage an entirely different campaign in 1870.[58] To insure his objective, White did more than write editorials; he joined an aggressive campaign to organize low-tariff sentiment.

On April 2, White helped gather over five hundred of "the most intelligent business men of Chicago" to discuss the subjects of national taxation and revenue reform. Speakers at the meeting called openly for an end of Civil War issues. "In contending for the equality of the negro," one speaker remarked, "they [Republicans] did not concede the inferiority of the consumer." Two days later the *Tribune* flatly declared, "The negro . . . has ceased to be an object of interest."[59] Shuttling between his newspaper office and the convention hall, White wrote and presented the resolutions for the assembly. He drew explicitly from David A. Wells's earlier report in recommending a reduction of fifty million dollars in taxation and a total abolition of the sales and income taxes. The resolutions blamed the tariff for high railroad rates and the lethargy of Great Lakes shipping and commerce. Appropriately, White concluded by resolving the assembly's support of David A. Wells. The businessmen passed the resolutions unanimously.[60]

This local effort was part of a concerted national campaign. White had been conferring with his friends in other areas on strategy for the fall elections. They had already mobilized the national Free Trade League.[61] To coordinate the total effort, David A. Wells summoned White and a bipartisan group of officials, editors, businessmen, and intellectuals to a conference in Washington on April 19.[62] White grew increasingly confident. Writing to Charles Ray after the Chicago meeting, he urged his old comrade-in-arms to redouble his efforts in the "free trade fight, which is now fairly opened, with every prospect of an early victory for our cause."[63]

The meeting in Washington consisted of a small but well-selected company: White, Edward Atkinson, Charles Nordhoff, Henry Adams, Mahlon Sands, Amasa Walker, David A. Wells, and a few others. They decided to concentrate their efforts on the election of Congressmen sympathetic to revenue reform regardless of party. There was to be, however, no open break with Grant or the Republican party. Instead the reformers would attempt to persuade Grant to back their cause, particularly by renewing the term of David Wells as Special Commissioner of the Revenue. Wells's appointment, unless renewed by Grant, was to end on the last day of June. White, as spokesman for the group, wrote Grant a "long and able letter," while others pleaded personally with the President.[64]

Grant refused to commit himself on the issue of the tariff.[65] At the same time he refused to interfere with the work of his Secretary of the Treasury and hinted that the reappointment of Wells did not suit Mr. Boutwell. White accordingly urged Wells to have his Congressional friends force the issue of reappointment. "Grant wants to temporize and follow the Good-Lord-good-devil policy," White observed, "and he ought not to be gratified in it."[66] Grant resisted the pressures: Wells had to step down from his office on June 30, 1870.

June 30, 1870, marked a crucial date in the disintegration of the Republican party. The rejection of Wells was a severe slap at the revenue reformers in the party, but it alone would not have caused the deep cleavages which eventually developed within Republican ranks at every level. Free-trade sentiment, except perhaps in the Midwest, was never so strong or so sharply focused as to have shattered the party structure. Nor, on the other hand, was Grant or his political entourage opposed to compromise on tariff reform. Something even more significant happened on June 30, 1870.

On that day, Charles Sumner led a successful rejection of a treaty to annex Santo Domingo to the United States. This was a question upon which Grant had definitely committed himself—he had placed the prestige of his administration behind the passage of this expansionist scheme. Its defeat stunned a commanding officer who had grown accustomed to victories. Embittered by what he felt was a broken promise of Sumner to support the treaty, Grant began careful preparations for a counterattack. Discarding his reasoned aloofness from politics, Grant decided to take an active role in disciplining his party.

The timing of Grant's partisan counterattack determined his selection of allies. White and other "Wells men" had proved themselves unreliable independents. Sumner, the idealistic Radical, was a marked enemy. Grant had to count on different men. In state after state, he began to draw reliable political lieutenants about him: John McDonald in Missouri; Ben Butler in Massachusetts; Roscoe Conkling in New York.[67] In each case, Grant made enemies by interfering in local squabbles; at the same time, he gained loyal compatriots for future battles. To win those allies, Grant distributed patronage freely. With cold realism he even asked for the resignation of one of his favorites in the Cabinet, Attorney General E. Rockwood Hoar, in order to win southern votes for his Santo Domingo scheme. Hoar had rendered himself expendable, moreover, by ruling that Grant's notorious private secretary, Orville Babcock, had no legal right to conduct diplomatic negotiations in Santo Domingo. For Hoar's replacement Grant nominated a political nobody, Amos T. Akerman of Georgia.

White did not perceive immediately the political machinations of the President. When rumors circulated that Grant was interfering in the Missouri elections, where Carl Schurz led a coalition of Republicans and Democrats against the regular Republicans, White refused to believe it.[68] White continued, therefore, to organize for a showdown on the tariff.

His campaign had already gained momentum. In 1869, Chicago had followed his lead. In 1870, Illinois did the same. The Illinois state Republican party allowed him virtually to dictate their platform on the issue of the tariff. Representing the First District on the resolutions committee, White helped frame a platform which condemned "the revival of the dead issues of reconstruction." On the tariff, the party pledged that "the best system of protection to industry is that which imposes the lightest burdens and the fewest restrictions on the property and business of the people." The platform continued: "It is wrongful and oppressive to enact revenue laws for the special advantage of one branch of business at the expense of another."[69] The *Tribune* gloated over its victory: "Protection," it insisted, "is a 'Lost Cause.' "[70] The defeat of the protectionist General Schenck, Chairman of Ways and Means, by a free-trader in Ohio's October election seemed to validate White's hopes.

It was not until after the October elections that White became aware of Grant's complicating interference. Shortly before the November elections (when most of the states voted), another reformer in Grant's Cabinet resigned—this time the Secretary of the Interior, J. D. Cox, who exposed Grant's heavy-handed use of the patronage. White did not pause long to contemplate the meaning of this new issue, for the exposé seemed only to help the cause of the revenue reformers. Many high-tariff Republicans lost their seats in Congress to low-tariff advocates. White viewed the result as one more advance in a growing reform movement.[71] In the victorious flush following the elections, he ran an editorial calling for the "reorganization of parties." The issue of anti-protectionism, he suggested, had the potential appeal of the old free-soil cause. Free traders from both parties could begin the reorganization by banding together in Congress in order to claim the Speaker, the organization of the House, and the appointment of committees.[72]

White and the free-trade reformers had prepared themselves to take advantage of the situation. A few days after the election, Mahlon Sands, secretary of the Free Trade League, sent out letters to key figures. Representing the officers of the League, Sands suggested an immediate conference "to determine whether an effort may not with advantage be made to control the organization of the new Ho. of Representatives by a union of Western Revenue Reform Republicans with democrats."[73]

Not many people knew of the secret conference, but thousands read White's threat of a bipartisan union of antiprotectionists in Congress and his specter of a possible new party. The Republican press blasted his proposals; even reform journals thought his suggestion of a new party premature. Facetiously, White marveled at the "unexpected excitement." He knew what he was doing; he was flexing his muscles. No paper reflected so powerfully the antitariff sentiment among Republicans in the West as the *Chicago Tribune.* The editor's brash maneuvers of 1869 seemed to be duplicating his bold course in 1865.

Influential Republicans began to fear that the editor was about to stage another political coup. The Speaker of the House, James G. Blaine, grew alarmed at the threatened free-trade alliance in Congress. He knew where to go. Before White left for the New York strategy session, Blaine came to Chicago in order to sound out the editor's demands. To assure his own election as Speaker, Blaine agreed to give the antiprotectionists the chairmanship and control of the Ways and Means Committee, where tariff measures originated in Congress. Both men picked Garfield as the appropriate chairman, and Blaine agreed to let White and his confreres in New York name two Republican members, who, with the Democrats, would form a majority of the committee.[74]

White reported his interview with Blaine to the New York gathering of twenty selected independent Republicans. Another member, Roeliff Brinkerhoff, told the group of an identical meeting with Blaine. There was some debate about compromising with Republicans on the question of congressional leadership, but finally the group accepted Blaine's offer. The views of the newspaper editors at the meeting prevailed over those of the officials of the Free Trade League. White made it clear that he did not intend to use the "new party" except as a threat. The threat had already forced Blaine's hand. There was not need yet to begin any dangerous flirtation with the Democrats.

White and the other editors carried one more point. They insisted that the movement should widen its platform to include Civil Service reform. Until the Santo Domingo fight, White had never emphasized that issue. The Free Trade League officials objected; they did not want to adulterate their cause. But Grant's flagrant use of the patronage in the fall elections had made Civil Service a major issue. The group could not pass up such a tempting weapon. For the time being, however, the revenue reformers decided to restrict their activities to the issues of the tariff and Civil Service reform, and they postponed any plans for a permanent political organization. They would put the administration "on its good behavior."[75] Brinkerhoff, however, was sent to Washington to keep an eye on James G. Blaine.[76]

The battle within the party went on—but not as White and his friends had so carefully planned. Grant did not make an issue of either civil service or the tariff. He said little about the tariff in his second annual message and even called for a Civil Service Commission to devise rules for his administration. Instead, Grant pushed ahead with his old hobby horse, the annexation of Santo Domingo. The intraparty feud therefore never took place precisely along the lines designed by Horace White and the revenue reformers. The Santo Domingo issue, rather than the tariff, brought about the major crisis in the Republican party. In March, 1871, the loyal agents of Grant attempted to purge Charles Sumner from his position on the Senate Foreign Affairs Committee.

White happened to arrive in Washington on the eve of the purge in order to confer with Congressman Allison of Iowa. Both of the men were protégés of the late Senator Grimes and had been working together closely on free-trade strategy.[77] While dining that evening, Allison told White of the decision of the Republican caucus to depose Sumner the next morning. Discussion of the tariff had to wait; the two men hurried to find Sumner. Locating the senator at the home of the Boston merchant, Samuel Hooper, the two men listened to Sumner's charges of injustice. From there they hurried to the apartment of Senator Howe of Wisconsin, who as Chairman of the Republican caucus was to announce the reorganized Republican committee assignments in the morning. White and his companion argued with Howe, late into the night, but the Wisconsin senator refused to challenge the decision of the caucus. White's predictions of "sorrows" for Howe's wing of the party had little effect on the senator's resolution. Sumner was deposed in the morning.[78]

Recalling earlier fratricidal battles, White dashed off, by telegraph, several lead editorials for the *Tribune*. The shrill items appeared for several successive days. White compared Sumner's exclusion to the removal of Stephen A. Douglas from the Committee on Territories in 1857 during the Democratic feud over the Lecompton constitution. White also reminded his readers of Sumner's earlier persecution at the hand of Congressman Preston Brooks. Rhetorically, White asked, "Will not this result in a political feud, which will not end until one or the other of the parties shall be driven into retirement by the indignant judgement of the public?"[79]

Returning to Chicago, White got news of removals closer to home. "The Presidential axe" fell "on the necks" of two local Treasury officials, closely identified with White's wing of the party in the city. The next day the editor pushed aside all former hesitations in criticizing Grant. He listed a long series of indictments against him. A President so accused, White concluded, "does not command entire confidence as to mental and moral fitness to be the ruler of a free people."[80]

The issues of the tariff, reconstruction, and finance had all steadily weakened White's devotion to Republican unity. It was the Santo Domingo imbroglio, however, which caused him to reject the party's president. Less than two weeks after Sumner's removal, White made an irrevocable decision: "The safety of the Republican party now depends upon . . . its selection of a sagacious, high-toned, genuine statesman as its standard-bearer in the next campaign."[81]

NOTES

1. *Chicago Tribune,* November 4, 1868.
2. Ibid., October 13, 1868.
3. Ibid., September 11, 1868.
4. Ibid., September 30, 1868.
5. Ibid., December 21, 1868.
6. Ibid., January 5, 1868.
7. Ibid., December 17, 1868.
8. Ibid., February 23, 1869.
9. Ibid., February 26, 1869.
10. Ibid., September 4, 1868. Joseph Medill, writing from New Orleans in April, 1869, expressed the new view of the *Tribune* managers toward the carpetbaggers: "The actual termination of the rebellion dates from the 5th of November, 1868. The South is now conquered, and peace has replaced war; prosperity will replace poverty, and happiness misery. Here are fair lands, sunny skies and magnificent opportunities for Northern capital and enterprise. The blacks are wholly inadequate to cultivate this country. They are beginning to work well, and to comprehend that freedom means hard work for wages. . . . The people of the South have been fearfully punished for their crime against the Union. The hardest heart could not wish them more punishment than they have suffered. They have been torn and bruised, battered and burned, slaughtered and lacerated, impoverished, humiliated, and, lastly ridden and robbed by carpetbaggers. They philosophically endure all the other stings of 'outraged fortune' except the carpetbaggers—the strolling, pilfering, political blacklegs of the North, whom they cannot bear, and they cry for exemption from this in-

fection. But this evil is of temporary duration, and is one of the gifts and legacies of Andy johnsonianism. Andy has gone back to his cabbage and his goose, and these carpetbagging birds of prey will soon scatter and disappear." Ibid., April 9, 1869.

11. Ibid., December 31, 1868.

12. Ibid., January 4, 1869.

13. Ibid., February 22, 1869.

14. White to Elihu Washburne, March 12, 1866, Washburne MSS.

15. William B. Hesseltine, *Ulysses S. Grant, Politician* (New York, 1935), p. 64.

16. White to Elihu Washburne, November 10, 1868, Washburne MSS.

17. White to Washburne, October 18, 1868, Washburne MSS. David A. Wells to James Garfield, November 13, 1868, James A. Garfield MSS, Library of Congress. Henry J. Raymond to White, November 17, 1868, David A. Wells MSS, Library of Congress.

18. The report was printed in full in the *Chicago Tribune*, January 6, 1869. Wells made the purpose of his report known to his friend, Congressman Garfield: "I have just completed my report. It will cause the Moorhead stripe to hate me more than ever, but they won't dare to bite openly. It seems to me, that the treasury is drifting to me inevitably. White writes that Senator Trumbull and E. B. Washburne will both support." David A. Wells to James A. Garfield, November 17, 1868, Garfield MSS. See Herbert R. Ferleger, *David A. Wells and the American Revenue System, 1865–1870* (New York, 1942), pp. 223–247.

19. White to Elihu Washburne, November 28, 1868, Washburne MSS.

20. *Chicago Tribune*, March 6, 8, 1869.

21. White to Elihu Washburne, March 6, 1869, Washburne MSS.

22. Ibid., letter and telegram, March 10, 1869, Washburne MSS. White felt that Stewart's offer to donate all his business profits to a charity during his term in office should have been a proper accommodation. For a more detailed account of this episode, see Hesseltine, *Grant,* pp. 146–148.

23. White to Elihu Washburne, October 18, 1868, Washburne MSS.

24. White had also been disturbed by Grant's bungling of the State Department choice. Grant first tapped James F. Wilson for the post. Wilson accepted but grew restless when Grant allowed Washburne to act temporarily as Secretary of State before Wilson assumed office. Washburne wanted the post to gain diplomatic prestige for his permanent appointment as Minister to France. Wilson understood that Washburne would make no diplomatic assignments during his brief reign over the department. Washburne made appointments nonetheless. Wilson then refused to serve as Secretary of State, and Grant had to name Hamilton Fish to the post. White claimed to have heard this version of the episode from Wilson shortly after it occurred. White, *Trumbull,* p. 334. White's recollection gives more detail than can be found in the standard accounts. See Hesseltine, *Grant,* pp. 147–148.

25. White to Elihu Washburne, March 20, 1869, Washburne MSS. White

urged Washburne to watch over the consular position which Washburne had given to Sherman Hill during his brief tenure as Secretary of State. Hill was their mutual friend. White apparently was not disturbed by Washburne's usurpation of Wilson's patronage powers.

26. White to Manton Marble, February 10, 1869, Marble MSS. Joseph Medill to Elihu Washburne, November 30, 1868, Washburne MSS.

27. White to Manton Marble, January 29, 1870, Marble MSS. The weekly edition of the *Tribune* declined mysteriously about 25 percent from the Civil War figure. White blamed it on the lessening prosperity of farmers.

28. *Chicago Tribune*, June 10, 1897. This "Golden Jubilee Edition" contains a fine succinct history of the *Chicago Tribune*.

29. Ibid., May 11, June 29, 1869.

30. Ibid., July 3, 1869.

31. White to John Caton, August 23, 1869, Caton MSS.

32. *Chicago Tribune*, May 25, 1869.

33. Ibid., July 1, 1869.

34. When Manton Marble, editor of the *New York World*, presented White with a complete set of the works of Bastiat, White replied, "Nothing could have pleased me more." White to Marble, August 21, 1867, Marble MSS.

35. M. Frédéric Bastiat, *Sophisms of Protectionism*, ed. Horace White (Chicago, 1869). *Chicago Tribune*, January 18, 1870.

36. *Chicago Tribune*, August 11, 1869.

37. Ibid., August 25, 1869.

38. Ibid., September 2, 1869.

39. Ibid., August 26, 1869.

40. Ibid., September 4, 1869.

41. Ibid., September 25, 1869.

42. Ibid., September 26, 1869.

43. Ibid., September 30, October 4, 11, 1869.

44. Ibid., October 6, 1869. Most of the Illinois Congressmen stayed out of the fray. Trumbull, urged to back the regular Republicans, bowed out gracefully. Lyman Trumbull to James Root, October 8, 1869, Lyman Trumbull MSS. J. Young Scammon and Norman Judd headed the regular Republican campaign. Scammon attacked White bitterly for the *Tribune*'s stand on reconstruction. Pointing to the case of Virginia, where Radicals were a minority, Scammon urged more Congressional action to safeguard the reorganization of that state. The *Tribune* retorted that Scammon was "fanatical" and stood "for keeping up the war and postponing peace and union indefinitely." White found it easier to meet the criticisms of the *Chicago Journal*, the only English-speaking paper supporting the Republicans. "We remember the present editor of the organ of the Barnacles was . . . a devout Johnsonite and strongly opposed to impartial suffrage or any form of negro suffrage." Ibid., October 6, 23, 1869.

45. Eight of the ten Republican papers in the city joined with the Democratic organ in advocating the Citizens' Ticket. Symbolic of the

rapprochement, the journalists formed the city's first press club. Ibid., October 14, 1869.

46. Ibid., October 12, 14, 1869. Corruption alone does not explain the rising municipal expenditures which caused these taxpayers' revolts. A serious study of municipal taxation in the nineteenth century could lead to a reevaluation of urban reform movements after the Civil War. They began in 1869. The Chicago movement led to changes in the Illinois constitution. Joseph Medill was elected at the time on a bipartisan slate to join the commissioners who drew up a new constitution in 1870. In explaining the moves to amend taxation powers to David A. Wells, Medill noted the problems of Chicago taxpayers: "Our state debt is now paid off. But our heavy onerous taxes are municipal taxes, which in Chicago alone amounts to $4,000,000 exclusive of special assessments amounting to as much more. The time has come to study the subject of state and municipal taxation. Four per cent on cash valuation of real estate is levied. The people 'groan' worse than ever the Britons did. The great problem is how to reduce local taxation against the bonded, professional tax-eaters." Joseph Medill to David A. Wells, March 7, 1871, Wells MSS.

47. *Chicago Tribune,* October 31, 1869.

48. Ibid., November 9, 1869.

49. Ibid., December 13, 18, 1869.

50. Ibid., December 22, 1869.

51. White to David A. Wells, December 24, 1869, Wells MSS.

52. J. W. Foster to David A. Wells, December 27, 1869, Wells MSS.

53. Symbolic of the new political priorities of White was his reconciliation with Charles Ray. The two men renewed their earlier effort to stimulate free-trade sentiment in Chicago. They both had a hand in organizing another branch of the Free Trade League in early November after a mass meeting in Chicago. Free-trade activity had been relatively dormant since Andrew Johnson's vetoes in the winter of 1866. *Chicago Tribune,* July 14, November 6, 1869.

54. Ibid., April 13, 1869.

55. Matthew Downey, "The Rebirth of Reform: A Study of Liberal Republican Movements, 1865–1872" (Ph.D. dissertation, Princeton, 1963), pp. 151–165. The strong business support which White received in Chicago undoubtedly helps to explain his boldness. When free traders in Boston, for example, hedged their views in order to stand in line with their city's Board of Trade, White lashed out at their pragmatism. "What we want is obedience to natural law. . . . The free traders of the Boston Board of Trade could have safely fallen back upon first principles, and left the protectionists to flounder alone in their syllogistic confusions." *Chicago Tribune,* January 18, 1870.

56. *Chicago Tribune,* February 4, 1869.

57. White to John A. Logan, March 6, 1879, Logan MSS.

58. Joseph Medill, growing uneasy about the new direction of White's leadership, demanded a change of editors. William Bross and Alfred

Cowles, however, decided to support White's decisions. Medill had come to oppose "prohibitory" tariffs but did not share White's willingess to work outside of national Republican circles. See Joseph Medill to White-law Reid, February 22, 1870, Reid MSS.

59. *Chicago Tribune*, April 4, 1870. When the Anti-Slavery Society announced its dissolution later in the week, White praised the group's wisdom and intelligence. He contrasted their "statesmanship" with the "fanatical" leadership of the "irreconcilables" in Congress. "Butler and Sumner," he noted, "have no faith in the influence of civilization and universal suffrage." Ibid., April 12, 1870. See also April 21, 1870.

60. Ibid., April 4, 1870. See also *Proceedings of the Meeting to Memorialize Congress in Favor of Revenue Reform held by the Citizens of Chicago, Farwell Hall, April 2, 1870* (Chicago: Free Trade League, 1870).

61. W. C. Bryant, Horace White, et al. to Theodore Woolsey, April 4, 1870, Theodore Woolsey MSS, Yale University. The League elected Woolsey, president of Yale, as their president. Well-subsidized, the League channeled propaganda all over the country for its free-trade cause. White's translation of Bastiat's *Sophisms of Protection* was only one of many works which the League distributed. See Chester M. Destler, "Western Radicalism, 1865–1901: Concepts and Origins," *Mississippi Valley Historical Review* 31 (December, 1944):342.

62. David A. Wells to Manton Marble, March 24, April 6, 1870, Marble MSS. Charles Nordhoff to Rutherford B. Hayes, April 1, 1870, Hayes MSS, Rutherford B. Hayes Library, Fremont, Ohio.

63. White to Charles Ray, April 4, 1870, Ray MSS.

64. Charles Nordhoff to Rutherford B. Hayes, May 12, 1870, Hayes MSS.

65. White never accused Grant of favoring high tariffs. "That he is perplexed by the situation is undoubtedly true, but we believe that he is in favor of lower duties rather than higher ones, and shall continue to believe so until he asserts the contrary." *Chicago Tribune*, May 13, 1870.

66. White to David A. Wells, June 3, 1870, Wells MSS.

67. Hesseltine, *Grant*, pp. 207–219.

68. *Chicago Tribune*, October 3, 4, 1870.

69. Ibid., September 2, 1870. A high tariff periodical in Chicago, the *Bureau*, sent up a howl when the party platform appeared: "But if the friends of protection are idle, its enemies are not. Never was so much effort made and money spent by the Free Traders as now; and the cloven foot shows itself in our recent State Convention, where a free trade plank was inserted by the editors of the *Chicago Tribune*." *Bureau* 2 (October 1870): 15. The *Bureau* began publication in 1869 heavily subsidized by iron manufacturers to counter the *Tribune*'s aggressive free-trade pronouncements. Frequently the editors of the monthly journal attacked White personally. "The revenue reformers of Illinois, consist of Mr. Horace White of the Chicago Tribune, and those who are afraid of him." *Bureau* 2 (October, 1870): 2.

70. *Chicago Tribune*, September 3, 4, 5, October 7, 1870.

71. There is some question whether the tariff issue itself caused the Republican turnover. Since there were many other issues involved, particularly in the border states where most of the changes occurred, the impact of the tariff itself is uncertain. See Downey, "The Rebirth of Reform," pp. 316–318.

72. *Chicago Tribune*, November 12, 1870.

73. Mahlon Sands to Carl Schurz, November 10, 1870, Carl Schurz MSS, Library of Congress. White must have known of this invitation before it was sent, as Sands promised White's attendance at the meeting.

74. There are conflicting stories about Blaine's meeting with White. Roeliff Brinkerhoff, writing much later, said that Blaine made these promises to White after he arrived in New York. White in his biography of Trumbull said that Blaine saw him in Chicago before he left for New York. Henry Adams in a letter written immediately after the free-trade gathering seems to bear out White's version. Roeliff Brinkerhoff, *Recollections of a Lifetime* (Cincinnati, 1904), pp. 205–206. White, *The Life of Lyman Trumbull*, p. 354. Henry Adams to J. D. Cox, November 28, 1870, in Harold Dean Cater, *Henry Adams and His Friends: A Collection of His Unpublished Letters* (Boston, 1947), pp. 49–51.
In his account of the Blaine interview, White did not mention Blaine's promise to make Garfield chairman of the Ways and Means committee. But it is apparent from letters at the time that Blaine did make such a promise to White. David A. Wells to James A. Garfield, May 14, 1871, Garfield MSS. Blaine did not mention this episode in his memoirs, *Twenty Years of Congress*, 2 vols. (Norwich, Conn., 1884). The omission, however, is understandable, since Blaine wrote his memoirs when he was running against the Mugwumps in 1884. He probably did not want to remind his readers of his own flirting with Democrats and independents in 1870.

75. Henry Adams to J. D. Cox, November 28, 1870, in Cater, *Henry Adams and His Friends*, pp. 49–51.

76. Brinkerhoff, *Recollections of a Lifetime*, pp. 206–209.

77. For a sketch of James W. Grimes's outlook, see Fred B. Lewellan, "Political Ideas of James W. Grimes," *The Iowa Journal of History and Politics* 42 (October, 1944): 339–404. Pages 395–404 show how Grimes, a Whig, became an outspoken free trader after the Civil War. See also William Salter, *James W. Grimes* (New York, 1876), and Leland Sage, *William Boyd Allison* (Iowa City, 1956).

78. White recalled this incident in his biography of Trumbull. White, *Trumbull*, pp. 346–348. A more accurate account, however, is probably found in a letter which White wrote to Sumner only a year after the event. White to Charles Sumner, April 13, 1872, Sumner MSS.

79. *Chicago Tribune*, March 10, 11, 12, 1871.

80. Ibid., March 13, 1871.

81. Ibid., March 24, 1871.

9
Liberal Republican

WHEN HORACE White sat down to write his public denunciation of Grant on the evening of March 23, 1871, the Republican insurgents had probably reached the apex of their
strength. The time seemed ripe to strike out against a blundering President. On that same day, James Garfield thought
Grant's power was "waning very rapidly" and the Washington
correspondent for the *New York Tribune* reported a growing
anti-Grant movement.[1]

Such optimism, however, could not have lasted more than
a day. White had actually chosen a very inopportune moment
to announce disloyalty to the Commander-in-Chief. It was
the same day that Grant had reluctantly called for powers
to quell the Ku Klux Klan violence that had broken out all
over the South after the 1870 elections. In a twenty-line address, Grant demanded legislation which would "effectually
secure life, liberty, and property and the enforcement of law
in all parts of the United States."[2]

Within a single day, the political plans of Horace White
virtually collapsed. He had firmly committed his paper to
nonintervention in the South. Such a stand had actually meant

little in the growing anti-Grant movement, since Grant himself had not taken any clear stand in the reconstruction debate. If anything, Grant had also demonstrated sympathy with the conservative approach to southern affairs. He gave no support, for example, to Senator Morton's efforts to delay the reentry of Georgia and Virginia into the Union. As a result, these states avoided any serious internal reorganization. But on March 23, 1871, Grant urged military action by the federal government to crush the Ku Klux Klan. Only a few days before, White had claimed that the South was "a case where the *Laissez-faire* doctrine is peculiarly applicable."[3]

Grant's speech isolated White and other discontented Republicans almost instantly. As racial violence in the South had discouraged Republican insurgency in 1866, further atrocities there postponed an imminent bolt within the party in 1871. Flirtation with Democrats suddenly became suicidal and demands for tariff reform appeared irrelevant. The Civil War was being waged once more by its leading general.

Many have wondered why the Liberal Republican movement fizzled after its strong start. The answer lies in these Ku Klux Klan disorders which disturbed so many northerners still living in the memories of the Civil War and southern intransigence immediately after it. Most Liberals, like White, had predicated their campaign openly on the conclusion of southern resistance. Some, like Carl Schurz, even staked their political careers on restored sectional harmony. The Liberals had not, by any means, abandoned their faith in the efficacy of the Reconstruction acts; they still defended Negro suffrage. Few of Grant's allies were any more devoted to that cause. But the Liberals had assured themselves and many who first followed them of the resignation of white southerners to reconstruction measures. The case for a "laissez-faire" policy in the South, however, seemed woefully inadequate after Grant focused national attention on the Ku-Klux Klan violence. When this southern resistance to national authority reasserted itself, few other issues could gain national attention before the Panic of 1873. Not only most of the northern electorate but significant numbers of the intelligentsia refused to heed the Liberal call. William A. Dunning insightfully recognized this fact although he could only view it as the result of duplicity and not a result, in part, of Republican conscience and ideals. "The time had not yet come," he wrote, "when an appeal to sectional feeling would fail to determine the political course of the northern masses. Butler and Morton and Hoar and the rest of the radicals who forced the Ku Klux issue to the front were more sagacious than the Liberals in their estimate of popular emotion."[4]

The *Tribune* could only protest feebly against the President's request, suggesting that "the remnant of the high tariff faction" was waging war against the KKK simply to divert attention from the financial questions of the day. Only weeks before such a charge might have won White the ear of Chicago businessmen or even prominent Congressmen. But when a Democrat read White's innuendo in the House of Representatives, the words drew a shout of laughter.[5] White could no longer convince many that Reconstruction was a matter of only secondary importance. Even Horatio Burchard, one of the Republicans chosen by White and the free traders to sit on the Ways and Means Committee, voted for the anti-Klan legislation.

As incontestable evidence of racial viciousness mounted, White himself had to admit the seriousness of the Klan-inspired disorders in South Carolina. By August, the editor almost allowed his paper to slip back into its old Radicalism. "The further continuance of these barbarities," the *Tribune* threatened, "should not be tolerated, even if it be necessary to place a soldier in South Carolina for every Ku Klux in the State."[6]

The Ku Klux Klan crisis enabled Grant to recapture a very strong political position. His declaration on March 23 seemed to end any hope for Republican insurgency in 1872, particularly when he followed it by an announcement of a major diplomatic victory in the nation's dispute with Great Britain over the *Alabama* claims. In the midst of the southern crisis, Grant also cut loose from his Santo Domingo albatross. By doing so he brought new unity to the party.[7] The divisive tariff issue meanwhile lost its importance, as it had in a similar crisis in 1866. There were few complaints when Congress tabled all issues except those dealing with reconstruction or when Blaine postponed reorganization of House committees until the second session of the Forty-second Congress.

Dissatisfied Republican Congressmen like Garfield, Allison, and Burchard fell into line.[8] They could not afford to flirt with Democrats besmirched by treason. Charles Sumner remained bitter, but he bemoaned his peculiar dilemma: "Must this President have a new lease? Greeley thinks he cannot be chosen,—but then, the Republican party is sacrificed. God forbid!"[9] Another dissatisfied Republican added a refrain: "That party is not free trade; it is Tammany. Whoever helps bring it into power does not only freedom of trade, but all liberty, an immense injury. No freedom is safe with a party herto [*sic*] justify slavery; and old issues are not dead so long as their hatreds survive."[10] The men who had been leading the battle for civil service and tariff reforms lost many sympathetic ears after the Ku Klux Klan crisis in 1871. The *Chicago Tribune,* in particular, remained rather silent that summer. The momentum of Republican dissatisfaction had lost its thrust.

On October 8, 1871, White wrote an editorial acknowledging that fact. Even though the Democratic party had sounded a call for a new departure—an acceptance of reconstruction—White could no longer safely accept their assertions.

The Democratic party now make a virtue of necessity and consent to yield acquiescence in the future, as they have *not* done in the past, to the principles of the Declaration of Independence. . . . But it is too soon to decide whether this change of head, this new departure is sincerely taken. The southern wing of that party has not yet been heard from. They must pass through another Presidential election, and suffer another national defeat, before it will be safe to depend upon their conversion to the great principles of Jefferson.[11]

Horace White did not have time to say much more about the disintegration of the bipartisan reform movement. Before the elections of 1871, a greater disaster struck his personal plans. In a matter of hours, the Chicago fire of 1871 burned, twisted, and scorched his journalistic empire. Few indeed ever read the editorial which he wrote for the October 9 issue of the *Tribune*. When White finished the editorial, he returned home as usual. That night he was awakened by a fire bell. There had been many fires in Chicago that fall. He ignored the alarm. But then the bell continued ringing after a fifteen minute pause—the signal of a general alarm! He jumped up to look out of his window. Above the South Division of the city a great light glowed from rows of burning tenements. Years in journalism left White no alternative. He rushed to the *Tribune* office to write something about the blaze.[12]

Once on the street, White found that panic had already gripped the city. Fighting his way through refugees to the newspaper office, he witnessed a scene "simply indescribable in its terrible grandeur." He recalled the spectacle several days later: "Vice and crime had got the first scorching. The district where the fire had got its first foothold was the Alsatia of Chicago. Fleeing before it was a crowd of bleareyed and drunken and diseased wretches, male and female, half naked, ghastly, with painted cheeks, cursing and uttering ribald jests as they drifted along."[13] Inside the *Tribune* building, White felt safe. Only two years earlier, he and Alfred Cowles had financed the construction of the fireproof structure. They were so assured of safety from fire that they scoffed at the notion of insurance. The events of the evening increased their confidence; their building stood unharmed while others around it melted to the ground. The only evidence that a fire had engulfed it was the shattered glass from the ground floor windows. After the blaze spent its force in the immediate neighborhood, the *Tribune* employees washed their faces and went back to their nocturnal chores in getting a morning paper out on the streets. White's editorials had already been composed and printed. The first and last pages of the four-sheet paper were kept open for the news that the reporting corps was to bring back about the fire. White, Bross, and Medill returned to their homes for breakfast.[14] George P. Upton, an employee who remained, described the early morning scene. Most of those who stayed in the office had already gone about their routine tasks. Sam Medill, the city editor, went off to a corner and fell asleep on a lounge waiting for his reporters to return. "The faith of every employee of the *Tribune* in the fire-proofness of the structure," Upton recalled, "was sublime."[15]

They were too confident. The fire was still raging and it suddenly, inexplicably doubled back toward the *Tribune* building. Bross and White could not return; they had to save their own homes and families. At the building, Joseph Medill and other members of the staff, steeled by the earlier crisis, continued to prepare the *Tribune* for their morning customers. While the "Tribune building stood as a lone isle in an ocean of fire," work on the paper proceeded apace. Sparks sputtering about in the air finally landed on the roof and started small fires, but men worked desperately and stamped out those minor threats, all along cursing the contractor who had topped the building with a "fire proof" material. Their efforts were in vain. The fortress succumbed when a wall of the McVickers theater "fell with a tremendous crash onto the roof smashing it in and also part of the alley wall." The cave-in exposed the interior—the press and paper rooms—to the flames. Once permitted to feast on those delicacies, the fire continued on its way throughout the interior, feeding on wood and paper until it gutted the entire structure.[16]

Almost everything was lost. Only the financial records in the vault survived. Much more could have been saved in that spacious fireproof compartment, but an absentminded employee had left the key to the vault at his home when he left the office temporarily for breakfast.[17] In abandoning the building, workers scurried out under Medill's orders, loaded down with volumes of the newspaper file, but they quickly dropped the heavy tomes in order to save their own lives. Someone managed to salvage a copy of the *Tribune* which never left the presses—the issue which documented Horace White's abandoned hopes for the 1872 national elections.[18]

After the fire White probably cared very little whether the public would ever read that editorial. He was too busy trying to save his own family and home. As the fire threatened his Michigan Avenue mansion, he, together with his wife, mother, brother, and servants, piled trunks and baskets onto a wagon. With a sizable load, he trundled off with the teamster. The others he left behind to prepare another shipment, which included his library and personal papers.[19] The wagon, however, got caught in a throng of refugees, some of whom taunted White for his privileged means of escape. It took White over an hour to reach a park along Lake Michigan where he had planned to unload his possessions. He attempted to return with the empty wagon, but halfway down Michigan Avenue he met his personal entourage, their arms filled with household goods. His wife described the destruction of their home and the macabre experience of stepping over corpses along the escape route. Panicked by rumors of fire all about them and fears of a "Commune" starting "incendiary fires," White and his family managed to get another wagon from a friend to take them all to a southern suburb where White's brother owned a modest cottage. The exhausted party fell asleep finally when they heard the welcome sound of rain tapping at their windows.[20]

White awoke to finish his nightmare. The morning light fully exposed the damage. The entire business district of one of the world's largest cities lay in ruins. In the midst of the charred mass, just the skeleton of the *Tribune* building remained standing. White found a dismal scene as he surveyed the horrendous spectacle. For miles around, the proud and stately city of yesterday had sunk into cellars and basements. Smoke still rose out of the landscape; occasionally some trembling ruin would fall to the earth, throwing up clouds of dust. The air was filled with suffocating smells of perishing property. After lingering about the disaster area for a while, White discovered that Joseph Medill had already taken the initiative and purchased a westside printing office which had escaped the fire.

There, in a dirty, oily machine shop, the owners of the *Chicago Tribune* began to rebuild their journalistic empire. On Wednesday morning, October 11, two days after the fire, the *Tribune* reappeared in a crippled single-sheet issue. Despite its form the paper urged its readers to "Cheer up." Furnished with a plank for a table and a soapbox for a chair, White composed an editorial which vowed to the world that "Chicago Shall Rise Again."[21]

After several days of such makeshift production, the *Tribune* owners held a conference to review their situation. They decided, first of all, to retrench on expenses. Their losses were phenomenal, probably over a half million dollars.[22] White alone lost over $100,000. To recover these losses, the stockholders began by firing unnecessary employees. White had to do the hatchet work. To Sidney Gay, the managing editor, whom White had lured away from Horace Greeley in 1868, the editor-in-chief expressed his regrets. "It is with the deepest pain," he began, "that I communicate to you the decision of the Directors of the *Tribune* Company that we must dispense with your services, in conjunction with those of a number of others heretofore in our employ." To soften what he had to say, White talked about his own grief:

> It is needless to tell you the reasons for this decision. The ruins of Chicago, the destruction of our machinery, the reduced size of our paper, all conspire to drive me back to my old position—the same that I held before you came to us, when I supervised the editorial, the make-up, the correspondence and all. I must begin again where I was five years ago, both as regards my labor and my fortune. It is harder for me to write these lines than it is to go back myself and begin again—harder than to look over the ashes of my burned home.[23]

The same day that White wrote Gay his almost tearful note, he speculated on the meaning of the fire. The disaster had stripped him of his affluent surroundings and smashed his magnificent enterprise. "All the eight hour strikers," he commented in evaluating his own predicament, "are possessed of more comfort and leisure."[24] In that mood White presented "The Lesson of the Fire" to his readers. "Then sudden disaster, which in a single night has reduced the rich to poverty and the poor to destitution," White began, "may furnish a profitable lesson to us all. We have all been living too expensively. . . . The War, with its sudden fortunes, its speculations, and the hot-house growth given to certain pursuits, gradually led us into habits of extravagance." White cataloged the sins of prosperity and hoped that any reformation in habits could be made permanent. "This great calamity," he surmised, "may prove to be a blessing in disguise."[25]

Poverty did not last long. Unlike others in the city, the *Tribune* owners had many wealthy friends and established credit. Murat Halstead, owner of the *Cincinnati Commercial*, provided type, and the *Chicago Journal* offered the use of its undamaged presses. Demand for advertising began just as soon as Chicagoans realized that the paper was being published. Merchants ran sales of damaged stocks; insurance companies inserted notices of failure or survival; and individuals printed personal items, searching for material and human losses.[26] By the end of the month, White could honestly boast, "The *Tribune* is making money faster than ever."[27] With his competition hurt even more seriously, White contemplated doubling the size of the paper.[28] Ironically, an even more secure journalistic power seemed to be rising from the ashes of Chicago.

Rebuilding political power, on the other hand, was not so easy for Horace White after Grant's crushing counterattack in the summer of 1871. But the fire in the fall did provide some ammunition for another attempt by White and his friends to gain ascendency within the Republican party.

Once more White began at the local level. The demands of a fire-ravaged city, he felt, required a suspension of partisan politics. On the morning of October 23, he presented a resolution to a meeting of Cook County Republicans. He moved that they cancel their convention and primaries. He suggested that, instead, they meet with the Democrats to draw up a nonpartisan slate of candidates. Norman Judd, still suspicious perhaps of his old protégé's bipartisan campaign in 1869, issued a strong objection. But White proved his authority in the city. On October 27, 1871, both parties contributed to a joint slate of candidates. With Joseph Medill heading the list as Mayor, the Fire Ticket won the day. Regular Republicans could do little but grumble at the *Tribune*'s continued dictation in the city's political affairs.[29]

On the state level, Governor John Palmer came out boldly against Grant for his interference during the Chicago fire. Intervention by the federal troops of General Sheridan angered the Illinois chief executive, and his protest did much to rekindle latent Republican dissent in Illinois. But he did not immediately join hands with the disaffected in Chicago. White, like most of the propertied men in the city, did not condemn the quick entry of the boys in blue. Indeed, he and other wealthy citizens of Chicago welcomed them with open arms.[30] The *Tribune* therefore turned a deaf ear to Palmer's cries of centralization and tyranny. White simply brushed aside the Governor's protests: "Granting that the Governor is technically right, we do not see the usefulness of such transcendentalism at the present time."[31]

For several months, the aftermath of the fire made it difficult for White to pay much attention to national affairs. He had to pass up one of the regular Washington strategy meetings of the revenue reformers in November. He could not leave the city until just before Congress assembled in December. He hoped then, he told Wells, "to look after the Com. of Way and Means, if my political influence has not been burned up."[32] When he went he was armed with new weapons forged in the Great Fire. Businessmen from Chicago petitioned Congress to exempt them from tariffs in rebuilding the city. White took every advantage he could of this sentiment in reopening the tariff battle.[33] A new optimism permeated the *Tribune* columns. When Congress returned to the Capitol, Blaine appeared to keep his promise: although the Speaker did not appoint Garfield chairman, revenue reformers dominated the new Ways and Means Committee. The *Tribune* duly complimented Blaine for his awareness of the tariff problem.[34]

Once more Grant maintained his aloofness from the tariff battle. His second annual message offered little for anyone to criticize. His performance only reemphasized the powerful position he had assumed within the party earlier in the year. The *Tribune* even noted some improvement in his attitude toward the tariff, as well as toward amnesty in the South and civil service reform.[35] Joseph Medill, for one, was convinced by his message. "With all his faults," Medill insisted, "Grant is a great man."[36]

In less than a week, however, White silenced the *Tribune's* praise of Grant. The editorial gag seemed to be related to certain actions taken by Congress. Senator Morton, an administration loyalist, introduced a motion to have Congress adjourn in May. White and others interpreted this as a move to "shut off all agitation" of economic matters until after the presidential elections in the fall.[37] Such an action would have undermined the pressure tactics of the revenue reformers, for they had been openly bartering their party loyalty for favorable action in Congress. White became furious with the "caucus junto" made up of "Morton and his clique—the Nyes, Stewarts, Spencers, Pomeroys, and carpet-bag misrepresentatives of the oppressed South."[38]

To counter this unexpected move, Republican revenue reformers held a strategy session in Arlington, Virginia, before the Christmas holidays. The group decided to intensify their free-trade pressure. White joined with Edward Atkinson, Colonel Grosvenor, David A. Wells and others in establishing the Tax-Payers Union to lobby in Washington. Grosvenor, architect of the 1870 Liberal Republican revolt in Missouri, took charge of the daily routine; he became the essential cog of the new machinery. In turn, Grosvenor delegated the editing of the *People's Pictorial Tax-Payer,* organ of the new group, to a bright young man, Henry Demarest Lloyd.[39] After this flurry of new activity, some of the reformers grew heady about the possibility of defeating Grant.

White was more realistic. He was no longer eager to declare war against Grant; he remembered too well his last impulsive attack on the General. Whatever hope there was for Grant's defeat depended on mistakes Grant might make during the winter. If the President's mistakes were serious enough, a conservative Republican like Trumbull might have a chance— but only if the candidate could avoid the stigma of the Democrats. To insure that end, the Democratic party would have to disband formally. White's set of prerequisites obviously left very little hope for Grant's defeat in 1872. Nevertheless, he held onto that hope. He told a close friend that Republican regulars had offered to let his wing of the party "make the platform what they please," but that his wing "declined the offer, preferring to await events and hoping yet to defeat Grant." "If they cannot," White's friend reported to a very interested David Davis, "they expect at the convention to have enough influence to dictate the platform if they must support Grant." In that case, the informer continued, "they calculate to make the platform and take their chances for power and control in 1876."[40]

Such were the views of Horace White on the second day of 1872, a presidential election year. White had more to tell his friends that afternoon. The editor indicated that Lyman Trumbull was his first choice to beat Grant; David Davis, his second. At the same time, White emphasized that there was little prospect of defeating Grant. Indeed, since the Ku Klux Klan message in March, 1871, the *Tribune* had no longer expressed White's personal dissatisfaction with the President. Nor had any contender for the presidency appeared from among conservative Republican ranks. Trumbull, White concluded, would never bolt the party. Yet a restlessness lingered among Republican insurgents. Charles Sumner and Carl Schurz remained bitter; Horace Greeley had begun to express his disapproval of the administration, and David Davis, Supreme Court Justice, flirted with both Republicans and Democrats. Yet no one knew when or how to strike. The concerted action and confident strategy which marked the activities of White's friends in 1870 had evaporated in the spring of 1871.

Finally William Grosvenor took the initiative. He mobilized the Liberal Republicans who had come to power in Missouri in 1870. Meeting in convention on January 24, 1872, the Missouri bolters adopted a platform for national affairs and called for a mass convention to meet at Cincinnati on May 2,

1872. Others in the country welcomed the initiative. A group
of Ohio free-traders led by J. D. Cox and Judge Stallo gave
an immediate second to the Missouri proposal.

Lyman Trumbull, after he got word of the Missouri action,
wrote to White. The Senator seemed ready to make his move.
He urged White to give the Missouri movement *Tribune* encouragement. Although Trumbull could list only a half-
dozen senators "inclined" to favor the meeting at Cincinnati,
he told White temptingly that "with the encouragement of
which I speak, it would at once assume formidable proportions, and enable those who participate in it, to dictate terms
to the June Convention, or present a candidate of their own,
who would sweep the country."[41]

White had already responded to the Missouri call. While
holding those who had bolted at arm's length, he commented
that "there is no difficulty in defeating party nominations
where public intelligence is insulted, or where the election
of better men can be accomplished without a sacrifice of
principle."[42] When Trumbull's letter arrived, White responded
by agreeing with the senator that this might be "the long
looked for opportunity for the Liberal Republicans to crys-
tallize upon."[43] He promised to see to it that Illinois brought
a respectable delegation to Cincinnati.

Within the next few weeks, the *Tribune* cautiously announced its willingness to oppose Grant. Editorials first began
a barrage of criticism against the legislative blockade established by the Senate "Regency."[44] Next, the paper wondered
why Grant did not use his patronage powers to pursue reforms in the same way he had when he gathered Congressional
support for the annexation of Santo Domingo.[45] Finally, the
Tribune questioned whether Grant could carry key states in
the next election. Such a ticket as Trumbull and Blaine, or
Wilson and Colfax, it suggested, might be able to save the
party.[47] Several reasons dictated his equivocal stance. First,
Grant offered the insurgents little room for criticism, as he

continued to make pronouncements for economy, retrenchment, and civil service reform.[48] Second, White fully understood that loyalties to the Republican party were still strong
among the masses. With good reason, therefore, he treated cooperation with Democrats as a sort of vile disease. Finally,
White's direction of *Tribune* editorial policy had its limitations.

White held only 15 percent of the *Tribune* Corporation
stock. William Bross, holding another 25 percent, was prepared to bolt the party with White; but Medill, with a share
about the same as that of Bross, stood opposed to any insurgency on the national level.[49] Alfred Cowles, therefore, remained the key to any decision concerning *Tribune* policy
toward the Cincinnati movement. Cowles himself was apol-
itical, but he was very sensitive to the paper's financial condition, and, with more than 35 percent of the *Tribune* stock,
he could theoretically throw the direction of the paper either
to Medill or to White.[50]

Advertising receipts would probably not be affected since
the paper's commercial position had become too powerful to
be easily upset by its editorial policies. The *Tribune* had
outgrown its dependence on party support.[51] Indeed, after
the Civil War, Republican politicians frequently complained
about the *Tribune*'s dictation. But flirtation with the Democrats could lose the paper many readers, and subscriptions
were important to the financial health of the paper.[52] Bolting
on the local level had not lost the *Tribune* any of its readers.
But no one could accurately foretell how readers would react
to bolting on the national level.[53] White's personal relationship with Cowles had enabled White to beat back frequent
dissents from Medill, but there were limitations to Cowles's
friendship. Bross and White, of course, also appreciated the
financial risks of party treason. White demonstrated just such
caution in silencing his editorial criticism after Grant reversed
his positions in 1871, even though he privately remained op-

posed to the President. White was not a totally independent journalist. Until early April, 1872, the *Tribune,* therefore, remained coy about the Cincinnati cabal.

Trumbull, in the meantime, had "burnt his ships," and he grew worried about the stragglers in his own constituency.[54] Since White did nothing to carry out his earlier promises to organize a delegation for the Cincinnati convention, Trumbull pleaded with various other persons to take the lead. But they, too, balked.[55] The supporters of David Davis, on the other hand, were not so hesitant. Democrats, first of all, who felt none of the pressures which constrained Republicans, advertised Davis's availability. A Labor Reform convention went one step further. Meeting in Columbus, Ohio, in February, its delegates nominated Davis for the presidency. Although Davis had not anticipated the nomination, he did nothing to renounce it.[56] The Supreme Court jurist thus quite suddenly took an early lead in the race for the Cincinnati nomination. His supporters were well organized before the reluctant Republicans in Illinois could even decide on the purpose of the May convention.

The dilemma of the Republican dissidents arose partly because they were so strong in Illinois. The open criticism of Grant by the governor, John Palmer, gave the Liberal Republicans a firmer base in Illinois than in almost any other state except Missouri. White explained the peculiar problem to Trumbull: "The one thing that has kept it down in this State is the belief entertained by many of our friends that we can carry the regular State Convention against Grant." Indecisive about the best strategy, White asked the already troubled and impatient senator for advice.[57] Eastern reformers who, like Trumbull, had already given their assent to the Cincinnati convention, kept up the pressure on White. Wells, Atkinson, Godkin, and other eastern intellectuals had provided essential leadership in the revenue reform movement, but they never had any significant political base in their own states. All along the West had provided the political muscle for the movement. The easterners therefore needed White's support. But as late as March 16, White, in reply to an anxious inquiry from Edward Atkinson, confessed that he was unsure whether he would even go to Cincinnati. He did, however, offer Atkinson some hope. "It seems most probable," White hedged cautiously, "that we shall sustain the Cincinnati movement to the bitter end."[58]

Leonard Swett, one of David Davis's managers, finally forced White's hand. In an open letter to the *Tribune,* Swett took the initiative in urging public support for the Cincinnati convention.[59] White grew alarmed; he could not equivocate much longer. "I shall have to give some attention to the matter soon," he wrote to Trumbull, "else the movement here will assume the character of a Davis movement." White confessed that his paper could lose all support with its readers if the movement was "embarrassed by Democratic complications or endorsements."[60] Still he allowed events to drift. Perhaps the movement was already too closely identified with Democrats.

Dragging his feet for a week after his letter to Trumbull, White revealed the cause of his dilemma. "The continued existence of the Democratic party is a menace of evils more important even than those which the Liberal Republicans seek to remedy."[61] At the same time, White rebuked regular Republican "Bungtown *Chronicles"* for their constant criticism of his political stance. Attempting to find some safe posture for himself, White compared the *Tribune's* independent position toward Grant with the position which the paper had taken toward Andrew Johnson.[62] But White must have known that the situation was different now. The recollection of Johnson must have stirred his fears: flirtations with the Democrats had destroyed Johnson, and they could also destroy Horace White and the *Chicago Tribune.* Caught in this tortuous dilemma, White made a pathetic plea to the

Democrats to end their embarrassing existence: "All that Liberal Republicans ask of the Democratic leaders is to disband their party organization."[63]

Finally, White made the fateful decision. On April 3, his paper announced that the easy Republican victories in February and March did in fact mean that the Democrats had disbanded. White was grasping at straws. "The result of the election in Connecticut," he maintained, "confirms the suspicion that the Democratic party . . . is no longer capable of sustaining a platform strong enough for candidates to stand upon,—in other words, that it is dead."[64] Having prematurely buried a still warm Democracy that had been embarrassing him, White hurried down to Springfield to take command of the Trumbull interests. The small group of men who gathered in his room at the Leland House agreed to an aggressive plan of action.[65] They decided to get fifty to one hundred prominent Illinois Republicans to sign a call advising sympathizers to go to Cincinnati. There were only about thirty who signed the document that day at Springfield, but White was confident that they represented the "heft of the party."[66] And they had represented it at one time. Most were the stalwart followers of the Lincoln-led party before the war. There was William Herndon and William Butler, Oziah Hatch and Jesse Fell, Jesse Dubois and William Bross—all founders of the Illinois Republican party. Few of these men, however, had been active in state politics in recent years. After circulating the petition among such men in Springfield, White sent the call to Belleville, the center of Trumbull's old constituency, where Gustave Koerner gathered additional signatures.[67]

Even as the call was being drawn up in his room at Springfield, White still wanted to equivocate. He refused, at first, to commit himself to an actual nomination at Cincinnati.[68] He wanted to use that convention simply as a weapon to pressure the Republican convention in June at Philadelphia. But most of the Springfield gathering were Trumbull enthusiasts and they were getting anxious and ambitious. White assented reluctantly to their inflated objectives for the Cincinnati meeting. The call committed the signers to a nomination.

White went beyond the consensus of the *Tribune* directors when he committed himself to a nomination at Cincinnati by signing the Springfield petition. The specter of bolting the Republican party was so unnerving that the owners held a conference when White returned from the state capital. They finally agreed to what White had done but refused to go beyond committing themselves to Trumbull until after the nomination was made.[69] Thus White could not give open *Tribune* support to the Missouri call until less than three weeks before the Cincinnati meeting. But once the decision was made, White moved quickly.

Joining a chorus of pleas to Charles Sumner, White urged the senator to cast off all doubts, as he had done himself only a little more than a week before. Evoking the memory of his attempt to help Sumner during the Santo Domingo imbroglio, White declared, "I, for one, am going to fight out the battle which I commenced in Senator Howe's room." Blaming all of the insurgents' discontents on the same "despotism" of party that had deposed Sumner from the Foreign Affairs Committee in 1871, White concluded (now a year later) that "the Cincinnati Convention became a necessity from that moment." "Can you do any less?" White inquired.[70] White and Sumner had long been on opposite sides of the party, but White realized that nothing would quiet the issue of Democratic involvement like the inclusion of Sumner, the foremost living Radical, into Liberal Republican ranks. White had even suggested the senator as a possible presidential candidate to insure the image of undefiled Republicanism for the Cincinnati movement.[71] But Sumner hesitated even longer than White. He remained silent until after the Cincinnati convention.

White had no choice; he had to continue what he had commenced at Springfield. After the owners' review of policy, the *Tribune* published the Illinois call for the Cincinnati convention.[72] The call included names from only twelve of the state's counties; ninety went unrepresented. But the lack of numbers was not White's chief concern, for the tardiness of the call could easily explain that. He was happy to emphasize what he felt was the most important characteristic of the group: it represented the "bone and gristle, brain and marrow, blood and muscle, of Republicanism in Illinois."[73] No one certainly could level the charge of copperheadism against these men.

David Davis's lieutenants were still a step ahead of the Trumbull supporters. Knowing now that they were to face a fight with the Trumbull men at Cincinnati, they laid practical plans for the convention. "Now we do not want a fuss if we can help it," John Wentworth wrote to Davis. "Hence we want numbers, *mere numbers*. We shall have experience and brains enough there, but what will they avail us without numbers, if that proscriptive and intriguing cabal are to keep us out of the convention?"[74]

White was indeed trying to keep Davis out of the convention. Davis and the Democrats seemed anathema to him. Republicanism was his only test. He had already begged the dedicated Radical Sumner to join the movement, and he welcomed his old foe, Horace Greeley, with open arms. Yes, even Horace Greeley, the leading prophet of protectionism, was admitted to Liberal ranks. Some revenue reformers lost faith when Greeley entered the Cincinnati movement, but White welcomed him. When Greeley published an ultimatum that he would support the convention only if it did not commit itself to free trade, White meekly surrendered. From that moment on, White frankly discarded free trade as a watchword of third party action. Magnanimity had little to do with this sudden rapprochement. White accepted Greeley because the New Yorker's association with the Liberal movement documented its Republicanism and gave it an eastern base of political support which it did not really have until that time. Publicly White listed Greeley as a possible vice-presidential candidate, and privately he even indicated Greeley's availability as an acceptable presidential nominee. The compelling logic of American politics had taken hold of the Liberal movement.[75]

White had another political purpose in abandoning the free-trade criterion. He realized that Trumbull's availability would be increased if the tariff issue could be muted. The already assembled New York and Pennsylvania delegations would never swallow both a free trader and a free-trade platform. Trumbull himself, in giving White his last-minute instructions before the convention, made it quite clear that the editor could best serve his chances for nomination by producing a meaningless platform on the tariff. Ignoring many years of his own arguments, Trumbull dished up a strange piece of double talk: "Free Traders and Protectionists differ more about the application of principles than the principles themselves in their effects."[76]

Other revenue reformers like David A. Wells and Carl Schurz also began to soft-pedal the tariff issue in order to insure a harmonious convention.[77] Only a handful of the free traders held firm, and, except in Ohio, they were without political influence.[78] The senators and the editors of the large dailies—the movers of the Convention—all agreed to equivocate on the tariff. They wanted Horace Greeley's support. In any case, much of the steam had already been taken out of the tariff issue. On April 17, 1872, the Ways and Means Committee announced a bill demanding a general reduction of tariffs. White praised the work of the Committee, and well he should—he had helped Blaine pack the Committee with low-tariff proponents.[79] Whether other free traders shared his appraisal of the compromise bill, none could blame a Congressional dictatorship any longer for refusing to consider lower tariffs.

Before White left Chicago for the convention, the resolution of the tariff, for all practical purposes, had already been decided. The Half-Breed Republicans, like Blaine, who were caught between the Grant Stalwarts and the insurgent Liberals, had carefully defused the battle over economic issues. Still the Liberals rushed towards a showdown with Grant even though the President held powerful weapons after the Ku Klux Klan disturbances. White knew the odds; yet he hoped to be able to avoid any charges of treasonous association with the Democrats. To insure the movement's respectability, he had to begin by eliminating David Davis and the Democracy at Cincinnati.

NOTES

1. William Hesseltine, *Ulysses S. Grant, Politician*, p. 243.
2. Ibid., p. 245.
3. *Chicago Tribune*, March 16, 1871.
4. William A. Dunning, *Reconstruction, Political and Economic, 1865–1877* (New York, 1907), p. 201.
5. *Chicago Tribune*, April 18, 22, 1871. *Congressional Globe*, 41st Cong., 2nd sess., pp. 805–806.
6. *Chicago Tribune*, August 1, 1871.
7. Hesseltine, *Grant*, pp. 249–251.
8. John Palmer, governor of Illinois, wrote Grant immediately after the Ku Klux speech and pledged his support. Grant's secretary acknowledged the letter and commented on the recent change in politics: "Four or five of them [Republican Senators] lately have great hopes of inaugurating a third party movement, but they got such a set-back in the President's last message that they are terribly demoralized." Horace Porter to John Palmer, April 18, 1871, John Palmer MSS, Illinois State Historical Library. See also Leland Sage, *William Boyd Allison*, pp. 119–121.
9. Charles Sumner to Carl Schurz, August 26, 1871, Carl Schurz MSS.
10. George William Curtis to David A. Wells, August 31, 1871, David A. Wells Collection, New York Public Library.
11. *Chicago Tribune*, October 9, 1871.
12. White recounted his experiences for the *Cincinnati Commercial* shortly after the fire. His letter to that paper was later reprinted in Mabel McIlvaine, ed., *Reminiscences of Chicago during the Great Fire* (Chicago, 1915), pp. 60–77.

13. White, Ibid., p. 63.

14. William Bross also related his experiences of the fire for an out-of-town newspaper. *New York Tribune*, October 14, 1871. His letter was also reprinted in McIlvaine, ed., *Reminiscences during the Great Fire*, pp. 78–91.

15. *Chicago Tribune*, February 1, 1891.

16. This account of the destruction of the *Tribune* building is taken from a letter of Joseph Medill to Murat Halstead, October 12, 1871, Murat Halstead MSS, Historical and Philosophical Society of Ohio.

17. William Christian to the Chicago Historical Society, October 5, 1915, William Christian MSS, Chicago Historical Society. Christian was the absentminded employee.

18. *Chicago Tribune*, October 9, 1871. This rare issue is kept at the Chicago Historical Society.

19. The papers of White, as well as those of Medill and Bross, were all destroyed by the Chicago fire of 1871.

20. White, in McIlvaine, ed., *Reminiscences during the Great Fire*, pp. 65–75.

21. This scene was recalled many years later by one of White's friends. W. A. Wyman to White, September 1, 1909, White MSS.

22. Sidney Gay to Samuel May, November 13, 1871, Gay Family MSS.

23. White to Sidney Gay, October 21, 1871, Gay Family MSS.

24. White, in McIlvaine, ed., *Reminiscences during the Great Fire*, p. 73.

25. *Chicago Tribune*, October 21, 1871.

26. Bross, in McIlvaine, ed., *Reminiscences during the Great Fire*, p. 89. By the third day of printing, the *Tribune* returned to its normal size. Advertising in that issue took up a good share of the paper. *Chicago Tribune*, October 13, 1871. See also advertisements for the rest of the week.

27. White to David A. Wells, October 29, 1871, Wells MSS. White noted that both A. T. Stewart and Senator John Sherman offered him money, but that his own income made their offers unnecessary.

28. White to Murat Halstead, November 15, 1871, Halstead MSS.

29. *Chicago Tribune*, October 24, 28, 1871.

30. Bross described the entry of Sheridan's troops on October 10, 1871: "in the morning . . . I saw Sheridan's boys, with knapsack and musket, march proudly by. *Never did deeper emotions of joy overcome me.* Thank God, those most dear to me, and the city as well, are safe. . . . *Had it not been for General Sheridan's prompt, bold, and patriotic action,* I verily believe what was left of the city would have been nearly, if not quite entirely, destroyed by the cutthroats and vagabonds who flocked here like vultures from every point of the compass." Bross, in McIlvaine, ed., *Reminiscences during the Great Fire*, pp. 90–91.

31. *Chicago Tribune*, November 17, 1871.

32. White to David A. Wells, October 29, 1871, Wells MSS. See also White to Murat Halstead, November 15, 1871, Halstead MSS.

33. *Chicago Tribune,* January 22, 23, 26, 1872.

34. Ibid., December 6, 1871. Not all the revenue reformers were as pleased with Blaine's performance as was White. See Roeliff Brinkerhoff, *Recollections of a Lifetime,* pp. 207-210. Brinkerhoff insisted that the majority of the committee were protectionists, including the chairman, Henry Dawes of Massachusetts. White, however, listed Dawes as a revenue reformer.

35. *Chicago Tribune,* December 6, 1871.

36. Joseph Medill to Murat Halstead, December 15, 1871, Halstead MSS. Medill had drawn closer to Grant when the President appointed him in June as one of the Commissioners of the Civil Service Commission. See Ari Hoogenboom, *Outlawing the Spoils* (Urbana, Ill., 1961), p. 90.

37. *Chicago Tribune,* December 14, 1871.

38. Ibid.

39. Chester M. Destler, *Henry Demarest Lloyd and the Empire of Reform* (Philadelphia, 1963), pp. 47-49.

40. L. G. Fisher to David Davis, January 3, 1872, Davis MSS.

41. Lyman Trumbull to White, January 27, 1872, Trumbull MSS.

42. *Chicago Tribune,* January 29, 1872.

43. White to Lyman Trumbull, January 31, 1872, Trumbull MSS.

44. *Chicago Tribune,* February 4, 1872.

45. Ibid., February 6, 1872.

46. Ibid., February 7, 1872.

47. About this time, Palmer, the Illinois governor, began to flirt with Liberal Republicans in his state. Through Lincoln Dubois, he sounded out White. White encouraged Palmer's growing dissatisfaction and even offered him advice on Grant's vulnerability. Yet White himself refused to promise any assistance. Nevertheless, Dubois concluded that "White himself is certainly as much in earnest as ever before against Grant & Co." Lincoln Dubois to John Palmer, February 19, 1872, Palmer MSS.

48. As White opened his cautious criticism of Grant, the President wrote Joseph Medill a letter declaring his "intention that Civil Service shall have a fair trial." Referring to this letter, a recent student of the Civil Service reform movement concluded: "Whatever his spoilsminded friends or reform-minded enemies may have thought, Grant was in the reformers' camp in early 1872." Hoogenboom, *Outlawing the Spoils,* p. 106. See also Grant to Medill, February 1, 1872, cited by Hesseltine, *Grant,* p. 264.

49. Although Medill had no control over the paper, his continued presence in the editorial rooms—despite his being Mayor of Chicago—embarrassed White. Medill's close contact with the Grant administration as a Civil Service Commissioner made the relationship particularly embarrassing. Jesse Fell, on a mission for David Davis, noted the strained atmosphere in the makeshift offices of the *Tribune:* "In pursuance of an agreement with White of the 'Tribune,' I called at 10 A.M. yesterday, and just as we got fairly to talking in walked Medill, and as White told me today—

I very adroitly turned the topic of conversation . . . called today and had a satisfactory talk with White and Bross." Jesse Fell to David Davis, March 4, 1872, Davis MSS.

50. Leonard Swett, another of David Davis's scouts, explained the motives of Cowles: "Coles [*sic*] looks at the paper from a money standpoint purely. The establishment is making more money than ever before. This is account of the abundance of new advertising matter. Still it cannot afford to lose its present subscribers list. In its editorials it is one day for the administration and the next shadows a support of the opposition." Leonard Swett to David Davis, February 25, 1872, Davis MSS.

51. In most large cities, newspapers eventually discarded their financial dependence on political parties. This ability explains the growth of "independent" journalism. See Bernard Weisberger, *The American Newspaperman* (Chicago, 1962), pp. 40–47.

52. For an interesting explanation of the importance of subscription lists in determining newspaper policy, see Eric McKitrick, *Andrew Johnson and Reconstruction*, pp. 439–442.

53. Trumbull, perhaps understanding White's dilemma, had the same fears of Democratic stigma. Trumbull insisted in a letter to White that the Cincinnati gathering had to be a "distinctively Republican convention." "The democrats,," he concluded, "must come to the Republican candidate." Trying to prod the editor into action he pointed out that "the N.Y. *Tribune*'s circulation has increased 25,000 since the liberal course." "The people are ready," Trumbull insisted, "and organization is all that is needed for complete success." Lyman Trumbull to White, March 6, 1872, White MSS.

54. David A. Wells to Manton Marble, March 7, 1872, Marble MSS. See also Mark Krug, *Lyman Trumbull: Conservative Radical*, pp. 309–312.

55. Trumbull to Gustave Koerner, March 9, 1872, Trumbull MSS. Koerner, however, was no more willing than White to take the initiative. In his memoirs he explained that he was opposed to the Liberals' nominating candidates before the regular Republican convention. He wanted the Liberals to wait until after the Republican convention before taking any action. Gustave Koerner, *Memoirs of Gustave Koerner* (Cedar Rapids, Iowa, 1909), p. 538.

56. Willard King, *Lincoln's Manager, David Davis* (Cambridge, Mass., 1960), pp. 278–9.

57. White to Trumbull, March 9, 1872, Trumbull MSS. The strength of the Liberals in the party leadership was made clear as the Grant faction attempted to force the dissidents into line by calling for an early convention. The majority of the State Central Committee beat down the motion. White to Lyman Trumbull, March 17, 1872, Trumbull MSS.

58. White to Edward Atkinson, March 16, 1872 Atkinson MSS.

59. *Chicago Tribune*, March 23, 1872.

60. White to Lyman Trumbull, March 24, 1872, Trumbull MSS.

61. *Chicago Tribune*, March 30, 1872.

62. Ibid.

63. Ibid.

64. Ibid., April 3, 1872.

65. Jesse Fell to Lyman Trumbull, April 18, 1872, Trumbull MSS.

66. White to Lyman Trumbull, telegram and letter, April 9, 1872, Trumbull MSS. White to Jesse Fell, April 10, 1872, Jesse Fell MSS, University of Illinois. Apparently rather impressed himself by the list of names, White tried to tempt Logan to bolt the party. Logan had on several occasions given support to the revenue reformers but had backed away from insurgency. White tried one last effort: "To my surprise I found nearly everybody hot for Cincinnati. . . . Unless I am greatly deceived by appearances the State of Illinois will be represented at Cincinnati by a larger and more enthusiastic crowd then was ever congregated at any convention except that of 1860 at Chicago. I thought you would like to know what is going on." White to Logan, April 9 1872, Logan MSS.

67. White to Lyman Trumbull, April 9, 1872, Trumbull MSS. See also David Donald, *Lincoln's Herndon* (New York, 1948), p. 262.

68. Oziah M. Hatch to Lyman Trumbull, April 11, 1872, Trumbull MSS.

69. L. C. Fisher to David Davis, April 17, 1872, Davis MSS. Fisher was angry when White told him of the *Tribune* directors' decision. Since White had given his assent to Davis's candidacy in January, Fisher felt that the reversal was "electioneering" for Trumbull "in a mean way." Fisher, however did not fully appreciate White's dilemma. White had, moveover, expressed his sympathy for Davis before the jurist received open support from the Democrats. If there was any "mean" campaigning, the Davis forces could certainly not claim clean hands. Leonard Swett in February told Davis of the strategy of their Democratic allies: "Whoever is nominated must be cordially supported by the democracy. Trumbull cannot get their support and when the time comes the movement can be checkmated there. Story [editor of the *Chicago Times*] thinks this but he is inclined to let it run far before making it known that the democracy will not support him. It strikes me to do this too soon takes away from Trumbull the motive for his action and weakens the general opposition." Leonard Swett to David Davis, February 25, 1872, Davis MSS.

70. White to Charles Sumner, April 13, 1872, Sumner MSS. See also Samuel Bowles to Sumner, April 14, 1872; David A. Wells to Sumner, 1872; Edward Atkinson to Sumner, April 13, 1872; F. W. Bird to Sumner, April 15, 1872: Charles Sumner MSS.

71. In March, White had written to Trumbull: "I doubt whether the *Chicago Tribune* could retain its influence with Republicans if it should attempt to carry him [David Davis]. No objection lies against yourself, or Sumner, or Greeley." White to Lyman Trumbull, March 17, 1872, Trumbull MSS.

72. *Chicago Tribune*, April 18, 1872. The list of signatures included those of many prominent political figures in the state. There were not many businessmen, but prominence seemed to make up for numbers. The

president as well as leading members of the Chicago Board of Trade, for example, joined in the bolters' appeal. The list was not particularly representative of the state. Most of the names came from Chicago, Springfield, and Belleville.

73. Ibid.

74. John Wentworth to David Davis, April 20, 1872, Davis MSS.

75. *Chicago Tribune,* March 19, April 6, 1872, and White to Trumbull, March 17, 1872: Trumbull MSS.

76. Lyman Trumbull to White, April 24, 1872, Trumbull MSS.

77. Lyman Trumbull to David A. Wells, April 24, 1872, Wells MSS. Lyman Trumbull to Sinclair Tousey, April 27, 1872, Trumbull MSS. William Grosvenor to Carl Schurz, May 26, 1872, Schurz MSS.

78. Destler, *Lloyd,* pp. 51–52.

79. *Chicago Tribune,* April 18, 1872.

10

Disappointment

THE Liberal Republican gathering in Cincinnati was the fourth national convention that White attended, but only the second that required him to leave Chicago. Both Lincoln and Grant had received their first nominations in his home town. In both of those conventions, the editors of the *Chicago Tribune* had played a major role; in both, they had secured the election of a favorite son. White hoped to maintain that tradition at Cincinnati.

Seldom had journalists played so dominant a role in the organization of any American convention. The very prominence of newspaper editors, however, revealed an ominous note as Cincinnati greeted her arrivals. Politicians, especially successful politicians, were shying away from the Liberal movement. True, politicians came, but almost all were losers of the battles which had been waged within the Republican party since 1869.

When White arrived at Cincinnati by train, four days before the convention began, a reporter from the *New York Herald* sounded him out. The flattery of recognition did not inflate the editor's hopes. He frankly confessed that the Liberal movement represented no political revolution. "The masses of the people are waiting in a half-curious way," White told the reporter, "to see what will be done here before they will make up their minds." If there was to be any upheaval, everything, according to White, depended on what would happen at Cincinnati.[1]

White had an immediate assignment in determining the eventual outcome at Cincinnati. As a lieutenant of the Trumbull forces, he had to secure support for his state's favorite son. There was a good chance that Illinois might take the prize once more. In the months before the convention, Trumbull had faced little real opposition, except for that of David Davis. Most of the revenue reformers had made Trumbull their candidate.[2] His fellow senators, Schurz and Sumner, had looked upon him as the likely choice of Republican dissidents.

Trumbull's strength dissipated quickly, however, in the final weeks before the convention. The eastern revenue reformers became infatuated with the candidacy of Charles Francis Adams. Adams's chilling condescension seemed only to warm their interest in his nomination.[3] One by one Trumbull lost his advance guard in the Northeast: David A. Wells, Edwin Godkin, Edward Atkinson, and Samuel Bowles. The same thing occurred in many parts of the Midwest. Carl Schurz and Grosvenor began to talk about *either* Trumbull *or* Adams for the nomination. The Ohio reformers led by William Grosbeck and J. D. Cox lined up their legions in Ohio and Michigan behind the acid-tongued Adams. Indeed the Ohio group looked upon Trumbull with some suspicion, since he had begun too noticeably to soft pedal the tariff issue. They did not even include him, therefore, as their second choice. All of these men no doubt had been attracted by the antique appeal of the Adams heritage. They had also probably noted the *New York World*'s public recommendation of an Adams ticket as the most favorable to eastern Democratic leaders. Manton Marble, the editor of the paper, reemphasized his advice in personal appeals to David A. Wells and Carl Schurz.[4] August Belmont, wealthy backer of the *World,* went one step further; he openly cultivated Adams support in Indiana, Kentucky, and Tennessee just before he stepped into Cincinnati to lobby among the delegates.

Trumbull also lost some votes by default. His supporters had made no concerted effort to secure sympathetic Southern delegations. Agents for Adams, Greeley, and Governor Brown of Missouri, had not been so negligent.[5] Trumbull, moreover, had alienated Southern support by a careless remark in his Cooper Union speech just before the Cincinnati gathering. There, in the traditional Republican place to announce one's availability, Trumbull inadvertently referred to the "traitors." White dashed off a note to Trumbull on the eve of the Convention observing that the expression had caused him "great harm at the South." But Trumbull refused to recant.[6]

Finally, White and other Trumbull supporters had lost ground to the Davis forces in their own state by hesitating so long in preparing for the convention. Davis, on the other hand, followed John Wentworth's advice and sent "numbers, mere numbers." Spending money freely, Davis's agents gathered dozens of delegates for the convention. These men gave the Cincinnati gathering the appropriate element for a normal American convention: the cigar-chewing politicians and the fun-loving delegates. Gustave Koerner, who arrived in Cincinnati a few days after White, found hotel lobbies crowded with people. "Their talk," he recalled, "was Davis, Davis."[7]

Davis, a mastermind of Lincoln's convention coup in 1860, had built up considerable momentum. Since the delegates were to be elected at state caucus meetings before the convention opened, Davis appeared the easy winner of the whole Illinois delegation. His supporters outnumbered the Trumbull men by the overwhelming ratio of four or five to one.

Davis had obviously gained the initiative. But his opponents were also able veterans of convention tactics. White countered Davis's numerical strength by using his influence with the convention managers, William Grosvenor and Stanley Matthews. Since his friends manned the credentials committee, White counterattacked confidently. He suggested that the Illinois delegation be appointed by Congressional districts. Although most of the Trumbull delegates came from Chicago and Springfield, a half dozen others were scattered about the state. The Trumbull supporters had also been careful in selecting their delegates. Some, though not all, had regular certificates from county conventions. The Davis men, on the other hand, were largely self-appointed and came almost entirely from an area around Bloomington, Davis's home town. White presented his plan and then offered a condescending compromise which gave Davis half the delegates and split up the rest equally between Palmer and Trumbull.[8] Davis's lieutenants protested the arrangement, but White held the power to enforce his threats. The Supreme Court judge therefore telegraphed his acquiescence.[9] White thus completed the first step of a brilliant strategy to halt the momentum of the Davis candidacy.

More remained to be done. Although Davis had lost half of the Illinois vote, he still had a strong following in the convention. The southern delegations were sympathetic with him, and Pennsylvania and New York, the two largest states (both with a high-tariff delegation), looked with favor upon him as an old Whig. In addition, Davis had large portions of the Indiana and Iowa delegations securely tied to him.[10] No candidate, moreover, had stronger support outside the convention among southern and western Democrats. Even after White's initial victory, Davis still stood as the convention's strongest candidate, rivaled only by Charles F. Adams. In order to forestall what seemed an inevitable victory, some anti-Davis interests tried to establish a two-thirds vote for nomination. But that attempt was beaten down. Ward Lamon confidently telegraphed Davis that the issue lay "between Illinois and New England."[11]

Davis's enemies were skillful and resourceful politicians. Even though they had procrastinated too long, they arrived in Cincinnati determined to make use of all their power. Four of the nation's top editors—White, Henry Watterson, Murat Halstead, and Samuel Bowles—agreed to cooperate in order to defeat the Davis campaign. They confidently dubbed themselves "the Quadrilateral" after the famous Austrian defensive position in the Alps. Although they were divided as between Trumbull and Adams, a consensus prevailed among them that Davis had to be defeated. Three of the editors had large Republican followings, and they could not afford to flirt with Davis's Democracy.[12] A different purpose impelled Watterson, editor of the *Louisville Courier-Journal*. Though a Democrat, Watterson felt that the convention in order to be successful had to nominate Adams.[13] All four, therefore, could agree that Davis had to be destroyed. They worked closely with Schurz and Grosvenor. To help them further, the four called on Whitelaw Reid, Greeley's editorial assistant and acknowledged manager at the convention.[14] White protested that move, but Watterson insisted that the influence of the *New York Tribune* could be decisive in their plan, particularly since Davis was the second choice of the New York delegation. Greeley, moreover, was a symbol of Republicanism, and White had already acknowledged his availability. Besides, what harm could it do? There was little chance, they all agreed, for Greeley to win the prize. The cabal determined to limit their support to three men—Greeley, Trumbull, and Adams. White, for some reason, would not let them include B. Gratz Brown, the Liberal Republican governor of Missouri.

The strategy was simple. Each editor would write an editorial for his paper. Pointing to the weaknesses of Davis's position—his lavish spending of money, his motley group of supporters, his taint of the Democracy, his overt presidential ambitions—each of the editors stressed a major point and then telegraphed his editorial home. The five "leaders" were then, in turn, reprinted in the *Cincinnati Commercial* which was distributed widely to delegates at the opening of the convention. The effect was deadly. White's editorial left Davis no quarter. He castigated the "obtrusive and impertinent interference of Democrats" in the Davis camp and condemned the "packing of a Convention by delegates picked up and shipped at a candidate's expense." "It is the candid judgement of everyone who witnessed the disgraceful scene," White concluded, "that the cause of Justice Davis has been irretrievably ruined in the country at large by these shameful excesses."[15]

Davis's agents angrily reported the impact of the editorials to their chief. They had to admit that the warnings of the Quadrilateral scared "a great many seats in the Hall. . . ." Although an even sweeter revenge would come for the Davis forces, John Wentworth could already speculate: "They may agree to kill Davis but then the assassins have got to fight for the man among themselves."[16]

As the convention assembled in an immense and well-decorated hall, the spectacle of 10,000 occupied seats no doubt swelled the imaginations of all the political movers. But the routine events of the first session evinced the controlling positions of the original revenue reform leaders. William Grosvenor, a chief among them, officially opened the convention by reading the call which in January he had prepared himself at the Liberal Republican assembly in Missouri. When he finished, Grosvenor passed the baton to Stanley Matthews, leader of the Ohio group of free traders, who in January had immediately seconded the Missouri call. As temporary chairman, Matthews read a resolution to confirm the already assembled committees: Horace White headed the crucial committee on the platform. Power obviously lay with the original reformers. They made no attempt to disguise that fact. After disposing of such matters, Matthews delivered "a very chaste and effective speech opening the convention." That concluded the activities of the first day, and the convention adjourned.

The second day continued with a further display of power by the Trumbull-Adams axis. The convention named Carl Schurz permanent chairman. Matthews happily passed the gavel to the Missouri senator, who was the inspiration for the Liberal movement. Schurz did not halt the surge of events. Instead, he fed the reformers' enthusiasm by delivering a powerful speech which presented a portrait of the convention's logical candidate. Only Adams or perhaps Trumbull could have fitted the specifications.[17] After Schurz concluded his masterful manipulation of the audience, cries for a nomination arose. A motion for balloting went to the floor.

At that moment Adams could have stampeded the convention. General Cochrane, a leader of the Greeley forces, tried to forestall the inevitable by requesting the delegates to table the motion. When it became apparent, however, that the two-thirds vote for tabling was unavailable, Cochrane withdrew his proposal. Pleas for nominations continued. Finally Gustave Koerner, chairman of the Illinois delegation and a Trumbull supporter, gained the floor. He boldly renewed Cochrane's motion, "insisting," as he later recalled, "upon the utter impropriety of nominating candidates before we had agreed upon the principles which we desired to prevail in the national councils."[18] Although White had virtually given up on Trumbull's candidacy by that time and offered no driving leadership for his candidacy, Koerner felt that Trumbull could still win.[19] The Adams men, knowing that they could not afford to alienate such a respected Trumbull spokesman, acquiesced in Koerner's advice. No nominations were made that day. Instead the convention, having been quieted by Koerner, adjourned and proceeded that evening with what he suggested—the platform.

The original Missouri call for the convention contained a set of principles which struck a consensus among those who assembled in Cincinnati. Only one point provided difficulty—the tariff. Many of the original revenue reformers, including White, had determined before the convention to blur the tariff issue. Still, a vocal minority led by the Ohio delegates refused to compromise. In the evening session, Stanley Matthews, now an Ohio floor leader, urged the convention to adopt a free-trade platform. There was some debate on the motion, but no vote. The convention deferred the issue to the platform committee.

As chairman of that important committee, White presided over the contenders well into the night. The disagreement was bitter. Irreconcilable free traders had threatened to bolt, and they now repeated their threat. The committee appeared deadlocked. At one point the members even considered reporting their irresolution to the convention. But finally, through the mediation of Schurz, a majority agreed upon a compromise offered by the Greeley forces—that the convention should refer the tariff question to the people in their respective congressional districts. Eastern free traders like Edward Atkinson, David A. Wells, and Judge Hoadly acquiesced in the decision, and Edwin L. Godkin, editor of the *Nation*, publicly absolved the committee of any deviousness. "It is right to add," he wrote from the convention, "that the sentiment of the convention was overwhelmingly in favor of this course. . . . and, at all events, nothing else was possible."[20]

When White left the committee room very late that night, he must have sighed in relief. The final barrier to a harmonious convention had been removed. But hardly had White gone to bed, when someone pounded on his door shouting: "Get up! Blair and Brown are here from St. Louis." It was

Grosvenor. He did not wait for White to answer; instead, he raced down the hall rousing others with the same alarm. White dressed quickly and awakened Dr. William Jayne, brother-in-law of Lyman Trumbull. Together they joined a half-awake group in the main lobby to discuss the meaning of the sudden appearance of B. Gratz Brown and Frank Blair at the convention.

Grosvenor told the supporters of Adams and Trumbull whom he had aroused that Brown had been meeting with some of the Missouri delegates. Brown was offended at having been read out of the convention by White, Bowles, and even his own Missouri compatriots, Schurz and Grosvenor. Now he was advertising his intention to withdraw as a candidate and to throw his support to Horace Greeley. Whether he and the Greeley managers ever came to any agreement, no one really knows.[21] The Adams and Trumbull supporters were startled but soon realized that there was little that they could do at two o'clock in the morning. One by one, therefore, they retired "to uneasy slumber."[22]

In the morning of its last day, the convention listened to the platform. White's work had been done well. The convention adopted the statement of principles "by a unanimous and enthusiastic" vote.[23] With that business out of the way, the convention moved on to the moment everyone was waiting for. The hall was crowded and hot; thousands of fans fluttered in a thousand different directions. A buzzing of conversation, shuffling, and exclamations filled the air. Hundreds of delegates now had to make up their minds. The gathering provided no concert of thought or motion. This was a bolter's convention. Loyalty to party or faction was nonexistent, and sharp divisions of principles had been purposely blurred. Only a few states maintained any discipline among their delegates. The choice of a candidate therefore remained uncertain. Politicians had been laying plans and forming combinations, but with the diversity of opinion and influence at work in a meeting of loosely united insurgents, it was still anybody's game.

The audience was so eager to move on to balloting that it quickly agreed to an unexpected motion by a Davis delegate to dispense with all nominating speeches. Only the waiting orators seemed disappointed; everyone else wanted ·to vote.[24] The chairman called the roll, and the first ballot began. Alabama led off with a majority of her votes for Horace Greeley. But when the balloting ended, Greeley finished well behind Adams. The stolid New Englander led the field with 205 votes. Greeley had 147. The favorite sons among them retained a majority, with Trumbull's 110 votes topping the list. Davis and Brown followed with 92 and 95 votes respectively. Pennsylvania's favorite son, Andrew Curtin, rounded out the field of serious contenders with all of his state's 62 votes.[25] The hard-core strength of the various candidates had been tested. Adams found his base not in New England, but in the center of the country—in Ohio, Michigan, Indiana, Tennessee, and Kentucky. A good number of the Northeastern states, headed by New York, voted for Greeley. The influential editor also received most of the votes of the Far West and won significant backing from the South, but he divided the votes there with both Adams and Brown. Now that the first ballot had clarified each candidate's base of support, begging and bantering began on the floor.

Before the second ballot could indicate the results of any reshuffling of ballots, the chairman of the convention, Carl Schurz, made an announcement: B. Gratz Brown wanted to make a statement. It was no surprise. Almost everyone in the auditorium knew what he was going to say.[26] Still there was a deep anxiety, for no one could foresee the effect of Brown's withdrawal upon Greeley's candidacy. What about Pennsylvania? Would the delegates desert Curtin and join in behind the protectionist Greeley? No one knew; they had to wait.

Brown gave Greeley one advantage. His rousing plea for the New York editor was the only speech made for any candidate. The galleries shouted their approval. Many in the audience were women, and since Greeley was a proponent of female suffrage, he became their favorite. But women did not vote. The second ballot would be a better test of the effectiveness of Brown's speech. Alabama began again by announcing all its votes for Greeley, and Arkansas followed by switching from Brown to Greeley. The Brown delegates from the South apparently heeded his advice and began to narrow Adams's lead over Greeley. But the real test of Brown's plea was in Missouri and Pennsylvania. And Missouri balked. Two-thirds of the delegation ignored Brown. Sixteen went to Trumbull; four to Adams; and only ten to Greeley. When the Pennsylvania delegates announced a change in their ballot, twenty-six went for Adams; eleven for Trumbull; and eighteen for Greeley. Although Greeley reached 245 votes (two more than Adams), Brown's move was considered a failure by some observers. In the shakeup of delegates, Trumbull and Adams together had picked up almost as many votes as Greeley, and they now jointly held 391 votes to Greeley's 245. The Trumbull and Adams men were actually relieved by the outcome of the second ballot.

The third, fourth, and fifth ballots increased their optimism. Adams progressed steadily, while Greeley did no more than stand still. At the end of the fifth ballot Adams had 309; Greeley, 258; and Trumbull, 91. Fifty-five other votes were divided between the two candidates from the Supreme Court, David Davis and Salmon Chase.

"Now was the time for Trumbull men to act," Koerner recalled.[27] Trumbull held the balance of power, and as Adams had drawn considerable strength from Trumbull on the fifth ballot, many considered Adams's nomination certain. Adams needed only a slight majority of the remaining Trumbull votes to take the convention prize. A large number of

Adams's cheering section, were so confident of victory that they left the hall, many in order to send telegrams which flashed the news of an Adams victory across the country.[28]

The Illinois delegates were among those that left the hall. They withdrew to poll themselves for a vote on the sixth ballot. The division within the Illinois delegation now began to tell; it had made it impossible for the Trumbull men to move adroitly during the convention.[29] Leadership and direction among the Trumbull forces were also missing; no one coordinated the Trumbull votes throughout the convention. Trumbull himself was in part responsible for this failure; he had been a cautious candidate, trying always not to offend the reformers' dislike of overt political ambition. He had carefully instructed White to keep outside of "rings and bargains" and told Koerner that he refused to be nominated "as the result of any combination or arrangements between rival interests." The loyalty of Trumbull's old associates and friends in the Illinois delegation, moreover, would not permit the withdrawal of his nomination any earlier than the sixth ballot. This group hoped to the last that a possible convention deadlock might lead to a Trumbull victory. All of this division and confusion among the Illinois delegates plagued the Trumbull leaders when they finally had to make their decisive move.

Going into a "sort of annex," Koerner and White urged the delegation to drop their favorite sons and unite upon Adams. The Davis leaders now had their revenge; they refused to fall in line. This prolonged the meeting, forcing Koerner to poll the delegation. Adams received twenty-seven votes; Greeley received fourteen; and Trumbull retained one. Illinois remained divided. Still, twenty-seven votes was more than half of the number needed by Adams to win. The delegation marched back into a screaming convention hall. Their bickering and cajoling had caused them to miss the entire sixth ballot.

Everyone had expected the sixth ballot to be the last; most felt that Adams would win. But the convention began to develop a logic of its own. Before balloting even began, the assembly had degenerated into a mob of yelling and screaming delegates. In this whirl of emotions, Greeley gained the advantage. The first three states—Alabama, Arkansas, and California—voted solidly for the New Yorker. Georgia, close behind, added its unanimous vote to the Greeley total. Illinois was next and it might have stopped the stampede by giving Adams twenty-seven votes, but its delegation was not in the hall. As the clerk skipped over Illinois, the balloting reached the loose Trumbull votes in Indiana, Iowa, Kansas, and Missouri. With Illinois and the Trumbull managers gone, these delegates had even less direction. Indiana, the first to vote, gave Greeley a majority of its support for the first time. The Greeley forces went wild. Hats filled the air and the cheers became overwhelming. As the roll continued, it became evident that Greeley, not Adams, was picking up a majority of the remaining ninety-one Trumbull votes. Under this strain, Louisiana, where the Adams vote was fickle, cast some votes for Greeley. The roll ended and the Illinois delegation had still not returned.

When they did return, they discovered that Greeley had taken the lead with 318 votes while Adams slipped to 293. The convention tensed as Koerner shouted out the vote: "Twenty-four for Adams." The Adams men roared their approval, as this put their candidate back into the lead by two votes. When order was restored, Koerner continued, "Fourteen for Greeley." Greeley only needed twenty-four more votes for nomination. All order ceased. Delegations converged on one another in complete disarray. The staccato beat of Schurz's gravel only twitted the throng. When some order finally returned to the floor, several delegations demanded recognition. Minnesota gained the floor and gave nine votes for Greeley. Pennsylvania followed that with fifty and put the New Yorker over the top. Other delegations followed suit.[30] In the midst of the confusion, a Davis man even called out a change of the whole Illinois delegation for Greeley. Though such a vote would only have been a formality at that point, Koerner went to the speakers platform to correct the enthusiastic delegate. It was still twenty-seven for Adams and one for Trumbull.[31]

While Koerner remained on the platform, the convention proceeded with the balloting for Vice-President. B. Gratz Brown won on the second ballot. Trumbull could have won the post easily, but Koerner arbitrarily announced that Trumbull would not accept the vice-presidency. Koerner had not recovered from Greeley's victory. He was still benumbed by the sudden turn of events.

The impossible had happened. All the Adams men were stunned. Some, like Schurz, scurried away from the crowds, but an earlier bargain forced White to eat crow that same night. He had promised to have dinner with the Quadrilateral before he went home. There was only one happy diner that evening—Whitelaw Reid. "Frostier conviviality I have never sat down to than Reid's dinner," Watterson recalled. "Horace White looked more than ever like an iceberg. . . . We separated early and sadly, reformers hoist on their own petard."[32]

White had good reason to be disappointed. He had worked hard for an Adams or Trumbull victory. Except for the last few moments, all had gone according to plan. What had happened, no one really knew. There was no easy explanation and certainly no rational one. The oft-quoted interpretation of crafty politicians snatching the prize from naive reformers, unskilled in convention warfare, is inadequate.[33] Although some free traders were anxious to point to the outcome of a Greeley-Brown ticket as the immediate result of early conspiracies, the detailed pattern of voting in the convention does not bear out any causal relationship between the two events. As disappointed as White was, he discounted that explanation. "The so-called Gratz Brown trick," White wrote Trumbull the day after the vote, "was simply a desperate throw of the dice—the gambler's last 'chip'—to humiliate Schurz. It had the least effect upon the convention. It changed scarcely anybody's mind."[34]

Chance, emotion, irrationality—all had conspired to make Greeley the candidate. It had happened before and would happen again in American political conventions. Samuel Bowles, who had attended many similar gatherings, resorted to metaphor to provide understanding. "What with Greeley's nomination and the killing of so many evergreens this winter," he advised a very bitter free trader, "we all need to study the higher philosophies."[35] In the weeks after the convention, many of the original revenue reformers continued to bewail Greeley's nomination. They devised all sorts of elaborate explanations. Horace White, however, could not afford the luxury of theorizing. He was the editor of a daily newspaper.

NOTES

1. Cited by Horace White, *The Life of Lyman Trumbull*, p. 378.

2. David A. Wells to Manton Marble, March 7, 1872, Marble MSS.

3. Adams wrote David A. Wells a letter which presented a long list of presumptuous prerequisites for his candidacy. To magnify his disdain for politics Adams departed for Europe on the eve of the convention. Adams, it is true, never expected the letter to be published. But Samuel Bowles thought Adams' apparent indifference to a nomination would increase his popularity at the Cincinnati gathering. Bowles took full responsibility for publishing the letter in his paper, the *Springfield Republican*. C. F. Adams to David A. Wells, April 18, 1872, Wells Coll. C. F. Adams, Jr., to Samuel Bowles, April 26, 27, 1872 Samuel Bowles MSS, Yale University. See also Martin Duberman, *Charles Francis Adams* (Boston, 1961), pp. 352–372.

4. Manton Marble to Carl Schurz, April 23, 1872, Schurz MSS.

5. The delegations from the South were well represented. Henry Watter-

son recalled that there was "a motley array of Southerners of every sort." Henry Watterson, "The Humor and Tragedy of the Greeley Campaign," *Century* 85 (November, 1912):30. For a detailed view of how several of the southern delegations were raised, see Frederick Bromberg to Carl Schurz, April 12, 1906, Schurz MSS.

6. White to Lyman Trumbull, April 25, 1872, Trumbull MSS. White had just spoken to David Goodloe of North Carolina who told White of the impact of Trumbull's remark. Mark Krug, *Lyman Trumbull*, p. 328.

7. Gustave Koerner, *Memoirs of Gustave Koerner*, p. 548.

8. Willard King, *Lincoln's Manager, David Davis*, pp. 281–282.

9. John Wentworth to Jesse Fell, May 2, 1872, Davis MSS. Davis apparently did not know, however, that Palmer had already withdrawn as a candidate in favor of Trumbull. John Palmer to Lyman Trumbull, April 13, 1872, Trumbull MSS.

10. King, *Lincoln's Manager*, p. 281.

11. Ward Lamon to David Davis, telegram, April 28, 1872, Davis MSS.

12. George S. Merriam, *The Life and Times of Samuel Bowles* (New York, 1885), 2:191.

13. Joseph F. Wall, *Henry Watterson, Reconstructed Rebel* (New York, 1956), pp. 99–101.

14. Royal Cortissoz, *The Life of Whitelaw Reid* (New York, 1921), 1:210–211, 223.

15. *Chicago Tribune*, May 1, 1872. The newspaper "chieftains" cabal was exposed many years later by Henry Watterson in an article, "The Humor and Tragedy of the Greeley Campaign," *Century* 85 (November, 1912):24–43 (hereafter cited as Watterson, *Century*).

16. J. Wentworth to Jesse Fell, telegram, May 2, 1872, Davis MSS. New York Senator Reuben Fenton, who had been working for the Davis cause, acknowledged defeat by leaving the convention. *Nation*, May 9, 1872.

17. Historians, relying on Godkin's report of the convention, have assumed that Adams was Schurz's choice. But White reported to Trumbull after the convention that Schurz had backed him. Earle D. Ross, *The Liberal Republican Movement* (New York, 1919), p. 97. *Nation*, May 9, 1872. White to Lyman Trumbull, May 4, 1872, Trumbull MSS.

18. Koerner, *Memoirs*, p. 551.

19. White to Lyman Trumbull, May 4, 1872, Trumbull MSS. A report from Cincinnati noting the unlikelihood of Trumbull's nomination was published in the *Chicago Tribune* on May 2, 1872. This report validates White's post-convention assertion to Trumbull on May 4: "My judgment was from the beginning of our arrival here that you could not be nominated."

20. *Nation*, May 9, 1872. See also Ross, *Liberal Republican Movement*, p. 95; Roeliff Brinkerhoff, *Recollections of a Lifetime*, p. 217; and White, *Trumbull*, pp. 381–383. Schurz's involvement in the dispute is noted in Frank W. Bird to Charles Sumner, May 7, 1872, Charles Sumner Papers.

21. There are conflicting explanations of this arrangement, none of them very satisfying. Samuel Bowles denied that Greeley participated in any deal with Brown, but Atkinson even gave the hour at which Greeley was informed of the deal. Samuel Bowles to F. L. Olmstead, May 11, 1872, Bowles MSS. Edward Atkinson to Carl Schurz, May 23, 1872, Schurz MSS. The Whitelaw Reid MSS supply no evidence about the May 2 negotiations, except a cryptic telegram from Greeley: "Let us await conclusion before deciding what shall be done." Horace Greeley to Whitelaw Reid, May 2, 1872, Reid MSS. The telegram does demonstrate, however, that Greeley was making decisions from New York.

22. White recalled the incident many years later. White to Frederick Bancroft, May 21, 1911, Frederick Bancroft MSS, Columbia University. White, *Trumbull*, pp. 382–383.

23. *Proceedings of the Liberal Republican Convention* (New York, 1872), p. 18. Koerner, *Memoirs*, p. 553.

24. Koerner, *Memoirs*, p. 553.

25. The vote totals have been taken from the official proceedings of the convention, *Proceedings of the Liberal Republican Convention*.

26. Not only had Grosvenor warned the Adams and Trumbull supporters the evening before, but Halstead reported the development in his morning paper. *Cincinnati Commercial*, May 3, 1872.

27. Koerner, *Memoirs*, p. 555.

28. Carl Schurz to E. L. Godkin, November 23, 1872, E. L. Godkin MSS, Harvard University.

29. Trumbull to White, April 24, 1872, Trumbull MSS. Koerner, *Memoirs*, p. 543. After the convention, White explained his paralysis: "If I had taken the responsibility of withdrawing your name as suggested by your letter, I should never have had any standing in Illinois again —certainly not among your friends." White to Trumbull, May 4, 1872, Trumbull MSS. At the same time, others found it impossible to switch to Trumbull to prevent a Greeley victory. When F. W. Bird, an Adams opponent, tried to switch the Massachusetts delegation to Trumbull, he received no response from the Trumbull men. F. W. Bird to Charles Sumner, May 7, 1872, Sumner MSS. There was simply never a realistic opportunity to make a switch to Trumbull. David A. Wells to Lyman Trumbull, May 8, 1872, Trumbull MSS. Even if there had been, the Ohio and Michigan delegations which had been supporting Adams refused to consider Trumbull. Edward Atkinson to Carl Schurz, May 23, 1872, Schurz MSS. See also Krug, *Trumbull*, pp. 331–334.

30. *Chicago Tribune*, May 4, 1872.

31. Koerner, *Memoirs*, p. 555.

32. Henry Watterson, *"Marse Henry": An Autobiography* (New York, 1919), 1:257.

33. Ross, *Liberal Republican Movement*, p. 102. This traditional view has been thoroughly examined and dismissed in an excellent review of

the convention. Matthew T. Downey, "Horace Greeley and the Politicians: The Liberal Republican Convention in 1872," *The Journal of American History* 53 (March, 1967):727–750.

34. White to Lyman Trumbull, May 4, 1872, Trumbull MSS.

35. Samuel Bowles to F. L. Olmstead, May 15, 1872, copy in the Samuel Bowles MSS.

11

Defeat

BACK IN Chicago the *Tribune* staff had been waiting anxiously for news of the convention. Cramped into their makeshift quarters in the loft of the machine shop, which the *Tribune* occupied after the fire, the staff stood poised to obey White's command. Finally his telegrams came. Their reaction to the news was a delayed duplicate of their chief's. Greeley's victory was a hard blow; they had been certain Adams would win. White knew they would be confused. A longer telegram followed.

James Sheahan, White's chief editorial assistant, read the message aloud to his colleagues: "The nomination of Mr. Greeley," White began, "was accomplished by the people against the judgement and strenuous efforts of politicians." Perhaps already anticipating the growling of the reformers over "duplicity" by politicians, White played down the effectiveness of Gratz Brown's switch to Greeley and insisted instead that the reason for Greeley's victory lay in his potential popularity among the masses of voters. He noted that the timing and momentum of balloting had not allowed the Illinois delegation to exert its full influence. "The gush and hurrah swept everything down." Summing up his conclusions, White inferred that "Greeley will be a popular candidate. . . . The opinion of the best judges this evening is, that the ticket will sweep the country."[1]

The telegram aroused no cheering among the attentive journalists. Yet it left them no choice. White had clearly swung the *Tribune* into line for Greeley. Sheahan, a masterful mercenary in Chicago journalism, promptly wrote an editorial to show that Greeley was the best of all possible nominations.[2]

All the members of the original Quadrilateral followed White in his support of Greeley. None were enthusiastic, but, as they were all editors of daily journals, they had to make a decision. Halstead could immediately write his own editorials in the *Cincinnati Commercial*. Samuel Bowles telegraphed his offices to fall into line, but he warned them "not to gush."[3] Watterson waited a few more days, until he had returned to Louisville, but he, too, fell into line.[4] All of them left the convention stunned and bewildered. Greeley's nomination had muddled their plans. So confused was the closing of the convention that White had to send a note to Schurz to remind him to give Greeley and Brown official notice of their nominations. After the convention had adjourned White remained in Cincinnati for two days, trying to tie up loose ends. When he returned to Chicago, he pumped new optimism into the editorial columns. "Horace Greeley is the People's candidate," he wrote, "and it is useless to oppose him."[5]

Whether it was useless or not, many opposed him; some were White's closest friends. The *Nation* ridiculed White's description of Greeley as "the People's candidate," and Wendell Phillips Garrison labeled White's actions "a surrender."[6] Garrison vowed to his brother that the *Nation* would not be "following in 'that crowd.'" Many of the eastern reform leaders agreed with Garrison.[7] A week after Greeley's victory,

Carl Schurz said that he still could not "think of the results of the Cincinnati Convention without a pang."[8] Some of the other reformers, like Trumbull, adjusted themselves slowly to Greeley's nomination before finally giving him their whole-hearted support.[9]

Because of the backwash of confusion and resentment among the Liberals themselves, White was forced to keep the *Tribune* on the defensive for several weeks. He had to fight both regular Republicans and rancorous reformers, and he had a worse time, by far, with the reformers. He began an almost daily debate with the *New York Evening Post* and the *Nation*.[10] Before long he grew exasperated with the free-traders who refused to join him in support of Greeley. He pleaded with Wells: "Don't you 'go and do it,' like the rest of them. If you do I shall tear my hair."[11] Perhaps trying to convince himself that, with Adams, the Liberals would have "been whipped out of our boots," White increasingly stepped up the *Tribune*'s enthusiasm for Greeley.[12]

White had more to do, however, than argue with his old friends. He faced the very practical task of establishing political machinery in Illinois. To offset the liability of Greeley's temperance beliefs among the Germans, White insisted that Gustave Koerner lead the Illinois ticket by running for governor. "The German vote, considerable exasperated by the nomination of Greeley, must be won back," he wrote to William Jayne, "and this is the only way I can now think of to do it." Palmer, White stated flatly, had to step aside.[13] After seeing to that matter, White helped set up a permanent group in Springfield to manage the Illinois effort.[14]

Having rolled up his sleeves and pitched into the battle, White grew even less patient than before with the eastern reformers who were outdoing the Republicans in their criticism of Greeley. He complained to Whitelaw Reid about the "horrid din" in his ears caused by the reformers' criticism.

"I confess I don't understand it," White snapped. "It seems to me that all these Reformers *allege* concerning Greeley could have been proven against Lincoln in 1860." White castigated his erstwhile comrades as " 'doctrinaires' who are not only destitute of political influence but who hold political influence in contempt." Despite their lack of real power, White admitted that the growing outcry had to be stopped before it became unanimous.[15]

The most important leader on the fence was Carl Schurz. If he rejected Greeley, disaster faced the Liberal movement. White knew it and his anxiety grew daily. On May 25, he dashed off a quick plea to Schurz: "Greeley is going to be elected. Let us not by our action, or our inaction, drive him to the embrace of those whose influence we dread." White followed that plea with another the very next day. "A dreadful rumor," he began, "comes to me from Washington which runs something in this wise: That Carl Schurz, having led his young friends up to the cannon's mouth, is about to leave them in the ditch—perhaps to win a victory[,] perhaps to perish without him." "I refuse to believe this dreadful rumor," White declared.[16]

Schurz was under furious pressure. His Missouri associate, Grosvenor, doubled the impact of White's letter. Writing on the same day, he begged Schurz not to desert his loyal friends, simply because the convention did not turn out "just the shape you want." "When Greeley wanted to come to the Convention," Grosvenor reminded Schurz, "you entered no protest—on the contrary, you were anxious to have him come, when I talked of getting along quite as well without him."[17] Poor Schurz! Yet, however bombarded he was by intimates, he refused to climb off the fence.[18] He waited in silence.

Meanwhile the irreconcilable free traders called for a conference at Steinway Hall in New York. At that time they decided on a number of alternatives to supporting Greeley but postponed a final decision until after the Republican convention.[19] In an attempt to avoid a total rupture among the original revenue reformers, White proposed one more meeting among all of them right after the Republican convention. Godkin agreed; they would talk.[20] For a full month after the Cincinnati convention, the battle with Grant seemed almost a minor motif of the Liberal Republican movement.

The Republican convention in Philadelphia finally brought the campaign back into focus. White went to the meeting as he had gone to every national Republican convention since the birth of the party. This time, however, he was an outsider looking on. The Cincinnati convention had shattered the antislavery coalition of the Civil War. Just before the Republicans assembled, Charles Sumner thundered out a long tirade against the party's titular head, U. S. Grant.[21] In response, another of the antislavery giants, William Lloyd Garrison, wrote a public letter castigating his fellow Bostonian. Sumner, deeply disturbed by the rupture in the antislavery ranks, refused even to read Garrison's rebuttal. White, therefore, felt obliged to answer. He replied as "A Western Abolitionist to William Lloyd Garrison."

White's open letter was published in the *Philadelphia Enquirer* on the second day of the Republican convention. He observed, first of all, that Garrison did not deny any of Sumner's criticisms of Grant—the nepotism, the executive aggrandizement, the imperialism. Instead, White noted, Garrison simply said, "What of it?" All of Sumner's criticisms, according to Garrison, were inconsequential in the face of the threat which Greeley's election posed to "impartial freedom." The old abolitionist did not share the Liberals' confidence that a laissez-faire policy would work in the South. The freedmen would need the continued protection of the federal government, and that protection, he felt, would be seriously jeopardized by a defeat of the Republican party. In meeting this position, White resorted to an ad hominem argument; he questioned Garrison's credentials as a critic.

How could he take Greeley to task over the issue of civil rights? Surely "after the year 1854," White maintained, "he was a less conspicuous leader of the antislavery column than Mr. Greeley." Pointing to the fact that Garrison had urged the abandonment of the Anti-Slavery Society because of the fulfillment of its principles, White wondered why Garrison had suddenly found new bogeymen among old antislavery crusaders. "Has the endorsement of the Cincinnati platform by the former opponents of impartial freedom in Tennessee, and New York, and California, so changed the complexion of the battle for impartial freedom, so changed it for the worse," White asked, "that the Anti-Slavery Society ought to reorganize, dust off its old banners, and sound the alarm anew? To my mind, the most hopeful sign of the present day is the disappearance of all organized opposition to impartial freedom."[22]

In his letter to Garrison, White probed the most sensitive issue of the campaign: was "impartial freedom" so secure that Democrats could be entrusted with power in the nation's capital? White may have felt that the Democrats no longer threatened the victories of the war, but not many other Republicans apparently felt the same. Certainly few abolitionists shared his optimism.[23] The nomination of the protectionist Greeley had neutralized the tariff issue and thereby forced the campaign to focus on the Southern question. Whoever had been nominated, however, it was probably inevitable that the issue of reconstruction would take precedence in the political debate. In 1870, White and the revenue reformers had won victories on the tariff and civil-service issues. But after the Ku Klux disorders in 1871, the southern question resumed its former importance. White had taken a bold departure in 1869 and 1870. In 1871, he was isolated and cut off; and in 1872, he suffered the inevitable consequences. The country was not prepared to forget the Civil War.

Still the campaign went on. After Grant's nomination, the

Liberal reformers reopened their bickering. On June 6 invitations were sent out by Henry D. Lloyd for Liberals to attend the conference which White had suggested. They were to meet at the Fifth Avenue Hotel in New York on June 20. Lloyd listed White as one of the sponsors.[24]

The conference proved to be a very delicate matter for White. While he went to Philadelphia and from there to New York, Alfred Cowles began to get nervous in Chicago. White's wife quickly warned him of the danger back home. Cowles, she wrote, was expressing "the most intense dissatisfaction with the 'Weavers' and declared that the *Tribune* should go with a party that was *firm* even if it had to go to Grant."[25] White was caught in the middle. The conference was a necessity if there was to be any harmony among the reformers, but Cowles was losing patience with their faltering. In an attempt to placate Cowles, White forbade Lloyd to use his name on any more invitations for the conference.

While in New York, White also went to see Horace Greeley. Greeley was in a magnanimous mood. Although he treated the politically impotent eastern free-traders with contempt, he could not afford, on the eve of the Fifth Avenue conference, to alienate White, who represented a significant political force.[26] White, therefore, was able to draw several promises from him. Concerned about Greeley's customary lack of discretion, White made him vow not to write any more political letters. Greeley also assured White that he would back civil-service reform as President. Waldo Hutchins, Greeley's confidant, made an even more sweeping guarantee. He gave White and Trumbull a veto on any cabinet appointments under a Greeley administration.[27] White came away flattered and convinced. "He is a sincere man," White told Schurz, "with right instincts upon all moral questions. Indeed I felt some sense of having wronged him in my thoughts."[28]

These reports must have had some impact on Schurz, for when the Fifth Avenue Conference assembled, he urged the conference to back Horace Greeley. Acknowledging that the tariff issue had been obliterated, Schurz instead stressed the promise of sectional reconciliation implicit in Greeley's candidacy. National reunion then would be the theme of the Greeley campaign. So persuasive were Schurz's arguments that a resolution of support for Greeley almost won unanimous support at the conference.[29] Only a handful of irreconcilables bolted this convention. Schurz and the great majority had finally accepted the results of the Cincinnati convention—six weeks after it adjourned.

White was maintaining a frantic pace. Hardly had he returned from one difficulty in New York when he heard of another in Illinois. While the Fifth Avenue Conference was in session, the Illinois Republican State Central Committee had read the *Tribune* out of the party: the committee in an official resolution urged Republicans to subscribe to other loyal papers in Chicago. In anticipation of just such a decision, J. Young Scammon, a wealthy loyalist, revitalized the fire-struck *Chicago Republican*. He rechristened it the *Inter-Ocean* and staffed it with new editors. The subscription-hungry new concern carried the resolution, purging the *Tribune,* on its front page.[30] Such action should have been expected, of course, but Alfred Cowles now grew even less enthusiastic about insurgency. White's nerves, as a result, wore thin.

The tension on the *Tribune* staff became evident when a letter of Greeley's appeared, dated June 11—only a few days after his promise to White to refrain from any more political correspondence. The note itself was harmless. Nonetheless, White exploded. "He had apparently shot an apple off our heads," White admitted to Whitelaw Reid. "But I cannot avoid asking whether he is going to continue shooting. Have we not anxieties enough resting upon us, without this additional and most unnecessary one?" White concluded with a threat: "My wife sails for Europe next month. If I supposed that the business of shooting apples off people's heads was to continue I would certainly go with her and remain until after the election."[31]

White's threat was serious enough. But Reid received a far more ominous note from Alfred Cowles. Cowles seldom wrote letters. He was a businessman, not a politician or an editor. From Cowles's letter, Reid must have received a good picture of the reticent power behind the *Chicago Tribune*:

> Mr. White and myself have put the Chicago *Tribune* earnestly at work in his behalf and are hazarding reputation and money on his election and I have too much at stake to have my interests fooled away. Mr. Greeley was not my preference at Cincinnati and I questioned his ability to make a president, but when I determined to support him I did suppose he had sense enough to "run" and keep his mouth shut. Now I propose to look out for myself, having sacrificed all that I propose to. Mr. Greeley may ruin himself if he wishes to but he can't take me or the Chicago *Tribune* along with him. I have made up my mind to just one thing. It is this. If the Chicago *Tribune* has not a candidate who knows enough to keep his mouth shut, it will find one who has just that amount of sagasity [*sic*]—if nothing more. It can find that man in just twenty four hours and if the name of Horace Greeley appears at the tail end of any other letter between this and the 9th of next November I will swing the Chicago *Tribune* around for Grant so quick that it will make your head swim. You have Mr. Greeley's ear I presume. Do as you please about showing him this.[32]

The campaign was not going well. Each day seemed to bring new complications for the *Tribune* owners. About the first of July, J. Young Scammon and other bankers in Chicago declared that Greeley's well-known insistence on specie resumption spelled disaster for the economy.[33] The *Tribune* appeared particularly pained by criticism from financiers, an interest which they and other revenue reformers had long protected. But rapid deflation was not popular among any western businessmen. It soon became obvious that the *Tribune* had to proceed in the campaign without the support of its usual business allies. Jacksonian threats only magnified the estrangement: "The banks are none to popular now," the *Tribune* noted, "and they should take care that they do not overstep their legitimate functions."[34]

White found little encouragement. The Liberal ticket was being assaulted from every quarter. It was not until the Democrats assembled in Baltimore that he received some ray of hope. Some observers had felt that the nomination of Greeley —an old Democratic nemesis—ended any possibility of cooperation from the Democratic party.[35] Greeley's forces moved deftly, however, and gained enough commitments to swamp the Baltimore convention. Of all people, southerners were the most enthusiastic for the venerable antislavery leader.[36] Of the 732 delegates at the gathering, only 58 dissented from Greeley's nomination on the first ballot, after they had enthusiastically endorsed the platform of the Liberal Republican's Cincinnati convention.

A new optimism flushed through the editorials of the *Tribune*. The editors had waited a long time for some encouragement. "It gives the final blow to the opposition. It gives new impetus to the revolution in popular sentiment."[37] Despite the *Tribune*'s exuberance, there is some question just how much the southern Democrats' enthusiastic embrace of Greeley helped the Liberal Republican cause. The war was too fresh in most memories to accept sectional reconciliation. True, the Democrats agreed to Charles Sumner's Cincinnati plank calling for an acceptance of the postwar amendments.[38] But not many Republicans in the North took that acceptance at face value. White used strained logic to bolster faith in southern promises: "Harmony between the races and the sections," he wrote, "can be had by the election of Horace Greeley. The ex-Rebel elements desire peace, and give a hearty assent to the amendments granting full political equality to their colored neighbors. They are honest and frank in their promise," White insisted. To reinforce his case, White added, southerners "will perform it as faithfully as they performed their promise to rebel in 1860 if Lincoln were elected."[39] White should have known that not many northerners would be comforted by that proof of steadfastness.

The first real test of Liberal strength came in North Carolina where state elections were held on August 2, 1872. Only several days before that election, Sumner finally spoke out in favor of Greeley, advising several Negro correspondents to support the New York journalist. White hoped that the appeal would aid the Liberal cause in North Carolina. He commended the letter to Negroes: "It comes from their best friend," he advised.[40] As returns came in from that state, White broadcast a victory. On August 3 he claimed that the election sounded "the death-knell to the hopes of Grant." For the next two days, conflicting reports began to drift northward. On August 6, 1872, White had to swallow his enthusiasm and contemplate defeat. Confirmation of a Republican victory did not come until August 8. The reversal of the returns in what was a close election brought White all the disappointment of a rout. Worst of all, the Negro vote apparently had turned the tide in the state. Neither the urgings of native Liberals nor the special pleas of Charles Sumner were able to split the Negro vote. This evident solidarity for the Republican party boded ill for the Liberal Republicans in the South—an area where they had hoped to sweep to victory.[41]

For White, the disillusionment ran particularly deep. The election in North Carolina probably marks his complete personal abandonment of the southern Negro. He had held on to threads of his antislavery past until that election, but now there was no reason to placate Sumner any longer, and the Negro seemed to him a threat to reform. White had never clearly articulated his attitudes on race. From the inception of his political maturity, he had found that the cause of black Americans dovetailed with his own concerns. He had resisted the open racism which marked the pronouncements of other Free-Soilers. On occasions, his enthusiasm even matched the idealism of advanced abolitionists. But that enthusiasm began to wane as White's objectives and status changed after the defeat of Andrew Johnson and when it became obvious that Negro votes supported his opponents. Still, he avoided an open appeal to racial inferiority. He usually fell back upon the socioeconomic status of southern blacks to explain his flagging enthusiasm for their continued political power. Defeat at the hands of southern blacks in 1872, however, exposed some racial antipathies.

After the results of the North Carolina election, White wondered publicly in the *Tribune* whether the political power of southern blacks did not pose a "serious menace to Republican institutions." The masses of freedmen, he felt, were "superstitious, ignorant, and brutal, governed only by the lowest instincts, and incapable of comprehending the issues of a political campaign." The large numbers of freed slaves, through the manipulation of "unprincipled men," had brought about "the domination, in a large section, of ignorance and barbarism over intelligence and civilization." This menace, White suggested, obliged "those in the North who have invested those Negroes with such dangerous powers to put them under better influences." The next day the *Tribune* criticized northern Negroes and recommended that the ignorant among them also be disenfranchised. Under heavy criticism, White eventually backtracked from these positions, but his initial remarks after the North Carolina defeat indicated that, already in 1872, he had given second thoughts to his opposition to the policies of Andrew Johnson after the Civil War.[42]

By September, the Liberals were desperate. Henry Watterson urged Greeley to try to turn the scales by taking to the speaker's circuit in the West. Greeley paused, since many—including White—insisted that he remain silent.[43] After consultations, he agreed that something had to be done. He began a long, hard speaking schedule. It seemed that only a miracle could save the Liberals.

On September 6, they thought just that had occurred. The *New York Sun* laid bare the Crédit Mobilier scandal in which many prominent Republicans were involved. The *Chicago Tribune* opened with a barrage of editorials. Listing the names of all the Congressmen involved, White demanded "a general cleaning out of the whole establishment."[44] Even this massive railroad scandal, however, backfired on the Liberals.

The main personalities supposedly involved in the scandal —James G. Blaine, Schuyler Colfax, and James A. Garfield—were men whom White considered the "best remaining representatives of the Republican party." They had not joined enthusiastically in the Republican campaign; they had flirted with the Liberals in the past. Now they fought for their lives. Garfield interrupted his thirty-day junket in the Far West to hurry home to "give what days" he could "to the Republican cause."[56] Blaine also stepped up his involvement in order to clear his name. These men centered their activities in Pennsylvania, Ohio, and Indiana, three "October states" which held their elections a month before the others. Even shrewd politicians like Garfield, however, could not accurately predict the outcome. The campaign had already been so full of surprises that no one knew what to expect. He admitted to himself, "We may lose it."[46] But they did not. The Republicans piled up overwhelming margins in both Pennsylvania and Ohio. The Liberals could salvage only Indiana.

Announcing the defeat was particularly difficult for the *Chicago Tribune* as the day after the election, October 9, had a double meaning. It was also the anniversary of the Chicago fire. To coincide with this date, the *Tribune* managers made a dramatic change in the appearance of their paper.

The issue of October 9 was an elegant quarto sheet, modeled after the *New York Times*. It was the first to be printed on the fire-damaged presses which had recently been returned from New York City after major repairs. The presses were installed, moreover, in a rebuilt and refurbished *Tribune* building.[47] A Greeley victory would have made a fine banner headline for the rebaptized journal. Instead, disaster celebrated disaster.

Whistling in the face of inevitable defeat, the melancholy editorial managed to generate some optimism at its conclusion: "The Liberal party is the party of the Future, notwithstanding the adverse result of yesterday's elections. We shall yield nothing in our zeal for Greeley and Koerner so long as there is a vote to be gained, or an inch of ground to contend for."[48] Public enthusiasm was mandatory since the major part of the national election, in addition to all of the Illinois contests, still had to be waged. Privately, however, White gave up. "Yes, Hiram Ulysses and the whole pack are coming in again," he wrote dejectedly to David A. Wells.[49] Even to Horace Greeley, White confessed his resignation: "We are not disposed to give it up yet, but we may have to, two weeks hence."[50]

With Grant's victory certain, White and other Liberals turned their attention to Illinois in order to salvage something from the campaign. Their chances, at least on the surface, seemed better there. On June 26, the Liberals and Democrats had held separate but concurrent conventions in Springfield. After nominating identical slates, they had concluded the day with a dramatic joint session.[51] The Democratic delegates from Illinois had gone to the Baltimore convention instructed for Greeley, and when the campaign officially had opened the united parties engineered enthusiastic rallies both in Chicago and Springfield.

Behind the scenes, however, the hastily constructed machine

faltered and at times almost broke down. The wealthy indus-
trialist, Cyrus McCormick, who was the Illinois Democratic
party chairman and leading contributor, became miffed at
what he felt were insulting exclusions of his presence. As a
result, he tied up his desperately needed contributions with
difficult qualifications. McCormick demanded that Governor
John Palmer be deposed from the chairmanship of the merged
Liberal-Democratic state central committee and that Palmer's
job be given to him.[52] Ignoring the warnings of White, Trumbull, and Palmer, that Republican votes would be frightened
away by the undue prominence of Democrats on the committee, McCormick argued that since the Democrats would
provide most of the votes and money, they should also manage
the campaign. For over two months the bickering continued.
Finally, on September 8, the Springfield Liberals surrendered.
Governor Palmer and Melville Fuller, the future Supreme
Court Justice, resigned and the headquarters was moved
closer to Chicago, "nearer to the dollars and dimes of McCormick."[53]

Up until that change of leadership, McCormick contributed
only $1,000. The lack of funds seriously hurt the Liberal
cause in Illinois. But when the money finally began to roll
in, it did not make up for the insult and irritation needed
to get it. After McCormick's power play, some of the Liberal
Republicans' most popular orators began to cancel their speaking appointments. Koerner, Palmer, and Black (the candidate
for Lieutenant Governor) either became ill themselves or reported illness in their families. Fusion thus was a failure in
Illinois; cooperation between old political foes proved virtually impossible.[54]

Third-party action, Horace White discovered, was no easy
business. The Liberals went down to a humiliating defeat in
November. The Republican majority, in fact, was the greatest
ever assembled by any party in the state's history. And the

outcome there was repeated in every other state north of Mason's and Dixon's Line. Only a handful of southern and border states went for Greeley.

On the day after the election, White could salvage nothing from the disaster. He could only speculate on the reasons for the overwhelming defeat. "The first thing that occurs to the reflecting mind in reviewing the recent campaign," he began, "is that the business men of the country took an early dislike and almost an alarm at Mr. Greeley's candidacy." "They feared that his election would produce hard times,—that he would do something with the currency,—that he would cause some precipitate action to be taken regarding specie payments. They feared the change."[55]

That was not White's only explanation for the lopsided vote. After the October elections, he admitted that "the cry that the liberties of the blacks are still in danger . . . has been the most potent weapon of the campaign."[56] But he insisted after the final returns that the opposition from businessmen who saw the "spectre of specie resumption" in Greeley's election was "on the whole the most important . . .—at least equal to the solid negro vote which was cast against him, and, perhaps, stronger even than that."[57]

White had anticipated the inevitable. Since the October elections he had been preparing for other contingencies. He wanted to know, for example, how the *New York Tribune* would respond to defeat. Would Greeley and the other owners move back into the Republican party after the November elections? He asked Greeley himself:

> The policy of the N. Y. *Tribune* will be a matter of interest to all of us. We shall go on as we have begun, irrespective of the course of any other paper, but if the N. Y. *Tribune,* through the short sighted views of stockholders who are not editors, should slink back to the Grant party and again become an "organ," our course would be a more difficult one to pursue.[58]

By that time Greeley no longer thought of such matters. Indeed he paid little attention, if any, to the approaching defeat. He faced a greater and more personal tragedy. His wife was dying. Just before the November elections, he stood at her bedside early in the morning darkness and watched her die. He shed no tears at the Liberal Republican defeat. Indeed, he shed no tears at all. "I am not dead," he wrote to a friend, "but I wish I were. My house is desolate, my future dark, my heart a stone. I cannot shed tears; they would bring some relief. Shed tears for me, but do not write again till a better day, which I know will never come."[59] He was right; that day did not come. The next day, he received an overwhelming setback at the hands of former Republican admirers. Before the month ended, the sage of Chappaqua got the relief he had wished; he died. Horace White would have to face the uncertain future without him.

NOTES

1. *Chicago Tribune,* May 4, 1872.

2. Alfred Bishop Mason to White, December 16, 1913, White MSS. Mason, who recalled the scene, was one of the employees in the office when White's telegrams arrived.

James Sheahan came to the *Chicago Tribune* when White took over the editorship in 1865. Before that he had been an editor of several Democratic papers in the city. During the Lincoln-Douglas debates he was an editor of the *Chicago Times,* but he left that paper in 1861 to edit a War Democratic daily. Under White, he specialized in antitariff propaganda.

3. George Merriam, *The Life and Times of Samuel Bowles,* 2:187.

4. Joseph Wall, *Henry Watterson,* pp. 107–109.

5. *Chicago Tribune,* May 7, 1872.

6. *Nation,* May 16, 1872. Wendell P. Garrison to William Lloyd Garrison II, May 4, 1872, Garrison Family Papers, Smith College. Garrison later told his brother-in-law, Henry Villard, then in Europe, of his disappointment with White. He suggested that anticipation of office had moved White to back Greeley. Although Villard agreed that his friend had been a "practical politician . . . all his life," he emphatically con-

tradicted Garrison's insinuations. "Whatever opinions of his course may prevail now, my own is not an admiring one—I feel confident that in case of Greeley's election, the dissolution of existing and formulation of new parties will be assured and lead to such results that White will yet be the object of universal admiration in the U. S. as one of the most far seeing and patriotic of men. For such are the ethics of politics!" Henry Villard to W. P. Garrison, July 11, 1872, Henry Villard MSS.

7. Carl Schurz to Horace Greeley, May 9, 1872, Schurz MSS. David A. Wells to Samuel Bowles, May 10, 1872, Whitelaw Reid MSS. Edward Atkinson to Carl Schurz, May 23, 1872, Schurz MSS.

8. Carl Schurz to Samuel Bowles, May 11, 1872, Schurz MSS.

9. Lyman Trumbull to William C. Bryant, May 10, 1872, William C. Bryant MSS, on microfilm at the New York Public Library. Trumbull took a rather fatalistic view of the outcome: "Having favored the Cincinnati movement and Greeley having rec'd the nomination I see no course left but to try and elect him." See also Charles Nordhoff to Carl Schurz, May 13, 1872, Schurz MSS.

10. *Chicago Tribune*, May 16, 1872. *Nation*, May 16, 23, 1872.

11. White to David A. Wells, May 17, 1872, Wells MSS.

12. Ibid. See also Chicago *Tribune*, May 21, 1872.

13. White to William Jayne, May 14, 1872, William Jayne MSS, Illinois State Historical Library.

14. White to Carl Schurz, May 23, 1872, Schurz MSS. White to Jesse Fell, May 28, 1872, Fell MSS.

15. White to Whitelaw Reid, May 26, 1872, Reid MSS. In the *Tribune,* White questioned the consistency of Stanley Matthews's criticism. "Judge Stanley Matthews, who was present, and who would have seen no objection to the Trumbull men going over to Adams as a body, or the Adams men going over to Trumbull in a body, finds a high moral imperfection in an unsuccessful attempt to transfer the Brown men to Greeley in a body." *Chicago Tribune*, May 27, 1872.

16. White to Schurz, May 25, 26, 1872, Schurz MSS.

17. William Grosvenor to Carl Schurz, May 26, 1872, Schurz MSS.

18. Gustave Koerner to Carl Schurz, May 27, 1872, and Whitelaw Reid to Schurz: Schurz MSS. Rather annoyed by editorials of the *New York Evening Post* inquiring of his position, Schurz wrote the editor, Parke Godwin, that he would not be "smoked out." Schurz admitted that he was looking for an alternative to Greeley but refused to think of Grant as a proper one. Carl Schurz to Parke Godwin, May 28, 1872, Bryant-Godwin Collection, New York Public Library.

19. Earle Ross, *The Liberal Republican Movement*, pp. 110–114. Edward Atkinson stated that his motive in encouraging this convention was to set up a third party to throw the election into the House. He admitted the obvious consequence: "I'm aware that Grant would then be elected, but I prefer Grant to Greeley, and with three parties in the field

we should get a strong Congress." Edward Atkinson to Carl Schurz, June 1, 1872, Schurz MSS.

20. Edwin L. Godkin to Lyman Trumbull, May 29, 1872, Trumbull MSS. Godkin to Carl Schurz, May 29, 1872, Schurz MSS.

21. Charles Sumner, *Works* (Boston, 1875–1883), 15:83–171. *Congressional Globe*, 42nd Cong. 2nd sess., 4110 ff.

22. *Chicago Tribune*, June 8, 1872.

23. Although White and some other abolitionists backed Horace Greeley, "more than three-fourths of the abolitionists favored the reelection of President Grant over his Liberal Republican challenger. James M. McPherson, "Grant or Greeley? The Abolitionist Dilemma in the Election of 1872," *American Historical Review* 71 (October, 1965):43.

24. Carl Schurz, Jacob D. Cox, William C. Bryant, Horace White, Oswald Ottendorfer, David A. Wells, and Jacob Brinkerhoff to Theodore Woolsey, June 6, 1872, Theodore Woolsey MSS.

25. White to Carl Schurz, June 8, 1872, Schurz MSS.

26. Greeley apparently thought that White might get involved in a plot to name another slate of candidates. See Henry Watterson's recollection of his interview with Greeley before the conference. *Chicago Tribune*, December 6, 1872.

27. White to Carl Schurz, June 9, 1872, Schurz MSS.

28. Ibid., June 15, 1872, Schurz MSS.

29. Roeliff Brinkerhoff, *Recollections of a Lifetime*, p. 220.

30. *Chicago Inter-Ocean*, June 21, 1872. The *Inter-Ocean* began on March 25, 1872. Labeling the *Tribune* the "Rebel Organ" and its managers "Benedict Arnolds and Iscariots," the editors of the *Inter-Ocean* relentlessly attacked White's actions and pronouncements. It frequently claimed that its increasing circulation was being taken from the *Tribune,* at one time saying it had as much as one-half of the rival's subscribers. That may have been a bit boastful, but by June (e.g., see issue of June 17, 1872) its advertising had easily doubled. Despite the *Tribune's* successful efforts to deprive the *Inter-Ocean* of press association services, the *Inter-Ocean* survived until the 1930s as an unabashed vehicle of protectionism and the Republican party. See *Chicago Inter-Ocean*, March 25, April 16, May 8, 18, 20, 24, 28, 1872.

31. White to Whitelaw Reid, June 27, 1872, Reid MSS.

32. Alfred Cowles to Whitelaw Reid, June 28, 1872, Reid MSS. White followed this letter with one more of his own. Just before he left for New York to bid farewell to his wife, White requested another conference with Greeley. He made clear what was still on his mind: "One thing is certain I am not going to stand in the range of his fire much longer." White to Whitelaw Reid, July 1, 1872, Reid MSS.

33. *Chicago Tribune*, July 2, 1872. See also *Chicago Inter-Ocean*, July 13, 1872.

34. *Chicago Tribune*, July 1, 1872. Although a few of the Liberal

strategists recommended a Jacksonian response, both the *Chicago Tribune* and Horace Greeley tried to calm businessmen's fears. See Whitelaw Reid to Jay Cooke, June 18, 1872, Reid MSS, and White to David A. Wells, August 26, 1872, Wells MSS.

On the specific issue of specie resumption, both White and Greeley publicly surrendered their positions: "We do not, for our own part, believe that there is any such thing as *growing* to specie-payments, nor do we believe that a continued suspension of specie payments is a good thing for the country. But we recognize the fact that a large majority of the mercantile and financial classes are of the opposite opinion, and we do *not* believe in going any faster in any fiscal policy than public opinion clearly authorizes and justifies. This is substantially what Mr. Greeley said for himself in his Franklin, Indiana speech." *Chicago Tribune,* September 25, 1872.

35. On May 3, 1872, just after Greeley's nomination, James A. Garfield wrote in his diary: "The nomination of Greeley at the Cincinnati Convention was a surprise to Members of the House. It appears tonight to insure a regular democratic nomination." MS diary, James A. Garfield MSS, Library of Congress.

36. See Earle D. Ross, "Horace Greeley and the South, 1865–1872," *South Atlantic Quarterly* 16 (October, 1917):324–328.

37. *Chicago Tribune,* July 11, 1872.

38. Ross, *Liberal Republican Movement,* pp. 115–116.

39. *Chicago Tribune,* August 2, 1872.

40. Whitelaw Reid, reviewing the campaign many years later, concluded that the North Carolina election was the turning point for the Greeley cause. Reid, "Comments," *Century* 85 (November, 1912):44.

41. *Chicago Tribune,* August 1, 1872.

42. Ibid., August 14, 15, 23, 1872.

43. Horace Greeley to Henry Watterson, September 1, 1872, Henry Watterson MSS, Library of Congress.

44. *Chicago Tribune,* September 10, 1872. See also September 9, 12, 17, 18, 24, 26, 27, 28, 30, October 1, 3, 1872.

45. James A. Garfield, MS diary, September 9, 16, 19, 1872, Garfield MSS.

46. Ibid., October 7, 1872.

47. The restored *Tribune* building had an additional story, and all wood, except in window sashes, was replaced by stone and tile. Besides these precautions, the owners this time took out insurance for $100,000. The cost of restoration amounted to $165,000. *Chicago Tribune,* October 9, 1872. White to Henry Villard, November 24, 1872, Henry Villard MSS.

48. *Chicago Tribune,* October 9, 1872. White's pessimism did seep into editorials on subsequent days. See *Chicago Tribune,* October 10, 12, 1872.

49. White to David A. Wells, October 16, 1872, Wells MSS.

50. White to Horace Greeley, October 21, 1872, Reid MSS.

51. Gustave Koerner, *Memoirs of Gustave Koerner,* pp. 560–564. About 600 delegates showed up at each convention. The display of strength,

particularly by the Republicans, encouraged Greeley. He congratulated William Bross: "Your Convention was of great value everywhere, because the wary were saying 'there is no *Republican* strength in the Cincinnati movement.' You answered that cavil." Horace Greeley to William Bross, June 30 1872, William Bross MSS, Chicago Historical Society.

52. In mid-July, the Liberal Republican state committee, headed by Governor John Palmer, met with the Democratic state committee and together they named a bipartisan executive committee to manage the state campaign. White had protested against this degree of fusion but was unable to stop it. See White to E. L. Gross, July 14, 1872, cited by William T. Hutchinson, *Cyrus Hall McCormack* (New York, 1935), 2:320.

53. *Illinois State Journal* (Springfield), September 9, 1872, cited by Hutchinson, *Cyrus H. McCormack,* 2:324.

54. Almost the whole account of Illinois politics is taken from Hutchinson, *Cyrus H. McCormack* 2:315–333.

55. *Chicago Tribune,* November 6, 1872.

56. Ibid., October 9, 1872.

57. Ibid., November 9, 1872. Trying desperately to offset these two forces, Trumbull had descended into an uncustomary demagogic appeal. Giving a speech in Chicago on October 30, he blamed Republican victories in Pennsylvania and Ohio on the "money-power and the colored vote." "Will the intelligent white people of this country consent that this great Republic, the hope of freedom throughout the world, shall fall under the control of the colored race, banded together as one man to hold the balance of power? . . . if you would surrender the Government of your country to those who owe their positions to the money-power and the combined negro element, then vote for General Grant." *Chicago Tribune,* October 31, 1872.

58. White to Horace Greeley, October 21, 1872, Reid MSS. For an examination of the internal problems of the *New York Tribune* at this time see Glyndon G. Van Deusen, *Horace Greeley* (Philadelphia, 1953), pp. 421–424.

59. Horace Greeley to Mrs. Margaret Allen, November 4, 1872, Horace Greeley MSS, Library of Congress.

12

Disillusionment

Not many were willing to face the future with Horace White. His reputation for political effectiveness came crashing down after the fall elections of 1872. Old associates mocked the "Chicago *Tribune*'s Influence," and erstwhile friends in the East savored the vindication of their judgment.[1] The *Nation* could not resist reminding White and others of their mistakes: "The knowing men who palmed off Horace Greeley on the Cincinnati Convention as 'truly popular,' even if nothing else, must surely long for a 'lodge in some vast wilderness.' "[2] Godkin was probably right. Indeed, afer the October state elections, White had told Wells he would like to go to Europe with him in order to avoid facing the inevitable disaster.[3] But White had to remain in Chicago; he still had too much at stake to run away. Right after the final defeat, he began to organize for a political comeback.

To reconcile the revenue reformers thrown apart by Greeley's nomination, White tried to arrange a meeting of "the old set." But Godkin flatly rejected any immediate rapprochement. "I don't see that we could come to any conclusion about the future," the editor of the *Nation* responded.

"The result of the Cincinnati movement has been so unfortunate, that there is at present a slight odor of ridicule hanging around everybody who had anything to do with getting it up. In short, the field is still covered with smoke, the dead unburied, the wounded to be cared for." Any reconciliation, Godkin concluded, would have to wait for a later time.[4]

Actually, White was unable to give much time to these political plans, since other matters quickly demanded his full attention. In some ways the diversion was fortunate. A huge fire in Boston on November 9, for instance, allowed the *Tribune* to turn away from its political critics and stir the feelings of Chicagoans who remembered their own conflagration. Thousands of people in other cities joined with Chicagoans in sending aid and relief. This national outpouring went beyond mere sympathy. The financial failures due to the fire in Boston caused real concern about the economic condition of the whole nation. Signs of a depression had been accumulating. Already during the campaign, businessmen had voiced their fears about tight credit and falling prices. How the Boston disaster would affect the nation's already fragile economy was of far greater importance to many than how Greeley's defeat would alter the pattern of national politics.

White sensed an economic disaster about the same time that he acknowledged Greeley's defeat. When he wrote David A. Wells of his wish to go to Europe to join his wife, he conjectured that a financial crash might come and "use me up." "Money," he complained, "is damnably tight here just now."[5] White had reason to worry about "tight money." Since he and Cowles had failed to secure insurance on the fire-ravaged *Tribune* building, they had to bear the total cost of repairs—a sum amounting to more than $165,000. To meet these obligations, the owners needed credit. They were able to obtain most of it, but in late October, 1872, they still needed $60,000. White found it almost impossible to secure the necessary loan from American sources, even at 10 percent interest. In desperation at one point, he wrote to his friend, Henry Villard, who was then beginning his financial wizardry in Germany.[6] Villard responded but confessed his helplessness. Economic conditions were no better in England or Germany than they were in the United States.[7]

The condition of the *Tribune* itself was excellent. Although circulation had decreased after the Cincinnati convention, it picked up again and climbed steadily after the appearance of the new format in October. White could soon boast that the paper had not lost a cent as a result of its political adventure. The hard times lessened commercial advertising slightly, but other advertising remained about the same.[8] Nevertheless, despite the paper's sound condition, White still had great difficulty securing reasonable credit. His stock in the corporation was not enough to induce a loan from the banks. "The fact is," White wrote Villard, "that the richest man in Chicago, (and in New York too), can scarcely borrow a dollar on commercial paper." Though White must have remembered the problems he once faced in raising money for his Kansas speculations in 1857, he observed that the winter of 1872 was "the worst time in that regard that I have ever known anything about."[9] White finally got his loans, but his troubles had only begun.

On January 14, 1873, White received a short European cablegram: Martha, his wife, had died. He was totally unprepared for this terrible blow. During the presidential campaign, he had sent her to Wuerzburg, Germany, to be treated by a European specialist for undiagnosed hemorrhaging. Her twice-weekly letters had left him with the comforting assurance that she was steadily improving, and these reports were reinforced by encouraging correspondence from Henry Villard and his wife who were staying nearby at Heidelberg. Mrs. White had persuaded them and other friends who knew her real condition to keep the truth from her husband. Remaining childless, she had always treated White with devoted selflessness. She thought that her ill health would only add to his political and financial troubles. When she lapsed into delirium, Fanny Villard finally broke her promise and told White "the harsh news" that he would probably never see his wife again. Fanny and her husband, who had to get up from his own sick bed, had gone to Wuerzburg to attend their dying friend. Before Fanny's letter reached White, however, the cablegram arrived announcing Martha's death.[10]

White could now appreciate Horace Greeley's grief. Political defeat and financial insecurity provided no comparable pain. White's plea, "God grant that I may soon follow her," echoed the pathetic wish of Greeley after the death of his wife.[11] In order to assuage his grief, White's friends pushed him away from his duties in Chicago and urged him to find a change of scene before his wife's coffin crossed the ocean. White followed their advice and sought escape in New Orleans but found no peace. Closeting himself, he penned a husband's confession of guilt. His busy public career had left him little time to share with her, he now wrote. He had been annoyed by her demands on his time and had failed to appreciate her daily affection. To remind himself forever of his present sorrow, he detailed his reaction to her demise, recalling his suicidal impulses and his feeling of imminent insanity. He searched for the meaning of existence and discovered that "the acme of all life is death." With his Calvinistic background, he managed to assure himself that there was a purpose in life: "To dispel ignorance, mental and moral, our own and others, is the highest labor we can put out hands to."[12]

After the funeral, White threw himself back into his work. With the dead buried, the wounded apparently cared for, and the field beginning to clear, he searched for a course of political recovery for the *Chicago Tribune.* Cowles and Bross left him a free hand. The three owners had agreed before Greeley's defeat that they would not seek reconciliation with the Republican party. Though some of the Liberal leaders, like John Palmer, drifted into the Democratic party, the *Tribune* proprietors gave no consideration to that alternative. None of them wanted to be "strapped down to a party organ-ship."[13] The *Tribune* declared: "The Liberal party must stand on its own bottom. There must be no partnerships; it must do business in its own name. If its principles are not sufficiently attractive to command a following it had better not attempt to be a party. If the Republican and Democratic parties are to continue, a new party can have no more affilia-tion with the one than the other."[14]

The course that White charted was reasonable enough. In the West, portents of political fragmentation were in the air. Farmers, alarmed by falling prices and rising costs, were shak-ing off their political apathy and beginning to make serious demands of their Congressmen and state legislators. Their resentment focused on the railroad corporations, which they felt were charging discriminatory freight rates. In taking advantage of this radical sentiment, White knew that he would be treading on dangerous ground. He condemned the "reckless legislation and revolutionary proceedings" of some agrarian spokesmen but at the same time maintained that the farmers' movement was "one of the most hopeful signs of the times, since it foreshadows an emancipation of the public mind from the tyranny of old party trammels, and the concentration of ideas upon new questions relating to the immediate wants of society."[15]

The *Tribune* became a cautious patron of the new move-ment. On the one hand, it warned farmers to discard their "hallucination" that "the State owns all railroads, and can, therefore, through its Legislature, fix the rates of freight and fare on them without consulting the real owners."[16] On the other hand, it warned the railroad owners to look at the "handwriting on the wall": "The demagogues are simply taking advantage of a deep-rooted conviction on the part of the people that they have been swindled."[17] Despite the

Tribune's usually conciliatory tone, it frequently echoed the farmers' radical rhetoric.[18]

White frankly admitted that he hoped to use the widespread rural resentment as a lever for his own political designs. The farmers, he felt, agreed with him that there was something more important than "the fight over the dead corpse of slavery." He insisted that they no longer cared "a fig for the Republican party and that their condemnation of railroad monopoly embraced the Liberal fight against governmental tariffs, subsidies, pay raises, and corruption."[19] White's decision to support and utilize the farmers' movement was a bold maneuver among Liberal journalists. He sent reporters scurrying all over the Midwest to report on rural resentment. The careful coverage was unique; no other major metropolitan paper exerted such an effort. The farmers recognized the unusual publicity and frequently expressed their gratitude. When the Illinois Grangers met in Bloomington, they presented a certificate to the *Tribune* as "the only paper that has the news."[20]

While White's sympathetic approach to the Granger movement won new support for the *Tribune* among western farmers, it enraged his old eastern associates. His action, in fact, precluded any chance for a reconciliation among the Liberal reformers. When Charles Francis Adams, Jr., attempted to call a conference of the Liberal leaders to take advantage of Republican setbacks in the fall elections of 1873, he received a cold shoulder from both White and E. L. Godkin. As a result, the meeting never materialized.[21] The two editors had taken opposite sides on the farmers' revolt, and for months they maintained a public controversy over the rural protest movement. When, for example, the *Tribune* endorsed a Granger demand for legislation to halt the "watering" of stock, the *Nation* exploded: "The application of any such rule now to roads already in operation would be spoliation pure and simple—spoliation as flagrant as any

ever proposed by Karl Marx." Those were strong words in
the Liberal camp.

White soon discovered that Godkin was right. In the spring
and summer of 1873, White had been playing with social
forces that he was unprepared to cope with. His political
expediency was quickly exposed, as the plight of the farmers
extended to other sectors of the economy in the fall of 1873.

White at first ignored the signs of economic collapse. When
Jay Cooke's firm climaxed a series of bank failures, the
Tribune scoffed at the fear of "any serious disturbance in
the business of the country." "The stringency of last autumn
and winter," the editor explained, "led to a vast curtailment
of liabilities. People have since then set their houses in order.
There is nothing to make a general panic out of."[22] But Jay
Cooke's failure did not conclude a mere "smashing of crockery
in Wall street." It signaled the beginning of a serious panic
which soon spread across the country.

As he became aware of the impending disaster, White suddenly turned on his favorites. The farmers' feud with the railroads, he now insisted, was responsible for the financial crisis.
Though still accusing the railroads of indifference to popular
feeling, he laid most of the blame upon the farmers. Their
program, he declared, "has been translated in Europe as a
communistic war upon vested rights and property." As a
result, American railroad bonds became a drug on the market.
"To wage war upon this vast property in a manner calculated
irreparably to damage it," White concluded, "was certainly
ill-advised, and must return upon the promoters of the hostility."[23] Chuckling over White's reversal, Godkin reminded
the Chicago editor of the encouragement he had given to the
movement he was now condemning: "When a public counsel-
lor in one mouth loudly demands confiscation, and the next
refers to its own demand as the hoarse cry of a demagogue,"
Godkin declared, "we can hardly wonder at the wild language
of those whom he advises."[24]

No more agrarian rhetoric appeared in the *Tribune* after the antimonopoly sentiment took on new meaning. The cry against corporations was no longer relevant to rural resentment only. In Chicago and in other cities, unemployed workers also took up the cry. When thousands of laborers, most of them recent immigrants, marched down Chicago streets demanding bread and public work, the *Tribune* indicated White's shock. The demands of these men, an editorial noted, "came upon the American portion of the population like lightning from a clear sky." "The denunciation of the rich and of the middle class of citizens was simply absurd. We have no privileged class in this country," the editor insisted.[25] Some of the speeches, he claimed, read like the "harangues that incited the Parisians of 1793."

As the weeks passed, bringing further demonstrations and protest, White wrote increasingly hysterical editorials. He branded demands of the workers as un-American and hinted that "the movements taking place in America are directed from Europe."[26] "We must no longer close our eyes to the dangers the International threatens," White cautioned. "In the United States the movement is heard like rumblings of a subterranean fire, warning the people of the danger of an irruption. The warning must not go unheeded. . . . Communism is constantly gaining organization, and has all the desperation of those who have nothing to lose and everything to gain. It is time that every State in the Union should go earnestly to work to prepare for the onset of the followers of Karl Marx, for they mean business,—not in Paris and Berlin merely, but in New York and Chicago."[27] Chicago was in the midst of a Red Scare—its first.

In later editorials White speculated that perhaps traditional American liberties might have to be altered in order to meet the challenge. Immigration might also have to be restricted. Better to act immediately, the *Tribune* warned, than "wait for some overt act on their part." "They may love American independence and the Stars and Stripes well; but they love the International and the red flag better."[28]

White soon used the same strong language indiscriminately in condemning not only foreign socialists but also labor unions and farm organizations. As strikes spread, he insisted, "The doctrine of the right to employment is the negation of property." As the associations of farmers and workers focused their discontent into a political demand for more greenbacks, he asked: "Can the Commune devise a more effective means for a redistribution of wealth than depreciated legal-tender units?" He was especially disturbed by the farmers' demand for greenbacks, since he had depended on the farmers to initiate a new political departure. Unable to support their protest after the onset of the depression, he confessed that the farmers' movement had "disappointed its best friends."[29]

The currency question had taken on exceptional importance for White. If it became an unreasonable cure-all for some reformers, it became an exaggerated bogey for men like White. Privately and publicly he expressed his fear that the "inflators" were "a numerical majority of this country."[30] That realization drove him into disillusionment with democracy itself. One *Tribune* editorial, for instance, observed that in their growing demand for greenbacks, the people were "demonstrating their incapacity to rule." Although gratified, White was quite surprised when Grant vetoed the bill to introduce more greenbacks into circulation.[31] He recognized that Grant's decision was unpopular; the veto did little therefore to abate his disillusionment with democratic government. "Universal suffrage has cheapened the ballot," White insisted. It has "taught ignorance that the franchise belonged to a man of right, was his property, instead of a trust committed to him by the State to be used for the State's benefit." Such a belief, the editor continued, "has nearly resulted already, and may yet result, in fastening the curse and crime of inflation upon the country. It has well-nigh destroyed American statesmanship."[32]

White's disillusionment with universal suffrage had been developing for some time. The popular support for inflation only brought his grievances into full expression. Although Republican support in the South for the inflation measures further convinced him of his earlier disenchantment with reconstruction measures,[33] his antidemocratic criticism was not limited to black voters. It was a worldwide concern. Havoc in France in the early 1870s led him to praise the good sense of the reactionary government which took charge and reversed democratic procedures. But it was chiefly in American cities that White found the clearest evidence of the failure of universal suffrage. "It seems to be the rule, in politics as in currency," White noted, "that the worse drives out the better. When the suffrage is universal, the worst classes will be represented in the city governments." However desirable reversals in universal suffrage appeared to him, White thought such action in the United States quite impossible. His solution was compulsory education and stronger law enforcement. The choice for him was simple: "Without universal education to prevent it, and without a militia to crush it, every large city lies at the mercy of a mob."[34]

White's intellectual dilemma had become acute. He found it difficult to identify with popular sentiment in America. This same crisis of thought faced other Liberal intellectuals. He was not alone. But as an editor, his problem was probably more painful than that faced by others. What role was the *Tribune* now to play? The newspaper needed popular support: it was not a low-budget journal of opinion; it was a commercial daily. White had rejected commitment to either of the major political parties and, after the outset of the depression, he could no longer support the rural protest movement. Subscriptions therefore declined at the same time that advertising revenues fell off as a result of the depression. A dispute with local Protestant ministers in the summer of 1874 only added to the *Tribune*'s difficulties.[35]

Alfred Cowles was naturally disturbed. In June, he began to send feelers to Medill, who was traveling in Europe. Through a "mutual friend" he informed Medill that possibly he could purchase a controlling interest in the *Tribune*.[36] At first, Medill hesitated to take the opportunity. He warned Cowles that "the damage had already been done, the usefulness and influence of the paper greatly impaired." As a consequence, he himself "would rather sell than bog in deeper." Communicating once more through a mutual friend, Cowles urged Medill to return home either to buy or to sell, in order to end the dissension among the paper's owners. Medill knew that he had the advantage now. Just before he embarked for the United States, he explained to Washburne: "I don't think that Cowles is serious in saying he will buy my stock if I don't purchase his. He wants to sell me a control. He wants me to take charge and restore the *Tribune* to its old relations with the Rep. party, and White is to step out—go abroad for a year or two. Cowles pocket nerve has been touched."[37]

When Medill returned to Chicago, he found that he had somewhat misjudged the relationship between Cowles and White. Although Cowles had insisted on a change in the management, he did not intend to do anything behind White's back. Indeed, he joined hands with White in the financial negotiations. The two men turned down Medill's first offer of $264,000 for 60 shares, which would have given him 107 out of a total of 200. White and Cowles demanded that Medill take all their 101 shares at half a million dollars. Finally, the parties all agreed to Medill's new offer of $300,000 for sixty shares. "I have 'met the enemy and they are ours,'" Medill gleefully wrote Washburne on November 1. "On the 9th inst. White retires and on that day, one Medill resumes his old 'throne and sceptre' in the Tribune 'kingdom.'"[38]

An era in the *Tribune*'s history was ending, an era in which White had brought the paper to maturity. Despite its political isolation, the *Tribune* had become one of the most important papers in America by the end of his nine-year term as editor-in-chief. Even Godkin, despite his recent battles with White, admitted that "Mr. White's management of the paper raised it to the highest rank of journalism, in the best sense of the term."[39] White's departure, coinciding as it did with Carl Schurz's political defeat in Missouri, silenced the main outposts of the Liberal reformers in the Midwest. On November 9, Joseph Medill announced: "The *Tribune* will be conducted as a Republican journal."[40]

White was probably relieved to cast off the burdens of the *Tribune* editorship. The daily routine of journalism had lost its appeal, and more enjoyable pursuits beckoned. Shortly after his retirement he married a beautiful young girl, Amelia McDougall, who was still in her twenties. They planned a honeymoon in Europe. In the midst of the depression, he had suddenly become a very wealthy man. At the age of forty, he looked forward to a life of leisure and financial independence. In the next several years, he received two flattering offers from Edwin L. Godkin to buy out the *Nation*, one from Henry Adams to edit a Boston daily, and another from Parke Godwin to purchase William Cullen Bryant's interest in the *New York Evening Post*. White turned them all down. "I suppose the Boston gentlemen . . . suggested me for the place because I had had so much experience," he explained to Carl Schurz. "I declined it for the same reason."[41] To Godkin, White confessed that even the weekly *Nation* looked like a "close anchorage." "I shrink from the confinement which it seems to imply."[42]

White made the most of his freedom. Within two months after his resignation, he was married and on a steamer for Europe, beginning a year-long tour of England and the Continent. This was his first trip across the ocean, and he planned to make the most of it. His travels made a profound impression upon him. Two months in Rome increased his dislike of Catholicism. "Before I came over here," White wrote Samuel Bowles, "I did not exactly sympathize with Bismark [*sic*] in his fight with the institution, but I do now."[43] European civil service systems, on the other hand, excited his admiration, particularly as he received the news of major scandals in Grant's second administration. "I find myself taking a rather gloomy view of our experiment of government," he wrote Carl Schurz, who had also sought respite in Europe after his own retirement from political warfare. "Frauds here, there and everywhere seem to be cropping out," White continued. "Our present constitution is a rope of sand. Anything may be done under it except punishing a culprit in office. I am not sure but the best thing that could happen would be to call a national convention and abolish it altogether and adopt something equivalent to the English system of governing the country by one legislative body."[44]

Of all European institutions, those of England made the most favorable impression upon White. Although the Liberal party in Britain had recently lost the national elections, politics and society had not witnessed the stress there which White had experienced in the United States. British Liberals, whom White had always admired, still retained their traditional following. The thrust of popular Radicalism lasted longer in Britain than it did in the United States. Gladstone remained a champion; and advanced Liberal forces, under the lead of such industrialists as Joseph Chamberlain, were refreshing the party's alliance of capitalists, shopkeepers, and important sections of the working class. Their longstanding enemy, the "titled and proprietary classes," still loomed as a target for further social reform.

The enemy in the United States, however, had lost its sinister appearance for many in the North. The southern slaveholding oligarchy which had once welded a growing political

force against them in the United States no longer appeared
to pose a significant threat to northern interests. White and
other American Liberals had tried to keep the Radical alliance together on other issues in the 1870s, but they failed.
Industrialists in America did all not have the same faith in
free trade as their British counterparts. Laborers and farmers,
moreover, saw the Republican prosperity vanish in the depression. Their subsequent questioning found no answers in
Liberal credos, and their angry political responses only drove
Liberals such as White into open opposition.

Doubtless, racial antipathies also made it impossible for anyone to keep alive the specter of the Southern oligarchy as a
force of unity within the old Radical coalition. English Radicals faced no similar racial problem in attacking their "land-
lords." They also did not operate within the same political
framework. The Liberal party had never opened political
leadership to the lower classes through spoils politics. Rigid
civil service requirements demanded significant education for
admission to the British bureaucracy, and that education was
hard to obtain outside of the exclusive and expensive Oxford
and Cambridge universities. The upper classes thus retained
a firm grip on the governmental establishment. Since suffrage
had not been extended to agricultural laborers or all of the
industrial workers, the British Liberal elite were also shielded
in the 1870s from the political forces that had been fully
unleashed by the American Radicals in 1867. When the Liberals in Great Britain finally pursued popular Radicalism to
its ultimate conclusion in 1885 by passing universal manhood
suffrage, they too, soon followed their American counterparts
into political impotence and futility.[45]

During White's visit in 1875, however, the Liberal party
was still a major power in Great Britain. To him the people
of England seemed to have made the correct decisions on "all
its great questions." He noted: "England has representative
government, free trade, a sound currency, and light taxation."

He found social misery in London during his tours of that city's slums but concluded that "a good degree of contentment pervades all classes—higher . . . than the United States can claim at the present time." He also recognized that there was land monopoly in England but concluded that it was "not an economic evil, unless we are prepared to admit that a perfectly natural and unconstrained course of trade is an evil —which no economist can allow." England's lack of universal suffrage no longer disturbed him as it had less than a decade ago. He now felt compelled to observe that England's "rule of expedience" was superior to America's "doctrine of abstract rights." "That it would have been better for us in America, especially in the large cities, if some such test had been adopted and adhered to, in place of universal suffrage," White told his English readers, "is the opinion of nearly all who have either education or property." The comparative results in government, White felt, proved his contention. "The English civil service . . . is a text upon which any American who has had to do with public affairs may preach a long sermon to his own countrymen." His praise was glowing: "I count it among the greatest advantages an American can derive from a visit to England, that he has the opportunity to put the two systems side by side, and to learn the detestable vices of his own by comparing it with yours [England's]."[46]

White could not give enough praise to European systems of civil service. The confidence which they imparted, he was convinced, made even government management of railway and telegraph companies practical. Such economic reforms would be impossible in America. "In our country," he responded to a direct inquiry, "I am satisfied that government meddling with either would only aggravate existing evils, of which I hear enough every day to almost make me ashamed of my native country."[47] As White returned to the United States, which was then celebrating one hundred years of independence, he apparently harbored doubts about the wisdom of withdrawal from the British Empire.

After the conclusion of his European sojourn, White tried for several months to continue writing for the *Chicago Tribune* but found his task impossible under Medill's dictation. Doubtless, that discovery was inevitable. He therefore put his house in order and left Chicago, where he had lived for over two decades, to take up permanent residence in New York City. In doing so, he closed an important chapter of his life.

Twenty-three years ago, he had come to Chicago determined to join the antislavery crusade. Into the next two decades, he had crowded more adventures than most men generally experience in a lifetime. He had taken part in such crucial events as the struggle for Kansas, the Lincoln-Douglas debates, and the Republican victory in 1860. He could claim as friends antislavery giants like Abraham Lincoln, John Brown, and Charles Sumner. After the Civil War he also played a major role in advancing the cause of the freedmen. When he insisted, however, that the Fifteenth Amendment had brought the antislavery struggle to a fitting conclusion, many Republicans and virtually all the former slaves disagreed. When the bulk of the Republican party refused to deal with other issues, White grew discouraged. When they crushed his attempt at a new political departure, he decided that the antislavery crusade had ended in failure.

His disappointments did not stop there. The centennial year found him deeply disillusioned. He was questioning not only the experiment of Negro suffrage but also democracy itself. The widespread corruption, social violence, and irrationality seemed to him the inevitable consequences of giving power to the urban and rural masses. America no longer looked as promising as it had when he arrived in Chicago in 1853. Now, in 1876, Horace White closed one part of his life and, by moving to New York City, opened another.

NOTES

1. *Chicago Inter-Ocean,* November 7, 1872.

2. *Nation,* November 7, 1872.

3. White to Wells, October 16, 1872, Wells MSS.

4. Edwin L. Godkin to White, November 1, 1872, Schurz MSS.

5. White to David A. Wells, October 16, 1872, Wells MSS.

6. White to Henry Villard, October 21, 1872, Henry Villard MSS.

7. Henry Villard to White, November 4, 1872, Henry Villard MSS. Villard described his own financial difficulties: "To give you an idea of the present dearness of money over here let me tell you that I obtained a loan of a million of a Berlin Bank for an American R.R. Co. in the early part of October at the rate of about 16% interest, the bank not being at all anxious to lend at that."

8. Martha White to Fanny Villard, November 12, 1872, Fanny Villard MSS, Harvard University. White to Henry Villard November 24, 1872, Henry Villard MSS. White to Horace Greeley, October 21, 1872, Reid MSS.

9. White to Henry Villard, November 24, 1872, Henry Villard MSS.

10. Fanny Villard to Helen E. Garrison, January 15, 1873, Fanny Villard MSS. See also *Memorial of Martha H. White* (Chicago, 1873), pp. 3, 13. The letter from Fanny Villard to White, January 10, 1873 is quoted in the memorial, pp. 3–5.

11. White to Henry Villard, January 23, 1873, Henry Villard MSS.

12. Excerpts of his long discourse were reprinted in the *Memorial of Martha H. White,* pp. 20–35.

13. White to Horace Greeley, October 21, 1872, Reid MSS.

14. *Chicago Tribune,* February 26, 873. White later defended this statement against Democratic criticism: "The folly of a double organization, working under all sorts of leaders, without a common agreement, and with the ideas of the old parties still clinging to them, cannot again be repeated." Ibid., March 10, 1873.

15. Ibid., March 3, 1873.

16. Ibid., March 11, 1873. "Take away the railroads," the *Tribune* warned, "and the business of the West would come to a standstill." Ibid., April 21, 1873.

17. Ibid., March 24, 1873.

18. "Corporations have overrun the country; have seized State and municipal governments; have placed whole counties, towns, and states under long mortgages to build their railroads; have stolen the proceeds of the bonds, and, while the white people of the country have been deluded with an imaginary battle to maintain the freedom of the blacks, they have themselves been delivered into a bondage that will grind them to death if they do not rise against it and throw it off." Ibid., April 7, 1873.

19. Ibid., July 10, 1873. See also May 24 and September 4, 1873.

20. Ibid., December 14, 1873. Solon Buck, the leading historian of the Granger movement, listed the *Tribune* (while it remained under White's direction) as one of the best sources for the political activities of Midwestern farmers in the 1870s. Solon Buck, *The Granger Movement* (Cambridge, Mass., 1913), pp. 288, 322.

21. C. F. Adams, Jr., to David A Wells, November 13, 1873, Wells Coll. C. F. Adams, Jr., to Carl Schurz, November 13, 30; and E. L. Godkin to Carl Schurz, December 5, 1873: Schurz MSS. "One of my objects," Adams wrote Schurz, "was to bring White and Godkin together again. . . . The failure of this part of my plan affects the whole of it." C. F. Adams, Jr., to Carl Schurz, December 22, 1873, Schurz MSS. See also Schurz's reply. Carl Schurz to C. F. Adams, Jr., December 25, 1873, Schurz MSS.

22. *Chicago Tribune*, September 19, 1873.

23. Ibid., September 26, 1873.

24. *Nation*, October 2, 1873.

25. *Chicago Tribune*, December 23, 1873.

26. Ibid., January 2, 1874, December 23, 25, 1873.

27. Ibid., January 5, 1874. See also January 10, 20, 1874.

28. Ibid., February 7, 1874. "This city has very many unemployed men today. . . . Under these circumstances, any increase in the number is a matter of lively concern. It means enforced idleness for some, more paupers, discontent, mutterings of communism, perhaps communism itself. There is a great danger to our system of government in the formation of large classes of the very poor. Such classes made Tweed a possibility. Such classes keep Butler in his seat. . . . Tweed, Butler, Rings,— these are the dangers to the Republic. . . . The foreign element, then, and the least Americanized part of it, is the most apt to be out of work. It greedily listens to the harangues of demagogues. It has come to this as a land of liberty, and to its untutored sense, liberty and license are much the same. Here is the danger. It will be wise for us to cooperate heartily in the efforts now being made by Germany and Great Britain to check the flow of immigration hither." Ibid., April 20, 1874.

29. Ibid., January 2, April 9, August 11, 1874.

30. Horace White to Herman Raster, March 31, 1874, Herman Raster MSS, Newberry Library, Chicago, Illinois.

31. *Chicago Tribune*, April 9, 1874. See also April 18, 1874. On April 13, 1874, the *Tribune* predicted Grant's approval of the bill. On April 23, the paper announced the veto and offered "high commendation."

32. Ibid., May 18, 1874. See also the editorial in the issue of April 25, 1874.

33. In analyzing the Senate vote for the release of more greenbacks into the national currency, the *Tribune* found that a majority of the senators came from the "Africanized States." This vote, an editorial insisted, proved that Negro suffrage hurt not only the South but also the whole nation. "The Republican party of the North," the editorial explained,

"is practically controlled by the Africanized States. The industry and production, the capital and wealth of the nation, have been put in peril to
satisfy the demands of the bankrupt and impoverished people of the
South, who, having wasted their capital and destroyed all their credit,
look to an issue of worthless paper to supply the need of both." Ibid.,
April 8, 1874.

34. Ibid., April 9, 18, 25, May 18, 1874.

35. Henry D. Lloyd, whom White hired in 1872 and later promoted to
literary editor, offended certain clergy in the city with his choice of topics
and reviews. The *Tribune's* scooping exposé of the Reverend Henry Ward
Beecher's extramarital affairs increased the hostility of the ministers in the
city. George A. Townsend, the paper's crack correspondent, broke the
story while White was on his summer vacation. Nevertheless, release of
the scandal hastened White's deteriorating position. Chester Destler,
Henry Demarest Lloyd and the Empire of Reform, pp. 86–89. See also
White to Whitelaw Reid, August 26, 1874, Reid MSS.

36. Joseph Medill to Elihu Washburne, September 25, 1874, Washburne
MSS. Washburne was in Paris as ambassador to France.

37. Ibid.

38. Ibid., November 1, 1874, Washburne MSS. White sold 14 shares and
Cowles, 45. See the *New York Tribune*, October 31, 1874. Whether White
knew of Cowles's indirect negotiations with Medill in the summer is
unclear. But there seems to have been continued rapport between White
and Cowles. When the A. P. announcement of the sale left the impression
that he had been forced out, White corrected the chief of the Associated
Press, William Henry Smith: "I don't care to have any correction made
of it, but I desire you to know that it was on my motion rather than
Mr. Cowles's that the trade was consummated. . . . I advised acceptance
of this proposition. This is the straight history of the transaction." White
to William Henry Smith, November 3, 1874, William Henry Smith MSS,
Ohio Historical Society. White gave a similar explanation to James
Blaine. See White to James Blaine, November 17, 1874, James Blaine MSS,
Library of Congress.

39. *Nation*, November 5, 1874. Until the panic, the *Tribune*, under
White's management, had produced an average yearly profit of $153,000.
See *New York Tribune*, October 31, 1874.

40. *Chicago Tribune*, November 9, 1874. Medill had boastfully anticipated his impact on the *Tribune's* fortunes, but his vows lost their force
after he spent six months at the helm. He expressed his disappointment
to Elihu Washburne: "It was not until after I had been at home several
months that I fully comprehended the extent and depth of the injury
inflicted on the business of this city and surrounding country by the
panic of 1873. . . . I slowly awakened to a painfully realizing sense of
the fact that I had paid too much for my stock—that I had gone too
deeply in debt, that the former rate of profits could not by any human
efforts be restored, chiefly because the advertising business had dropped

off and could not be gained back until there was a revival of trade, commerce, and speculation. The panic following the fire had left this city
in a sad plight. . . . So you may imagine I felt a little blue." Joseph
Medill to Elihu Washburne, June 5, 1875, Washburne MSS.

41. White to Carl Schurz, March 10, 1876, Schurz MSS. See also Henry
Villard to White, February 26, 1876, Henry Villard MSS. The offer to
edit the *Post* came about the same time. White to Samuel Bowles, February 18, 1876, Bowles MSS.

42. White to Edwin L. Godkin, October 3, 1878, typed copy in the
Horace White Family Papers. Information concerning an earlier offer for
White to edit the *Nation* can be found in a letter from White to William
Henry Smith, October 3, 1878, Smith MSS. The ideological and political
debates between the two men did not seem to hurt their personal relations. In his letter to Godkin, White referred to a $6,000 loan which he
had made to the New York editor.

43. White to Samuel Bowles, April 13, 1875, Bowles MSS.

44. White to Carl Schurz, August 21, 1875, Schurz MSS.

45. Although abundant, the general literature on British Liberal
thought and politics is not altogether satisfactory. W. Lyon Blease, *A
Short History of English Liberalism* (London: T. F. Unwin, 1913) is still
useful and *The Liberal Tradition* (London: A. & C. Black, Ltd., 1956),
edited by Alan Bullock and Maurice Shock, provides valuable insights.
Among the many other important works are G. Kitson Clark, *The Mak-
ing of Victorian England* (Cambridge, Mass.: Harvard University Press,
1962); Keith Hutchinson, *The Decline and Fall of British Capitalism*
(New York: Charles Scribner's Sons, 1950); H. J. Hanham, *Elections and
Party Management* (London: Longmans Green & Co., Ltd., 1959); and J.
L. Garvin, *The Life of Joseph Chamberlain* (London: Macmillan & Co.,
Ltd., 1933).

46. Horace White, "An American's Impressions of England," *Fortnightly
Review* 18 (September, 1875): 291–305. White met the editor of this journal, John Moreley, while he was in England. He agreed to Moreley's
request for the article. Their friendship was maintained for many years
afterwards.

47. White to William Henry Smith, October 8, 1875, Smith MSS.

13

The *New York* *Evening Post*

Horace White disliked New York. About a year before his arrival, the very thought of calling Manhattan home had made him reluctant to consider the editorship of the *Nation*.[1] This time, however, he had been called there by another occupation, one that he could not refuse. His closest friend, Henry Villard, needed his assistance in managing a wide-flung, mushrooming railroad enterprise.

The friendship of White and Villard had begun in Washington during the Civil War, when they were fellow reporters. From the time they formed their maverick agency to gather and distribute wartime news, they seldom lost touch of one another. One of White's first acts as editor of the *Chicago Tribune* in 1865 was his appointment of Villard as the *Tribune* correspondent in Washington. When Villard resigned from that post after a year's tour of duty and returned to his native Germany, White paid him handsomely for articles about European events.[2] During the late 1860s and early 1870s, the two men continued to assist each other in their individual careers. When Villard became secretary of the American Social Science Association, White joined the Liberal group and recruited others in the West for the research society. Villard, in turn, invested money in White's growing interest in the *Chicago Tribune* and helped the newspaper through the financial scare in the winter of 1872–1873.[3] The friendship of the two men was further strengthened by the tragic death of White's wife in 1873. In caring for Martha White in Germany, Villard and his wife sympathetically shared those desperate moments with their grief-stricken friend. The emotional crisis forged a lifelong bond; Villard became White's "beloved friend."[4]

While he was in Germany in the early 1870s, Villard had gained the confidence of German investors in American railways and became their troubleshooter for several shaky speculative adventures in the United States.[5] As soon as he began his long career in railroad promotion and development, Villard turned to White for assistance. When he first offered White the promise of large commissions in 1872 to act as his agent in the Midwest, the busy editor had to turn him down.[6] But when White retired from the editorship of the *Tribune,* he quickly focused his attention on Villard's railroad promotions. He invested $65,000 of his own money in bonds of the Oregon and California Railroad, one of the firms under Villard's supervision. Apparently he trusted Villard's pledge to double the investment within two years.[7]

Villard had grandiose plans for transportation development in the Northwest, beginning with an attempt to consolidate and monopolize the transportation facilities of Portland, Oregon. Within a year he was able to inform White of his election to the presidency of the three major railroad and steamship facilities serving the Portland area.

Villard's involvement in railroads did not stop there; soon it expanded beyond the Pacific Northwest. His connections with German bondholders drew him into a battle with two titans in the transportation world—Jay Gould and the Union

Pacific Railroad. In the fall of 1876, Villard was appointed as a receiver of the defaulting Kansas Pacific Company, a line connecting Kansas City with Denver, Colorado. From Denver a feeder line, the Denver Pacific, brought Kansas Pacific shipments to Cheyenne, whence they could proceed by the Union Pacific main line to California. Through various technicalities of the federal laws regulating the Union Pacific Railroad, Villard managed to divert some of the west coast traffic monopolized by Gould's line over the Kansas Pacific. Forced into a compromised situation, Gould finally rid himself of the competition by taking control of the bankrupt Kansas Pacific corporation. To win this control, however, Gould had to pay all interest in arrears on the bonds belonging to Villard's employers.[8] The transaction caused those securities almost to triple in market value. One commentator questioned "whether any other great railroad property in this country, which has been actually in the hands of a receiver, can show so remarkable an advance as this."[9]

Once the Kansas Pacific matters were settled, Villard was able to turn with renewed vigor and prestige to his Pacific Northwest properties. During the summer of 1879, he proceeded with an ambitious plan to dominate the transportation facilities not only of the Portland area but of virtually the whole of the Pacific Northwest. Eastern capitalists were more than eager to supply this new railroad wizard with capital. In his first major move—consolidating several steamship firms to form the Oregon Railway and Navigation Company—Villard received, as he told White, "over a million more than we wanted."[10] White demonstrated his personal confidence in Villard by turning over large portions of his own available funds to the ambitious promoter.[11] The nation was pulling out of the depression, and the flush times had returned to Wall Street.

Not until late in 1880 did Villard unfold his full financial program. Through another bold and gigantic move, he secured enough money from bedazzled Eastern capitalists to purchase a majority interest in the Northern Pacific. This transaction provided him with sweeping continental holdings that extended from the Pacific to the thriving Midwest. Villard had become one of the nation's leading financial tycoons.

White played a key role in several of Villard's manuevers. In Washington, he had successfully lobbied before Congress and won favors from his friend, Carl Schurz, then Secretary of Interior under Hayes.[12] He had also assisted in the bargaining with Gould, drawing up gentlemen's agreements and profit pools.[13] Finally, he served as treasurer of a major Villard holding, the Oregon Railway and Navigation Company. In this position, he kept watch over the financial front in New York while Villard was away on the Pacific coast building a transportation empire.[14] As a Liberal reformer, White clearly showed no alienation from modern finance or big business. He remained quite close to the nation's centers of social and economic power.

White's first love, however, remained journalism, an enthusiasm which Villard also shared. The two men therefore prepared to reenter the world where they had originally become partners. Flushed with capital and confidence, they looked about for a major newspaper to represent their interests. After a respite of more than six years, Horace White was ready to return to his first calling. Backed this time by a financial giant rather than the political masses, he hoped once again to champion Liberal reform.

New York was the acknowledged capital of American journalism. Despite White's frequent boasts about the prestige of the *Chicago Tribune,* he always considered New York the center of the nation's fourth estate. The roster of active newspapers in the city seemed endless, and the competition among them was severe. Yet adventurers continued to enter the market. White had no intention of assuming the daily burdens of a newspaper enterprise by himself. He still remembered too well the onerous busy work and long hours of a chief editorship in Chicago, and journalism in New York, he recognized, offered even greater challenges and responsibilities. Besides, he did not want to divorce himself from Villard's Wall Street affairs; he hoped, rather, to return to journalism on a part-time basis—to write when he wished, "without the strain of daily tasks."[15] Someone else would have to take up the day-to-day management of any paper he and Villard might purchase.

Villard and White had "someone else" in mind—Carl Schurz, who was about to step down from his Cabinet post in March, 1881. Schurz's editorial experience as well as his national reputation made him the obvious choice. In February, when White broached the subject to him, Schurz fired back a request for more information.[16] White explained that he and Villard, along with Edwin L. Godkin, had been shopping around for a daily newspaper "with a view of offering it to you on terms which would have you on a footing of independence as editor."[17]

Absorbed in railroad affairs, Villard allowed White to manage the negotiations for the purchase of a suitable daily paper. White first spoke with the owners of the *New York Commercial Advertiser* but eventually turned away from that journal. A morning paper like the *Chicago Tribune,* it demanded evening work which he expected Schurz would no more want than he did. Then, too, since the *Commercial Advertiser* was "an enemy organ," the necessary shift in editorial policy by the new proprietors would make for an awkward transition of control.[18] Fortunately, within a week after White informed Schurz of these reluctant negotiations, word came that a large interest in the *New York Evening Post* was up for sale.

The *Evening Post* met every specification that White had in mind. It was an evening paper with a grand tradition. Begun eighty years earlier by Alexander Hamilton, under the editorship of William Cullen Bryant the paper had won an enviable reputation in American journalism. The career of the literary-minded Bryant, White once confessed, had provided him with a "mark of emulation."[19] No paper in the city, moreover, had an editorial policy more in tune with White's own thinking on public questions. With delight, therefore, he opened negotiations with Parke Godwin, who had assumed the editorship after Bryant's death in 1878. Godwin, in turn, was almost as pleased as White with the possible transfer. In financial straits, Godwin had been anxious to sell the paper to like-minded intellectuals. John Bigelow, a former associate of Bryant, had pressed that obligation of tradition upon Godwin: "Don't let the dynasty of Bryant end in a Hastings—nor our most glorious temple of newspaper justice be converted into a house of prostitution."[20]

If White and Godwin had been able to make the decision by themselves, the sale would have proceeded without delay. But the ownership of the *Post* complicated the transaction. Godwin could transfer only twenty-five of the fifty shares in the company. The other twenty-five shares were controlled by the business manager, William Henderson, who had been at odds with Parke Godwin over the management of the paper. Henderson, burdened neither by undue concern with tradition nor by financial difficulty, had not considered selling his shares. If anything, he was interested in gaining full control of the *Evening Post* in order to transfer the editorship to members of his family. White's negotiations with Godwin, therefore, had to remain secret. All along, however, White kept Schurz informed.[21]

Buying a newspaper was not much different from buying a railroad. White immediately put Villard's reservoir of legal talent to use: C. F. Southmayd, Villard's chief corporation lawyer, checked whether White could control the paper's editorial policy with only 50 percent of the stock. In the meantime, Godwin made overtures to purchase Henderson's shares,

without letting the business manager know of White's interest in the purchase. White also sought help from various other
sympathetic parties.[22] He had become a shrewd businessman.
With tactics he had learned well from his relations with Villard, White offered ready cash and lots of it. Using about a
hundred thousand dollars of his own and three quarters of
a million from Villard, he purchased outright control of the
New York Evening Post.[23] On May 23, 1881, the reorganized
Board of Trustees appointed Carl Schurz editor-in-chief,[24]
and on May 25, the *Post* announced the purchase and change
of editors. Having appointed the talented *Nation* editor,
Edwin L. Godkin, as associate to Schurz, the new management began with high expectations of success.

The public reaction was quite favorable to the change.
Other newspapers, as one would expect, welcomed the new
editors, and powerful politicians expressed their pleasure.
Public leaders generally expected Schurz to speak with great
authority. Recognized as the leader of the scattered Liberals,
the former senator and Cabinet officer now seemed to be in
a position to pronounce the opinion of an influential bloc
of voters. James G. Blaine, who had cooperated with the
"Independents" in electing Garfield in 1880, wanted to pre-
serve the alliance; he therefore responded immediately to
the announcement of Schurz's elevation to the editor's chair.
"I congratulate you on your return to journalism under
such flattering auspices," Blaine wrote.[25] From a different
vantage point, John Bigelow commended Parke Godwin for
the moral distinction of the *Post* and confessed to E. L.
Godkin his satisfaction that his "foster-mother is no longer
in immediate danger of dying like an oak tree at the top."
Bigelow agreed with Godkin that the return of Schurz and
White to journalism bolstered the "somewhat optimistic view
of our political future."[26]

At first, few knew that Henry Villard was the major owner,
but journalistic gossip in New York soon passed that tidbit

down the line. David Goodman Croly, a knowledgeable work-horse in the city's newspaper world, was able to announce almost immediately the proprietary power behind the sale. Reflecting upon the recent removal of newspaper giants from the New York scene—Bryant, the elder Bennett, Henry J. Raymond, and Horace Greeley—Croly praised the reappearance of strong personalities. Yet, with a profound insight, Croly added a dissent to the optimistic public reception; he saw serious problems facing the new enterprise. Evening journals, he pointed out, worked under various handicaps: circulation was limited, fresh news coverage was confined to only a few hours of the day, and advertising profits were slim. Croly regretted that the men did not pick up a morning daily and concluded with an insightful comment: "Those who know the new editors of the *Evening Post,* doubt whether they will be able to pull together. They are opinionated and crotchety gentlemen, in whom the critical faculty has been inordinately developed. They would naturally criticize one another, to begin with; but the disagreement if there is one, will end with a survival of the fittest. Mr. White would do well to issue a morning edition of the *Post* and edit it himself.[27]

The triumvirate began happily enough. They anticipated not only a command of the public ear but also substantial financial rewards. Their success on both fronts seemed doubly insured when they hammered out arrangements to tie the influential *Nation* to the *Evening Post.* They counted on a full 10 percent annual return on their investment.[28]

White and Villard purchased the *Nation* a few weeks after Schurz took over the *Evening Post.* Godkin, at first, tried to get better terms from Parke Godwin but eventually accepted the $40,000 offered by White and Villard, a price far less than the $60,000 originally invested in the weekly.[29] White drove this hard bargain after thoroughly checking the books of the struggling *Nation.*[30] As part of the consolidation, White agreed to retain Godkin's former assistant, Wendell Phillips Garrison, as editor of the reorganized *Nation*. That was an easy decision, since Garrison, besides being an able editor, was Henry Villard's brother-in-law. On June 30, 1881, the *Nation* itself announced its new role: "Beginning with the next number the *Nation* will be issued as the weekly edition of the New York *Evening Post*. It will retain its name . . . but its contents will in the main have already appeared in the *Evening Post*."[31]

On the surface, the new enterprise did show promise of strength and vitality. Family, friendship, and philosophic agreement seemed to bind all of the parties together. Yet, from the very beginning, there were signs of the dissension which David G. Croly had expected. Edwin L. Godkin entered the enterprise with apparent reservations. When the negotiations were drawing to a close for the purchase of the *Evening Post,* Godkin described to a friend the unsatisfactory basis on which White and Villard invited him to join the editorial staff. "They ask me to join, on the same terms as Schurz, but as 'associate editor.' "[32] Both Schurz and White had battled with Godkin in the past. The *Nation* editor had excoriated them both for their support of Horace Greeley as well as for some of their subsequent political activities. White had settled his argument with Godkin over the Grangers, but the relationship between Godkin and Schurz never found a firm footing. After only a few months on the job, Godkin expressed open dissatisfaction with Schurz's editorial lead. He repeated criticism to Schurz which he claimed came from Villard and others to the effect that the *Post* "ran some topics into the ground—that for instance there were so many articles on Conkling, and on Civil Service reform. I think there is some ground for this," Godkin continued, "and that we ought to beware of harping too much in one key."[33] To others, Godkin expressed even graver reservations about the direction of the paper. In correspondence with Henry Adams, Godkin accused

Schurz of being "sentimental"—a very harsh adjective in Godkin's vocabulary. Adams, a minor investor in the *Post,* understood Godkin's meaning; he countered the remark firmly but good-naturedly:

> You relieve me greatly by telling me that Schurz is sentimental. If you dry one of his tears, I will denounce you at a stock-holders meeting. Every tear he sheds is worth at least an extra dollar on the dividends. Cultivate them! collect them! point to them! you are no good yourself in the sobbing business, but you can affect a decent respect for real sympathy. I have always told you that your fatal defect was the incapacity to make a *popular* blunder. Not that you can't blunder as others; we are all quick enough at that; but all your blunders are on the wrong side; they don't even make friends. What I want to see is some good, idiotic, gushing, popular blundering. We shall thrive on that.[34]

Schurz paid little attention to Godkin's criticism. Lengthy articles on civil service reform and Republican rascals continued to dominate the editorial pages; the material, nevertheless, stirred up considerable excitement. Indeed Schurz's attacks on Jay Gould and Roscoe Conkling created an uproar. The victims responded by raking over Schurz's activities during the Hayes administration and accusing him of official misdeeds.[35] Despite this hubbub, however, the circulation of the *Post* failed to grow, and earnings proved very disappointing. David Croly had pointed out this difficulty as the inevitable consequence of running an evening journal. Still, the slow gains tended to reinforce Godkin's criticism of the management of the paper.

Minor incidents now began to aggravate the delicate harmony. When Schurz went on his vacation in the summer of 1882, Godkin was left, by chance, in sole control of the editorial office. Godkin first opened an intemperate attack on James G. Blaine, which destroyed the recent understanding between Schurz and the senator.[36] He also reversed the *Post*'s stand on a matter in New York politics which involved Schurz's two favorite whipping boys, Roscoe Conkling and Jay Gould. Since Godkin's action embarrassed and irritated him, Schurz dashed off a complaint to White. White confessed that he had also been chagrined but explained that new evidence justified Godkin's independent action. White cautioned at the same time that "only one man on the editorial force should be gone at one time."[37]

White was caught in the middle. Occupied with his duties on Wall Street, he substituted only occasionally for one or the other of the editors.[38] Yet as a major owner, he became increasingly involved in their quarrels. They called on him frequently to mediate between them. On one occasion, Schurz complained of Villard's interference with the paper. Villard had arranged for the publication of a long article in the *Post* in the interest of "certain railway enterprises." "You can imagine my sensation," Schurz complained to White, "when . . . in spite of the objections made by me, after discovery, on the ground of inconvenience as well as manifest impropriety, the publication was still insisted upon, until I peremptorily refused. . . . This matter is vital. The idea of that banking house . . . being permitted to think that the columns of the Ev. Post could be disposed of in such a way, is simply inadmissable." Schurz added that his financial losses as editor of the *Post* did nothing to help matters.[39]

All three editors of the Post were involved in Villard's railroad speculations.[40] This did not disturb Schurz, since he felt it did not interfere with his independence as director of the paper. When Villard complained that the *Post*'s criticisms of the Arthur administration embarrassed him, Schurz sent back a stinging note: "I'm very sorry indeed to learn that you have been embarrassed on account of the conduct of the *Evening Post.* . . . Having been a journalist yourself you will readily understand that we cannot permit the independence of our position to be questioned."[41]

By the end of the second year, dissension on the *Post* reached a crisis. The lack of an increase in either circulation or profits had already undermined Schurz's authority, and his disputes with Villard did nothing to improve his position. Godkin, whether he understood the situation or not, picked the right moment to press his complaints. He delicately avoided Schurz's name in spelling them out for White:

> I have pretty much decided, under the circumstances not to go over this summer, as I had proposed. I should not be easy leaving the Post and Nation, with the force there would be, or is likely to be in the office. The Post suffers from dreariness and monotony, from which the people are too ready to seek relief in the cheap light evening paper. The result of our two year experiment from this point of view troubles me a good deal. We are not gaining circulation, and I can say I think we deserve it. Half our editorial matter every day is dull reading on uninteresting subjects. I certainly should never think of reading it if I could help it, and I know the same is the case with the average New Yorker.[42]

The letter apparently shocked White into action. A meeting with Godkin clarified the fiery Irish editor's determination to have drastic changes. First, he demanded the chief editorship. If that were out of the question, he then wanted to buy back the *Nation* and resign from the editorial staff of the *Post*. White now had to play the role of diplomat. Since he had scheduled a trip to Europe in June, he had only a few weeks to resolve the matter.

Without fully informing Schurz of Godkin's ultimatum, White somehow managed to get the principled German to step down and give way to his associate. Since Godkin and Schurz were not discussing the matter between themselves,

White relayed the news to Godkin before embarking upon his European tour:

> Schurz assented to the proposed arrangement without hesitation or reluctance and we said good bye with cordiality. He requested that the change would take place when he goes for his summer vacation, to which I assented. He said he would consult with you on the subject. Nothing was said about H. V. and indeed H. V. declined to interfere but said we must decide the question although he concurred in the views I presented.

In a postscript to this letter, White explained the conditions which helped make the transfer palatable to the proud editor of the *Post*. "I said to S.," White added, "that if the new arrangement did not prove a success I should take my turn at the bellows two years hence and that if any comment were made inside the office it should be understood that this turnabout was part of our original plan."[43]

When White departed, Godkin and Schurz had to iron out the details of the transfer of authority. After waiting for a week to hear from Schurz, Godkin opened the conversation. He expressed his impatience with Schurz's silence, and then detailed to Schurz, for the first time, the grievances and ultimatums which he had earlier presented to White. Hoping that Schurz would view his comments "in the friendliest spirit" and "as simple business," Godkin bluntly stated that the *Post* under Schurz's management was a "failure." "In brief, though you and I agree on most public questions," Godkin continued, "we differ greatly in opinion as to the *quality* of writing, and I am unwilling longer to father a great deal of writing that appears in the Post." Godkin concluded by asking Schurz for the precise date of his retirement.[44]

Schurz replied with a terse note. He explained that he failed to say anything "about the matter opened to me by White because I expected, as I thought I might, that you would speak to me. In fact," Schurz complained, "I was inclined to think it would have been better had the whole plan from the beginning been discussed between us without any reticence. Of course, I do not object to anything thought necessary or desirable for the furtherance of interests which are those of others as well as my own. I told White that I had intended to begin my vacation about the 1st of August, which he thought would be satisfactory."[45]

Tensions ran high as Schurz finished his last six weeks as editor-in-chief. When Villard suggested, after consultations with Godkin in July, that Schurz go to Europe for a year as correspondent for the paper, Schurz refused.[46] Later that month, the friction between Godkin and Schurz blazed into a fiery controversy. Without consulting one another, the men wrote and published conflicting editorials on a general strike of the nation's telegraphers. Neither had ever been sympathetic to strikes, but Godkin had always been extreme in his hostility to organized labor. He scoffed therefore at the moderation with which Schurz analyzed this particular labor outburst. The *Post*'s contradictory stance ended temporarily when Godkin left for a short vacation at a private club in the Berkshires. He sent an editorial by mail, but Schurz refused to publish it without some major revisions. Under those terms, Godkin canceled its publication. He dismissed Schurz's suggested alterations as "simply that elusive balancing of rights and duties we see often in party platforms."[47]

After writing to Schurz, Godkin explained the row to his intimate associate, *Nation* editor Wendell Phillips Garrison. He also outlined the role which he contemplated for the newspaper: "The Post ought to make a specialty of being the paper to which sober minded people would look at crises of this kind, instead of hollering . . . platitudes like the *World* and *Times*." The *Post* might have to wait for this new direction, but Garrison saw no reason to postpone such an editorial line in the *Nation*. He exercised his prerogative and published Godkin's article—uncensored.[48]

As the editorship of the *Evening Post* changed on August 1, in the midst of the strike, argument led to schism. As soon as he gained power, Godkin transformed the paper into his contemplated instrument. He came down heavily against the strikers. Despite his extreme views, Godkin regarded himself as an impartial critic. He had frequently lashed out against irresponsible corporations and "monopolies." At one point in this strike, for instance, he suggested that the nation's telegraph system be brought under the control of the United States Post Office. Reform of the civil service under the Pendleton Act, he felt, removed the "greatest objection to the assumption of the telegraph business by the Government."[49] Godkin, however, was not truly neutral. He warned the striking telegraphers not to misinterpret criticism which "responsible people" leveled against monopoly—even against a Jay Gould monopoly like Western Union. "No disgust with corporate mismanagement has ever, or probably will ever bring the business community to believe that the strikes of the employees, ordered or superintended by trades unions, are a proper cure for it."[50]

Schurz fumed as he read Godkin's editorials at his vacation retreat in the Catskill mountains. Godkin's continued insistence that telegraph and railroad workers "had to be governed on the same principles as an army" infuriated Schurz.[51] He wrote a long and emphatic dissent to Godkin's position; he challenged the analogy of workers and soldiers. The employee's relationship to his employer, Schurz insisted, was one of "simple contract," not military enlistment. The *Evening Post,* he argued, dare not indiscriminately defend corporations which "indulge in such practices as stockwatering and the like and then seek to grind out dividends by cutting down the wages of their working men." From Schurz's point of view criticism of corporations or subsequent demands for reform by the *Post* would not be enough to present a balanced view as long as the *Post* "put the most odious demands the corporations might make (and which so far they have not even dared to make) in the most odious form." Schurz concluded with an ultimatum: "if the Ev. Post assumes . . . the character of . . . a 'corporation organ,' I shall have to sever my connection with it at any cost."[52]

Godkin drafted a reply in which he intended to inform Schurz that he held "the editorship and the responsibility of the paper," and that he was "not afraid of being thought the organ of a corporation." Godkin never mailed the letter; instead he spoke to Schurz in person. He remained adamant. Indeed, as if to throw down the gauntlet to Schurz, Godkin wrote a blistering editorial reply to those who sympathized with the strikers. He directed his criticism against the *New York Times* and the *New York Herald* but took up the charges which Schurz had made in his letter. Freedom of contract, Godkin declared "leaves the operators free to go, and the company free to do without them." Godkin also lashed out against those who sided with the strikers because the Western Union watered its stock. Watered stock, Godkin claimed represented nothing more than "the fact that the profits of the Western Union are large." The insistence that "a man or a company was bound to pay wages in proportion to his profits," Godkin warned, planted "the seeds of great and far reaching mischief." "If it turns out they have raised the devil with their 'sympathy,' . . . we trust they will be sorry."[53]

Schurz might have resigned at this point, but the crisis was avoided. Horace White returned to New York just as Godkin left on a six week's excursion celebrating the opening of the Northern Pacific's main line to the Far West.[54] During the respite afforded by Godkin's absence, White managed to dissuade Schurz from any official resignation but was unable, on the other hand, to persuade him to resume his work on the paper. When Godkin returned, White drew a written apology from the Irish editor and promptly relayed it to Schurz. To this, Schurz responded with a note of his own saying that he did not "harbor any ill feeling." Neither of the antagonists, however, budged from his declared position on the strike. White's mediation, therefore, could not bring about a working agreement between the two men. "All we can do now," Schurz concluded in his reply to Godkin, "is to find the pleasantest possible way out of this difficult situation which, of course, cannot remain long in its present state."[55]

The break finally came in early December. It was not pleasant. Schurz insisted on giving his reasons for resigning from the paper. Godkin, in turn, threatened to humiliate him by exposing his earlier demotion from the chief editorship. At that, Schurz went into a rage and, for the first time, spoke bluntly to Godkin. He lambasted Godkin for the "underhanded way" in which he had taken over the editorship. Unperturbed by Godkin's threat, Schurz dared him to publish whatever he wished but insisted that he would, at the same time, publish his version "of that story." Facetiously, he wondered why Godkin was reluctant to have the public know of their respective views about the strike.[56]

Schurz called Godkin's bluff. With White's permission, he published his reasons for leaving the paper. Godkin, as Schurz expected, did not follow through with his threats. Instead, both he and Schurz continued their bitter private quibbling over their respective journalistic abilities and social outlooks. The argument continued well into January, even after Schurz insisted: "By all means, let us have peace and take my good wishes."[57] The two men parted in anger and did not meet again on friendly terms for many years.[58]

Horace White's sympathies had been muted in this battle. Over the matter of editorial policy, he was drawn to Godkin. Since their own editorial debates in the early 1870s, White had come to accept Godkin's general approach to social problems.[59] Over the clash of personalities, on the other hand, White was drawn to Schurz. White always maintained a warm friendship with him but only strained relations with Godkin. After his failure to patch up the quarrel in October, White assumed an impartial role and allowed the situation to drift to Godkin's advantage. The timing of the feud had handicapped Schurz. Godkin still had another year to serve of his two year trial term as editor-in-chief of the *Post*. Schurz was unwilling to wait that long for a change. Besides, White and Villard were in no mood for another change at that moment.

White and Villard had more important matters on their mind. A much larger investment than the *Post* dominated their attention. The celebrated opening of the Northern Pacific main line to the West masked the serious financial troubles of the railroad firm. Panic had hit Wall Street in the middle of the summer of 1883 and alarmed Villard and his friends. When anxious notes first reached Villard asking about the stability of his railroad stocks, he answered them all with optimistic replies.[60] When White got news of the panic in London, he made immediate preparations to hurry home. Villard did not disguise the situation to him but cabled: "Your account is fully protected."[61]

From the moment White arrived in New York, the seriousness of the financial panic dwarfed the importance of the Godkin-Schurz feud. By September, the handwriting was already on the wall for the Northern Pacific. Villard ordered his bankers to transfer White's account to one under his personal guarantee.[62] His railroad empire was falling apart. Despite his earlier wizardry, Villard did not know what to do. His operation had become so large that even he no longer understood its workings. Early in November, he sat down with White to search through the accounts. Even before they finished, they recognized that the financial structure could not withstand the panic. It was a hasty, unreliable consolidation.

Villard humbled himself before William Endicott, his major source of capital: "It is hardly necessary for me to confess that I did not understand the Company's position."[63] On December 17, 1883 (not long after Schurz's official resignation from the *Post*), Villard resigned from the presidency of the Northern Pacific. He left for Europe several months later.

White also retired from Wall Street. Because of Villard's foresight, he luckily did not lose the money which he had invested in Villard's promotions. Nor was the *Evening Post* threatened, since it had been financially divorced from Villard's railway speculations. That much at least had survived Villard's first storming of Wall Street. White therefore gave little thought to his next job; he turned to full-time work on the *Post*. The inflated dreams of an unrivaled Liberal journal had vanished after Schurz's departure from the paper. Still, the *Post* and *Nation* remained powerful vehicles of reform. Although White never enjoyed the prospect of working with Godkin, unlike Schurz, he usually shared Godkin's general outlook. The approach of another presidential election year, moreover, enabled the editors to overlook personal differences and concentrate their attacks on a common foe—James G. Blaine.

NOTES

1. White to William Henry Smith, October 8, 1875, Smith MSS. "I *don't* like New York as a place of residence. That is the most serious obstacle on my side to the plan."

2. White offered Villard an annual salary of $5,200 for his services as a foreign correspondent—a rate which his brother-in-law, Wendell P. Garrison, considered "stiff for any paper." The *Nation*, Garrison explained, paid only $1,300 for "the very best." White apparently could not justify that large an expenditure and reduced it somewhat during the summer. Wendell P. Garrison to William L. Garrison II, August 18, 1867, in the Garrison Family Papers.

3. *Journal of Social Science* 1 (June, 1869): 200. Henry Villard to Fanny Villard, June 9, 1870, Henry Villard MSS.

4. When Henry Villard seemed near death himself in 1877, White recalled for Fanny Villard the bond which his wife's death had fastened upon their friendship: "I can hardly tell you the emotions that have filled my breast during the painful days that your dear husband, my beloved friend, has been so near death. I received the telegram which seemed to me fatal of all hope, on Sunday morning. . . . ["Mr. Villard is sinking rapidly—there is hardly a chance of recovery left." Fanny Villard to White, July 28, 1877, Fanny Villard MSS.] Coupled with our grief which overwhelmed me was the remembrance of another and more distant scene when you watched over the departing soul of one who was dearest to me of time and eternity, and I thought, O, that I might do anything, to relieve your distress, or to share it with you! . . . if for no other purpose than to testify the love and gratitude I bear to you both." White to Fanny Villard, July 31, 1877, Fanny Villard MSS.

5. Henry Villard, *Memoirs of Henry Villard*, pp. 271–283. James Blaine Hedges, *Henry Villard and the Railways of the Northwest* (New Haven, Conn., 1930), pp. 11–17 (hereafter cited as Hedges, *Villard*).

6. White to Henry Villard, January 24, 1872, Henry Villard MSS.

7. Henry Villard to White, May 11, 1875, January 13, 1876, Henry Villard MSS. See also White's account with Villard, December 14, 1875, Henry Villard MSS.

8. Julius Grodinsky, *Jay Gould* (Philadelphia, 1957), pp. 142–143. Grodinsky elaborates in detail the in-fighting between Gould and Villard. See ibid., pp. 138–144, 167–168, 170–171. With less detail, the story is also told in Villard, *Memoirs*, 2:281–283. White was kept informed of these private negotiations. Henry Villard to White, June 6, 1878, Henry Villard MSS.

9. *Public*, March 13, 1879, p. 176, cited by Grodinsky, *Jay Gould*, p. 171.

10. Henry Villard to White, June 16, 1879, in the Henry Villard MSS. All the affairs of Villard in the Pacific Northwest are detailed in Hedges, *Villard*. The same ground is covered inadequately in Villard, *Memoirs*, 2:272–367.

11. Finley Anderson to White, June 7, 1879; Henry Villard to White, June 10, July 2, 3, 8, 1879, Henry Villard MSS. White probably had over $200,000 in investments at this time, most of which he purchased on credit. Villard backed most of White's credit in his own name. White, under Villard's advice, also invested in Pullman Company stock, Edison's electric enterprises, and New York railways. Much of it was speculation. As the nation finally pulled out of the depression, many made fortunes in Wall Street. In one operation, the New York City and Northern Railroad, White made a 55 percent profit on a two-year investment of about $15,000 by selling out at a higher price. He explained the speculation in a letter to David A. Wells, February 4, 1881, Horace White Misc. Papers, New York Public Library. White's original holdings in this com-

pany are described in a letter from George Saxer to White, July 14, 1879, Henry Villard MSS.

12. Henry Villard to White, January 15, February 12, Henry Villard MSS. Horace White, "Union Pacific Railroad Discriminations," 45 Cong., 2d Sess., House Committee of the Pacific Railroads. See Henry Villard to Finley Anderson, February 13, 1878; Henry Villard to White, March 8, 20, April 5, June 3, 6, 8 [2 letters], 12, 1878; Henry Villard to Robert Carr, June 8, 1878: Henry Villard MSS. White to Carl Schurz, April 10, May 11, May 31, June 22, October 2, December 1, 1877, December 10, 1879, Schurz MSS.

13. White to Henry Villard, July 5, 1877, Henry Villard MSS.

14. George Saxer to White, July 7, 1879; White to George Saxer, August 1, 1879; George Saxer to White, August 18, 1879; Henry Villard MSS.

15. Fanny Villard to White, January 31, 1903, Fanny Villard MSS. Fanny Villard, just after White's retirement, recalled the arrangements made for the White's reentry into journalism in 1881.

16. White to Carl Schurz, February 17, 1881, and Schurz to White, February 19, 1881: Schurz MSS.

17. White to Carl Schurz, February 21, 1881, Schurz MSS.

18. Ibid.

19. White to W. C. Bryant, February 28, 1875, Bryant-Godwin Coll. Allan Nevins, *The Evening Post* (New York, 1922).

20. John Bigelow to Parke Godwin, February 24, 1881, Bryant-Godwin Coll.

21. White to Carl Schurz, March 17, 18, April 18, 19, 1881, Schurz MSS.

22. White to Gordon L. Ford, May 6, 1881, Horace White Misc. Papers.

23. White's tough business tactics are evident from his own post-mortem explanation of the transaction to Parke Godwin: "Your note of this date is received. In reply I beg leave to say that my purchase of your interest in the *Evening Post* property (the Wm. C. Bryant Co.) was predicated entirely on your ability to transfer to me four of the five trustees, that is to say, a control of the corporation—that this was an essential part of our written contract—that after consulting counsel upon the feasibility of continuing control in this way while owning only one half of the shares I was strongly inclined to accept your offer to cancel the contract. Whether I would have so cancelled it in the case Mr. Henderson had refused to sell I cannot now say, but I can say that I would not have bought 25 shares without control at anything like the rate I agreed to pay for 50 shares with the control." White to Parke Godwin, May 26, 1881, Bryant-Godwin Coll.

24. Bryant-Godwin to Carl Schurz, May 23, 1881, Schurz MSS.

25. James G. Blaine to Carl Schurz, May 26, 1881, Schurz MSS.

26. John Bigelow to Parke Godwin, June 13, 1881, Bryant-Godwin Coll. John Bigelow to E. L. Godkin, June 9, 1881, copy in the John Bigelow MSS, New York Public Library.

27. *Real Estate Record and Builders Guide*, May 28, 1881. David G.

Croly, the father of Herbert Croly, had been the managing editor for the *New York World* and several other papers in the city. Both he and his wife, Jane Cunningham Croly, were veteran journalists. David Levy, working on a long needed biography of the Croly family, found this editorial by D. G. Croly about the sale of the *Evening Post*.

28. E. L. Godkin to Thomas W. Higginson, June 9, 1881, Godkin MSS.

29. Parke Godwin to E. L. Godkin, May 28, 1881; Godkin to Thomas W. Higginson, June 9, 1881; W. P. Garrison to Thomas W. Higginson, September 17, 1881: Godkin MSS.

30. White to Carl Schurz, June 9, 1881, Schurz MSS. White gave a full accounting to Schurz. The *Nation* could show only a $1,200 annual profit on its capitalized worth.

31. *Nation*, June 30, 1881. All editorial and news items after this date were reprinted from the *Post*. Only some of the literary notices and book reviews were original material. W. P. Garrison gave an account of the negotiations and reorganization to his brother. Wendell P. Garrison to William L. Garrison II, June 27, July 9, 1881, Garrison Family Papers.

32. E. L. Godkin to Frederick L. Olmstead, April 21, 1881, F. L. Olmstead MSS, Library of Congress, cited by William M. Armstrong, "The Godkin-Schurz Feud, 1881-83, over Policy-Control of the *Evening Post*," *New York Historical Society Quarterly* 48 (January, 1964): 11. Although Schurz was editor-in-chief, both he and Godkin received identical salaries ($8,000) and identical options on stock ($100,000), as well as guaranteed annual dividends of four percent on whatever stock they decided to retain.

33. E. L. Godkin to Carl Schurz, August 12, 1881, Schurz MSS.

34. Henry Adams to E. L. Godkin, September 23, 1881, Godkin MSS.

35. Carl Schurz to Thomas Bayard, January 18, 1882, Schurz MSS. The most serious of the charges was that Schurz had made improper favors to Henry Villard's railroads.

36. Carl Schurz to Joseph Medill, September 21, 1882, in *Speeches, Correspondence and Political Papers of Carl Schurz*, ed. Frederick Bancroft (New York, 1913), 4:154.

37. White to Carl Schurz, August 26, 1882, Schurz MSS.

38. Ibid., September 6, 11, 1882, Schurz MSS. White handled the business affairs of the paper. Neither Godkin nor Schurz had much experience in this field. White, for example, organized the evening papers and presented a united front in bargaining with the powerful morning dailies in New York *(Herald, World, Times, Tribune)*. His contacts with western editors also enabled him to use their influence in winning rights from his New York competitors. George Jones to White, December 5, 1881, Schurz MSS. White to William H. Smith, March 9, April 3, 30, 1883, and White to Richard Smith, June 2, 1883: Smith MSS.

39. Carl Schurz to White, October 14, 1882, Schurz MSS. Villard had legally denied himself any editorial control of the paper by allowing a trust headed by David A. Wells and Benjamin Bristow to manage his investment. Nevertheless he did, on occasion, let his opinion be known.

The editors could, however (as Schurz did in this case), claim their rights of independence.

40. White frequently quoted prices of Villard's securities for Schurz and advised him on purchases. White to Carl Schurz, September 6, 11, 12, 1882, Schurz MSS. Henry Villard's brother-in-law, Wendell Phillips Garrison, seemed a bit more squeamish about his connection with Villard's railroad speculations. On one occasion, when Villard sent him $5,000, the railroad magnate also sent a note of mocking apology: "I know that you do not think much of the Oregon Improvement Co. But you may form a better opinion of it while enjoying the proceeds of the accompanying check which represents the fruits of an operation in Improvement securities which I ventured to make for your account without your 'knowledge or consent' so as to leave your conscience entirely free from moral responsibility for the evil deeds." Henry Villard to Wendell P. Garrison, January 25 [1883], Henry Villard MSS.

41. Carl Schurz to Henry Villard, February 15, 1883, Schurz MSS.

42. E. L. Godkin to White, May 20 [1883], Horace White MSS.

43. White to E. L. Godkin, June 8, 1883, Godkin MSS.

44. E. L. Godkin to Carl Schurz, June 18, 1883, Schurz MMS.

45. Carl Schurz to E. L. Godkin, June 18, 1883, Godkin MSS. There is a draft of this letter in the Schurz MSS. It is dated June 17, 1883, apparently in error, since it is obviously in reply to Godkin's letter of June 18. Both were in New York City, and their letters were probably carried by private messenger.

46. Henry Villard to White, July 17, 1883, Henry Villard MSS. Perhaps in response to this matter, White sent a quick postal card to Schurz: "Yours received. Your decision is undoubtedly right." White to Carl Schurz, July 30, 1883, Schurz MSS.

47. E. L. Godkin to Carl Schurz, n.d. [c. July 24, 1883], Schurz MSS. Although many more letters passed between Schurz and Godkin over this matter, no more are found in the Carl Schurz MSS. The quarrel is also ignored in the published papers of both Schurz (*Speeches, Correspondence of Carl Schurz*, ed. Bancroft) and Godkin (Rollo Ogden, *Life and Letters of Edwin Lawrence Godkin*, 2 vols. [New York, 1907]). Some of the correspondence remains in the Godkin MSS, but what once existed in the Schurz MSS was purposely removed. An undated note written by Frederick Bancroft on a scrap of paper left in the unorganized papers of Schurz at the Library of Congress explains that absence: "Letters about personal differences, June-Dec., 1883, not being of public interest, are removed from this collection and retained by the Schurzes. Copies of C. S. to G. made in February, 1912, and covering June-Dec., 1883, are sent to Miss Schurz, Mar. 5/12. F. B."

48. E. L. Godkin to W. P. Garrison, July 24, 1883, Godkin MSS. Garrison had taken sides before when he published Godkin's editorials on the strike, but not Schurz's. Garrison, no doubt, aggravated the feud between the *Post*'s editors by his actions. *Nation*, July 19, 26, 1883.

49. E. L. Godkin, "The Telegraph and the Post-Office," *Nation*, August 2, 1883.

50. E. L. Godkin, "The Last Stage of the Telegraphic Strike," Ibid., August 9, 1883.

51. *New York Evening Post*, August 8, 1883, cited by Nevins, *Evening Post*, p. 456, and by Armstrong, "Godkin-Schurz Feud," p. 20. "Divided authority is fatal to discipline," Godkin had insisted in an earlier editorial. "No employer can manage an army of officials such as our corporations employ, if they have two masters to serve, or if they can be withdrawn from duty any day by blowing a whistle on the order of a committee of outsiders." *Nation*, August 9, 1883.

52. Carl Schurz to E. L. Godkin, August 9, 1883, Godkin MSS.

53. E. L. Godkin, "The Strike and the Monopoly," *Nation*, August 16, 1883.

54. Villard had invited Godkin earlier in the summer to join him in a "select company" for the trip. Many prominent men were invited. Henry Villard to E. L. Godkin, June 11, 1883, Henry Villard MSS. Replies to Villard's invitations can be found in Henry Villard Misc. MSS, New-York Historical Society.

55. Carl Schurz to E. L. Godkin, October 3, 1883, Godkin MSS.

56. Ibid., December 11, 1883, Godkin MSS.

57. Ibid., December 14, 1883, Godkin MSS.

58. Allan Nevins was in error when he suggested that the two men quickly resumed cordial relations. Nevins, *Evening Post*, p. 457.

59. White's changed position on corporate "stockwatering" is given in White, "Railroad Stockwatering," *Nation*, August 14, 1884.

60. To Godkin, Villard wrote: "The decline in O & T [Oregon and Transcontinental] stock is due to scalping operations,—not to any untoward occurrence. The stock is far more valuable than ever today." Henry Villard to E. L. Godkin, July 30, 1883, Henry Villard MSS. See also Henry Villard to James G. Blaine, August 11, 1883, and Henry Villard to William Endicott, Jr., August 14, 1883: Henry Villard MSS.

61. Henry Villard to White, August 14, 1883, Henry Villard MSS. White's fearful reaction to the "unaccountable stock panic" is detailed in a letter he wrote to Edmund C. Stedman, August 16, 1883, E. C. Stedman MSS, Huntington Library.

62. Henry Villard to Messrs. Decker, Howell & Co., September 28, 1883, Henry Villard MSS.

63. Henry Villard to William Endicott, Jr., November 7, 1883, Henry Villard MSS. James B. Hedges explains the weaknesses of Villard's railroad empire. Hedges, *Villard*, pp. 109–111.

14

Mugwump

BLAINE WAS A bogy for the bumptious editors of the *New York Evening Post*. The antagonism between them and the Plumed Knight extended well back into the 1870s. Blaine was more than a hated adversary; he had become a symbol for all their political frustrations and resentment. His very political longevity and persistence constantly haunted them. Horace White's personal reaction to Blaine reveals in large measure the Mugwumps' attitude toward American politics since the Liberal debacle in 1872.

Until that critical juncture in the 1870s Blaine's political sentiments had been remarkably similar to White's. As young antislavery activists, both men had moved before the Civil War from a short sojourn in the Whig party to the ranks of Radical Republicans. And they both remained there until 1867. Then, like White, Blaine called a cautious halt to further reorganization of Southern society. For a while, Blaine had also cooperated with the Liberal reformers, even joining their prestigious Social Science Association. He approved amnesty for Confederate leaders, supported civil-service measures, and opposed the Stalwart effort to annex Santo Domingo.

Although very cautious on both the money and tariff questions, he spoke out firmly against repudiation and assisted the Liberals, as Speaker of the House, in appointing a sympathetic low-tariff majority to the Ways and Means Committee. Those appointments were largely responsible for the subsequent tariff reductions in 1872.

In making these decisions, Blaine had proved himself an extremely amiable and clever politician. He had an uncanny ability to sense the pulse of the Republican party. He had ridden the crest of Radicalism and later cooperated with the Liberals while they had strength. Some Liberals distrusted him even then, but most, like White, genuinely admired the affable Congressman. They urged him to follow their bolt in 1872 lest the political vanguard pass him by. But Blaine knew better; he recognized that the northern masses were not ready to cooperate with Democrats in 1872. He remained a loyal Republican.

After the depression of the 1870s blunted the antislavery thrust within the Republican party and shattered its majority coalition of forces, Blaine worked diligently to repair Republican fortunes. No leader was able again until 1896 to assemble a majoritarian party; but unlike White and other Liberals who, in reaction to agrarian and urban radicalism, became disillusioned with democratic institutions, Blaine proved remarkably deft in reassembling the discordant elements of depression America. Holding firmly to small-town, middle-class Republican loyalists in the North and West, the Maine Congressman appealed to labor, immigrants, and the growing business class. While continually proclaiming his adherence to sound currency, he managed to explore the widespread inflationist anxieties of the Republican Midwest. In the tariff, he also found a facile tool not only to satisfy the needs of industrialists, but also to promise workers a means for improving wages and Irishmen a weapon for damaging British commerce.[1]

Blaine was clearly able to make the transition from the politics of the revolutionary Civil War era to the more normal pattern of party politics in the Gilded Age. His major concerns were personal advancement and party survival. White could not make that transition. He wanted greater reform; government scandals, financial nostrums, labor violence, and Reconstruction disorders all called, in his mind, for more than Blaine's loyalty to party and juggling of discordant interests. But White never found the issues which could seize the imaginations of the voting masses. Rather than examine the limitations of his own Liberal program, he blamed his failure on the rigidity of party loyalties and the corrupting influences of industrial America.

When White returned from Europe in 1876, the view from abroad had convinced him that only major civil service reform could break the power of politicos and restore virtue and good sense to American government. His first letter to Carl Schurz upon his arrival to New York expressed the major lesson he had learned from his year abroad: "Unless we can reform the civil service the country will go to the dogs."[2]

As the nation approached another election, White asked Schurz for advice, acknowledging him as the "leader" of the remaining Liberal forces.[3] Not all the Liberal reformers, however, were as willing as White to follow Schurz's lead. A continuing conflict showed up in their search for a presidential candidate. For a moment, Charles Francis Adams seemed to strike a consensus among them, as they hoped to capitalize on centennial sentiment; but they soon recognized the elder statesman's unavailability after he failed to win the Republican nomination in Massachusetts for the Senate seat vacated by the death of Charles Sumner.[4] Once Adams was removed from contention, division among the Liberals reappeared. Most of the eastern intellectuals turned to a Democrat, Samuel Tilden, the reform governor of New York. Others, like White and Schurz, searched for a suitable Republican.

Democratic appeals to Jeffersonian notions about state rights did not draw White's sympathy. As a Liberal, he had frequently recommended government withdrawal from many economic and social matters, but he always wanted quick and responsive protection for property and felt that only federal power would suffice in that regard. To an English audience, he reaffirmed certain of his recently strengthened Whiggish notions of government and society. "The birth of the nation," he insisted, "does not really date from the 4th of July, 1776, but from the day whereon the theories of Thomas Jefferson were crushed by force and arms."

> Mr. Jefferson's desire for a rebellion oftener than once in a century and a half has been gratified beyond his most sanguine expectations. Considering the state of the world at the time he played his part in it, we need not blame him for the views he held, but in awarding the palm of statesmanship, which is the gift of seeing in advance how institutions will operate upon society, we must pass him by and place it on the brow of his great rival.[5]

White and others of the Republican-minded reformers finally focused their attention on Benjamin Bristow, Grant's Secretary of the Treasury, who had exposed some of the frauds in the administration.[6] They passed over the other Republican front-runners: James G. Blaine and Elihu Washburne. White, for one, quickly dismissed his old friend Washburne as a disciple of Grant.[7] Though once an admirer of Blaine, White now was repelled by the Maine Congressman. Two speeches by Blaine in early 1876 convinced him of the Congressman's perverseness. One called for action by Congress to meet the currency needs of citizens in the Midwest; the other spoke out against the inclusion of Jefferson Davis in a Democratic amnesty bill which intended to remove all remaining proscriptions against Confederate leaders. The latter speech, which refreshed northern memories of the war, catapulted Blaine into national prominence and won him a large following in Republican strongholds. But it infuriated Liberal reformers.

About the same time, White heard rumors about Blaine which implicated the Congressman in improper railroad manipulations. These rumors had been circulating ever since the Crédit Mobilier scandal, which had threatened to implicate Blaine. This time the rumors did not die. Some of Blaine's Republican opponents allied to Senator Oliver P. Morton of Indiana found former railroad officials of the Union Pacific who declared that Blaine had received a "loan" on some worthless bonds of the Little Rock and Fort Smith Railroad. This gossip circulated around Republican editorial offices for months before it became public. Poking his nose in the *Chicago Tribune* offices before his move to New York, White got full wind of the rumor and alerted Schurz. "The danger in the West," he wrote, "is from the Blaine movement. I am satisfied now that Blaine would be at bottom no better than Grant but probably worse. . . . A year ago I thought much better of B. than I do now."[8]

White urged Schurz to give leadership to their "Liberal friends of 1872" and to warn the public "against tricky politicians, without mentioning names." Schurz did just that. Over the signatures of White and several other Liberal sponsors, he called a conference in New York at the Fifth Avenue Hotel on May 15. Schurz clearly shared White's view of Blaine. To one of the invited guests he explained, "I must confess that I look upon Blaine as one of the most dangerous enemies of genuine reform, the more dangerous as he is shrewd enough to cover his manipulations of the machine under the fairest pretences. I would not support him under any circumstances."[10] When the Liberal reformers met, they ruled out third party action and avoided their disagreements over possible candidates by recommending no specific nominee for either major party. Instead, they did just what White suggested: they warned the public about "tricky politicians, without mentioning names." Their long "Address to the People" condemned corruption and spoils politics and declared that those assembled at the conference would "support no candidate, however conspicuous his position or brilliant his ability, in whom the impulses of the party manager have shown themselves predominant over those of the reformer."[11]

Simultaneously, a Congressional investigation probed into Blaine's involvement with the Little Rock and Fort Smith Railroad. The evidence was at first inconclusive but, on May 31, a bomb exploded. A new witness, James Mulligan, who had been a clerk in the firm which built the defunct railroad, told the investigators that Blaine had indeed received $64,000 from the Union Pacific for his worthless bonds. He mentioned, moreover, that he had letters between Blaine and William Fisher, his former employer, to prove his allegations. Through some skulduggery, Blaine obtained the letters before they were admitted to the record. Under public pressure, he finally rose up in righteous anger and read them himself in a dramatic display before the House. But, in his selective reading, he garbled their real content. His gambit won temporary applause but undermined his drive for the Republican presidential nomination in 1876.[12]

The defeat of Blaine gave White and Schurz considerable gratification. Both approved the dark-horse choice, Rutherford B. Hayes, who was eventually selected by the Republicans. "Your letter of acceptance," White wrote to Hayes, "is the most encouraging poltical document promulgated since the war." White was in no position, however, to aid the Republican candidate. Except for a few letters of advice to Schurz, who campaigned aggressively for Hayes among German voters, White stayed on the sidelines. He had hoped that Hayes's candidacy would give a "healthy and clarifying tone . . . to the atmosphere of American politics." The inconclusive outcome of the election, however, quickly ended that hope. Politics became hopelessly muddled. The disputed returns dispelled what optimism White had briefly recovered after his return from Europe. "The trouble," he wrote to Schurz, "is that the virus in the civil service had eaten nearly to [the] heart of our institutions."[13]

While politicians tried to resolve the electoral dispute, White opened his offices in New York to assist Henry Villard's railroad enterprises. One of his first letters from his new home was to Carl Schurz, who had just written to him claiming that the Republicans had won the election, since Democrats in the South had kept Negroes from the polls illegally, by force. In a harsh reply, White challenged his friend's rediscovered Radicalism: "It is evident to my mind that the attempt to give leadership, precedence, supremacy, in political affairs [in the] South, to the ex-slave population has failed, and that though there were no Democratic party in the North, it would still be a failure."[14]

At first, White insisted that Tilden, the Democratic candidate, should be allowed to take the presidency, but finally resolved himself to the election of Hayes. The president's appointment of Schurz as Secretary of the Interior together with his support for civil service reform and sound currency convinced White that the best man had been selected. He also heartily endorsed the move by Hayes to withdraw federal troops from the South; never again did White support intervention on the behalf of southern blacks. He had indeed, as he wrote to Schurz, closed that part of his life.

When Blaine led a drive to defend federal protection of southern Republicans, White met such appeals with scorn. "Civil Service reform and pacification of the South," he wrote to Schurz, "must go hand in hand."[15] White's criticism of continued federal intervention had little to do with any aversion to the use of army bayonets to enforce law and order. His position was clarified later that summer when a massive national strike by railroad workers released lower class resentments in several large American cities.

White's hysterical reaction during the strike was no doubt amplified by his involvement in railway affairs. Villard's Kansas Pacific, like most other railroads, was shut down. And although White was secure on Wall Street, his friend Villard got caught in the middle of one of the strike's worst outbursts, in San Francisco. Villard had contacted pneumonia and was near death while the city was torn by strife all around his hotel. His wife described the scene: "The rioters here made his last night very horrible. I feared for fires in all directions and that even we might have to seek flight. The great fire at a lumber wharf presented the greatest spectacle I ever beheld."[16]

To meet this revolutionary strife, White called for a standing army to put down labor violence. "Such a condition of things," he advised *Nation* readers, "is intolerable, and can be amended only by an increase of the military establishment of the nation. The elements of the recent outbreak are still in a state of effervescence, and may develop into new riots and further destruction of life and property at any time, unless confronted by trained bodies of men in sufficient numbers to overawe or crush them at the first outset." Follow Britain's lead was his advice, for "if the truth must be confessed, we have more of the spirit of communism and turbulence to deal with than the mother country."[17]

In this call for a standing army to put down violent strikers, White took care, however, to soothe southern fears of military intervention. "No Democrat," he wrote, "however zealous for states rights, can pretend that such a force would be dangerous in the hands of an Administration which has remitted Packard and Chamberlain to their own resources, and withdrawn all its troops from the South. The doings of the Electoral Commission will exert a faint influence on politics, as compared to the doings of a possible Commune holding the commerce of the country by the throat and sitting in judgment over the rights of property."[18]

Some abolitionists who maintained their devotion to fair elections in the South gained considerable satisfaction from the twisted reasoning of Liberals like White. William Lloyd Garrison II noted the paradox of such thought in a letter to his father: "In one point of view the situation is interesting. Many who were so shocked at the sight of Federal troops in So. Carolina are clamorous for them in Penna. and N. Y."[19]

The late 1870s was a terrifying period for White. While looking out for Villard's railroad affairs in Washington, he also witnessed at close hand the rising demand for "cheap money." To the familiar call for greenbacks, some Congressmen had added a new twist—the free coinage of silver. White's public and private reaction to this was almost as frenzied as his reaction to labor violence. "The foes of communism," he wrote in the *Nation,* "must meet the Toledo rabble at some time. . . . They have got to fight Mr. Bland as a crammer of greenbacks down people's throats, anyhow. They must defend the rights of property and the present system of society and government sooner or later, and defend themselves with whatever weapons their assailants arm themselves withal."[20]

All these fears further alienated White from popular government and severely circumscribed his field of reform. In 1879, he explained to English intellectuals that America should never discard its arrangement of checks and balances for parliamentary government because of the nation's "system of universal suffrage." The vetoes of Presidents and the conservatism of the Supreme Court were needed to moderate Congressional action, for not only had suffrage been granted to a "vast body of blacks" but it was also being granted "every day to a still more mischievous class from the Old World, who have brought the doctrines of Lassalle and Karl Marx into an atmosphere where they cannot be so summarily dealt with as at home. As the population of cities increases, a pernicious sort of dogmatism gains ground. The idea that the majority have a right to govern tends to expand into the idea that what the majority wants is *ipso facto* right."[21]

White found it very difficult to respond politically to depression-ridden America. When a powerful group brought ex-President Grant forward for a third term, he grew alarmed and bewildered. Although he felt that this movement was based on the fear and frustration of northern conservatives, which he shared, he refused to welcome Grant's return as a reactionary messiah. The cure under the General's renewed administration could be worse than the disease itself. Besides, White doubted Grant's fidelity to the antigreenback cause and did not share the desire of the Grant protagonists for renewed law enforcement in the South. "The more champions of this unreasoning sort capital has," White advised, "the worse it will be in the long run for capitalists."[22]

The demand for Grant's reelection to the White House did not diminish. When the Pennsylvania state convention met in 1880 and pledged its support to Grant's candidacy in the national convention, White sounded another alarm in the *Nation*.[23] The old Liberal Republican alliance, however, was even less prepared to face Grant for a third term than they had been for a second. No one wanted to take the lead. The organized strength which the Liberal reformers had once held in the West was gone. Grosvenor, White, and Schurz had drifted East. The Liberals, moreover, were bereft of issues which would stir the political masses, and as the nation began to pull out of the depression, the specter of Grant did not cause much concern among businessmen normally sympathetic to a Liberal campaign. "We cannot raise money," White complained to Schurz, "till the people who have money and who are inclined to agree with us see something going on. . . . The arguments on our side are but imperfectly understood by even the more intelligent portion of the business community." Still something had to be done. White and a group of "independents" hit upon an idea—a series of lectures by prominent reformers to advertise their cause. "We must have meetings of some kind to make a sign of our existence," White wrote to Schurz.[24]

Some sign of existence was made, but little more. The New York reformers organized into the Independent Republican Association and chose White as their president. White did not want the post, since he still considered his involvement with the 1872 bolt a kiss of death to any political organization. "The Machine," he felt, "will make scare crows of the 1872 men. I would not have taken a leading part in the Ind. movement here," White explained, "if the young men who started it could have found anybody of prominence to take hold—but they could not. All who sympathized with them were either too busy or too timid, to 'take a stand.'" The campaign of 1880 pointed painfully to the political isolation of White and his like-minded reforming friends. They could not even find a candidate to support. "We must make a James G. Birney campaign," White told Schurz. But White could follow his assertion only with an embarrassing question: "Who is our Birney?"[25]

Conferences and conventions were called in New York and St. Louis to consider strategy and candidates, but the reformers could do little more than agree upon their opposition to Grant. White expressed their thinking as he led off the New York Independents' lecture series at Steinway Hall in New York City. He had no use for the "lazy rich," the "disgusted millionaires" who with an allied "class of educated and fastidious cynics . . . tell each other that self government is a failure . . . and that it cannot last long. . . ." He insisted that the business of government was no joke and condemned the "degenerate sons of noble sires" who found the only solution in a "stronger government than the United States constitution provides for." No thinking man, White insisted, could ignore the imminent threat to American politics—the election of

Ulysses S. Grant to a third term in the White House. Self-government itself, White claimed, was at stake. "The American Republic . . . is even now . . . bound in powerful coils —the coils of the Machine." A remedy was at hand: "To defeat the third term will be a staggering blow to the Machine."[26]

Grant, however, seemed to grow stronger. Desperate at what appeared a Grant victory just a few weeks before the Republican convention, White even considered looking to the Democrats for a suitable candidate. When Benjamin Bristow duplicated his pessimistic frame of mind, the two men praised the former Illinois governor, John M. Palmer, to Schurz.[27] Schurz, instead of flirting with Democrats, concentrated on organizing an anti-Grant bloc at the Republican convention in Chicago. The coalition strategy worked. The combined efforts of the reformers and "half-Breeds," like James G. Blaine, stopped Grant's thrust.

Blaine, the Liberals felt, would be no threat as a candidate himself; they were certain that his presidential ambitions were thoroughly destroyed by the Mulligan exposures in 1876. White, who went to the Chicago convention representing the New York Independents, thought the convention would settle on John Sherman, Secretary of the Treasury under Hayes.[28] As in 1876, however, another dark horse from Ohio, Senator James A. Garfield, won the nomination. And it was James G. Blaine who insured his victory.

The reformers were initially pleased. Although Garfield had broken ranks with the Liberal Republicans in 1872, he had been one of their own; he spoke their language. They expected him now to clean up the party and institute civil service reform. With that expectation, White and his New York group began to organize in Garfield's behalf. But the nominee's letter of acceptance dashed their hopes. It relegated civil-service reform to a position of minor importance. After he read Garfield's letter, White predicted to Schurz that the Republican candidate's expressions would alienate the New

York independents and throw the state to the Democrats. Schurz, carefully crossing out White's adjective, "contemptible," sent the letter to candidate Garfield as "an expression of widespread opinion."[29]

White's hasty reaction was typical; he soon reconsidered his initial hostility. Although visibly disappointed by Garfield's set of political priorities, he and the other New York independents backed Garfield rather than the Democratic candidate, the Civil War general Winfield Scott Hancock.[30] The Democrats had never offered White any real alternative. From his point of view, their control of Congress in the late 1870s —their first in nearly twenty years—was an unsatisfactory experiment. "The bulk of the party," he found, insisted on "supporting schemes for debasing the currency and impairing the public credit."[31] On the crucial issue of silver coinage, "the conclusion is irresistible," White wrote, "that . . . the Republican party is the safer of the two, and, if not wholly trustworthy, is more so than its antagonist, while the course of General Garfield himself has left nothing to be desired."[32] Therefore, when a decision had to be made, White threw his support to Garfield and the Republicans. Both he and his New York band campaigned vigorously for Garfield, culminating their efforts in a rally at Cooper Institute on the eve of the election.[33]

The narrowness of Garfield's victory gave White and the independents a new sense of power. The Republicans' slim margin in New York, White noted, "happens . . . to be the deciding factor between the two parties in national politics." Civil-service reform, he added, would be the test for continued support. To consolidate and capitalize on their victory, White and the other Liberal reformers formed various agencies to propagandize their causes.[34]

The Liberals' sense of power and effectiveness was probably undeserved. Doubtless, Blaine's efforts in the convention and

Roscoe Conkling's support in New York were far more important than their meager contributions. Garfield expressed his own view of their strength by turning increasingly to Blaine for advice and support. In 1881, he made the senator his Secretary of State. The appointment infuriated the reformers. When Schurz became editor of the *New York Evening Post,* Blaine congratulated him and held out his hand: "I hope all the opponents of the Grant-Imperial crowd, or rather *'gang,'* now understand each other better than ever before and are better prepared to work in harmony to one common patriotic end." The *Evening Post* editors, however, rejected this overture and scoffed at his professed willingness to work for civil service reform. Although Schurz was not as arrogant in his criticism as Godkin and White, he mocked Blaine by treating his new reform attitude as a "rich joke." The difference between Blaine and the reformers, Schurz declared, went beyond the civil service question. "The author of the Mulligan letters will, in spite of 'booms' and 'plumes' and reform professions, never get votes enough to be elected President of the United States."[35]

The arrogance of the reformers grew. Their powerlessness was masked, no doubt, by Garfield's assassination. Not only was Blaine removed from his post by Garfield's successor, Chester A. Arthur, but more importantly, civil-service reform won a major victory in 1883. The public outcry at the President's assassination by a disappointed office-seeker forced Congress to pass the Pendleton Act—a landmark in civil-service reform. Basking in the satisfaction of this victory during a period of national prosperity, Horace White and his friends paid little attention to the signs of both economic recession and a Blaine resurgence.

White was surprised, at first, by the Blaine boom; he, too, thought the 1876 revelations of railroad speculations in the Mulligan letters had forever ruined Blaine's future as a presidential candidate. But when he got word from Illinois in April, 1884, that Blaine was winning strength in that state, he began to treat his candidacy as a sober possibility.[36]

Well before the Republican convention in June, White issued an ultimatum to the Grand Old Party. After reminding his readers of the alleged balance of power held by the independents in New York, White stated flatly:

> Mr. Blaine is the one candidate about whom the minds of the great body of New York Independents is made up. What they know of him they have learned from his own testimony, and not from the accusations of enemies. Their misgivings are, therefore, unappeasable. Their repugnance toward him is more deep-seated and irreconciliable than it is towa d Mr. Arthur. The nomination of the latter would not lead to rupture or revolt in the party. The nomination of the former would.[37]

White meant what he said. In the next several weeks, he started mobilizing the New York Republicans whom he had headed in 1880 for a bolt in 1884. He patched up his difference with Schurz, who had departed the *Post,* and once more joined hands with his old comrade. White provided the active link between the writings of the *Evening Post* editors and the workings of the independents. Godkin generally stood aloof from political organization and his relationship with Schurz remained tense.[38]

After reorganizing the Republican mavericks of 1880, White and several other independents went to the Republican convention. There, despite their own assurance of potential influence in the election, they were extremely weak. They had few delegates and no candidate. Neither John Logan nor President Arthur was a real alternative to Blaine. Blaine's convention strength, on the other hand, was impressive, and he made no move to conciliate the dissidents.[39] The platform offered no quarter. It supported protective tariffs, the pro-

hibition of imported contract labor, federal regulation of
railroads, and the enforcement of an eight-hour day. After a
few ballots, Blaine scored an easy victory. Although Blaine in
accepting his nomination agreed to civil service reform and
"pacification" of the South, the *Evening Post* editors felt this
change of mind only proved his political expediency and
perverseness. Godkin labeled the whole Republican gathering
"a debauch."[40]

As soon as White and other disaffected Republicans retreated from Chicago, they mapped out their next move. On
June 17, they assembled once more and decided against third-
party action. Instead they indicated their willingness to support two Democrats for the presidency, either Delaware
Senator Thomas Bayard or New York Governor Grover Cleveland. The independent movement was unquestionably far
stronger than it had been in 1880. The prosperity of that year
was gone, and the subsequent panic brought the old insurgents
new converts. Large numbers of wealthy businessmen, some of
them millionaires, joined the Independent Committee which
was formed in New York City on June 18. George William
Curtis, chairman of the new group, had led the New York
delegation to the Republican convention in Chicago. Since
the 1870s he had steadfastly resisted flirtation with the Democrats; his willingness now to bolt indicated the proportions of
the movement. In addition, the *Evening Post* now had a significant ally in New York City. George Jones, owner of the
New York Times, pulled his powerful paper out of the regular Republican ranks.[41]

White met the Republican charge that the Mugwump revolt
was just another "bolt of 1872" with a rather perceptive
analysis of the two campaigns. "The single point of resem-
blance which the present revolt bears to that of 1872," White
wrote, "is that it is a revolt against a party nomination incited by public misdemeanors. The similarity begins and ends
there." In explanation, White pointed out that Greeley was

not the choice of the Democrats but an unsuitable former opponent foisted upon them. More importantly, however, the issues had changed: "In 1872 the reconstruction of the Southern States was, in the minds of the great body of Republicans, incomplete. Tales of Kuklux outrages filled the public ear. . . ." But twelve years and the new demands for "reform of the public service," White insisted, had changed the nation's mood. "The issues of slavery have ceased to excite men's passions. The wand which conjured Republicans to the support of Grant in 1872 has lost its power. Whoever wins this year must win by his personal character."[42]

The Mugwump campaign against Blaine certainly was focused on personality. In a brief examination of the Republican platform, White found "a plain streak of communism running through it." The eight-hour day, he insisted, was "one of the most arrant communistic delusions of the day."[43] After this particular outburst, however, White paid little attention to specific issues of the Republican platform. His main target was the character and personality of James G. Blaine.

White insisted that everything be subordinated to the single question of Blaine's immorality in office. In this, he followed the lead of Carl Schurz who asserted that Blaine stood "convicted of having traded upon his high official position and power for his own pecuniary advancement. Of this the notorious 'Mulligan letters' leave no doubt. . . . I therefore consider the defeat of Mr. Blaine a moral necessity. . . ." After the nomination of Grover Cleveland by the Democrats, White delineated the major issue in the *Evening Post*: "The character and record of the candidates nominated will be the real platform. . . ." His friend David A. Wells was disappointed; Wells wanted to do battle over Blaine's commitment to higher tariffs—but found little support. Democratic leader Manton Marble tried to explain to him: "Undoubtedly White is right in thinking Blaine's character as a public man is the winning issue, and we ought not to alter the issue as shaped by the exposures of him which no where else have been so formidable as in the *Eve. Post.*"[44]

In late July the independents' strategy seemed to backfire. A Buffalo clergyman accused Cleveland of having a bastard son.[45] The truthfulness of the charge stunned the fastidious reformers. At first they ignored the scandal; then, they simply increased their attack on Blaine.[46]

Godkin finally made a weak attempt to meet the charge. "Chastity," he said, "is a great virtue, but every man knows in his heart that it is not the greatest of virtues. . . . We will not for our part support the Republican party at this crisis in an attempt to capture the Presidency for a trickster, as Joshua captured Jericho, by the aid of a harlot." Schurz, who was out on the political hustings, knew that something more than sarcasm was needed. He conferred with White and they concluded that their candidate needed the moral cloak of ministerial pronouncement. White met with a Reverend Mr. Collyer who agreed to join with several other clergymen and write "a letter on the subject of the relative importance to the Republic of official integrity and personal chastity." Such measures as these, when reinforced by the publication of a new batch of Mulligan letters, allowed White and Godkin to resume an offensive in the *Post* and *Nation* before the election.[47]

The vote was close. The returns fluctuated, as more than a half dozen crucial states remained in doubt for several days. Neither side was confident of victory. Cleveland finally emerged the winner but not until almost a week after the election. The returns of New York, giving Cleveland a plurality of 1,149 votes, decided the outcome. The state's thirty-six electoral ballots defeated Blaine by a mere eighteen-vote margin. White was jubilant: the victory vindicated all his boasts.[48] The triumph gave him a sense of political power and exhilaration that he had not known since his days with the *Chicago Tribune.* He completely overlooked other factors which helped to decide the issue. The Protestant minister's call in Blaine's presence for a victory over "Rum, Romanism and Rebellion" undoubtedly alienated thousands of Catholic Irish voters who had been strong supporters of Blaine until that time. The effects of the national recession and the last minute willingness of Roscoe Conkling to help his old intra-party enemy also had much more influence in New York, especially in upstate areas, than the Mugwump moral crusade.[49]

Cleveland, however, appreciated the assistance of the Mug-wumps and let them know it. After a visit with the newly elected President, Senator Thomas Bayard wrote David A. Wells: "He fully respects and values the 'Independents' and I do not think Horace White and his friends and associates will feel themselves without weight or just influence." Democratic leaders asked White's advice on Cabinet positions and governmental policy. He gave it freely.[50]

As a result of its important role in the campaign, the *Evening Post* reached new heights in advertising and circulation. It began to give evidence finally of the financial promise which the owners had hoped for in 1881. Everything thus seemed bright for the editors. They viewed the election of Grover Cleveland as the opening of a new day. That they were convinced on an important and necessary role for themselves was indicated by White in a letter to Carl Schurz after he visited the President: "As to the great mass of National questions, which will come up for daily treatment, his information is extremely defective. . . . he is liable to make many and even serious mistakes unless his daily advisers and associates are men of experience and proved political ability." When Edwin L. Godkin came back from the nation's capital shortly after the inaugural, he was "greatly refreshed and encouraged by everything he saw—a new heaven and new earth for Washington."[51]

In the midst of all these optimistic signs, personal tragedy struck White again. On June 6, 1885, just before he intended to start on a vacation, his second wife died from an overdose of morphine. Like many others of the time, she regularly took the powerful drug for severe headaches. This time, however, a physician unfamiliar with her case prescribed a fatal dose. Once more White sustained a loss, and once more it came with a stunning shock. He buried his second wife in the tomb he had built for his first wife. Leaving his children with a relative, he tried to find relief by a change of scene.[52] Three young daughters, one only a few months old, gave him a reason to return. On July 11, he was back at work.

The lines of authority on the *Post* were now unclear. Godkin's two-year term as editor was drawing to a close. No new agreement had been made. For all practical purposes, Godkin remained at the editorial helm, but he was not truly editor-in-chief after 1885. He and White were dual editors. They divided editorial management, Godkin handling political and social topics and White taking charge of financial and economic questions.[53]

Under White's direction the *Evening Post* championed laissez-faire economics in a rapidly changing industrial society. His writings during the last hectic years of the nineteenth century brought him into sharp conflict with the forces of change. The defeat of James G. Blaine, he soon found, had not brought a "new heaven and a new earth." As one of the nation's most celebrated and damned political economists, White's reactions to the new challenges demonstrate the thorough disintegration of Liberal ideology in the 1890s.

NOTES

1. There is no satisfactory biography of Blaine. A competent study is needed; it would reveal much about politics in the Gilded Age, since

Blaine represented the core of Republican support for more than three decades. Three biographies remain useful: Gail Hamilton (Mary Abigail Dodge), *The Biography of James G. Blaine* (Norwich, Conn., 1895); Edward Stanwood, *James Gillespie Blaine* (Boston, 1905); and David S. Muzzey, *James G. Blaine* (New York, 1934). Blaine's autobiography, *Twenty Years in Congress* (New York, 1884–1886), is valuable but contains understandable omissions. For an excellent examination of the Republican party during the late nineteenth century, see Vincent DeSantis, "The Republican Party Revisited, 1877–1897," in *The Gilded Age: A Reappraisal*, ed. H. Wayne Morgan (Syracuse, N.Y., 1963), pp. 91–110.

2. White to Carl Schurz, December 28, 1875, Schurz MSS.

3. Ibid., March 10, 1876, Schurz MSS.

4. John G. Sproat, *"The Best Men," Liberal Reformers in the Gilded Age* (New York, 1868), pp. 90–91.

5. White, "The American Centenary," *Fortnightly Review* 26 (October 1, 1876): 514.

6. E. Bruce Thompson, "The Bristow Presidential Boom of 1876," *Mississippi Valley Historical Review* 33 (June, 1945): 3–30.

7. White to Samuel Bowles, February 8, 1876, Bowles MSS.

8. White to Carl Schurz, February 25, 1876, Schurz MSS. See also White to Schurz, February 14, 17, 22, March 3, 11, 1876, Schurz MSS.

9. White to Carl Schurz, February 25, 1876, Schurz MSS. William C. Bryant, et al. to Francis A. Walker, April 6, 1876, in Schurz, *The Writings of Carl Schurz*, ed. Frederick Bancroft, 3:228–229.

10. Schurz to Francis A. Walker, April 17, 1876, in *The Writings of Carl Schurz*, ed. Bancroft, 3:232. See also Schurz to L. A. Sherman, May 3, 1876, in Ibid., 3:239.

11. Carl Schurz, "Address to the People," in Ibid., 3:245. White had to miss the conference because of a miscarriage of his new wife's first pregnancy, but he advised Schurz and helped recruit participants from the Midwest. He fully endorsed the address. White to Schurz, February 14, April 8, 10, 11, May 17, 1876, Schurz MSS.

12. Muzzey, *James G. Blaine*, pp. 83–115.

13. White to Rutherford B. Hayes, July 12, 1876, Hayes MSS. White gave public commendation to Hayes's letter of acceptance in a signed statement inserted in the *Chicago Tribune*, July 12, 1876. White to Carl Schurz, August 4, 1876, Hayes MSS. White to Carl Schurz, September 2, December 5, 1876, Schurz MSS.

14. White to Carl Schurz, December 21, 1876, Schurz MSS. With less directness than he used in his rebuff of Schurz's reasoning, White publicly challenged the Republican position on the disputed returns from the South. His article appeared as an editorial in the *Nation*—an article which initiated his frequent contributions to that journal. White, "The Rationale of Intimidation," in the *Nation*, December 28, 1876.

15. White to Schurz, March 12, 1877, Schurz MSS.

16. Fanny Villard to Wendell P. Garrison, July 26, 1877 and Fanny

Villard to White, July 25–31, 1877, Fanny Villard MSS. For a detailed account of this national strike, see Robert V. Bruce, *1877: Year of Violence* (Indianapolis, 1959).

17. Horace White, "The Rioters and the Regular Army," *Nation,* August 9, 1877. James F. Rhodes took note of White's article when he wrote his history of the period several decades later. Rhodes recalled that "many reflecting men found a capital expression of their own sentiments" in White's call for troops. James F. Rhodes, *History of the United States from the Compromise of 1850* (New York, 1900–1928), 8:48.

18. Rhodes, *History of the United States,* 8:48.

19. William L. Garrison II to William Lloyd Garrison, July 24, 1877, Garrison Family Papers.

20. *Nation,* March 14, 1878. Letter from Washington dated March 11, 1878. While in Washington, White contributed several reports of affairs in the city. See Ibid., February 25, 1878, March 21, 1878, March 27, 1879, November 13, 1879, and February 12, 1880.

21. White, "Parliamentary Government in American," *Fortnightly Review* 32 (October 1, 1879): 515.

22. *Nation,* March 14, 1878. Letter from Washington dated March 11, 1878.

23. White, "The Harrisburg Convention and its Consequences," Ibid., February 12, 1880. This was an unsigned letter written by White from Washington and dated February 9, 1880.

24. White to Carl Schurz, March 20, 1880, Schurz MSS.

25. Ibid., April 10, 1880, Schurz MSS.

26. White, *Third Term Politics* (Lecture delivered in Steinway Hall, New York, April 5, 1880).

27. White to Carl Schurz, May 20, 1880, Schurz MSS.

28. White to Carl Schurz, telegram, June 5, 1880, Schurz MSS. Ari Hoogenboom, *Outlawing the Spoils,* pp. 182–83. Hoogenboom gives a good sketch of the reformers' campaign in this book, pp. 132–186. Before the elections, White provided a detailed examination of the Republican convention and the maneuvering which preceeded it. White, "The Nominations," *International Review* (1880): 171–184.

29. White to Carl Schurz, July 14, 1880, and Carl Schurz to James A. Garfield, July 20, 1880: Schurz MSS.

30. White to Schurz, September 28, 1880, Schurz MSS.

31. White, "The Democratic Caucus," *Nation,* March 27, 1879. His disillusionment with the Democratic failure to alter the tariff is evident in a letter he addressed to the *Nation* from Washington on February 25, 1876. Ibid., February 28, 1878.

32. White, "The Silver Question in the Campaign," Ibid., October 14, 1880.

33. *New York Tribune,* October 29, 1880. White to Whitelaw Reid, October 29, 1880, Reid, MSS.

34. White, "General Garfield and the Bosses," *Nation,* November 18,

1880. Hoogenboom, *Outlawing the Spoils*, pp. 186–191. One group which White helped form after the election was the Society for Political Education. The roster and prospectus for the group can be found in the White MSS.

35. J. G. Blaine to Schurz, May 26, 1881, Schurz MSS. Schurz to Joseph Medill, September 21, 1882, in *The Writings of Carl Schurz*, ed. Bancroft, 4:155–156.

36. Horace White, "The Logan Campaign," *Nation*, April 3, 1884. Godkin catalogued Blaine's faults in the "The Blaine Boom," Ibid., April 10, 1884.

37. White, "New York in National Politics," Ibid., April 24, 1884. White's raking over of Blaine's record caused Blaine supporters to make some investigations of their own. Whitelaw Reid, editor of the *New York Tribune*, let White know that they knew of his whiskey speculations during the Civil War. White fired back a note to Reid insisting that he had not used his "official position" or "official knowledge" to enrich himself or anyone else. White to Whitelaw Reid, May 12, 1884, Reid MSS.

38. Schurz did no writing for the *Post* since he and Godkin were still unreconciled. But he cooperated with White, who supplied him with advice and materials for his oratorical stumping among the Germans in the West. White to Carl Schurz, July 28, 1884, Schurz MSS. See also H. V. Boynton to White, May 7, 1884; S. P. Butler to Carl Schurz, May 7, 1884; White to Carl Schurz, May 8, 1884: Schurz MSS. Wendell Phillips Garrison approved the new cooperation of Godkin and Schurz: "Mr. Schurz is speaking with singular power in the West, and is the right man in the right place. Mr. Godkin, meantime, is the right man in his place." Wendell P. Garrison to Fanny Villard, September 13, 1884, Fanny Villard MSS.

39. White got into a minor row with Theodore Roosevelt when he reported that Roosevelt wanted to bolt. Roosevelt repudiated the interview, and White countered with a reaffirmation of Roosevelt's original remarks. This sort of criticism embittered Roosevelt's relations with the Mugwumps for some time to come. See Henry F. Pringle, *Theodore Roosevelt* (New York, 1956), pp. 60–62 and Muzzey, *James G. Blaine*, p. 288n.

40. *Nation*, June 12, 1884.

41. A profile of the Mugwump adherents in 1884 shows their significant support from business and upper class groups in New York. Gerald W. McFarland, "New York Mugwumps of 1884" (Master's thesis, Columbia University, 1962), pp. 98–112.

42. White, "The Bolt of 1872," *Nation*, July 17, 1884.

43. White, "Communist Features of the Chicago Platform," Ibid., June 26, 1884. White later defended these remarks against a letter of criticism. Ibid., July 10, 1884.

44. White, "The Democratic Platform," Ibid., July 17, 1884. White did not like the Democratic platform either. Its only good point, he wrote,

was that "it embodies less demagogism than the Republicans!" White, "The Bolt of 1872," Ibid., July 17, 1884. Manton Marble to David A. Wells, n.d., 1884, David A. Wells MSS. George Curtis concurred with White: "The paramount issue of the Presidential election this year is moral," cited by McFarland, "New York Mugwumps," p. 17. Carl Schurz to W. D. Dickham, June 25, 1884, and Schurz to J. W. Hoag, June 29, 1884, Schurz MSS.

45. Just after this revelation, Blaine won the support of the female suffragettes. *Nation*, August 7, 1884.

46. White wrote most of the editorials on the charges stemming from the Mulligan letters. He had been one of the first to hear the details in 1876. To embarrass Medill, who was supporting Blaine in the *Chicago Tribune* in 1884, White publicly recalled that Medill had been so disturbed by the charges in 1876 that he refused to support Blaine for the Republican nomination that year. White, "A Political Reminiscence," Ibid., August 14, 1884.

47. Godkin, "What We Think about It," Ibid., August 7, 1884: White to R. R. Bowker, September 3, 1884, James Freeman Clark MSS, Harvard University. White, "More Light from Mulligan," *Nation*, September 18, 1884.

48. White to David A. Wells, November 17, 1884, Horace White Misc. MSS.

49. For a perceptive analysis of the election returns in New York, see Sproat, "*The Best Men*," pp. 140–141.

50. Thomas Bayard to David A. Wells, December 10, 1884, David A. Wells Coll. White's main demand of the administration was a satisfactory Secretary of the Treasury. He wanted Cleveland to pick Thomas Bayard for the post. When Bayard, however, accepted the post of Secretary of State, White had no other candidate. His advice thereafter was negative. He apparently helped dissuade Cleveland from appointing William Whitney to the post but was compelled to acquiesce to the appointment of Robert Manning. Manning, perhaps in return, made efforts to gain White's favor. White to Carl Schurz, January 5, 13, 24, 30, 31, February 1, 2, 6, 9, 11, 21, 27, 28, March 1, 1885, Schurz MSS. White to Manton Marble, January 20, 29, February 1, 3, 14, 20, March 1, 6, 1885; Robert Manning to Manton Marble, January 29, 1885: Marble MSS.

51. White to Schurz, January 24, 1885, Schurz MSS. Wendell Phillips Garrison to Fanny Villard, March 28, 1885, Fanny Villard MSS.

52. Wendell P. Garrison to Fanny Villard, June 7, 21, 1885, Fanny Villard MSS. The many telegrams and letters of condolence can be found in the Horace White Family Papers.

53. The editorial writings of the two men are distinguished in Daniel Haskell, *Index to Titles and Contributors of the Nation* (New York, 1953). William M. Armstrong has delineated (though not quite correctly) the roles of the two men. Armstrong, *E. L. Godkin and American Foreign Policy* (New York, 1957), pp. 30, 163. Their salaries were the same; White

was never considered a subordinate. When Godkin demanded a raise in pay in 1894, Wendell P. Garrison explained the problem to Henry Villard: "I regarded it as an amendment to the original constitution of the editorial staff, and that I for one should give no vote upon it, pro or con, till you had been heard from. Godkin admitted that his extra allowance would destroy the dual editorship, and make him obviously the editor-in-chief—which he had been in fact from the beginning. A decent regard for Mr. White's feelings dictated laying the matter before you—all the more because, with his customary impulsive liberality, he at once consented to be made second fiddle on the books." Wendell P. Garrison to Henry Villard, December 13, 1894, Fanny Villard MSS. For a more detailed explanation of the working relationship between White and Godkin during these years, see Wendell P. Garrison to Oswald G. Villard, July 14, 1901, Oswald G. Villard MSS.

More than White's liberality and lack of egoism enabled him to work with Godkin. White apparently isolated himself from frequent social intercourse with anyone on the editorial staff. As a result, few of the employees even knew that he was Godkin's equal in authority. Wendell P. Garrison explained White's behavior to his sister: "Neither Frank (Garrison) nor myself had heard of the death of Mrs. White's mother till you wrote; but then Mr. W. is a peculiarly secretive man, and lives very much aloof from his colleagues." Wendell P. Garrison to Fanny Villard, November 15, 1885, Fanny Villard MSS.

15

Political Economist

BELOIT COLLEGE had given White his first training in political economy. The president of the school, Aaron L. Chapin, personally directed the program; he taught a course for seniors entitled "Moral Philosophy." It might have been appropriately called, "Political Economy," but the actual title reflected some of its basic assumptions.[1] Chapin had been an intimate friend and devoted disciple of the Reverend Francis Wayland, a pioneer in American economic theory; he used Wayland's influential book, *Elements of Political Economy,* as the text for his course at Beloit. Wayland saw the laws of Adam Smith as closely related to the laws of God.[2] The title of Chapin's course therefore was appropriate to the subject matter.

A quarter of a century later Horace White reviewed, in the *Nation,* a new edition of his first text, revised by his former teacher, Aaron Chapin. In reviewing the book, White indicated a great deal about the development of his own thinking on economic questions in the years since he had left the Beloit campus in 1853.

White began with a generous commendation: "The greater part of his textbook may be truly called a model of close and clear statement of economic truth." Yet White noted, quite correctly, "that scarcely any attempt has been made to bring the science down to date, or to a later period than the work of Wayland." No attention, White observed, was given to Ricardo or Malthus—men who had provided "the foundation stones of modern political economy." White illustrated his point:

> Dr. Chapin says that "the minimum rate of wages is the rate neces-
> sary to support the laborer and his family—the maximum limit is
> the rate determined by the market value of the product." This is
> one of the maxims of the old school, but it has been shown to be
> erroneous by later writers, and indeed a moment's notice of the
> condition of things existing in India last year, or in Ireland to-day,
> must convince anybody that there is no such thing as "a minimum
> rate of wages." The rate of wages may be and often is not merely
> at starvation point but below it, so that large numbers of the pop-
> ulation who would gladly work perish for want of any wages what-
> ever. These, and some other defects . . . seem to have resulted
> from too close adherence to Wayland and those contemporary
> with him.[3]

White was himself a recent convert to "modern political economy." His adherence to Wayland had continued for some time after he left the portals of Beloit College. Indeed, many classical economists in the United States and elsewhere ignored the laws of Malthus and Ricardo, even though these laws had been propounded decades before White entered college. Despite the pessimistic notions of Ricardo and Malthus, many remained convinced that the application of traditional laissez-faire doctrines would yield a perfect harmony of interests.[4] While editing the *Chicago Tribune,* White, for one, did not look so much to the English exponents of the classical tradition but instead turned to the Frenchman Frédéric Bastiat, who maintained the optimism of Adam Smith. As a result,

White could submit laissez-faire proposals to his readers as programs for social amelioration. Free trade and the general reduction of government interference in the economy could all be presented as a program to reverse the trend of the rich becoming richer and the poor becoming poorer.

As in the case of his Whig associates who had also learned laissez-faire theory in college but who frequently demanded tariffs and internal improvements, White's practice did not always match his theory.[5] The demands of White's midwestern business allies often adulterated his theoretical notions. In his *Tribune* editorials, he justified government regulation of warehouses and railroads; indeed, he insisted upon it. He also compromised his bullionist theories to satisfy his readers' urgent requests for the retention of greenbacks. Optimism and contradictions thus characterized White's laissez-faire notions until the depression of 1873.

The depression had a profound impact on his thought. The radical demands for governmental assistance by agrarians and workingmen forced him to reconsider his theoretical inconsistency. The hard facts of want and suffering during the extended crisis of the seventies ended his complacency about social harmony and American uniqueness. Away from the pressures of daily journalism, he examined his thinking in the surroundings of "depression, discouragement, and even dismay." The depression was a watershed for White. "At all events," he confessed, "we have lost our distinction among nations as the country in which there is work and bread for all."[6] After the depression, White no longer considered himself an uncritical adherent of Chapin or of Wayland. Experience had schooled him in the pessimistic dogmas of Malthus and Ricardo.[7] The rigors of iron laws replaced his innocent belief in inevitable progress; Christian morality, moreover, had little relevance any longer to his theories of social and economic behavior. The evangelical moral insistence which infused his early antislavery attitudes simply vanished from his social outlook. Morality no longer had any place in his economic analysis. Already by the 1870s, White would have seriously questioned the title of his first college course at Beloit.

Not all of his former associates, however, went through this same change of opinion. Some, like Edward Daniels, his anti-slavery comrade, dabbled in one reform movement after another, calling for continued government action and currency inflation even after the outset of depression. But their careers had diverged after the Civil War. White became a wealthy businessman and entered the nation's elitist political and cultural circles, while Daniels vainly chased fortune and took up reform as a carpetbagger in Virginia.[8] White's departure from the Midwest also played a part in shaping his new outlook. The perspective from Wall Street was different from that of State Street. His former associates in Chicago, many of whom were also wealthy, continued to demand railroad regulation and to resist currency contraction and the gold standard. White, on the other hand, assisted in railroad collusion and became one of the nation's leading champions of a sound currency and the gold dollar. Thus, social status and a change of residence combined with the depression to refashion his thought.[9]

White was not an original or systematic thinker. Current political and economic questions, for the most part, determined the focus of his writings. He never wrote as a detached economist; he wrote primarily as a journalist in response to contemporary issues. The question which absorbed him most after his departure from Chicago was the threat of a silver currency. Grant's veto of the bill to increase the supply of greenbacks and the subsequent Resumption Act had stilled the inflationist offensive from the greenbackers. The new attack came from those who insisted on a bimetallic currency. Congress had quietly taken the nation off a bimetallic standard in 1873. Few were opposed to that move, since silver, because of its scarcity, had demonstrated little effect on the nation's money supply. New silver strikes in the Far West a few years later, however, made the metal a potential vehicle for currency inflation, particularly if it were minted at its former market value, established then at a 16 to 1 ratio to the market value of gold.

Convinced that governmental interference with the currency would only aggravate the depression, White joined in the fray. In 1876, at his own request, he presented a paper on the silver question to the American Social Science Association at their annual meeting in Saratoga, New York. He obviously had done a great deal of research in tracing the background of "the rapid and unexampled fall of silver." The market relation of gold and silver he noted was 17½ to 1. Unrestricted coinage of silver at the old legal ratio of 16 to 1, he maintained, would "not bring better times, but rather the reverse," White painted a gloomy picture. "This new calamity, this silver crisis," he warned, "has an ugly look of permanence about it."[10]

White continued his writing on the question in the following years. He established himself as an expert on the problem. When inflationists mobilized to resume coinage of silver at the 16 to 1 ratio, editors and public figures called on him for advice. He responded quickly to their calls.[11] Edwin L. Godkin, in particular, opened the columns of the *Nation* for White to attack the positions of the bimetallists. Despite White's predictions of gloom, Congress passed the Bland-Allison Act, which resumed silver coinage on a limited basis. White predicted the bill would jeopardize the conversion of greenbacks into gold—a program which was to begin in 1879 under the terms of the 1874 Resumption Act. He urged, therefore, that the Bland-Allison measure be repealed.[12]

Largely as a result of his writing on silver, White gained a reputation as an economic authority in the United States.[13] When he entered into the *Evening Post* combine, in 1881, he became the paper's economic expert. When Schurz departed from the staff of 1883, the loose division of tasks—political and economic—was therefore a natural one for Godkin and White. White's writings over the next two decades won him the reputation as one of the nation's foremost exponents of laissez-faire. Although he had little academic training, he was welcomed as an equal by the laissez-faire academics and as a worthy foe by the trained critics of classical economics.[14]

Monetary theory continued to be White's major concern while he was editor of the *Evening Post*. That was to be expected, since monetary problems dominated most of the political fighting in the last years of the nineteenth century.

When Grover Cleveland assumed office, in 1885, White hoped that the new President would reverse the errors which had been committed in public finance. Up until Cleveland's election, White had little faith that the Democrats would renounce their Jacksonian "hostility to capital."[15] He felt, however, that Cleveland had no other choice than to bring a new persuasion to the White House. For White, "the anomalous silver coinage" crippled industry and deterred investment. The issue of silver was in his mind "of more immediate importance than the tariff question."[16]

Since fiscal problems dominated White's attention, he considered the choice of a Secretary of the Treasury Cleveland's crucial Cabinet decision. He applied pressure to secure the appointment of Senator Thomas Bayard, a known gold-standard advocate. Cleveland, however, in an interview with White, questioned Bayard's credentials as a civil-service reformer.[17] Ordinarily White might have accepted that criticism, but the silver crisis overshadowed his fears of spoils in office. "He has so many other invaluable qualifications," White said, "that I would be willing to take the risk of that."[18] Bayard did not get the post; instead he became Secretary of State. After heated wrangling, White finally gave his assent to the appointment of William Manning, a Wall Street banker, as Secretary of the Treasury.[19] White considered him safe.

During the next few years, White kept in close contact with Manning and gave him advice freely. Since Manton Marble made most of Manning's decisions and actually wrote many of his reports, White often communicated with Manning through Marble. White made his point immediately:

> It strikes me that the boldest form of words, to repeal the silver appropriation, will be the best, as for example: "The permanent appropriation heretofore by the . . . act for the purchase of silver bullion to be coined into standard silver dollars is hereby repealed."[20]

The matter was not quite so simple. Support for silver legislation ran strongly through both parties. Cleveland and Manning, therefore, straddled the issue. Rather than repeal the Bland-Allison Act, Manning dragged his feet in enforcing its provisions and cooperated with New York bankers in devising methods to avoid using silver in their exchange. When attacks on Manning's policy came from a Democratic senator from Kentucky, James Beck, White came to the Secretary's defense.[21] Manning thanked White for his services: "I realize that your clear and comprehensive arguments will do a great good by educating the public mind to a proper sense of the impending financial dangers and disasters that threaten the people and their business, unless the enforced coinage of silver dollars is stopped."[22]

Manning also sent White his annual report, which called for the cessation of silver coinage. White was quite naturally delighted with Manning. When Manning later attacked a congressional resolution insisting that he vigorously enforce the silver bill, White expressed his pleasure: "Your reply to the resolution is thunder and lightning. It *may* split the Democratic party but if it does, nobody can charge that the wedge was put there by you. . . . Those who have attempted to erect a lie into the forms of law, and make swindling a national crime, must answer for all their consequences."[23]

Neither Cleveland nor Manning was able to get Congress to repeal the silver law. Yet no calamity followed. Chagrined, White admitted later that his "predictions of panic fell under popular ridicule."[24] The return of prosperity absorbed the silver money without any appreciable affect on the nation's gold supplies. White had no real explanation for the anomaly; he simply ignored the silver question for several years.

Most Americans forget about monetary questions during boom years. White got involved himself in the speculative excitement of the late 1880s. His friend Villard stormed back into Wall Street in 1887 and resumed the presidency of the Northern Pacific. The flush times of the early 1880s had returned. White, like many others, backed his friend's ambitious enterprises with large outlays of cash.[25] The excitement, however, lasted for only a few years, and then a panic followed the boom. In the fall of 1890, several of Villard's grand constructions threatened to fall apart.[26] In search of an explanation, White and Villard found their perfect villain—silver.

When the Republican-controlled Congress of 1890 passed the Sherman Silver Purchase Act in the summer, White did not send up the shrill alarm with which he had greeted the Bland-Allison Act in 1878. Still enjoying the prosperity of the late eighties, he was grateful that Senator Sherman prevented the passage of a worse measure.[27] But when the rumblings of a financial panic reached his ear about five months after Congress passed the bill, White once more began to predict dire consequences. The growing demand in Democratic circles in the West for extending the coinage of silver alarmed him even more. He spoke of "the most tremendous financial crash the world has ever seen" and an economic "slaughter."[28] "It is easy to say," he wrote, "that the trouble . . . predicted [in 1885] has not come to pass. The truth is that it was only postponed, and it is not far distant now if the present programme of silver-men is to be carried out."[29]

Cleveland once more emerged as White's champion. Defeated by the Republicans in 1888, Cleveland published an open letter in 1891 calling for an end to silver coinage. Already armed with national resentment over the Republican's passage of the restrictive McKinley Tariff, Cleveland, in White's mind, seemed destined to reenter the White House as a financial Messiah.[30] Getting the Democratic party to follow Cleveland's lead, however, was difficult. White joined Villard in forging a strategy with Cleveland to commit the party platform to the repeal of the silver legislation.

In New York and Massachusetts a panicked Villard temporarily set aside his business activities and recruited a contingent of businessmen and financiers for the Democratic cause.[31] Largely as a result of their influence, the Democratic parties in both of these states drew up platforms supporting the repeal of the recent silver legislation. Villard then used his influence in Wisconsin, where he had large investments, to frame that state's Democratic statement on silver. Working with White and Schurz in New York, Villard actually drafted the silver plank in the Wisconsin platform. White did most of the writing. Cleveland went over it himself, making a few minor changes.[32] The *Post* deceitfully praised the platform as an expression of western sentiment: "If there has ever been a disposition in the Eastern States to sneer at the West as a region destitute of culture and absorbed in purely material interests, the platform adopted last week by the Democrats of Wisconsin gives notice to the world that the day for such sneers is past." White continued his self-praise:

The most important planks are of course those relating to silver. The denunciation of the disgraceful law of 1890 is like a blow delivered straight from the shoulder and striking squarely between the eyes. . . . On this subject the Wisconsin Democrats have certainly "nailed their colors to the masts." . . . If the party acts up to this platform, it will give the country good government; and where so much sincerity is shown in framing a platform, there is every reason to expect that the party will act up to it.[33]

The national Democratic platform did call for the repeal of the Sherman Silver law; and when Cleveland was elected, he pressed for action.[34] White insisted that, with repeal, "daylight will appear."[35] He was wrong. The nation, instead, continued its descent into a severe depression. When the repeal went through Congress, White published a triumphant editorial entitled "Exit Silver." "There will be no more contests over free silver coinage or over new purchases," he glibly predicted. "Silver will no longer be a persecuted sister, but an inconvenient ghost."[36] He was wrong again.

Although the debate over silver dominated White's writing on the economic problems of the day, other public issues also drew his attention. The tariff question, in particular, continued to trouble him. Free trade had been his major economic crusade in the Midwest, but the abortive campaign of 1872 and the panic of 1873 clouded the importance of that objective and shattered its well-organized pressure groups. He continued his membership in free-trade organizations,[37] but only in the last years of the depression did he begin to do much writing again on the American protective system.

In a speech delivered before the American Social Science Association in 1877, he attributed the severity of the crisis of 1873 to high tariffs. The protective system, he claimed, made it impossible for American manufacturers to market their surplus manufactures abroad. There was no reason that the United States, with its "natural resources, capital, and skill, together with an over supply of cheap labor," could not compete with England and western Europe "in any market whatsoever." Freedom of trade, he insisted, was the *"sine qua non"* of the revival of American business. The United States was "too large for protection," he told his audience. "Its resources, both natural and acquired, are swelling with the pains of a giant against the artificial barriers which now close them in."[38]

The nationalism expressed in White's speech was not feigned. Two years later he said the same thing to a Cobden Club audience in London. He frankly warned his English audience that as soon as America lowered its tariff barriers in search of foreign markets, his country would overtake and outstrip Great Britain on the international scene.[39] Four years later White had the satisfaction of hearing the same warning from Joseph Chamberlain at a similar Cobden Club gathering. White remarked that Chamberlain did not need to derive his ominous opinion of American capabilities from his own earlier speech. Chamberlain's personal experiences as a manufacturer and as president of the British Board of Trade were probably sufficient to give him an understanding of America's economic threat.[40]

Congress had shied away from the tariff for over a decade after making minor revisions of the schedule in 1872. In 1883, a special Congressional committee recommended a general reduction of 20 percent, but the House and Senate raised some rates while lowering a few others. Although Cleveland entered office in 1884 as a low-tariff advocate, he did not tackle the issue until the last year of his administration. Congress rejected his proposals. Nevertheless, in reopening the issue, Cleveland pushed politics off dead center. White, like many others, responded to the new excitement.

White's antitariff writings made a plea to the poor and dispossessed. He could do this without jeopardizing his laissez-faire consistency. To a Harvard audience, he explained: "I think that if we can once get the ear of the plain people there are few who cannot be made to understand that taxes on consumption are undue and disproportionate burdens on the poor."[41] Through their free-trade propagandizing, White and other socially conservative Mugwump economists were also able for a time to join the outcry against monopoly powers of the new industrial giants. But White and his friends refused to consider any legislation regulating monopoly; such a program ran counter to their ideology.[42] In the case of White, personal involvement, no doubt, also influenced his condemnation of a positive governmental response to monopoly. He had assisted Villard in the formulation of railroad pools; he himself served as a "trustee" of some of Villard's elaborate constructions. Besides, some of the Wall Street directors of the trusts were his close friends.[43] When Congress began serious consideration of national railroad regulation, White insisted that "the wisest thing Congress can do is to keep hands off altogether."[44]

Consolidation in industry obviously perplexed and befuddled White. Though at times he warned against the evils of monopoly, he frequently countered the threat of government regulation with praise for the efficiency and lower prices resulting from unobstructed consolidation.[45] He berated the Interstate Commerce Commission for trying to enforce lower rates among railroads and congratulated the group when it retreated from a policy of strict enforcement.[46] He recognized the tensions and contradictions in his thought. The lowering of tariffs was not a solution for every monopoly; not every consolidation brought lower prices and efficiency. The Standard Oil Trust gave him no end of trouble. It had circumvented the laws of competition without any direct governmental assistance. Lowering tariffs on an industry already dominating the world market offered no solution. Nor was there any evidence that the firm provided consumers with lower prices than its former competitors. "Trust monopolies," White admitted, "are new things under the sun in the fact that they do not have their origin in any act of Government." Old notions of laissez-faire offered no solution. "To say that competition will overthrow trusts is a wholly unwarranted assumption. . . . Now that experience has proved the contrary, the burden of proof is shifted upon the other side to *show* how competition will do the thing which is admitted to be best for the interests of society."[47] White had become the victim of his own ideology. Governmental authority was anathema, but unrestrained competition itself had brought about monopoly. When pinned down for a solution, White was stymied: "The Standard Oil Trust," he weakly surmised, "will be put to death somehow and sometime, most probably by its own vaulting ambition."[48]

Other men were offering solutions to the threatening corporate giants, but White and his colleagues would have none of their suggestions. New economists—some trained by German universities, others by native experience—demanded government action. But White refused to consider their negations of "economic laws." He and his colleagues treated the new economists with the same scorn that English Liberals reserved for the Radicals who were moving outside the respectable pale of classical economics in order to meet the social problems of the day.[49] The new intellectuals were labeled "sentimentalists," "socialists," and "fomentors of strikes." Both Godkin and White called for and defended the removal of Richard T. Ely and certain other new economists from American universities.[50] In 1893, White clarified what he felt were the basic errors of the new theorists. Addressing himself to an audience at a memorial service for A. L. Chapin in Beloit (not far from Richard T. Ely's University of Wisconsin), White digressed from his remarks:

A new school has arisen which insists upon giving a place to religion and the higher moral nature of man in the domain of economics, with which they have no more to do than they have to do with mineralogy or chemistry. . . . When anybody tells us that it is a part of political economy to pay higher wages than the market rate, or to "sell all that thou hast and give to the poor," or to turn the left cheek, when the right one has been struck, we reply that all these things may be a part of our duties, and yet political economy may refuse to consider them. This is not saying that political economy merely teaches how to get rich. . . . It shows you how wealth comes into the world, how it moves about, and how it disappears and reappears.[51]

White could and frequently did write dispassionate appraisals of the work of the economists of the new school.[52] His lengthy reviews of Henry George's work were calm and deliberate. He noted, for instance, that George was no "agrarian, or a communist, or in any sense a disturber of the peace and good order of society." White confined his accusation to a critique of what he felt was utopianism and impracticality. He commended some of George's ideas but challenged his negation of the wage-fund theory and the Malthusian law of population. George's concepts of land scarcity, according to White's view, were irrelevant in the United States.[53] White countered that if taxation were to assist in alleviating social problems, taxation of corporate income was more practical than taxation of land values.[54]

White, however, did not always remain so calm. Whenever the new intellectuals became social activists, he challenged them with frenzied attacks. When George, for example, ran for Mayor of New York in 1886 on his Single Tax program, White called his movement "revolution" and accused George of advocating socialism.[55] Although the *Evening Post* had campaigned vigorously against Tammany Hall in 1884, it approved the alliance between the wealthy Mugwump reformers and the Tammany politicos to elect George's Democratic opponent, Abram Hewitt.

The rise of these new reform movements in the late 1880s paralyzed the normal political activity of White and his fellow Mugwumps. After mobilizing to attack the McKinley tariff in 1890, they drew back because more radical groups threatened to flood their organization. In 1889, White was chosen as the chairman of the Committee on Propaganda by a tariff-reform convention held in Chicago.[56] The group had plans to form local committees all around the country. Villard, members of the Kuhn-Loeb firm, and other New York financiers were ready to back the movement.[57] But it died in stillbirth because followers of Henry George insisted on participating. Rather than let them join the movement, White and others scuttled the whole operation. J. Sterling Morton, businessman from Kansas, summed up their feelings: "I agree with David A. Wells. We had better omit the Convention for 1890. The Single Tax men would swarm in and dilute results. It was difficult to prevent the absorption, by them, of the last convention. . . . And now, I feel quite certain, the George men would take control and . . . ruin for the occasion, Tariff Reform and its earnest advocates."[58]

Although White continued to urge lower tariffs, he never again tried to mobilize mass support for their adoption. Nor did he again suggest free trade as a method of resolving social problems in the United States. When Cleveland returned to the White House, only minor adjustments were made in the tariff. The editors of the *Evening Post* did not demand that the president take his fight to the people. They had larger problems on their minds after 1893.

The late nineteenth century was not an opportune time for dispassionate discourse on political economy. A great deal of what White wrote was filled with cataclysmic forebodings. He looked out upon a society plagued with depression, panics, riots, strikes, and boycotts; his thought cannot be understood unless it is placed in this context. Ever since the Panic of 1873, his own fortune, as well as those of his friends, had been threatened by bankruptcy and ruin. With each depression came demands for the reordering of society or the redistribution of income. With each depression the demands grew louder and the exponents more articulate. With each depression

White became less secure and more frightened of those demanding radical change.

In the 1870s White had lashed out against the agrarians and the strikers; and, unlike Schurz, he had accepted Godkin's flaying of the telegraphers in 1883. Godkin handled the *Evening Post*'s editorial response to most of the strikes for the remainder of the nineteenth century, but it is obvious that White sympathized with Godkin's reactionary pronouncements. White hoped that some noncompulsory system of arbitration could be developed to avoid labor outbursts,[59] but when those outbursts occurred he invariably sided with the employer. He granted the legality of unions, but he deplored those that became aggressive. National organizations, like the Knights of Labor, he considered dangerous.[60] When the Haymarket riot exploded in Chicago in 1886, White joined Godkin in applauding the order to execute the anarchists. The disturbances in 1886 obviously upset White. To Cleveland's Secretary of State, Thomas Bayard, he wrote: "It is hard to keep civilization going. Sometimes I think that Bismark's [sic] way is best." When anarchists paraded a few months later in New York, White urged city officials to frame ordinances to restrict such processions. He considered models for emulation the ordinances which Chicago had passed after the Haymarket massacre. He urged the New York legislature to grant the city full powers to halt "a polygot foreign rabble" from marching "through the streets with black flags and red flags."[61]

In the 1890s White happened to be in sole direction of the paper when the most celebrated of the strikes occurred. Since most of these disturbances usually took place in mid-summer when Godkin was off to Europe on two-month vacations, White measured the *Post*'s response to the labor outbursts. The language of his editorials was more restrained than Godkin's, but the content was the same.[62] When the Homestead strike took its violent turn in the summer of 1892, White came down hard against the strikers and approved the Pennsylvania militia's intervention "to end the anarchy . . . , to restore the works to the owners of the property, and to protect them in their right to operate them."[63] When Senator Palmer of Illinois deprecated the Carnegie Steel Company's use of the lockout and private armies, White accused his old friend of being in league with the followers of Edward Bellamy and "the Socialists of the school of Marx."[64] When a House Committee later issued an official report absolving Congress from any responsibility in the strike and defending the actions of the employers, White praised the chairman of the special study group: "Mr. Cates is entitled to the thanks of the community for daring to say the right word."[65]

Perhaps the most important strike in the nineties took place two years later at the town and works of Pullman, Illinois, just outside of Chicago. White had known the owner, George Pullman, when they were neighbors in Chicago several decades earlier. He subsequently invested in Pullman's firm and frequently met with him both in New York and Chicago. On one occasion, White toured Pullman's elaborate industrial empire. Shortly thereafter, in 1895, he defended the paternalistic establishment, where Pullman owned the homes and businesses, against the criticism of the "new school" economist Richard T. Ely. Pullman's town, according to Ely, was a repulsive and forbidding feudalistic barony.[66] White, on the other hand, considered it "the most notable existing combination of labor and capital in the world." "The idea at the bottom of the enterprise," White answered, "was neither philanthropy nor avarice, but an intelligent conception that the highest rate of profit for capital was consistent with the highest state of comfort for labor." White concluded: "So much has been done for them [the workers] that the future may be trusted to care for itself."[67] From the workers' point of view, however, the future came laden heavy with hardships, suffering, and, in 1894, the shedding of blood.

Under the leadership of Eugene V. Debs and his American Railway Union, the Pullman workers struck against lowered wages and high rents. As other railroad workers joined in a sympathy strike, the nation's railroads came to a halt. The employers refused to negotiate and stiffened in order to annihilate Debs's organization.[68] Cleveland's Attorney General, Richard Olney, broke the deadlock by securing an injunction against the union and reopening the railroads through the use of federal troops. The Governor of Illinois, John Altgeld, protested against this move but to no avail. White, on the other hand, considered Olney's action "worthy of the highest praise." The strikers, in his mind, had no just complaint. He expected them to accept the wage reduction with "a grin and bear it" attitude. "Wages," he said, "do not grow on trees and cannot be had except upon the condition of meeting the market. These conditions are sometimes hard. In fact, they are so hard in some countries that large numbers of people perish for want of sufficient nourishment every year. Anybody who fights against them, or who spends his time cursing the 'iron law of wages,' will go supperless to bed and will get no other reward for his pains."[69]

The *Post* under White's management questioned Debs's sanity and called Altgeld the "friend and champion of disorder."[70] There was no question about the legality of Cleveland's decision to intervene; the *Post* editors insisted that he had not only the "power to suppress mobs, but to overcome anarchist governors."[71] In December, when a federal judge sentenced Debs to six months in jail under the Sherman Antitrust Act for interfering with interstate commerce, White thought the sentence "mild" and only a "token of what society has in store for this class of offenders."[72]

Cleveland's election in 1892 had obviously brought neither peace nor prosperity. Although Cleveland's administration had ended the coinage of silver, it proved unable to still silver demands. Indeed, as the depression grew worse the demands grew louder. To more and more of the discontented, free silver became a rallying cry for widespread reform.[73] In 1895, White took notice of the renascence of the free-silver movement. An address signed by William Jennings Bryan and thirty other recently defeated Democratic members of Congress sounded the alarm. The address called for unrestricted coinage of gold and silver at a ratio of 16 to 1. The disgruntled Democrats cursed the leadership of both parties. White accepted their challenge: "One way or the other," he reasoned, "either by putting a new party in the field or by putting the Democratic party on a free-coinage platform—it is to be hoped that the issue may be squarely made in the next Presidential election. . . . Let us hope that it may not be postponed beyond 1896."[74]

White got his wish. When Governor John Altgeld took command of the Illinois Democratic party and silver-minded Democrats gained control in Ohio, White urged Gold Democrats to make preparations for a bolt from their party. Though such a move might mean the election of a tariff-minded Republican, White did not care. "In any case," he explained, "a McKinley tariff is a curable evil, as we have already seen, while a fifty cent dollar is not."[75] There would be another compensation: "We can still find satisfaction in the prospect that all the cheap-money men, repudiators, Populists, anarchists, and Coxeyites are ranging themselves under one banner where they can all be raked by one fire."[76]

White was displeased when the Republicans supported a tariff and nominated its symbol, William McKinley. But he rejoiced when the GOP came out for the gold standard and when McKinley pointed to free silver as *the* issue of the campaign.[77] When the Democrats pledged an administration to free silver, as White knew they would, he declared the campaign a major crisis: "If the party of repudiators cannot be put down, the republic cannot be preserved and is not worth preserving."[78] Bryan's nomination, he considered a catastrophe. He disowned the Democrats: "The decadence of the party in the past few years since the Tillmans, Altgelds, Bryans, and Blackburns came to the front and took the leadership, has been melancholy in the extreme."[79]

White and other Gold Democrats girded for the battle. They called for third-party action. Their purpose in taking this course was clear. They were neither neutrals nor escapists. They intended to elect McKinley but keep their hands clean in doing so. Moorfield Storey summed up their thinking in a few sentences: "I am very anxious for an independent movement or a bolt. I think it is necessary to divide the Democratic vote and more necessary in order that there may be some trustworthy organization to which the voters can turn when the reaction which is sure to follow McKinley's election sets in."[80] White expressed the same muffled partisanship when he urged Schurz to speak out "in order to instruct ten thousand Republican stump speakers who want to say something on the money question but don't know how." Without proper coaching, the Republicans might "lose the election," White warned.[81] Schurz took to the campaign trail, and once more White supplied him with facts and figures for his speeches.[82] White had many at his disposal. To counter the popular propaganda of the silverite William "Coin" Harvey, he had already published *Coin's Financial Fool*.[83] In the same period of excitement, he had also prepared and written his larger treatise, *Money and Banking Illustrated by American History*.[84]

The Gold Democrats nominated John Palmer of Illinois as their candidate for the presidency and fostered Sound Money Clubs to propagandize their antisilver sentiments. These organizations did not garner many votes, but they did collect a great deal of money. The traditionally Democratic financiers of New York were alarmed. James Loeb of Kuhn, Loeb and Company expressed their concern to Schurz: "Things have grown worse, and apprehension as to the outcome of the election, is, I think steadily growing in well informed circles." Loeb agreed to help with the organization of the anti-silver campaign. He suggested that the effort "must not be known to have originated in New York or in the East." It should begin, rather, in "Indiana, Kentucky and Maryland or Missouri." Two days later, Loeb reported on the progress of his work among fellow businessmen in the city: "I have just seen Schwab of the Chamber of Commerce Sound Currency Committee and he thinks well of the plan. A great deal of money must and can be raised. People's blood is up."[85] A great deal of money was raised and most of it was diverted directly to the National Republican Campaign Committee. Campaigning by the Gold Democrats was also coordinated with the Republican effort in order to field "one well equipped army of fighters rather than a lot of separate organizations."[86]

By early August, White regained confidence and thought that the chances of Bryan's election were "diminishing rather than increasing."[87] To the end, however, he persisted in a hysterical campaign. The Populists certainly had no monopoly on unreasonable exaggeration and irrationality. Both Schurz and White considered the election as dangerous as the contest of 1860. "We have faced other campaigns," White explained, "in which feelings were powerfully enlisted, and in which it seemed to some of us as if an adverse result could not easily be borne, but we have never seen one where a false step was so void of remedy and recall. The election of Mr. Bryan is a step that can never be recalled, because it is a lapse from virtue. . . . To talk about retracing such a step is like attempting to put new life into a corpse."[88]

Bryan's defeat did not restore full confidence to White. The victory was too close; too many had supported radical reform. As a result, White was not quick to jettison the coalition which the Gold Democrats had fashioned with the

Republicans during the campaign. "Our policy now," he wrote to one enquirer, "is not to worry the Republicans tariff-wise but to keep them, as far as we may to reach right conclusions."[89] For the assistance given by the Gold Democrats, White asked just one concession: security of the gold standard. White made the selection of a Secretary of the Treasury a test of Republican financial convictions. In the *Evening Post* and in a letter to McKinley, White made clear the Gold Democrat's choice for the post, Lyman J. Gage, a Chicago banker and personal friend.[90] Gage got the cabinet seat.[91]

In 1900, the Republican leaders justified White's expectations: they passed the Currency Act which legalized the gold standard. White's long struggle thus had ended in victory. His own contribution to that triumph was not forgotten. The next year, at a banquet celebrating the hundredth anniversary of the *Evening Post,* Wall Street banker Joseph C. Hendrix threw him a verbal bouquet:

> While Mr. Godkin's strife in the thirty years' war for civil-service reform is very laudable, let me say from the banking world . . . that we recognize and appreciate the service to this country of the luminous editorial writer in all of the fight for the preservation and final adoption, and the perfect maintainance [sic] of the gold standard in this country—Mr. Horace White. . . . It is my privilege and my honor to be able to be here in behalf not only of the bankers of New York, but in behalf of the bankers of the United States, to testify [turning to White] to your splendid services in the final establishment of the gold standard in this country.[92]

White had reason to be grateful to the Republicans. Yet, even before they established the gold standard, he was already damning the McKinley administration and preparing for its defeat. The imperialist adventures of the new President had stimulated Horace White's last crusade.

NOTES

1. Gladys Bryson, "The Emergence of the Social Sciences from Moral Philosophy," *International Journal of Ethics* 42 (April, 1932): 304–323, cited and discussed by Sidney Fine, *Laissez Faire and the General Welfare State* (Ann Arbor, Mich., 1956), p. 11.

2. Fine, *Laissez Faire*, p. 11.

3. White, "Political Economy for Schools," *Nation*, April 1, 1880. Aaron L. Chapin, *First Principles of Political Economy* (New York, 1880). When Chapin died in 1893, White praised him as a teacher and a scholar of economics. See *Alumni Memorial Service. Aaron L. Chapin, July 20, 1893* (Beloit, 1893), pp. 23–27. Joseph Dorfman discusses Chapin in his book, *The Economic Mind in American Civilization* (New York, 1949), 3:74–75.

4. Dorfman, *The Economic Mind*, 3:49–50.

5. White later recalled this dichotomy in his own thought before he joined the free-trade movement after the Civil War: "When I was in college . . . the tariff was not a political issue. There was no controversy about protection and free trade. We learned from our text-book and our instructor that free-trade was the system most conducive to the national well-being, yet we learned it in a languid sort of way. . . . But after some years protection had a revival in the legislation of the country and began to be talked about. It became my duty as a journalist to know the reasons for and against it. As a Republican in politics I had a leaning toward protection; as a pupil of Dr. Chapin I had a leaning toward free trade. I was not slow in discovering that all, or nearly all, the men who had any reputation as writers and teachers of political economy agreed with Dr. Chapin." *Alumni Memorial Service. Aaron L. Chapin*, p. 26.

6. White, "The Tariff Question," *Galaxy* 24 (October, 1877): 501–502. See also White, "The Financial Crisis in America," *Fortnightly Review* 25 (June 1, 1876): 810–829.

7. His acceptance of Malthus is evident from an editorial in the *Nation*. Criticizing legislative proposals voiced before a special committee, White insisted: "The question pressing upon the committee, and upon the whole world, at all times, is nothing else than the problem of supporting an unlimited—potentially unlimited—number of people upon a limited amount of produce." White, "Mr. Hewitt's Committee on the Depression in Business," *Nation*, August 15, 1878. Brought before this committee about a week later, White scoffed at the suggestion of public works: "There is no place to stop. There is nobody to say what employment I shall be engaged in, or how much money I shall earn." U.S., Congress, House, *Depression in Labor and Business*, 45th Cong., 3d sess., H. Misc. Doc. 29, p. 569 [August 23, 1878].

8. For a sketch of Daniels's postwar career, see David Montgomery, *Beyond Equality*, pp. 436–439. His letters to his wife and his diaries

vividly portray his failure to move, like White, into the citadels of status and power. Boxes 1–4, Edward Daniels MSS.

9. The impact of the depression and a change of residence changed Henry D. Lloyd's outlook too, except in a different way. Much more consistent in his advocacy of strict laissez-faire before the election of 1872, Lloyd's coming to Chicago and the outbreak of the depression caused him to accept bimetallism and to sympathize with lower class demands. His recent biographer notes the change. "While the *Tribune*'s free silver campaign obliged Lloyd to differ from the Gold Standard economists, his fight for railroad reform led him to abandon laissez-faire completely. . . . Ethical and power considerations combined with Chicago's and regional interests in determining his policy." Chester Destler, *Henry Demarest Lloyd and the Empire of Reform*, p. 103.

10. White, *The Silver Question* (New York, 1876), pp. 3, 4–23, 25.

11. White "Present Phases of the Currency Question," *International Review* 4 (1877): 750. White to Carl Schurz, September 27, 1877, November 7, 1878; White to John Sherman, November 15, 1877; White to John Morley, July 17, 1878; White to Thomas M. McDonough, September 3, 1878: copies of all these letters are in the Horace White Family Papers.

12. White, "After Specie Resumption—What?" *International Review* 5 (1878): 833–846. The House bill of Bland was emasculated by Senator Allison's amendments. Allison, an old friend of White, had made his move largely out of expediency. He was no advocate of silver coinage. White sent him a copy of his article and insisted "that Bill Allison will have to repeal the Allison Bill if he can." White to William Allison, October 29, 1878, copy in the Horace White Family Papers.

13. When John J. Lalor planned his comprehensive *Cyclopedia of Political Science*, 3 vols. (New York, 1881–1884), he asked White to contribute articles. White, "Commercial Crises," 1:523–530; "Money and Its Substitutes," 3:730–752; and "Paris Monetary Conference," 3:58–68.

14. White and several other "popular economists" (David A. Wells, Edward Atkinson, Manton Marble) met frequently with the academics in an informal group called the Political Economy Club. J. Lawrence Laughlin founded the group in 1883. The unity of the popular and academic laissez-faire theorists was social as well as intellectual. They were a tightly knit group. White arranged most of their meetings in New York. White to Manton Marble, March 12, 1884; April 3, 1885, Marble MSS. White to David A. Wells, November 17, 1884, Wells MSS. White to E. R. A. Seligman, April 23, 1889, E. R. A. Seligman MSS, Columbia University. White to Carl Schurz, December 27, 1886, Schurz MSS. See also Fine, *Laissez Faire*, pp. 49–51.

15. White, "The Democrats and the Finances," *Nation*, November 23, 1882.

16. White, "Silver Dollars," Ibid., March 1, 1883. White stressed that, if Cleveland were able to stop silver coinage, the move would "be only second in importance as a financial achievement to the resumption of

specie payments in 1879." White, "The Next Administration and the Silver Bill," Ibid., February 5, 1885. See also White, "The Silver Crisis," Ibid., February 28, 1884.

17. White to Carl Schurz, January 24, 1885, Schurz MSS. For a discussion of this interview, see Charles C. Tansill, *The Congressional Career of Thomas Francis Bayard, 1869-1885* (Washington, D.C., 1946), p. 338.

18. White to Carl Schurz, February 1, 1885, Schurz MSS.

19. White to Manton Marble, February 20, 1885. Marble MSS. White gently prepared the *Evening Post* readers for the appointment before announcing it. Still it brought some angry dissent. This was a case in which White obviously ran the policy of the paper. Henry Adams to E. L. Godkin, February 23, 27, 1885, Godkin MSS.

20. White to Manton Marble, March 1885, Marble MSS.

21. *New York Evening Post,* January 13, 1886, later reprinted in pamphlet form. White, *The Silver Coinage Question, A Review of Senator Beck's Speech.* Marble helped White get his article reprinted in the *Washington Post* in order "to search Beck and his crowd where they live." White had to pay $100 to get it republished in that newspaper. After reading White's retort, Abram Hewitt asked White to write some material for him. White to Manton Marble, January 14, 18, 1886, and White to Mr. Webster, January 14, 1886: Marble MSS. *Washington Post,* January 17, 1886.

22. Daniel Manning to White, January 18, 1886, Horace White Family Papers. Manning followed Marble's advice in sending White this letter of gratitude. White kept in close contact with Manning, going to Washington frequently to confer with him. Daniel Manning to Manton Marble, January 18, 1886, and White to Manton Marble, January 30, 1886: Marble MSS.

23. Manning copied portions of White's letter in a letter of his own to Marble. Manning to Manton Marble, March 4, 1886, Marble MSS.

24. White, *Money and Banking* (Boston, 1902), p. 199. White insisted that the prophecy was true: "The fulfillment was delayed by the shrinkage in the national bank circulation and by the retirement of small greenbacks." As a result, he claimed, there was no increased pressure on the gold reserves.

25. James Hedges, *Henry Villard and the Railways of the Northwest,* p. 148. Villard, *Memoirs,* 2:321-337. Villard came back to the United States refortified with German capital. He expanded his involvement into electricity and coal as well as railroads. White invested in all his promotions from Edison's companies to a Far Western coal syndicate. He also served as a trustee of some of Villard's financial constructions. C. A. Spofford to White, July 25, 29, September 12, 1887; August 6, 1888; February 14, June 3, 1889; February 11, 1892: Henry Villard MSS. White's business accounts are listed under the following dates in Villard's record books, January 1, July 1, 1889; January 1, 1890; January 1, February 26, 1892: Henry Villard MSS. White had up to $70,000 invested through

Villard at various times. Carl Schurz, who got involved in a wide range of speculative adventures in these boom years, had almost $100,000 invested in Villard's enterprises. See his account with Villard, January 16, 1890, Henry Villard MSS.

26. Fanny Villard to Oswald Garrison Villard, September 24, November 17, 27, 1890. Henry Villard MSS. Villard had to hurry to Europe to obtain enough capital to shore up his American enterprises.

27. White, "The Silver Compromise," *Nation*, July 10, 1890.

28. White, "The Money Question," Ibid., December 18, 1890.

29. White, "Senator Sherman on Free Coinage," Ibid., January 8, 1891.

30. White, "Mr. Cleveland's Letter," Ibid., February 19, 1891.

31. Villard, *Memoirs* 2:360–364. See also Matthew Josephson, *The Politicos* (New York, 1938), pp. 488-491.

32. Henry Villard to White, April 23, 1892, and C. A. Spofford to White, May 6, 1892: Henry Villard MSS. See also E. C. Wall to William F. Vilas, April 18, 25, 27, May 23, 1892, William F. Vilas Papers. Horace S. Merrill, *William Freeman Vilas* (Madison, Wis., 1954), pp. 192–193.

33. *Nation*, May 5, 1892. Villard had his secretary tease White about the feigned editorial. C. A. Spofford to White, May 6, 1892. The editorial first appeared in the *Post* and was reprinted later in the *Nation*. It is evident from a telegram from Villard to Schurz (July 20, 1892, Henry Villard MSS) that White and Villard continued to act as important advisers for Cleveland. "Arranged strictly confidential conference with Cleveland to consider serious subjects. . . . Only Fairchild, Grace, White, yourself and myself will be present."

34. White kept up the propaganda campaign after Cleveland's election. White, "Silver Legislation," *Nation*, November 17, 1892, and "Repeal the Silver-Purchase Act," Ibid., December 1, 1892. In one of his rare speaking engagements, he also called for the repeal before the Congress of Bankers and Financiers at their meeting in Chicago on June 20, 1893. White, *The Gold Standard* (New York, 1893). See also White, "A Substitute for Silver," *Harper's Weekly* 37 (July 22, 1893): 698.

35. White, "Financial Whimseys," *Nation*, July 27, 1893. See also White, "Constitutional Government," Ibid., October 19, 1893. White was convinced that the money panic which preceded the depression of 1893 was caused by the withdrawal of European investment, brought on by the passage of the Sherman Silver Purchase Act of 1890. "What may be affirmed with positiveness," he explained, "is that our present scarcity of money would certainly be relieved by the surplus of Europe but for the silver scare. For the first time within my recollection has it happened that the offer of high rates of interest in this country has not proved an attraction to foreign capital. The reason why it has not must be coupled, in the minds of foreigners, with some danger of the loss of principal. The repeal of the Sherman law will remove that danger and nothing else will." White, "India's Action and the Sherman Bill," *The Forum* 15 (August, 1893): 656.

36. White, "Exit Silver," *Nation*, November 2, 1883.

37. The Free Trade Association withered away in the United States in 1872. That same year, however, White joined the international Cobden Club and frequently attended their annual dinner meetings in London. In 1875, he did not attend but sent a letter commenting upon the lack of any special free-trade agitation in the United States. He predicted that the hard times of the depression, however, might bring a revival of free-trade sentiment. *Report of the Proceedings at the Dinner of the Cobden Club, July 17, 1875* (London, 1875), p. 104.

38. White, "The Tariff Question and Its Relations to the Present Commercial Crisis," *Journal of Social Sciences* 9 (January, 1878): 117–131. The *Galaxy* magazine picked up the speech delivered on September 7, 1877, before it was printed in the American Social Science Association's official proceedings. White, "The Tariff Crisis," *Galaxy* 24 (October, 1877): 501–511.

39. White delivered his speech at the Cobden Club's annual dinner in 1879. G. H. B. Jackson, *The History of the Cobden Club* (London, 1939), p. 74.

40. White, *Surplus and the Tariff* (Boston, 1888), p. 8. [An address before the Harvard Financial Club, February 27, 1888.] Chamberlain's doubts about continued British superiority under a policy of free-trade caused serious divisions in the Cobden Club when he was elected chairman at the annual meeting in 1883. His concern with domestic problems irritated many of the internationally minded free traders. White attended that meeting and enjoyed the fireworks. He described the affair in a long letter to the *Nation*. His letter was dated July 1, 1883, and was published in the July 19, 1883, issue of the *Nation*.

41. White, *Surplus and the Tariff*, p. 11.

42. White, "Trusts, Tariffs, and Wages," *Nation*, November 10, 1887.

43. Henry Villard to White, March 5, 1891, Henry Villard MSS. Villard wrote the *Nation*'s first editorial responses to the passage of the Interstate Commerce Bill. He considered the law "crude and incomprehensible." Continuing with the unsigned editorial, Villard predicted: "We deem it as certain as anything, in the solution of the railroad problem in the United States, that the national Government and the public will, after a short period of trial, unite in adopting the correct view of pooling." Henry Villard, "How the Inter-State Commerce Bill Will Work," Ibid., February 3, 1887.

44. White, "Railway Regulation," Ibid., May 5, 1885.

45. White, "The Railroad Problem," Ibid., February 12, 1885, and "Interstate Commerce Bill," Ibid., December 23, 1886.

46. White, "The Inter-State Commerce Report," Ibid., December 28, 1887, and "The Railroad Agreement," Ibid., January 17, 1889.

47. White, "The Competition of Trusts," Ibid., December 20, 1888.

48. White, "Trusts and Confidences," Ibid., May 5, 1887.

49. E. L. Godkin, "Socialistic Tendencies of English Radicalism,"

Nation, July 9, 1885. For an examination of the "new school" of economic theory, see Joseph Dorfman, *The American Mind in American Civilization,* pp. 141–212, and Fine, *Laissez Faire,* pp. 198–251.

50. The *Nation* and *Evening Post* led the drive to remove Richard T. Ely from the University of Wisconsin. *Nation,* July 12, 19, 1894. The humiliating failure in this instance did not deter White and Godkin from approving other academic purges. When E. Benjamin Andrews was dismissed from Brown University, White wrote the *Post's* commendation of the purge. He explained to Villard: "I did write the article on the Andrews Case. . . . The only doubt I had about the matter . . . was whether the trustees should be sustained on financial grounds or on the ground that Andrews was a political agitator and had overstepped the line of academic propriety by his speeches in Colorado and elsewhere. In Colorado I am credibly informed that he wore a silver pin in his shirt front and called attention to it, as an indication of his soundness, like a demagogue politician. But I concluded that if the trustees were to be sustained at all they must be sustained on their chosen ground." White to Henry Villard, July 30, 1897, Henry Villard MSS.

51. *Alumni Memorial Service. Aaron L. Chapin,* p. 27.

52. See, for example, White's review of Henry C. Adams, *Public Debts,* a work by a "New School" economist. *Nation,* September 8, 15, 1887,

53. White, "Progress and Poverty," *Nation,* July 22, August 12, 1880. White [Social Problems] Ibid., pp. 237–238. White, "Agriculture and the Single Tax," *Popular Science Monthly* 36 (February, 1890): 481–500. White knew George personally and had corresponded with him over the years. Both had been Liberal Republicans. Like Henry D. Lloyd, however, George parted company with the laissez-faire Liberals after the depression of the 1870's. See Charles A. Barker, *Henry George* (New York, 1955), pp. 144, 159, 316, 323, 560, 607.

54. Luigi Cossa, *Taxation, Its Principles and Methods,* ed. Horace White (New York, 1888), pp. iii–v, 143–149.

55. White, "The New York Mayoralty," *Nation,* October 21, 1886. See also White, "Chief Arthur and Mr. George," Ibid., October 28, 1886.

56. George L. Houghton to White, April 20, 1889, Horace White Family Papers. The convention met on February 21, 1889.

57. Henry D. Baldwin to White, January 31, 1890, Horace White Family Papers.

58. J. Sterling Morton to White, August 5, 1890, Horace White Family Papers. See also similar statements from Emerson Judd, secretary of the New England Reform League, and Franklin McVeagh, a Mugwump from Chicago. Emerson Judd to White, August 19, 1890, and Franklin McVeagh to White, August 29, 1890: Horace White Family Papers.

59. White, "Mr. Weeks on Arbitration," *Nation,* April 8, 1886.

60. White, "President Cleveland on Arbitration," Ibid., April 29, 1886. White, "The Law and the Boycotters," Ibid., July 22, 1886. White, "Mr.

Powderly at Richmond," Ibid., October 7, 1886. White to Thomas Bayard, December 13, 1886, Thomas Bayard MSS, Library of Congress.

61. White, "The Right of Procession," *Nation*, November 17, 1887.

62. Wendell Phillips Garrison missed Godkin at those moments. After one such strike in August, 1890, he wrote to his sister: "By Wednesday we expect to see our chief again. I wish he had been here at the time the N. Y. Central strike began, for Mr. White's treatment of such subjects is feeble in comparison." Wendell P. Garrison to Fanny Villard, August 24, 1890, Fanny Villard MSS.

63. *Nation*, July 14, 1892.

64. White, "Senator Palmer on the Rights of Labor," *Nation*, July 14, 1892.

65. White, "Congressman Oates's Report," Ibid., August 11, 1892.

66. Almont L. Lindsay, *The Pullman Strike* (Chicago, 1942), p. 86.

67. White, "The Pullman Experiment," *Nation*, May 7, 1885.

68. Lindsay, *The Pullman Strike*, p. 139.

69. White, "The Pullman Boycott," *Nation*, July 5, 1894.

70. *Nation*, July 5, 1894.

71. Ibid., July 2, 1894.

72. White, "The Punishment of Debs," *Nation*, December 20, 1894.

73. The worldwide depression gave a renewed impulse to bimetallism in Europe as well as the United States. White was in communication with the leaders of the gold standard proponents in England. He even did some writing for their pressure group. Charles W. Mills to White, May 2, 23, December 21, 1895, January 2, 27, 1896; George Pell to White, August 7, September 16, October 3, 1896: Horace White Family Papers. White, *The Monetary Issue in the United States*, Pamphlet No. 19 in the Gold Standard Defence Association Series (London, 1896). White also corresponded with a leading German gold standard advocate, Ludwig Bamberger. See L. Bamberger to White, March 27, 1895, Horace White Family Papers.

74. White, "A Silver Party," *Nation*, March 14, 1895.

75. White, "Prospects of a Bolt," Ibid., May 21, 1896.

76. White, "The Prospect at Chicago," Ibid., June 4, 1896.

77. White, "The St. Louis Platform," Ibid., June 25, 896. White, "The Issue of the Campaign," Ibid., July 2, 1896. Since Godkin was in Europe during July and August, White managed the paper by himself during those months.

78. White, "The Chicago Platform," Ibid., July 16, 1896.

79. White, "The Chicago Nominee," Ibid., July 16, 1896.

80. Moorfield Storey to Carl Schurz, July 8, 1896, Schurz MSS.

81. White to Carl Schurz, July 9, 1896, Schurz MSS.

82. Ibid., July 27, 30, August 3, 19, 1896, Schurz MSS.

83. White, *Coin's Financial Fool. A Reply to Coin's Financial School* (New York, 1895). Since White felt that Harvey's "unmeaning drivel"

gained a wide audience because of its cartoons, he had his work illustrated by the *Evening Post* cartoonist, Dan Beard. See White, *Coin's Financial Fool*, p. 110. The Sound Currency Committee of the Reform Club of New York reprinted and circulated 300,000 copies of a condensed version of White's work. White, "Coin's Financial Fool," *Sound Currency* 2 (May 1, 1895): 1–20. See Stanley L. Jones, *The Presidential Election of 1896*. (Madison, Wis., 1964), pp. 33–34, 357n.

84. White, *Money and Banking* (Boston, 1895). This work went through ten succeeding editions, serving as a standard text in American colleges.

85. James Loeb to Carl Schurz, July 20, 1896, Schurz MSS.

86. Ibid., July 22, 27, 1896, Schurz MSS.

87. White to Carl Schurz, August 3, 1896, Schurz MSS.

88. White, "The Gravity of the Crisis," *Nation*, October 15, 1896. See also Carl Schurz to William McKinley, November 7, 1896, Schurz MSS.

89. White to Worthington Ford, November 17, 1896, White Misc. Papers. Republican leaders seemed ready to cooperate. White continued in his letter: "Wells [David A.] told me the other day that Dingley had asked him to make suggestions touching the best method of raising necessary revenue."

90. White, "For Secretary of the Treasury," *Nation*, January, 1897. See also White to William McKinley, March 2, 1897, William McKinley Papers, Library of Congress.

91. Lyman Gage to White, February 6, 1897, Horace White Family Papers. Gage remarked shortly after the notice of his appointment: "This morning a Chicago man . . . showed me the matter referring to my appointment with this remark. 'I could give more for that endorsement than for the endorsement of all the other papers in the U. S. put together,' and it is not saying too much to say that I sympathize with his remark." During the next several years, Gage conferred with White on financial matters. Lyman Gage to White, December 16, 1897, July 19, 1898, May 25, June 3, 1899, Lyman Gage MSS, Library of Congress.

92. *The Evening Post Hundredth Anniversary* (New York, 1902), pp. 128–29.

16

Anti-Imperialist

WHITE'S RECORD on imperialism had been consistent. While working on the *Chicago Tribune,* he never succumbed to Joseph Medill's fancies of American hegemony over the whole of North America. Indeed, when White assumed control of the *Chicago Tribune,* he put a damper on such appeals to Manifest Destiny. He criticized Seward's acquisition of Alaska, opposed Grant's attempt to annex Santo Domingo, and denounced Blaine's flagrant use of force as Secretary of State in the 1880s. While serving on the *Evening Post,* White and his colleagues applauded Cleveland's halt to American annexation of Hawaii, but they did not spare Cleveland when in 1895 he threatened to open hostilities with Great Britain over an embroilment in Venezuela. They rebuked him for his "extraordinary break with his own best traditions" and labeled him the "greatest international anarchist of modern times."[1]

White and Godkin derived their attitudes on foreign policy from the same source as their views on domestic affairs—the liberalism of Cobden and Bright. They prescribed free trade as the remedy for ills both at home and abroad.

They had often wrung their hands with British Liberals over growing governmental interference in the domestic economy, and they joined with their British counterparts to deplore colonialism and the use of international force. After the *Post* sent up a lonely protest against Cleveland's threats toward London late in 1895, one British Liberal thanked White for his "sane and intelligent view."[2]

American experience had also conditioned White's reaction to colonization and the use of force in foreign policy. His antislavery zeal had led him to advocate the forceful reconstruction of the South after the Civil War. At that time, he had called for thorough governmental interference. His subsequent disillusionment with that experiment only reinforced his laissez-faire notions, and his disappointment with the postwar efforts of southern Negroes colored his condemnation of colonization among nonwhites. After his experience with the South, White challenged the glib optimism of extending democracy abroad.

Anticolonialism for White did not, however, mean American isolationism. He and his colleagues, Godkin and Schurz, believed that American business was destined to dominate world markets. White had predicted American economic hegemony before a British audience in the 1880s. He and Godkin continued to talk about it in the *Nation* throughout the 1890s.[3] Carl Schurz reflected this optimism about American economic expansion by publishing an export almanac for American businessmen in the late 1880s.[4] White and his friends felt that to win these world markets, the United States would have to avoid pitfalls of colonialism. Only if the United States renounced the military force, the enlarged bureaucracy, and the heavy taxes needed to run a colonial empire, would it achieve world economic predominance.[5]

When the Republicans returned to the White House in 1897, White added one more charge to his indictment of imperialism. Another effort to annex Hawaii evoked his dormant political idealism. The American republic, he insisted, could not morally alter a foreign government "without asking the consent of the governed." White found this argument particularly useful against Republican leaders; it enabled him to turn their heritage of Radical rhetoric against them. He was, of course, well acquainted with the heritage. His use of it now, however, had a hollow ring.

> That Senator Morgan of Alabama should argue this question as though the people of Hawaii have no rights which white men are bound to respect, is not to be wondered at. He belongs to a class who are in office by virtue of suppressing the votes of the black men and also of such whites as do not vote their ticket. . . . It is easy, we say, to understand how men who believe in this system should . . . talk about England and Japan, and naval power in the Pacific, and every other conceivable thing except the foundation principle of government. . . . But that the liberty loving North, and especially the Republican party, which fought a four years' war to establish this principle, and contended for thirty years after the war to maintain it, should now join in tramping upon it, is something that would not have been believed by any former generation of Americans.[6]

Such an argument may have been applicable against American involvement in Hawaii. White had a more difficult time, however, countering American cries for intervention in Cuba. Many demanded that America assist the Cuban revolutionists in their attempt to throw off Spanish tyranny. But if imperialists could change their argument, so could the anti-imperialists: White and Godkin responded with a defense of Spain. For every tale of cruelty by "Butcher" Weyler, the editors printed an account of brutality by Cuban nationalists. White was relieved when President McKinley seemed to oppose the popular outcry in his annual message in 1897. "The Cuban question," the editor commented, "is considered . . . upon the whole in a satisfactory manner. The present Government of Spain is treated with marked deference; its plan for Cuban autonomy is commended. The terms offered by Spain are recited. They are the same as the rights enjoyed by Canada."[7]

Even after the destruction of the *Maine,* White called for moderation. He challenged the American infatuation with the Cuban rebels. Cuban independence, he declared, was undesirable. The guerrilla leaders did not have the sympathy of the "cultivated people of Havana and the property classes of the other cities." Rhetorically he queried, "Shall we plunge into the calamity of war for the sake of a few straggling bands who are hiding in the mountain fortresses, burning cane-fields and sugar-mills, and stopping the industries of the peaceful inhabitants, and who probably represent only a minority of the people of the island. . . . It seems incredible," he concluded, "that such a step can be desired by any thinking person in the United States."[8]

There were, White added, too many hazards for the United States itself. American involvement in Cuba would shatter "the prosperity which has just dawned upon us after the panic of 1893."[9] The nation would also become hopelessly involved in Cuba's domestic affairs after Spain's departure. White evoked the memory of Reconstruction: "We have no way of ruling a dependency except by the ballot. We should be obliged to impose upon Cuba . . . what we actually imposed on the South after the civil war—that is, carpet-baggers, negro suffrage, and a chaos of institutions."[10]

White's allusions to Reconstruction probably did not have much appeal to a new generation of Americans. They were too young to recall the Civil War era; they wanted only to "Remember the *Maine.*" They knew that Spanish officials had insulted the President, and they suspected now that those same authorities had destroyed an American battleship in the Havana harbor. In this atmosphere, the *Nation* and *Evening Post* were issuing a muffled dissent to the drift of American policy. When McKinley later changed his stance and endorsed the popular frenzy by requesting Congress to approve American intervention in Cuba, White could only bewail the "national hysteria."[11]

Once hostilities had begun, the *Evening Post* refrained from opposing the war itself and turned its attention to the blunderings of amateur American warmakers. War brought remuneration to the press. A new member of the *Evening Post*'s staff, Oswald Garrison Villard, reported to his Europe-bound parents, still the paper's major proprietors: "Mr. Cook reports that the circulation is going onward and upward. The edition of Saturday was 34,000." Although young Villard had initially opposed the war, he could not restrain his enthusiasm over an early American victory. "When you reach the other side," he wrote to his parents, "you will hear the great news of Commodore Dewey's dashing exploit at Manila, which really seems to have been carried out with extraordinary daring and spirit."[12]

White, an older man, able to recall an earlier war, did not share his subordinate's glow over the paper's finances or America's victories on the high seas. White was much more concerned with the nation's finances and the implications of military involvement across the globe. Recalling the introduction of greenbacks during the Civil War, he warned against another effort to inflate the nation's money supply.[13] He was distressed but not really surprised by the extension of the war into the Pacific; indeed, he had predicted such a turn several weeks before American intervention in Cuba.[14] But White gained little satisfaction from his success as a seer. What was America to do with its new possessions?

As soon as the debate opened on that question, White took an irreconcilable position. "The thought," his argument began, "of admitting the Philippine natives to the Union as a self-governing community, with representation in our Congress . . . does not enter the mind of a single human being."[15] Yet White would consider no other basis for annexation than full Constitutional equality. His blend of racism and political idealism therefore made territorial expansion unthinkable.[16] Administration efforts to annex Puerto Rico forcefully, he labeled "criminal aggression." His anti-imperialist enthusiasm almost matched his earlier antislavery fervor:

> The imposition of a hateful government upon an offending people, in violation of our own theories of government, in the teeth of the Declaration of Independence, becomes a very simple matter when the roar of cannon deafens our ears. It is impossible, however, that such inversions of the principles of republican government, such shameless departures from our own declared purposes and intentions, should take place without impairing the love of liberty in our own breasts and producing internal changes most deleterious to ourselves.[17]

In refusing to budge from his unconditional attitude, White broke ranks with other anti-imperialists. This division became evident before the end of the war, when a conference of intellectuals met at Saratoga, New York, in August, 1898, to discuss the disposition of the Philippine Islands. Both imperialists and anti-imperialists were present. A consensus emerged: there should be temporary American jurisdiction until the capability of the natives for self-rule could be demonstrated. Carl Schurz stated the reasoning of the anti-imperialists. Positing the immorality and the impracticality of holding the Philippines forever, he agreed to an interim American government which would "not annex, but secure the opening to our activities of the territories concerned. Holding to this principle," Schurz continued, "we shall gain commercial opportunities of so great a value that they will more than compensate for the cost of the war. . . ."[18] The common tenet of economic expansionism therefore drew the imperialists and some anti-imperialists together.[19]

White dissented. He had innocently believed that the gathering was a "protest against colonial acquisitions." But anyone who could read the unanimously adopted resolutions, he complained, could see that they "practically surrendered the whole case to the expansionists." He explained his position in a lead editorial:

> We say this because when you affirm that "we should not be justified in returning the islands to the misrule and oppression from which we have relieved them," and that "the rescued and liberated people . . . are in a sense temporarily the wards of the conquering nation," you practically invite and endorse the whole colonial policy. Not to return the islands is to keep them, . . . and to treat their inhabitants as "wards" is to govern them according to *our* ideas, not their own, of what is for their best good.[20]

Carl Schurz could not understand his comrade's lack of understanding. After reading White's editorial he wrote a letter of explanation: "The sentences quoted in your article are meant to say that our protecting rule over the conquered populations is to be only temporary. 'Not to return the islands' is by no means necessarily 'to keep them.' "[21] White's view did not change. "I cannot agree with your interpretation of the Saratoga resolutions," he replied to Schurz. "If we are to retain the Philippines till we can decide by joint debate in this country, 10,000 miles from the scene, whether or not they are or are not fit to govern themselves, we shall hold them forever."[22]

That prospect was unthinkable for White. Inclusion of ignorant nonwhites as equals would disrupt American society; inclusion without equality would undermine the nation's democratic ideals. The vital question, White therefore declared, "was not, What shall we do with the Philippines? but, What will they do with us?"[23]

While cruising in the Mediterranean, White learned what the Filipinos would do with the Americans; they began to kill them in an armed insurrection. Violence, in this case, instead of making White more cautious, had the opposite effect. "I judge the Filipinos intend to fight for their independence," he wrote to Schurz while aboard ship. "I fervently hope they will do so. I shall say as Lord Chatham did in a similar crisis, 'If I were an American as I am an Englishman I would welcome them [the invaders] with bloody hands to hospitable graves.' "[24]

When White returned to the United States, anti-imperialism was only a minor concern of the *Evening Post*'s editors. Edwin L. Godkin, at the moment, was busy directing the scorn of the paper at customs officials rather than at American soldiers. In 1897, the McKinley administration had limited to one hundred dollars the duty free purchases of returning American tourists. The law did not arouse much excitement until customs officials began examining the tourists' baggage in order to insure compliance with the edict. Godkin, a habitual European traveler, damned the new activity as an outrageous invasion of privacy. A covering news story, explaining the low cost and superiority of English clothes, expanded the controversy by irritating New York dry goods merchants.[25] As a result, the angry retailers, led by John Wanamaker, withdrew their heavy advertising from the *Evening Post*. Godkin retaliated, in turn, by ballyhooing the boycott and defending independent journalism in the United States.[26] Numerous cosmopolitan New Yorkers then backed Godkin's protest by joining a selective buying campaign. Godkin, in turn, helped them by drawing up lists of his former clients who had deserted the paper.[27]

Henry Villard did not share Godkin's enthusiasm. Retired now from Wall Street and taking a more intense interest in the paper, he openly disagreed with the editor's actions. Only a short time before the advertisers' boycott, the *Post* had suffered a serious setback when two of the paper's best reporters, Lincoln Steffens and Norman Hapgood, left with the talented city editor, Henry J. Wright, to manage a competing New York daily.[28] Fearful of another reversal, Villard refused to let Godkin's principles interfere with his profits.

As soon as White's boat docked in New York, Villard told him about the "most serious turn" in the "affairs" of the *Evening Post* "which you should understand thoroughly before you meet E. L. G."[29] After conferring, the two men arranged for a parley between Godkin and a Wanamaker representative.[30] A compromise emerged. Wanamaker agreed to reinstate advertising and write a letter indicating that he had never intended to infringe on Godkin's editorial independence.[31] Several days later Godkin dropped his protest campaign.[32] In the next several weeks advertisements from a few more major New York merchandisers appeared in the *Evening Post.*[33] The battle seemed over, but its consequences were not.

Godkin did not resign immediately. He waited until his European summer vacation and then sent a note to White indicating his unwillingness to return to the United States.[34] Although Godkin contributed signed editorials for the next two years, he and his compatriots who stayed on the editorial staff remained embittered over the way White and Villard handled the advertising boycott.[35] Godkin's departure from the *Evening Post,* under these circumstances, was far from a graceful retirement.

Of the talented trio of editors who had begun the enterprise in 1881, only Horace White now remained to serve in the twentieth century. Unfortunately, he was now too old to give the *Evening Post* the personal imprint that he might have given it as a younger man. His editorial staff, aware of his declining powers, resented the credit he received for their work. With Godkin gone, the younger editorial writers— Oswald Garrison Villard, Joseph B. Bishop, and Rollo Ogden —all coveted the chief editorship for themselves. The office consequently was rife with jealousy and dissension.[36] But White insisted on leading the paper through one last battle —laying out the "Pecksniffian administration" of William McKinley in 1900.[37]

Even before White gave much thought to a likely opponent to the incumbent President, he dismissed the candidacy of William Jennings Bryan. "The chasm," White declared, "between himself and the Gold Democrats . . . is still so wide that if he had ignored the silver question altogether they could not take him for their candidate next year."[38] The selection of a suitable candidate continued to be a quadrennial dilemma for White. Once more he turned to Carl Schurz for advice. "I suppose you have had your thinking cap on during the past six weeks," White began. "Evidently we cannot support McKinley. Nothing that he can do hereafter will atone for what he has already done, since nothing can change the character of McKinley. Do you think the time has come, or will come next year, for a third party movement?"[39]

Schurz responded with a program of action. The already organized Anti-Imperialist Leagues, he recommended, should form the nucleus for a political opposition. A good Republican, he added, such as the former governor of Massachusetts, George S. Boutwell, should be put in the lead. White agreed.[40] But Bryan complicated Schurz's and White's plans when, at Chicago, he came out strongly against McKinley's Philippine policy. White had to admit that Bryan "now stands with Senator Hoar and the Anti-Imperialist League, and he is in a position where he can do much more effective work than they, because he can carry a party with him, while they cannot."[41]

After Bryan's declaration at Chicago, White's dilemma hardened. Bryan offered an opportunity to defeat the imperialist program of William McKinley, but at considerable cost. On every other issue Bryan stood in opposition to White's convictions. To use the columns of the *Post* effectively, White had to make a choice, and yet, in 1900, he remained pathetically indecisive.

Schurz urged him to act—if for no other reason than to emphasize the divisions within the Republican party in the hopes of unseating McKinley. But White hesitated. Who was the Republican alternative to McKinley? White knew full well. He replied to Schurz: "Another thing moving to delay on our part is the chance that Roosevelt and not McKinley may be nominated by the Republicans next year. Roosevelt's little finger," he wrote, "would be thicker than McKinley's loins as regards Imperialism and kindred enormities, but he would be better than McKinley in every other way, and so far as Civil Service reform goes we could not say a word against him."[42]

Since White postponed any decision on the upcoming presidential race, Carl Schurz acted alone.[43] He did not openly advocate Bryan's candidacy, but his attacks on McKinley gave Bryan implied support.[44] Some of the anti-imperialists reacted immediately. Charles F. Adams, Jr., for one, refused to be forced into virtual support of the hated Populist candidate:

The break between us is, I fear, coming on the practical question of "what to do." It is that which has been uppermost in my mind for the last six months. I find myself unable to follow the apparent drift of yourself and many of my other friends. I am not prepared to jump out of the frying-pan into the fire; and, in this case, I prefer distinctly to bear the ills I have than fly to others of which I have not even the comfort of being ignorant. I refer, of course, to the political alternative. I have no use whatever for Mr. Bryan, Mr. George Fred Williams, Mr. Croker, Mr. McLean, Mr. Goebel of Kentucky, Mr. Altgeld of Illinois or any others of that crew.[45]

White waited longer to make his decision. When finally forced by a direct question, he fell into line with Adams. In March, 1900, Erving Winslow, secretary of the American Anti-Imperialist League, sent out a letter to various sympathizers proposing a more favorable attitude toward Bryan.[46] Discussing the Winslow letter with Schurz, White replied: "If I should answer it at all I should say that I have no confidence in Bryan. I do not consider him a man of principle, but rather of momentary impulse and temporary expediency. I should have no confidence that he would surrender the Philippines to the Filipinos."[47]

White had reasons for this charge of insincerity against Bryan. He pointed to Bryan's crucial support of the treaty which gave the Philippines to the United States in 1898 and scorned Bryan's explanation for that decision.[48] Despite Bryan's increasingly forthright statements against colonialism, White refused his anti-imperialist credentials. He continued to justify his opposition by deprecating Bryan's anti-imperialist line.[49] When Bryan, however, committed his party to a forceful indictment of McKinley's Philippine policy at the Democratic convention, White praised that platform decision. Nonetheless, the editor-in-chief made the stand of his paper inflexible: "The *Evening Post* does not intend to support William J. Bryan for President under any circumstances. . . ." In taking this position White shifted the grounds of his opposition. The continued adherence of the Democratic party to free silver, White now declared, left no room for equivocation.[50]

A tale brought home from the convention allowed White to retreat easily to his former reasons for resistance to Bryan. In a triumphant mood, he related the full story to Schurz.

A returning Democratic delegate, A. B. Hepburn, told White of a conversation he had held with Daniel S. Lamont and Senator Jones of Arkansas, chairman of the Democratic National Committee. "It was assumed by both Lamont and Hepburn," White wrote, "that if Bryan were elected our forces would be soon withdrawn from the Philippines. 'By no means,' replied Jones. 'The South is in favor of Expansion, and if Mr. Bryan should make any movement toward giving up the Philippines the South would rise up as one man and prevent it.' "[51]

Schurz was disturbed by this revelation. Immediately he sent an inquiry to Erving Winslow, architect of the Anti-Imperialist and Democratic coalition. Winslow just as quickly responded but could only question the validity of the story. Unsatisfied, Schurz now helped White and other editors of the *Post* to look for a suitable third-party candidate.[52] It was an eleventh-hour move. Winslow had already persuaded the anti-imperialist Liberty Congress, about to meet in Indianapolis, to throw its support to Bryan. Oswald G. Villard tried desperately to arrange for a concurrent third-party gathering in Indianapolis, but his efforts fizzled as only eighteen of two thousand invited guests arrived.[53] Still White and Villard did not give up; they tried to arrange another third-party conference in New York City in September.[54] Their effort, however, came to naught again, as Schurz and several others who had been cooperating earlier with the *Evening Post* editors now acknowledged the impossibility of forming an effective third party.[55] Only a small gathering was held, and Senator Caffery of Louisiana was nominated as the candidate.[56] Schurz ignored the meeting and decided to give a qualified endorsement to Bryan.[57] White, on the other hand, disagreed with Schurz and advised him against such action.[58]

White remained adamant in his refusal to support Bryan. When Herbert Welsh, Secretary of the New England Anti-Imperialist League, circulated a petition in support of Bryan,

White refused to sign it.[59] He was more polite than the others who sent back the petition with curt notes. Some, including William Graham Sumner, Fulton Cutting, and Charles Dudley Warner, even indicated that they intended to vote for McKinley. The Anti-Imperialists' endorsement of Bryan at Indianapolis quite obviously won few votes for the Democratic candidate.[60] So discouraging was the response to Welsh's petition that Schurz thought the best policy would be "to drop the matter in silence."[61]

White anticipated Bryan's disaster weeks before the outcome. In the last days of the campaign, he therefore suggested that the Anti-Imperialist League circulate another petition, this time in support of McKinley with a reservation against his Philippine policy. Schurz pointed out the ineffectiveness of such a frantic gesture but suggested that it should be acted upon after the election. Defeated, divided, and discouraged, the anti-imperialists thus prepared to continue their efforts after McKinley's return to the White House.

White thought that the leadership of the post-election battle would have to come from anti-imperialists who voted for McKinley. On the eve of the election, he therefore wrote to the influential Republican anti-imperialist, Andrew Carnegie, and urged him to direct a new movement. "Men like Schurz, Boutwell, Edwin Burritt Smith, etc." White emphasized, "will help of course but they will expect somebody else now to take the laboring over." Carnegie's support was deemed crucial, for he not only had the necessary influence with the administration, but he also had the money needed to support anti-imperialist propaganda. He was therefore invited into the anti-imperialists' inner councils.[62]

Postelection strategy was worked out in an executive committee meeting of the American Anti-Imperialist League at the Plaza Hotel in New York City, on December 1, 1900. Carnegie, Schurz, White and a few others attended the meeting as invited guests. Carnegie laid down a program of patience and accommodation with the McKinley administration. He felt that, at that late date, probably only the Supreme Court could stop colonialism, by insisting that the new possessions be given the same Constitutional rights as were held by previous American territories. White had agreed to that strategy several weeks before the meeting. "Like yourself," White wrote to the steel baron, "I have been looking eagerly to the Sup. Court to let us and the Administration out of the present *impasse*. I would not only build a golden bridge for the latter but would have it studded with diamonds and rubies." Voluntarily, the anti-imperialists thus spiked their guns while Carnegie went to Washington to negotiate with the victors.[63]

The capture of Aguinaldo, the leader of the Philippine insurgents, in the spring of 1901 also helped to quiet the anti-imperialists by bringing the Philippine revolt to an end. When the Anti-Imperialist League prepared an address to the newly elected Congress, White was able to demand certain revisions in the document. He felt that the "harsh and rasping tone" of the address would "irritate the Republican party" and "prevent us from making any headway in the only quarter where we can hope for gains." To Schurz, White emphasized that "this is the only logical position for the *Evening Post,* and is the one that we will contend for, irrespective of the decision of the anti-Imperialist League." Schurz did not fully agree with White's caution but nonetheless urged Edwin Burritt Smith, president of the Anti-Imperialist League, to ask for White's alterations, since he felt that it was "of great importance to have the *Evening Post* on our side." White gave them his recommended changes. They were accepted.[64]

White thus had adjusted himself to a policy of accommodation before McKinley's assassination. At first he viewed the succession of Theodore Roosevelt as a calamity, since the Vice-President had been one of the most outspoken imperialists in the previous campaign. Obviously upset at Roosevelt's elevation, White hastily wrote to the Secretary of State, John Hay, inquiring about the possible repercussions on American foreign policy. White had long admired Hay's "Open Door" expansionism.[65] Hay himself was worried but responded to White's inquiry with a diplomat's note: "I think you need have no apprehensions for the present. The President has asked us all to stay, and to me has been most kind and considerate. I know of nothing in which we are at variance. I shall stay as long as I can feel I am doing the work."[66]

A few days later, the uneasy *Post* editors received word directly from the new President. He gave their Washington correspondent, Frances F. Leup, a confidential interview. Roosevelt explained that he intended to get out of Cuba as soon as possible. The Secretary of War, Elihu Root, was only withholding official approval of the Cuban constitution "until certain Tammanyized features of it are altered." "Roosevelt," Leup continued, "is thoroughly in earnest in his desire to get out. He feels the same way about the Philippines, though all his private advices from Taft and others whom he trusts indicate that that may take a considerable period. He regards, as the E. P. does, the retention of the Philippines as a source of weakness to us as a nation and liable to embroil us in wars with other countries, which he declares must be avoided during his administration by any means consistent with national honor."[67]

Roosevelt had never feared or respected the anti-imperialists; he had been one of their foremost opponents during the 1900 campaign.[68] Nevertheless, once in the White House, he and Root managed to disarm some of the most important anti-imperialist leaders.[69] When another minor rebellion broke out in the Philippines in 1902, several of these leaders refused to participate in a protest against the methods used by Roosevelt in putting down the insurgency. One, Wayne McVeagh, was related to Root; another, Henry Higginson, was a close friend of T. R.'s and another, Jacob Schurman, president of Cornell University, expressed his confidence in the "high-minded and very able and resolute President."[70]

The most important defector, however, was Andrew Carnegie. He had become reconciled to the administration's Cuban policy after Elihu Root explained: "The trouble about Cuba is that, although it is technically a foreign country, practically and morally it occupies an intermediate position, since we have required it to become part of our military and political system, and to form a part of our line of exterior defense." Carnegie, along with increasing numbers of anti-imperialists, could see nothing wrong with that sort of domination, as long as the United States left the country with a semblance of self rule. Few anti-imperialists, for example, would sign a remonstrance against Roosevelt's methods in gaining canal rights in Panama.[71]

White and others, however, did continue their campaign against American rule in the Philippines. Indeed, after he retired from the *Evening Post* in February, 1902, White assisted various anti-imperialist groups. In 1906, he became president of the Filipino Progress Association. But the very name of that organization indicated a change of tactics. Organized by Edward Ordway, this group of anti-imperialists broke from the already emaciated Anti-Imperialist League in 1905. They took the bulk of contributing members and formed their own more cautious agency.

Their chief objective was limited. Since no American newspaper had a correspondent in the Philippines, they hoped to raise enough money to send an agent to the islands and then sell his syndicated reports to major American journals. At first they tried to get Lord Bryce to accept the position, but he turned it down. Subsequently they arranged for the services of Dr. David Doherty, an expert on the Philippines.[72]

Even this limited operation, however, ran into trouble. A number of the major contributors to anti-imperialist causes saw no purpose in the endeavor. They felt that matters in the

Philippines were "moving in the right direction" and that it was undesirable to "agitate the subject."[73] Despite White's personal pleading to Carnegie during a visit at his castle in Scotland, the millionaire also refused to cooperate.[74] He had already explained his motives to Roosevelt himself: "I decline to contribute for an agent to be sent since you and more recently Judge Taft have stated your aims to be 'As Cuba.' "[75]

White responded to these pressures. He recognized that his association could not win support for Doherty's mission if it was to be a check on administration procedures. He therefore began to bill the operation as a simple effort "to restore communications between that people and the people of the United States."[76]

Charles Francis Adams, Jr., one of the hesitant contributors, opened another question: what was the ultimate objective of the Filipino Progress Association? Adams, like Carnegie, had become amenable to Roosevelt's Cuban policy. After a trip to Egypt, he had, moreover, become enthusiastic about the settlement worked out in that country by Britain's Lord Cromer. On the basis of this experience, Adams explained to White what he now felt should be done in the Philippines:

> I hope that the 'veiled protectorate', or Lord Cromer, policy of dealing with Egypt may be adopted as respects San Domingo; and as a corollary and natural sequence thereto, in the case of the Philippines. It is very much the policy we are now adopting towards Cuba;—the system of home rule of dependencies, subject to potent influence through advice judiciously conveyed.[77]

Adams subsequently detailed his suggestions in an article in *Century*. The article was, for Adams, a philosophic self-repudiation. Having seen Africans in their native continent, "the scales," he wrote, "fell from my eyes." Americans, "especially we philanthropists and theorists of New England," have "wallowed in a bog of self-sufficient ignorance. . . . The Negro, after emancipation, should have been dealt with, not as a political equal, much less forced into a position of superiority; he should have been treated as a ward and dependent,—firmly, but in a spirit of kindness and absolute justice," His new knowledge of Africa, where slavery could not be used as an excuse for apparent racial inferiority, convinced him that the "theoretical rights of man and philanthropical African-and-brother doctrines were all 'rot';—'rot,'" he added, which he had "indulged in to a considerable extent" but had now outgrown. This new wisdom, Adams felt, allowed him to think clearly about Santo Domingo and the Philippines. In his opinion, only disaster faced Taft's policy to hold the Philippines indefinitely, in order to develop "'the prosperity and self-governing capacity of the Philippine people.'" Roosevelt's recent policy in Santo Domingo, Adams suggested, was closer to a Lord Cromer formula in dealing with dependent, non-European peoples. He admitted the need of holding "those we shield territorially up to a reasonable sense of their debt to civilization" even if such action demanded greater naval armaments. Veiled protectorates, Adams concluded, "may for all concerned most advantageously displace and replace foreign domination."[78]

White did not fully approve of the article. He did not personally challenge Adams' explicit racism but indicated that some in his organization could not follow such an argument. His own disagreement arose, because Adams' position was "on all fours with San Domingo and his [Roosevelt's] naval policy, as to both of which I non-concur."[79] White refused to capitulate to all of Roosevelt's programs and insisted that there was still essential disagreement between him and Roosevelt. The latter's involvement in Santo Domingo, White felt, was wrong. "Supposing that it would be better for Santo Domingo that we should interfere in her affairs it does not follow that it would be better for us. I look at the affair primarily as it affects the U. S. I think that the consequences are most dangerous in their influence upon the national character."[80]

White did not, on the other hand, completely disagree with Adams or Roosevelt. A month before Adams' article appeared, White had already dedicated the Filipino Progress Association to "putting the Philippines in the same relation to the United States as Cuba now stands." He frankly maintained that his group favored "self government under a Protectorate of the United States."[81] Expediency, he explained to Adams, had driven him to that decision. "The reason why I favor a protectorate over the Philippines with independence a la Cuba, is that it seems to me the most feasible way out of the dilemma that we are now in. I think that it is more practicable and easy of attainment than the neutralization policy advocated so nobly and eloquently by Moorfield Storey."[82]

White had already opened private discussions with the Roosevelt administration. After a meeting with William Howard Taft, Roosevelt's Secretary of War, in April, 1906, he came away in sympathy with the objectives of the former Philippine governor. "I was very agreeably impressed," White related later to Ordway, "with his sincerity and his aims respecting the Filipinos. He spoke in high terms of Dr. Doherty, and is glad that we found so good and competent a man to represent us in the islands."[83] Further reports about the administration's objectives in the Philippines encouraged White and his associates in their willingness to continue their cooperation with Roosevelt and Taft.[84] More than expediency obviously determined their motives. By December, 1906, White could write to Adams that "weighty truths" expressed by him "have been gaining lodgment in my own mind of late." He admitted that the same was true of others in the Filipino Progress Association.[85]

Whatever the reasons, White and his group began to work

in close contact with the administration. In August, 1907, they finally sent a private memo to Taft expressing a plan worked out by the Filipino Progress Association for self-rule in the islands. "The fundamental object of the United States in temporarily governing the Philippine Islands," the report began, "is to educate the Filipinos in self control to that degree that the withdrawal of the control of the United States would not precipitate anarchy in the islands, but, on the contrary, result in the establishment of a stable government." Since White had already acknowledged this principle to be the aim of Roosevelt, he and his associates recommended only that certain steps, designed to accomplish that end, be drawn up and advertised to assure Americans and Filipinos of the administration's objectives. That an American protectorate would be compatible with these objectives, the report made clear in its final paragraph:

All questions of the future relations of the ultimate federation with the United States and with the other great powers of the world would be of course postponed to the future, such as the provision of a coaling station for the United States, or the regulation of trade relations by treaty, or of consular and judicial rights of foreign nations within the Philippines. The successful erection of states for the management of their own affairs within specified lines would not prejudice the wise settlement in the future of all questions which have a national scope.[86]

This "declaration of principles" was duly sent to Taft for his use. It was neither made public nor referred to the Filipinos. Entrusting the Philippines to Roosevelt's safekeeping, the Filipino Progress Association disbanded.[87]

White and his friends did not view themselves as surrendering in 1907. On the contrary, they felt that they had made an honorable truce. They had never opposed American expansionism nor the practicality of American protectorates;

they had never opposed the racist assumptions of the imperialists nor the inevitability of American economic hegemony. They had opposed colonialism only—the annexation of distant lands and inferior peoples. Roosevelt agreed with them. Both he and the anti-imperialists like White saw the superiority of "Open Door" expansionism. They both saw the Philippines as a handicap and agreed on a *gradual* program of transforming the islands into a protectorate "like Cuba." Succeeding Presidents also agreed to that program; none encouraged colonialism. True, White and his friends were disappointed with Taft's failures to implement their Philippine policies during his term in the presidency, but they were convinced that his successor, Woodrow Wilson, would carry them out.[88] The Philippines were a beginning and an end of a colonialist adventure.[89] Some historians have felt that the Anti-Imperialists lost their battle.[90] Horace White would not agree.

NOTES

1. *Nation,* December 26, 1895.

2. Charles W. Mills to Horace White, January 2, 1896, Horace White Family Papers. "I am sure that the heartfelt thanks of every right thinking man are due to you, and to others who have had the strength of mind and courage to preach reason and righteousness amid the din of a war excitement." See also Charles W. Mills to White, December 21, 1895 and January 27, 1896, Horace White Family Papers.

3. See, for example, *Nation,* September 6, 1894.

4. Alonzo Bell to Carl Schurz, May 3, June 9, 1888, Schurz MSS. Until the depression of 1893, Schurz was involved in mining enterprises in Mexico and Dutch Guiana, in German shipping, and in an American electrical firm trying to push its sales in Australia. E. W. Little to Schurz, September 1, 9, 1892; Ulysses D. Eddy to Schurz, December 22, 1892; Samuel DeCoursey to Schurz, December 31, 1892, January 20, 1892: Schurz MSS.

5. White, "The Uses of a Large Navy," *Nation,* April 18, 1889. See also White, "Eighteenth Century Politics," Ibid., February 15, 1894; and

"Commerce and Big Guns," Ibid., December 16, 1897. The similarity between these views and those of English Liberals can be seen in John Gallagher and Ronald Robinson, "The Imperialism of Free Trade," *Economic History Review* Ser. 2, 6 (1953): 1–15. For an attempt to gauge the importance of this sentiment among American Mugwump anti-imperialists as a group, see Robert Beisner, *Twelve Against Empire* (New York, 1968), pp. 84–106.

6. White, "Hawaiian Annexation," *Nation*, November 25, 1897.

7. White, "The President's Message," Ibid., December 9, 1897.

8. White, "Cuban Autonomy or Independence," Ibid., March 10, 1898.

9. Ibid.

10. White, "After Intervention—What?," *Nation*, March 17, 1898.

11. White, "National Hysteria," Ibid., April 21, 1898.

12. Oswald Garrison Villard to "mother and father," May 3, 1898, Oswald Garrison Villard MSS. See also Michael Wreszin, *Oswald Garrison Villard* (Bloomington, 1965), pp. 19–21.

13. White, "The New Greenback Diversion," *Nation*, June 2, 1898.

14. White, "Duration of the War," Ibid., April 14, 1898.

15. White, "Holding the Philippines," Ibid., June 9, 1898.

16. Christopher Lasch, "The Anti-Imperialists, the Philippines, and the Inequality of Man," *Journal of Southern History* 24 (August, 1958): 319–331. In this article, Lasch points out quite appropriately that most of the anti-imperialists combined racism and political idealism. This combination, he notes, made it difficult for them to counter the arguments of the imperialists.

17. White, "Forcible Annexation," *Nation*, July 28, 1898.

18. *New York Evening Post*, August 19, 1898. Northwestern University professor Henry Wade Rogers presented the unanimous resolutions of the gathering. Ibid., August 22, 1898.

19. Samuel Gompers, labor leader and member of the conference, perhaps best expressed the shared enthusiasm of the delegates: "That nation which dominates the markets of the world will surely control its destinies." Ibid., August 20, 1898. For recent discussions of the consensus of the imperialists and the anti-imperialists, see Walter LaFeber, *The New Empire* (Ithaca, N.Y., 1963), pp. 412–417 and John Rollins, "The Imperialism of Anti-Imperialism, *Studies on the Left* 3 (1962):9–24. See also John Rollins, "The Anti-Imperialists: A Reappraisal" (Master's thesis, University of Wisconsin, 1960).

20. *New York Evening Post*, August 22, 1898.

21. Ibid., August 24, 1898. The letter was reprinted in the paper with the anonymous signature, "A Member of the Saratoga Conference," but it was obviously from Schurz.

22. White to Carl Schurz, August 24, 1898, Schurz MSS.

23. White, "Our New Citizens," *Nation*, November 10, 1898.

24. White to Carl Schurz, January 13, 1899, Schurz MSS.

25. *New York Evening Post*, March 6, 1899.

26. Ibid., March 28, 1899.

27. Ibid., April 11, 1899.

28. Wendell P. Garrison to Henry Villard, May 6, 1897; Fanny Villard to Oswald Garrison Villard, May 6, 1897: Fanny Villard MSS. See also Norman Hapgood, *The Changing Years* (New York, 1930), pp. 107–133; Lincoln Steffens, *The Autobiography of Lincoln Steffens* (New York, 1931), 1:169–178, 311–319; and Oswald G. Villard, *Fighting Years* (New York, 1939), pp. 115–117.

29. Henry Villard to White, April 3, 1899, Henry Villard MSS.

30. Oswald Garrison Villard to Fanny Villard, April 19, 1899, Oswald Garrison Villard MSS. See also Wendell P. Garrison to Fanny Villard, April 9, 1899, Fanny Villard MSS.

31. *New York Evening Post*, April 20, 1899.

32. Ibid., April 24, 1899.

33. Oswald Garrison Villard to Henry Villard, July 31, 1899, Oswald G. Villard MSS. Not all of the merchants, however, returned. As a result, the paper suffered financially for some time. In the spring of 1900, the *Post* completely abandoned Godkin's position and apologized to the merchants. *New York Evening Post*, April 2, 1900. Even then some of the advertisers held out until White had Andrew Carnegie intervene with the retailers two years later. See White to Andrew Carnegie, January 25, March 10, 1902, Andrew Carnegie MSS, Library of Congress.

34. White to E. L. Godkin, September 6, 1899, Godkin MSS.

35. J. B. Bishop to E. L. Godkin, July 9, September 11 [1900], Godkin MSS.

36. After White insisted on remaining editor-in-chief, J. B. Bishop left the *Evening Post* in anger. Oswald Garrison Villard did not give up his ambitions until he received a long letter of advice from his uncle, *Nation* editor Wendell P. Garrison, July 14, 1901, Oswald Garrison Villard MSS.

37. White to Edward L. Godkin, September 6, 1899, Godkin MSS.

38. White, "The Candidacy of Bryan," *Nation*, April 20, 1899.

39. White to Carl Schurz, July 21, 1899, Schurz MSS.

40. Ibid., July 24, 1899, Schurz, MSS.

41. White, "Bryan at Chicago," *Nation*, July 27, 1899.

42. White to Carl Schurz, August 4, 1899, Schurz MSS.

43. *New York Evening Post*, February 10, 24, 1900.

44. Fred H. Harrington, "The Anti-Imperialist Movement in the United States, 1898–1900," *Mississippi Valley Historical Review* 22 (September, 1935):226. *New York Evening Post*, February 15, 23, 24, 1900.

45. Charles F. Adams to Carl Schurz, November 3, 1899, Schurz MSS. For a thorough examination of Adams's position, see Beisner, *Twelve Against Empire*, pp. 107–137.

46. Erving Winslow to Carl Schurz, March 23, 1900, Schurz MSS.

47. White to Carl Schurz, March 23, 1900, Schurz MSS.

48. See the editorial, "Bryan as a Candidate," *New York Evening Post*, April 11, 1900. White was not alone in his suspicions of Bryan's stead-

fastness as an anti-imperialist. See Harrington, "The Anti-Imperialist Movement," pp. 221–222.

49. White, "Mr. Bryan's Platform," *Nation*, June 7, 1900. This article dealt with an article written by Bryan in the *North American Review* shortly before the Democratic convention.

50. *New York Evening Post*, July 6, 1900. See also the issue of July 5, 1900, as well as White, "Bryanism at Kansas City," *Nation*, July 12, 1900.

51. White to Carl Schurz, July 21, 1900, Schurz MSS. See also White's editorial the same day in the *Post*. White, "The South and the Philippines," *New York Evening Post*, July 21, 1900.

52. White to Carl Schurz, July 25, August 11, 1900; and Carl Schurz to Erving Winslow, July 26, 1900: copies in the Schurz MSS. See also the *New York Evening Post*, July 18, 25, August 8, 1900.

53. Carl Schurz's absence was a special blow. See Oswald Garrison Villard to Fanny Villard, August 14, 1909, Oswald G. Villard MSS. See also Edwin Burritt Smith to Carl Schurz, August 18, 1900, Schurz MSS. See also *New York Evening Post*, August 14, 15, 16, 17, 1900.

54. *New York Evening Post*, August 28, 1900.

55. Carl Schurz to Moorfield Storey, August 20, 1900; Moorfield Storey to Carl Schurz, August 21, 1900; J. B. Henderson to Carl Schurz, August 24, 1900: Schurz MSS.

56. *New York Evening Post*, Sept. 5, 1900.

57. Ibid., September 29, 1900.

58. Oswald G. Villard to Carl Schurz, August 30, 1900, Schurz MSS.

59. White to Herbert Welsh, October 2, 190, copy in the Schurz MSS.

60. See letters of Franklin Carter, R. Fulton Cutting, William G. Sumner, and Charles Dudley Warner to Herbert Welsh, all dated October 2, 1900, copies in the Schurz MSS. Warner was particularly harsh in his reply to Welsh: "In turn I cannot refrain from expressing my surprise to see a man so identified with good government devoting himself to the most dangerous and shallow demagogue of our day." Some prominent anti-imperialists resigned from the American Anti-Imperialist League as soon as the Liberty Congress endorsed Bryan. See J. Laurence Laughlin to Hermann von Holst, September 14, 1900, Hermann von Holst MSS, University of Chicago.

61. See Schurz to Edwin Burritt Smith, October 4, 1900, copy in the Schurz MSS. See also Schurz to Herbert Welsh, October 5, 1900, copy in the Schurz MSS.

62. White to Andrew Carnegie, November 4, 1900; Erving Winslow to Andrew Carnegie, November 7, 1900; Edwin Burritt Smith to Andrew Carnegie, November 16, 1900: Andrew Carnegie MSS, Library of Congress.

63. White to Andrew Carnegie, November 4, 1900, Carnegie MSS. White to Carl Schurz, January 5, 1901, Schurz MSS.

64. White to Carl Schurz, June 17, 1901; Carl Schurz to Edwin Burritt Smith [copy], June 26, 1901; White to Carl Schurz, June 17, 1901; Edwin Burritt Smith to Carl Schurz, June 22, 1901: Schurz MSS.

65. White, "Chinese Logic for the Philippines," *New York Evening Post,* July 19, 1900. See also "Mr. Hay's Great Stroke," *New York Evening Post,* March 28, 1900.

66. John Hay to White, September 18, 1901, Horace White Family Papers. The note was marked "private."

67. Frances E. Leup to Oswald Garrison Villard, September 20, 1901, Schurz MSS. Villard sent the letter to Schurz with a note expressing his relief. "I thought it would interest you to know how the new President really feels. Of course it is easy for him to say these things and the test is yet to come. But how much better to have him take this line than to go into office breathing fire and slaughter." Oswald Garrison Villard to Carl Schurz, September 23, 1901, Schurz MSS.

68. Howard K. Beale, *Theodore Roosevelt and the Rise of America to World Power* (Baltimore: Johns Hopkins University Press, 1956), pp. 14-80. Roosevelt's letters to the embittered former editor of the *Evening Post,* Joseph B. Bishop, give his candid views of the editors. Roosevelt thought their actions "amusing," but admitted that "that whole *Evening Post* gang excites me in a way disproportionate to their importance." See Theodore Roosevelt to J. B. Bishop, October 21, 1901, April 23, 1902, August 5, 1903, J. B. Bishop MSS, Harvard University. Bishop, a protégé of Godkin, eventually became one of Roosevelt's administrators in Panama.

69. Oswald Garrison Villard was very much impressed by Root's plans for Cuba after an almost two-hour talk with the Cabinet officer. See Villard's reaction to this interview in a letter to his mother. Oswald G. Villard to Fanny Villard, September 26, 1901, Oswald G. Villard MSS.

Another anti-imperialist, Josephine S. Lowell, even circulated a petition backing Root's policy in Cuba. She was censured by some members but also received some support. See Josephine S. Lowell to Carl Schurz, December 23, 1901; George F. Peabody to Carl Schurz, December 27, 1901: Schurz MSS.

70. Charles F. Adams, Jr., to Carl Schurz, April 30, 1902, and Jacob Schurman to Carl Schurz, May 3, 1902: Schurz MSS.

71. William James to Edward W. Ordway, December 6, 1903, Edward W. Ordway Collection, New York Public Library.

72. James Bryce to White, July 20, 1905, Ordway Coll.

73. Charles F. Adams, Jr., to White, January 22, 1905, copy in the Charles Francis Adams MSS, Massachusetts Historical Society.

74. White to Edward Ordway, December 23, 1905, Ordway Coll.

75. Andrew Carnegie to Theodore Roosevelt, February 5, 1905, Carnegie MSS.

76. White to Edward Ordway, January 19, March 28, 1906, Ordway Coll.

77. Charles F. Adams, Jr., to White, January 30, 1905, copy in the Charles F. Adams, Jr., MSS.

78. Charles F. Adams, "Reflex Light from Africa," *Century Magazine* 72 (1906):101–111.

79. White to Charles F. Adams, Jr., April 29, 1906, Charles F. Adams,

Jr., MSS. Speaking of his article, White warned Adams that Roosevelt "will roll it as a sweet morsel under his tongue. . . ." White was correct. Roosevelt gloated in a letter to Henry Cabot Lodge that Adams and other anti-imperialists were finally understanding his purpose abroad. Roosevelt, too, had become an admirer of Lord Cromer. Lodge sent the long letter to Adams. See Theodore Roosevelt to Henry Cabot Lodge, April 30, 1906, Charles F. Adams, Jr., MSS.

80. White to Charles F. Adams, Jr., May 1, 1905, Charles F. Adams, Jr., MSS. Not all of the former anti-imperialists agreed with this truce. Some, like Moorfield Storey, kept up their organizations and attacked the foreign policy of the Federal government until the 1920s. But that resistance was only a muted dissent after 1906.

81. White to Edward Ordway, March 28, 1906, Ordway Coll. Once the group concurred on this purpose, both Adams and Carnegie eventually contributed to its efforts. See Charles F. Adams, Jr., to White, December 13, 1906, a copy in the Charles F. Adams, Jr., MSS.

82. White to Charles F. Adams, Jr., May 1, 1906, Charles F. Adams, Jr., MSS.

83. White to Edward Ordway, April 6, 1906, Ordway Coll. The Filipino Progress Association told newspaper editors interested in publishing Dr. Doherty's reports that Doherty had Taft's "confidence and support." White to C. C. Burlingham, July 21, 1906, Ordway Coll. White even tried to get Doherty appointed to an official commission overseeing the islands. Taft turned down that application but suggested that he might find some other post for Doherty in the Philippines. William Howard Taft to White, October 20, 1906, Ordway Coll.

84. White to Carl Schurz, April 11, 1906, Schurz MSS. See also White to Edward Ordway, January 12, 1907, Ordway Coll.

85. White to Charles F. Adams, Jr., December 18, 1906, Charles F. Adams, Jr., MSS.

86. Horace White to William H. Taft, August 10, 1907, a copy with enclosure in the Ordway Coll. The committee drawing up the report for Taft consisted of White, Charles W. Eliot, Moorfield Storey, George F. Seward, Felix Adler, and James H. Blount.

87. White to Edward Ordway, October 6, 13, 1907, Ordway Coll.

88. Ibid., December 18, 1912, June 21, 1918, Ordway Coll.

89. Max Beloff, "Anti-Colonialism in American Foreign Policy," *Commentary* 24 (September, 1957):204-211. "The United States, having acquired the embryo of an empire, then set to work getting rid of it; so that the Schurzes and the Bryans now appear to have triumphed," p. 210.

90. Both standard accounts of the anti-imperialist movement end in 1900 and, thus, fail to cover the understanding worked out between Roosevelt and many of his former opponents. See Harrington, "The Anti-Imperialist Movement in the United States, 1898-1900," and Beisner, *Twelve Against Empire, The Anti-Imperialists, 1898-1900.*

17

Historian

HORACE WHITE had outlived most of his generation. None of his partners on the *Chicago Tribune* lived to see the twentieth century, and his partners on the *Evening Post* saw very little of it, for Henry Villard died in 1901, Godkin in 1902, and Schurz in 1906. White retired from active journalism in 1902 but still had more than a decade of leisure to review the past, contemplate the present, and wonder about the future.

His very survival compelled him to ponder the past. As one of a handful of men who could claim intimate knowledge of Civil War heroes, he became a minor celebrity as the semicentennials of the era began. To various historians, he gave assistance and advice; they found him a cooperative witness to the past.[1] Only regarding John Brown did he indicate some reticence. He pleaded with Oswald Garrison Villard not to "give unnecessary circulation" to his "foolishness" in 1860 in predicting "the probable success of Brown's uprising if he had taken a little more time for his preparations."[2] Before audiences in Illinois, Massachusetts, and New

York, White gladly recalled all of his experiences in the company of Abraham Lincoln.

Lincoln remained White's political idol, yet White never succumbed to a simple romantic recollection of the Republican saint. True, he advised historians to ignore base rumors of Lincoln's bastard birth, but generally he insisted that Lincoln be portrayed with both his faults and his virtues.[3] He could not forget, for example, Lincoln's pragmatic, amoral handling of political patronage. He thought that another generation would recognize a "certain degree of moral obtuseness in Abraham Lincoln."[4] He insisted, however, that none of these criticisms would ever impair the essential greatness of the man, namely, "his refusal to countenance any compromise" on the extension of slavery. "The election of Lincoln," he explained, "decided that a war which was unavoidable should take place in 1861 instead of later."[5] Fifty years had failed to alter White's view of the fratricidal war as a just and necessary conflict.

Time, however, had seriously altered his view of the postwar years. He confessed that change of mind after he finished writing the biography of his contemporary, Lyman Trumbull. Somehow everything had gone wrong after the Civil War. Perhaps allowing the Radicals to seize power was the basic mistake. Although Andrew Johnson was not his ideal leader, White admitted that he had erred in opposing Johnson. Most of White's friends agreed.

White and his fellow Mugwumps had an almost uncanny monopoly on the historical interpretation of their own era. They and their fathers may have lost control of the industrial and political machinery of the nation, but they retained control of its intellectual apparatus. They directed the major universities, the journals of opinion, and the leading publishing firms in the United States. From these bastions, they wrote and disseminated their views of the past. James

Ford Rhodes, a former Liberal Republican, and William A. Dunning, an intimate of the eastern social elite, presented the broad outlines of the Mugwump view.[6] Others filled in the details, frequently writing congratulatory biographies of their friends and condemnatory biographies of their foes.[7]

Their view of the Civil War, of Reconstruction, of the Gilded Age went unchallenged for decades; and this dominance continued despite the fact that the Mugwumps were neither objective nor impartial. Indeed, they had been important partisans of the period.[8] White had actually made his judgment on Reconstruction in the 1870s, not in 1912. He merely reaffirmed that judgment in his biography of Lyman Trumbull. He had good reason to look for validation of his views of Reconstruction in the works of Rhodes and Dunning. In writing their accounts, those younger men had used such journals as the *Nation,* the *Chicago Tribune,* and the *Springfield Republican* as reliable nineteenth-century authorities. Theirs was a mutual-admiration society.[9]

After White received his laurels from Rhodes and Dunning for his confession of errors in 1865, he was taken aback by criticism from an unexpected quarter.[10] Two forgotten men, one a former carpetbagger and another an unrepentant scalawag, challenged his glib generalizations about the Reconstruction era. The carpetbagger, James Shaw, a retired printer in Aurora, Illinois, wondered how White could accept such blatant distortions of the Republican effort in the South. None of the comments in the Trumbull biography, he claimed, fit his experience in Alabama. Frederick Bromberg, a Mobile lawyer and friend of Shaw, joined the dissent. White reacted by bringing forth his accusers: Walter Fleming, a Dunning student, and William Garret Brown, a former Harvard professor—both of them experts on Reconstruction in Alabama.[11]

After a barrage of detailed replies from the two Radical relics, White had to agree that Brown and Fleming were not impartial observers of the postwar southern scene. Admitting that "Mr. Brown's employment by Harvard University had much to do with my bias in his favor," White assured Bromberg, "I shall not make that mistake again."[12] This exchange led White to conclude that perhaps the "sins" of the Negroes and carpetbaggers "have been much magnified and lied about."[13] The reading public, however, never learned about his new wisdom.

White quietly modified other of his nineteenth-century convictions during the twentieth century. In correspondence with Henry Demarest Lloyd, he admitted the inequity of applying laissez-faire standards to labor disputes.[14] Some form of arbitration, he now felt, was needed. When the coal strike of 1902 broke out, he allowed Lloyd to use the columns of the *New York Evening Post* to advertise the viewpoint of the mine workers.[15] White also began to moderate his long held convictions on governmental regulation and banking enterprise. In step with certain large bankers after the panic of 1907, he called for the government to establish a central institution to control the nation's finances.[16] Later he also agreed to head a blue-ribbon committee appointed by Governor Charles Evans Hughes to investigate the New York securities market. After months of deliberation, he submitted a long list of recommendations for both voluntary and legislative action to correct widespread Wall Street abuses.[17]

Only a decade before, White would have condemned his new concepts as contradictions of "economic laws." The late nineteenth century, however, had not provided him with an atmosphere for rational discussion. Instead, those years provided him with a stake and position in society which compelled him to defend the status quo.[18] Fears aroused by radical reformers after 1873 eventually had dispelled his youthful idealism, transformed his tolerant view of human affairs, and negated his humanitarian impulses. As a result, he had frequently perverted his Liberal credo to satisfy the particular needs of big business. The bulk of his writings in those years left him open to warranted charges of bigotry and hypocrisy.

The prosperity and relative social calm of the Progressive period, however, allowed him to moderate his views. By accident, in 1901, civil-service reform found a champion in the presidency. Once White had made his peace with Roosevelt on overseas expansion, his only complaint involved those occasional flashes of impetuosity which were the trademark of the Rough Rider. White found even that objection removed, however, when William Howard Taft entered the White House. White admired the new breed of reformer. Reason and moderation had triumphed. Politicos and populists had temporarily disappeared; and cultivated gentlemen now occupied the White House. He could therefore turn his attention to the careful correction of the nation's economic and social problems—something which he had failed to do in the previous century. If his life was any indication, much of Progressive reform was more the result of new circumstances than of a new generation.

How dependent his moderate views were on the security of the Progressive period became obvious with the approach of World War I, when fear once more replaced reason and prejudice superseded tolerance. At first, White stood against aggressive nationalism; he joined the New York Peace Society. Horrified at the outbreak of the war, he wrote to Oswald Garrison Villard:

> The war is too horrible for words. I dread to open a newspaper. I lie awake o'nights thinking about the agony that it brings to men, women and children in other lands who have had no share in bringing it about, and can never derive any advantage from it,

but only the wounds and destruction and anguish that attend all wars. And all this comes like a thunder blast out of a clear sky. It is too dreadful.[19]

The possibility of a French defeat and a German victory soon caused White to abandon his neutrality and fears of war. When over three hundred editors and publishers of foreign language newspapers called for the cessation of American arms shipments to the Allies in the interests of peace, White could not restrain his anger. "The distinction between right and wrong should never be lost sight of in weighing the claims of neutrality," he declared in the *New York Times*. He warned the editors of the "queer publications" to guard their appeals. "Germany is the quintessence of imperialism and militarism," he insisted. "If our polygot editors do not know this fact their ignorance will naturally prompt Americans to be more careful about admitting more of them to our shores." The Civil War offered an appropriate parallel to White. He recalled for his readers the moral determination of Abraham Lincoln to wage a righteous war a half century ago. He urged them now to follow that leader's example.[20]

With these remarks, White seemed to echo the moral certitude of his youth. Yet before America entered the European conflict, his conviction crumbled. Writing to a fellow octogenarian, he documented his refreshed cynicism. He had just read a book on the European war from which he drew the quotation, "all nations are natural born fools." Recalling the disappointing aftermath of the Civil War, he wrote to Manton Marble: "Methinks . . . that you and I thought something akin to it about the Americans in 1872." Convinced that Americans had made little progress since their rejection of Liberal advice in 1872, he gave little hope for improvement in the future:

This is the day of the Preparedness parade in New York. Preparedness for what? you may ask. Preparedness to fight Germany. This is what everybody in the marching column means, although nobody knows when or how. They all intend to 'foil the foul fiends' somehow and sometime.[21]

Horace White did not live to witness the conclusion of the crusade. He died on September 16, 1916. Others would have to scorn the failures of another generation of postwar Americans.

NOTES

1. White had taken a hand in history writing in 1890 when he rewrote the chapter on the Lincoln-Douglas debates for the third edition of William Herndon's biography of Lincoln. White also played a major role in securing an eastern publisher for the work. See David Donald, *Lincoln's Herndon*, pp. 337–342.

2. White to Oswald Garrison Villard, July 29, 1908, Oswald Garrison Villard Coll., Columbia University. Villard was just one of many historians who asked White about John Brown and the free-soil operations in Kansas.

3. White had known about the suspicions of Lincoln's illegitimate birth for some time. In 1871, he learned that Leonard Swett and David Davis forced Ward Lamon to suppress any innuendo about Lincoln's parentage. Refusing to believe the rumor himself, White later convinced both Herndon and Jesse Weik to ignore the whole question. White to William Herndon, January 18, 1890, Herndon-Weik MSS. William Herndon to White, October 26, 1890, Horace White MSS. See also White to Jesse Weik, February 27, July 23, 1907, April 14, 1909, Herndon-Weik MSS.

4. White to Jesse Weik, August 12, 1914, Lincoln-Weik MSS.

5. White to J. R. B. Van Cleave, March 15, 1909, Lincoln Coll., Brown University.

6. White acknowledged his debt to Rhodes in providing a context for the biography of Trumbull. Dunning's contribution was more direct; he read the manuscript and gave White advice. White knew Dunning very well, both professionally and socially. He helped Dunning enter the

fashionable Century Club and frequently discussed the postwar era with him. White, *The Life of Lyman Trumbull*, p. vii. White to William Dunning, October 21, 1893, January 11, 1906, William A. Dunning MSS, Columbia University.

7. White urged, for example, that Frederick Bancroft prepare a multivolume edition of Carl Schurz's works as a "monument" to his old friend. In keeping with that objective, he recommended that Bancroft not publish all of Schurz's famous report to Andrew Johnson on the condition of the southern states after the Civil War. "I have lately read that report," White advised, "and I am convinced that it was a misleading document, although I did not so consider it at the time it was made." White to Frederick Bancroft, February 12, 1912, Frederick Bancroft MSS.

8. Rhodes recognized his partisanship when he wrote to E. L. Godkin in 1896: "I read your article, 'Social Classes in the Republic,' last Sunday and so consonant is it with my own views, some of them finding expression in words for the first time, that I hesitated to write you my warm approval of it, fearing that surroundings and education might have made me too glad to receive the ideas for which your cogent sentences stand." James Ford Rhodes to E. L. Godkin, November 25, 1896, Godkin MSS.

9. See the commendations of White's biography of Trumbull by Dunning and Rhodes. William A. Dunning to White, November 6, 1912, and James F. Rhodes to White, November 6, 1913, White MSS. The creation of Reconstruction myths by Liberals is discussed in John Sproat, *"The Best Men," Liberal Reformers in the Gilded Age*, pp. 29–36.

10. White's view of Reconstruction in the Trumbull biography had been challenged earlier by a son of William Lloyd Garrison. White probably expected his remarks: "Whatever the sins of the Reconstructionists, they planted the common schools in the South and imbedded the 15th Amendment in the Constitution, and while the latter is nullified and flouted now, it will stand and the nation must live up to it, as it has had to be dragged and driven to live up to the principles of the Declaration of Independence. Both are shirts of Nissus which we cannot tear from us." Francis J. Garrison to White, November 10, 1913, White MSS.

11. White to Frederick Bromberg, May 10, 1914, Frederick Bromberg MSS, University of North Carolina. Bromberg began the correspondence at the suggestion of Shaw. Shaw urged that Bromberg send White his two pamphlets on Reconstruction in Alabama. Frederick Bromberg, *The Reconstruction Period in Alabama* (Mobile, 1911).

12. White to Frederick Bromberg, May 17, 1914, Bromberg MSS. Bromberg had sent White a letter he received from Harvard president, Charles W. Eliot, deprecating the work of Brown. Charles W. Eliot to Frederick Bromberg, April 28, 1914, a copy in the White MSS. See also James Shaw to White, May 20, 1914, White MSS.

13. White to Frederick Bromberg, May 17, 1914, White MSS. Shaw

continued the correspondence, finally sending White a copy of his reminiscences in Alabama. *Aurora Daily Beacon-News*, July 31, 1915. For a biography of Shaw and excerpts of his memoirs, see Joseph Logsdon, "An Illinois Carpetbagger Looks at the Southern Negro," *Journal of the Illinois Historical Society* 62 (Spring, 1969):53–64.

14. White to Henry D. Lloyd, May 26, 1900, Henry D. Lloyd MSS, State Historical Society of Wisconsin. See also Chester Destler, *Henry Demarest Lloyd and the Empire of Reform*, p. 412. White demonstrated his new doubts when a steel strike broke out in 1901. He blamed the strike on the "consolidation of capital." He did not lash out against the strikers as he had so often done in the past. Instead he withheld judgment. *New York Evening Post*, August 5, 1901. Oswald G. Villard could not understand this neutrality. He thought that White had gone "to pieces over this strike." Villard was encouraged, however, when Rollo Ogden, in White's absence the next day, "came to our rescue . . . with a ringing editorial on the strike which had the old Evening Post flavor." Oswald Garrison Villard to Fanny Villard, August 6, 1901, Oswald Garrison Villard MSS.

15. Destler, *Lloyd*, pp. 482, 486.

16. White, *Address on the Need of a Central Bank* (delivered in New York, November 17, 1909). White to Andrew Carnegie, August 28, 1908, Carnegie MSS. See also George M. Reynolds to White, September 29, 1913; A. Barton Hepburn to White, September 27, 1909, White Family Papers.

17. *Report of the Governor's Committee on Speculation in Securities and Commodities. State of New York* (Albany, 1909). The official correspondence which White received while directing this committee can be found at New York Historical Society. The collection indicates that the committee acted in order to avoid more drastic action. See also Nelson W. Aldrich to White, April 16, 1909, and William Endicott to White, December 20, 1908; White Family Papers. For a discussion of the influences of this committee, see Joseph Dorfman, *The Economic Mind*, 3:320–321.

18. White was listed in every issue of the *Social Register* (New York, 1887–1916) published during his lifetime. Although never a millionaire, he lived comfortably. His assets at his death amounted to over $300,000. See "Horace White's Will" (New York City, Liber 1042, proved September 29, 1916), pp. 212–216.

19. White to Oswald G. Villard, August 13, 1914, Oswald G. Villard MSS.

20. White to the Editor of the *New York Times*, April 6, 1915, *New York Times*, April 7, 1915. For the full-page advertisement of the editors, see the *New York Times*, April 5, 1915. White's ambivalent peace position was shared by others in the New York Peace Society. Its secretary, W. H. Short, read White's letter and wrote him that he took "an un-

sanctified satisfaction in it." Short continued: "It is with great difficulty that I have restrained myself many times this year from saying or writing things which would be considered unneutral by a portion of our constituency." W. H. Short to White, April 8, 1915, White MSS.

21. White to Manton Marble, May 12, 1916, Marble MSS.

Bibliography

Manuscript Collections

Academic Records, Archives of Beloit College.

Adams Family Papers, Massachusetts Historical Society.

Edward Atkinson MSS, Massachusetts Historical Society.

Frederick Bancroft MSS, Columbia University.

William Barnes MSS, Kansas State Historical Society.

Thomas Bayard MSS, Library of Congress.

John Bigelow MSS, New York Public Library.

Joseph B. Bishop MSS, Harvard University.

James Blaine MSS, Library of Congress.

Samuel Bowles MSS, Yale University.

Frederick Bromberg MSS, University of North Carolina.

William Bross MSS, Chicago Historical Society.

William C. Bryant MSS (microfilm), New York Public Library.

Bryant-Godwin Collection, New York Public Library.

William Butler MSS, Chicago Historical Society.

Zachariah Chandler MSS, Library of Congress.

Aaron L. Chapin MSS, Beloit College.

Andrew Carnegie MSS, Library

of Congress.

John D. Caton MSS, Library of Congress.

A. L. Chapin MSS, Beloit College.

William Christian MSS, Chicago Historical Society.

James Freeman Clark MSS, Harvard University.

Ellery Crane MSS, Beloit Historical Society.

Edward Daniels MSS, State Historical Society of Wisconsin.

David Davis MSS, Illinois State Historical Library.

James Doolittle MSS, State Historical Society of Wisconsin.

William A. Dunning MSS, Columbia University.

Jesse Fell MSS, University of Illinois.

William P. Fessenden MSS, Library of Congress.

William P. Fessenden Family Papers, Bowdoin College.

Lyman Gage MSS, Library of Congress.

James A. Garfield MSS, Library of Congress.

William Lloyd Garrison Family Papers, Smith College.

Sidney Gay MSS, Columbia University.

Edwin L. Godkin MSS, Harvard University.

Horace Greeley Collection, New York Public Library.

Horace Greeley MSS, Library of Congress.

Murat Halstead MSS, Historical and Philosophical Society of Ohio.

Osiah M. Hatch MSS, Illinois State Historical Library.

Rutherford B. Hayes MSS, Rutherford B. Hayes Library, Freemont, Ohio.

Herndon-Weik Collection, Library of Congress.

Hermann von Holst MSS, University of Chicago.

Thaddeus Hyatt MSS, Kansas State Historical Society.

W. H. Isley MSS, Kansas State Historical Society.

William Jayne MSS, Illinois State Historical Librray.

Andrew Johnson MSS, Library of Congress.

Abraham Lincoln Collection, Brown University.

Robert Todd Lincoln Collection, Library of Congress.

Henry D. Lloyd MSS, State Historical Society of Wisconsin.

John A. Logan MSS, Library of Congress.

Hugh McCulloch MSS, Library of Congress.

Manton Marble MSS, Library of Congress.

John S. Mill MSS, Yale University

Justin Morrill MSS, Cornell University.

Bronson Murray MSS, New-York Historical Society.

Charles E. Norton MSS, Harvard University.

Edward W. Ordway Collection, New York Public Library.

John Palmer MSS, Illinois State Historical Library.

Edward L. Pierce MSS, Harvard University.

Herman Raster MSS, Newberry Library, Chicago, Illinois.

Charles Ray Collection, Chicago Historical Society.

Charles Ray MSS, Henry Huntington Library.

Whitelaw Reid MSS, Library of Congress.

Charles Robinson MSS, Kansas State Historical Society.

John A. Rockwell Papers, Henry Huntington Library.

Carl Schurz MSS, Library of Congress.

E. R. A. Seligman MSS, Columbia University.

John Sherman MSS, Library of Congress.

William Henry Smith MSS, Ohio Historical Society.

Edwin L. Stanton MSS, Library of Congress.

Edmund C. Stedman MSS, Huntington Library.

Eli Thayer MSS, Brown University.

Lyman Trumbull Family Papers, Illinois State Historical Library.

Lyman Trumbull Family Papers, Illinois State Historical Library.

Fanny Villard MSS, Harvard University.

Henry Villard MSS, Harvard University.

Henry Villard Misc. MSS, New-York Historical Society.

Oswald G. Villard Collection, Columbia University.

Oswald G. Villard MSS, Harvard University.

Elihu Washburne MSS, Library of Congress.

Henry Watterson MSS, Library of Congress.

Jesse Weik MSS, Illinois State Historical Library.

David A. Wells Collection, New York Public Library.

David A. Wells MSS, Library of Congress.

Horace White Collection, Beloit College.

Horace White Committee Papers, New York Historical Society.

Horace White Family Papers. Miss Amelia White and Mrs. John Mead Howells, the daughters of Horace White, have recently presented the bulk of these papers to the Illinois State Historical Library.

Horace White Misc. Papers, New York Public Library.

Horace White MSS, Illinois State Historical Library.
Theodore Woolsey MSS, Yale University.
Richard Yates MSS, Illinois State Historical Library.

Newspapers

Beloit Free Press, 1848, 1856–1860, 1872–1873.
Chicago Bureau, 1870–1872.
Chicago Evening Post, 1869–1872.
Chicago Inter-Ocean, 1872–1874.
Chicago Journal, 1853–1866.
Chicago Republican, 1865–1871.
Chicago Times, 1854–1874.
Chicago Tribune, 1853–1876.
Nation, 1868–1914.
New York Evening Post, 1881–1902.
New York Tribune, 1859–1874.
Springfield (Mass.), *Republican,* 1868–1876.

Other Sources

Alumni Memorial Service. Aaron Lucius Chapin, July 20, 1893. Beloit, 1893.

Ander, O. Fritiof. *Lincoln Images.* Rock Island, Illinois: Augustana College Library, 1960.

Andrews, J. Cutler. *The North Reports the Civil War.* Pittsburgh: University of Pittsburgh Press, 1955.

Angle, Paul. *Created Equal.* Chicago: University of Chicago Press, 1958.

Armstrong, William N. *E. L. Godkin and American Foreign Policy, 1865–1900.* New York: Bookman Associates, 1957.

——. "The Godkin-Schurz Feud, 1881–83, over Policy Control of the *Evening Post.*" *New York Historical Society Quarterly* 45 (January, 1964): 5–29.

Barker, Charles A. *Henry George.* New York: Oxford University Press, 1955.

Bastiat, M. Frédéric. *Sophisms of Protectionism.* Edited by Horace White. Chicago: American Free Trade League, 1869.

Bates, David H. *Lincoln in the Telegraph Office.* New York: Century Co., 1907.

Baxter, Maurice. *Orville H. Browning*. Bloomington, Ind.: Indiana University Press, 1957.

Beale, Howard K. *The Critical Year*. New York: Harcourt, Brace & Co., 1930.

Beisner, Robert L. *Twelve Against Empire: The Anti-Imperialists, 1898–1900*. New York:McGraw-Hill, 1968.

Beloff, Max. "Anti-Colonialism in American Foreign Policy." *Commentary* 14 (September, 1957) : 204-211.

Blaine, James G. *Twenty Years in Congress*. 2 vols. Norwich, Conn.: Henry Bill Publishing Co., 1884–86.

Book of Beloit. Beloit, 1936.

Brinkerhoff, Roeliff. *Recollections of a Lifetime*. Cincinnati: Robert Clarke Co., 1904.

Brock, William R. *An American Crisis: Congress and Reconstruction, 1865–1867*. New York: St. Martin's Press, 1963.

Bromberg, Frederick. *The Reconstruction Period in Alabama*. Mobile: Iberville Historical Society, 1911.

Bross, William. *The History of Chicago*. Chicago: McClure's, 1888.

Bruce, Robert V. *1877: Year of Violence*. Indianapolis: Bobbs-Merrill, 1959.

Buck, Solon J. *The Granger Movement*. Cambridge, Mass: Harvard University Press, 1913.

Catalogue of the Officers and Students of Beloit College. Beloit, 1850, 1851, 1852, 1853.

Cater, Harold D. *Henry Adams and His Friends. A Collection of His Unpublished Letters*. Boston: Houghton Mifflin, 1947.

Chapin, Aaron L. *First Principles of Political Economy*. New York: Sheldon & Co., 1880.

"Chicago in 1856." *Chicago History* 4 (Fall, 1956) : 257-285.

Cleveland, H. I. "Booming the First Republican President: A Talk with Abraham Lincoln's Friend, the Late Joseph Medill." *Saturday Evening Post* 172 (August 5, 1899) : 84–85.

Cohen, Stanley. "Northeastern Business and Radical Reconstruction: a Re-examination." *Mississippi Valley Historical Review* 46 (June, 1959) : 67–90.

Cole, Arthur C. "President Lincoln and the Illinois Radical Republicans." *Mississippi Valley Historical Review* 4 (March, 1918) : 417–436.

Congressional Directory. Washington, D.C., 1863.

Cortissoz, Royal. *The Life of Whitelaw Reid.* 2 vols. New York: Charles Scribner's Sons, 1921.

Cossa Luigi. *Taxation, Its Principles and Methods.* Edited by Horace White. New York: G. P. Putnam, 1888.

Cox, John H. and LaWanda. *Politics, Principles, and Prejudice.* Glencoe, Illinois: Free Press, 1963.

Curtis, Asher. "Personal." *The Round Table* 38 (September 25, 1891): 10–14.

Dante, Harris L. "Reconstruction Politics in Illinois, 1860–1872." Ph.D. dissertation, University of Chicago, 1950.

Davis, Granville D. "Douglas and the Chicago Mob." *American Historical Review* 54 (April, 1949): 553–556.

Destler, Chester M. *American Radicalism.* New London, Conn.: Connecticut College, 1946.

——. *Henry Demarest Lloyd and the Empire of Reform.* Philadelphia: University of Pennsylvania Press, 1963.

——. "Western Radicalism, 1865–1901: Concepts and Origins." *Mississippi Valley Historical Review* 31 (December, 1944): 335–368.

DeWitt, David M. *The Impeachment and Trial of Andrew Johnson.* New York: Macmillan Co., 1903.

Donald, David. *Lincoln's Herndon.* New York: Alfred A. Knopf, 1948.

Dorfman, Joseph. *The Economic Mind in American Civilization.* 5 vols. New York: Viking Press, 1959.

Douglas, Stephen A. *The Letters of Stephen A. Douglas.* Edited by Robert W. Johannsen. Urbana, Illinois: University of Illinois Press, 1961.

Downey, Matthew T. "The Rebirth of Reform: A Study of Liberal Republican Movements, 1865–1872." Ph.D. dissertation, Princeton University, 1963.

Duberman, Martin. *Charles F. Adams.* Boston: Houghton Mifflin, 1961.

Dunning, William A. *Reconstruction, Political and Economic, 1865–1877.* New York: Harper & Bros., 1907.

Eaton, Edward D. *Historical Sketches of Beloit College.* New York: A. S. Barnes & Co., 1928.

The Evening Post Hundredth Anniversary. New York: N. Y. Evening Post, 1902.

Fehrenbacher, Don E. *Chicago Giant.* Madison, Wisconsin: American History Research Center, 1957.

——. "The Judd-Wentworth Feud." *Journal of the Illinois State Historical Society* 45 (Autumn, 1952) : 197–211.

——. "Lincoln, Douglas and the 'Freeport Question.' " *American Historical Review* 66 (April, 1961) : 599–617.

——. "The Origins and Purpose of Lincoln's 'House Divided' Speech." *Mississippi Valley Historical Review* 45 (March, 1960): 615–643.

——. "Political Attitudes in Illinois, 1854–1860." Ph.D. dissertation, University of Chicago, 1951.

——. *Prelude to Greatness.* Stanford, California: Stanford University Press, 1962.

Ferleger, Herbert R. *David A. Wells and the American Revenue System, 1865–1870.* New York: Columbia University, 1942.

Feuss, Claude M. *Carl Schurz, Reformer.* New York: Dodd, Mead & Co., 1932.

Fine, Sidney. *Laissez Faire and the General Welfare State.* Ann Arbor Michigan: University of Michigan Press, 1956.

First Annual Report of the Trustees of Beloit College. Beloit, Wisconsin, 1849.

Grodinsky, Julius. *Jay Gould.* Philadelphia: University of Pennsylvania Press, 1957.

Hamilton, Gail. *The Biography of James G. Blaine.* Norwich, Conn.: Henry Bill Publishing Co., 1895.

Hapgood, Norman. *The Changing Years.* New York: Farrar & Rinehart, 1930.

Harlow, Ralph V. *Gerrit Smith.* New York: H. Holt Co., 1939.

——. "The Rise and Fall of the Kansas Aid Movement." *American Historical Review* 41 (October, 1935) : 1–25.

Harper, Robert S. *Lincoln and the Press.* New York: McGraw-Hill, 1951.

Harrington, Fred H. "The Anti-Imperialist Movement in the United States, 1898–1900." *Mississippi Valley Historical Review* 22 (September, 1935) : 211–230.

Haskell, Daniel. *Index to Titles and Contributors of the Nation, vols. 1–105: New York, 1865–1917*. 2 vols. New York: N. Y. Public Library, 1953.

Heckman, Richard A. *Lincoln vs. Douglas*. Washington, D.C.: Public Affairs Press, 1967.

Henderson, John B. "Emancipation and Impeachment." *Century* 85 (January, 1913) : 192–211.

Hedges, James B. *Henry Villard and the Railways of the Northwest*. New Haven, Conn.: Yale University Press, 1930.

Herndon, William, and Weik, Jesse. *Abraham Lincoln: The Story of A Great Life*. 2 vols. New York: Appleton & Co., 1892.

Hesseltine, William B. *Ulysses S. Grant, Politician*. New York: Dodd, Mead & Co., 1935.

Hinton, Richard J. *John Brown and His Men*. New York: Funk & Wagnalls Co., 1894.

Holbrook, Steward H. *The Yankee Exodus*. New York: Macmillan, 1950.

Hoogenboom, Ari. *Outlawing the Spoils*. Urbana, Illinois: University of Illinois Press, 1961.

"Illinois in 1856." *Chicago History* 4 (Summer, 1956): 225–255.

Isley, W. H. "The Sharps Rifle Episode in Kansas History." *American Historical Review* 12 (April, 1907) : 546-566.

Jackson, G. H. B. *The History of the Cobden Club*. London, 1939.

Jaffa, Harry V. *Crisis of the House Divided*. Garden City, N. Y.: Doubleday, 1959.

Jellison, Charles. *Fessenden of Maine*. Syracuse, N. Y.: Syracuse University Press, 1962.

Johnson, Samuel A. "The Emigrant Aid Company in Kansas." *Kansas Historical Quarterly* 1 (November, 1932) : 429–41.

———. "The New England Emigrant Aid Company." Ph.D. dissertation, University of Wisconsin, 1935.

Jones, Stanley L. *The Presidential Election of 1896*. Madison, Wisconsin: University of Wisconsin Press, 1964.

Josephson, Matthew. *The Politicos*. New York: Harcourt, Brace & Co., 1938.

King, Willard L. *Lincoln's Manager, David Davis*. Cambridge, Mass.: Harvard University Press, 1960.

Kinsley, Phillip. *The Chicago Tribune: Its First Hundred Years*. 3 vols. Chicago: Alfred A. Knopf, 1945.

Koerner, Gustave. *Memoirs of Gustave Koerner.* 2 vols. Cedar Rapids, Iowa: Torch Press, 1909.

Krug, Mark. *Lyman Trumbull: Conservative Radical.* New York: American Book Co., 1965.

LaFeber, Walter. *The New Empire.* Ithaca, New York: Cornell University Press, 1963.

Lalor, John J. *Cyclopedia of Political Science.* 3 vols. New York: C. E. Merrill & Co., 1881–1884.

Lamon, Ward. *Ward Lamon and the Chicago Tribune.* n.p., 1866.

Lasch, Christopher. "The Anti-Imperialists, the Philippines, and the Inequality of Man." *Journal of Southern History* 24 (August, 1958) : 319–331.

Lewellen, Fred B. "Political Ideas of James W. Grimes." *Iowa Journal of History and Politics* 42 (October, 1944) : 339–404.

Lincoln, Abraham. *The Collected Works of Abraham Lincoln.* Edited by Roy Basler and others. 9 vols. New Brunswick, N. J.: Rutgers University Press, 1953–1955.

Lindsay, Almont L. *The Pullman Strike.* Chicago: University of Chicago Press, 1942.

Lomask, Milton. *Andrew Johnson: President on Trial.* New York: Farrar, Straus & Co., 1960.

Luthin, Reinhard H. *The Real Abraham Lincoln.* Englewood Cliffs, N. J.: Prentice-Hall, 1960.

McFarland, Gerald W. "New York Mugwumps of 1884." Master's thesis, Columbia University, 1962.

McIlvaine, Mabel, ed. *Reminiscences of Chicago During the Great Fire.* Chicago: R. R. Donnelley & Sons, 1915.

McKitrick, Eric. *Andrew Johnson and Reconstruction.* Chicago: University of Chicago Press, 1960.

McWhinney, Grady, ed. *Grant, Lee, Lincoln and the Radicals.* Evanston, Illinois: Northwestern University Press, 1964.

Mallan, William D. "The Grant-Butler Relationship." *Mississippi Valley Historical Review* 46 (September, 1954) : 259–76.

Matthews, Lois Kimball. *The Expansion of New England.* Boston: Houghton Mifflin, 1909.

Memorial of Martha H. White. Chicago, 1873.

Merriam, George S. *The Life and Times of Samuel Bowles.* 2 vols. New York: Century Co., 1885.

Merrill, Horace S. *Bourbon Democracy of the Middle West, 1865–1896*. Baton Rouge: Louisiana State University Press, 1953.

——. *William Freeman Vilas*. Madison, Wisconsin: State Historical Society of Wisconsin, 1954.

Merrill, Sereno T. *Narrative of Experiences in the Life of Sereno T. Merrill*. n.p., 1900.

Milton, George F. *The Age of Hate*. New York: Coward-McCann, 1930.

Monaghan, Jay. *The Man Who Elected Lincoln*. Indianapolis: Bobbs-Merrill, 1956.

Montgomery, David. *Beyond Equality: Labor and the Radical Republicans 1862–1872*. New York: Alfred A. Knopf, 1962.

Morgan, H. Wayne, ed. *The Gilded Age: A Reappraisal*. Syracuse, New York: Syracuse University Press, 1963.

Morrow, Robert. "Emigration to Kansas in 1856." *Transactions of the Kansas State Historical Society* 8:302–315.

Murphy, Lawrence E. *Religion and Education on the Frontier, a Life of Stephen Peet*. Dubuque, Iowa: Telegraph-Herald, 1942.

Muzzey, David S. *James G. Blaine: A Political Idol of Other Days*. New York: Dodd, Mead, 1934.

National Cyclopedia of American Biography.

Newman, Ralph G. "The Douglas 'Deal' Lincoln Spurned." *Chicago Tribune Magazine* (October 4, 1964) : 20–29.

Ogden, Rollo. *Life and Letters of Edwin Lawrence Godkin*. 2 vols. New York: Macmillan, 1907.

Past Made Present, Presbyterians in Wisconsin. Milwaukee, 1901.

Pierce, Bessie L. *As Others See Chicago*, Chicago: University of Chicago Press, 1933.

——. *A History of Chicago*. From Town to City, 1848–1871, vol. 2. New York: Alfred A. Knopf, 1940.

Pringle, Henry F. *Theodore Roosevelt*. New York: Harcourt, Brace & Co., 1956.

Proceedings of the Liberal Republican Convention. New York: New York Tribune, 1872.

Proceedings of the Meeting to Memorialize Congress in Favor of

Revenue Reform Held by the Citizens of Chicago, Farwell Hall, April 2, 1870. Chicago: Chicago Free Trade League, 1870.

Quarter-Centennial Anniversary of Beloit College. Beloit, Wisconsin, 1872.

Report of the Governor's Committee on Speculation in Securities and Commodities. State of New York. Albany, 1909.

Report of the Proceedings at the Dinner of the Cobden Club, July 17, 1875. London, 1875.

Rhodes, James F. *History of the United States from the Compromise of 1850.* 8 vols. New York: Macmillan, 1900–1928.

Richardson, Robert K. *Centenary History, First Congregational Church in Beloit.* Beloit, Wisconsin, 1938.

——. "How Beloit Won Its College." *Wisconsin Magazine of History* 28 (March, 1945): 290–306.

——. "The Mindedness of the Early Faculty of Beloit College." *Wisconsin Magazine of History* 19 (September, 1935): 32–70.

——. "The Non-Sectarian Clause in the Charter of Beloit College." *Wisconsin Magazine of History* 22 (December, 1938): 127–155.

Rollins, John. "The Anti-Imperialists: A Reappraisal." Master's thesis, University of Wisconsin, 1960.

——. "The Anti-Imperialists and Twentieth Century American Foreign Policy." *Studies on the Left* 3 (1962): 9–24.

Ross, Earle D. *The Liberal Republican Movement.* New York: H. Holt & Co., 1919.

Ross, Edmund G. *History of the Impeachment of Andrew Johnson.* Santa Fe, New Mexico: New Mexico Printing Co., 1896.

Sage Leland L. *William Boyd Allison.* Iowa City, Iowa: State Historical Society of Iowa, 1956.

Salter, William. *James W. Grimes.* New York: D. Appleton & Co., 1876.

Sanborn, F. B. *The Life and Letters of John Brown.* Boston: Roberts Bros., 1885.

Schurz, Carl. *Speeches, Correspondence and Political Papers of Carl Schurz.* 6 vols. Edited by Frederick Bancroft. New York: G. P. Putnam's Sons, 1913.

Scott, Franklin W. *Newspapers and Periodicals of Illinois 1814-1879.* Collections of the Illinois State Historical Library, vol. 6 (1910).

Scripps, John L. *Life of Abraham Lincoln.* Edited by Roy P. Basler and Lloyd A. Dunlap. Bloomington, Ind.: Indiana University Press, 1961.

Semi-Centennial Anniversary of Beloit College. Beloit, Wisconsin, 1897.

Semi-Centennial Anniversary of the First Congregational Church. Beloit, Wisconsin, 1888.

Sharkey, Robert. *Money, Class and Party.* Baltimore: Johns Hopkins University Press, 1959.

Social Register. New York: Social Register Association, 1887-1916.

Sproat, John G. "Party of the Center: the Politics of Liberal Reform in Post-Civil War America." Ph.D. dissertation, University of California, 1959.

———. *"The Best Men": Liberal Reformers in the Gilded Age.* New York: Oxford University Press, 1968.

Stanwood, Edward. *James Gillespie Blaine.* Boston: Houghton, Mifflin, 1905.

Starr, Louis M. *Bohemian Brigade.* New York: Alfred A. Knopf, 1954.

Steffens, Joseph Lincoln. *The Autobiography of Lincoln Steffens.* New York: Harcourt, Brace & Co., 1931.

Strevey, Tracey E. "Joseph Medill and the *Chicago Tribune* during the Civil War Period." Ph.D. dissertation. University of Chicago, 1930.

Sumner, Charles. *Works of Charles Sumner.* 15 vols. Boston: Lee and Shepard, 1875-1883.

Tansill, Charles. *The Congressional Career of Thomas Francis Bayard, 1869-1885.* Washington, D.C.: Georgetown University Press, 1946.

Thompson, E. Bruce. "The Bristow Presidential Boom of 1876." *Mississippi Valley Historical Review* 33 (June, 1945): 3-30.

Trefousse, Hans L. *Benjamin Franklin Wade.* New York: Twayne, 1963.

———. *The Radical Republicans.* New York: Alfred A. Knopf, 1969.

Unger, Irwin. *The Greenback Era.* Princeton, N. J.: Princeton University Press, 1964.

U.S., Congress, *Congressional Globe,* 1859–1873.

U.S., Congress, House, *Depression in Labor and Business,* 45th Cong., 3d. Sess., Misc. Doc. 29.

U.S., Congress, Senate, *Report of the Select Committee on the Harper's Ferry Invasion.* 36th Cong., 1st Sess., Rept. 278.

Van Deusen, Glyndon G. *Horace Greeley.* Philadelphia: University of Pennsylvania Press, 1953.

Villard, Henry. *Memoirs of Henry Villard.* New York: Houghton, Mifflin, 1904.

Villard, Oswald G. *Fighting Years.* New York: Harcourt, Brace & Co., 1939.

——. *John Brown.* New York: Alfred A. Knopf, 1943.

Wall, Joseph F. *Henry Watterson, Reconstructed Rebel.* New York: Oxford University Press, 1956.

Washburne, Elihu. "Abraham Lincoln in Illinois." *North American Review* 141:318–319.

Watterson, Henry. "The Humor and Tragedy of the Greeley Campaign." *Century* 85 (November, 1912): 27–43.

——. *"Marse Henry": an Autobiography.* 2 vols. New York: G. H. Doran, 1919.

Weisberger, Bernard. *The American Newspaperman.* Chicago: University of Chicago Press, 1962.

——. "The Newspaper Reporter and the Kansas Imbroglio." *Mississippi Valley Historical Review* 36 (March, 1950): 633–56.

——. *Reporters for the Union.* Boston: Little, Brown and Co., 1953.

White, Horace. *Abraham Lincoln in 1854.* Springfield, Ill.: Illinois State Historical Society, 1908.

——. "An Address." *The Round Table.* 50:171.

——. Address on the Need of a Central Bank. New York, 1909.

——. "After Specie Resumption—What?" *International Review* 5 (1878): 833–846.

——. "Agriculture and the Single Tax." *Popular Science Monthly* 36 (February, 1890): 481–500.

——. "The American Centenary." *Fortnightly Review* 26 (October, 1876): 496–516.

———. "An American's Impressions of England." *Fortnightly Review* 18 (September, 1875) : 291–305.

———. "The Beginnings of Beloit." *Semi-Centennial Anniversary of Beloit College*. Beloit, Wisconsin, 1897.

———. *Coin's Financial Fool: A Reply to Coin's Financial School*. New York: J. S. Oglivie Publishing Co., 1895.

———. "Coin's Financial Fool." *Sound Currency* 2 (May 1, 1895) : 1–20.

———. *An Elastic Currency, "George Smith's Money" in the Early Northwest*. New York: The Evening Post Publishing Co., 1893.

———. "The Financial Crisis in America." *Fortnightly Review* 25 (June 1, 1876) : 810–829.

———. *The Gold Standard*. New York: The Evening Post Publishing Co., 1893.

———. "India's Action and the Sherman Bill." *Forum* 15 (August, 1893) : 649–656.

———. *The Life of Lyman Trumbull*. Boston: Houghton, Mifflin, 1913.

———. *The Lincoln and Douglas Debates*. Chicago: University of Chicago Press, 1914.

———. "Lincoln and the Tariff." *Magazine of History* Extra No. 77 (1921) : 61–63.

———. *The Monetary Issue in the United States*. Pamphlet No. 19 in the Gold Standard Defence Association Series. London, 1896.

———. *Money and Banking*. Boston: Ginn & Co., 1902.

———. "Parliamentary Government in America." *Fortnightly Review* 32 (October 1, 1879) : 505–17. Reprinted in *Library Magazine* 2 (1880) : 527–539.

———. *Plans for Monetary Reform*. New York, 1912.

———. "Present Phases of the Currency Question." *International* 4 (1877) : 730–750.

———. "Recollections of Abraham Lincoln." *Evening Post*, February 12, 1905.

———. *The Silver Coinage Question, A Review of Senator Beck's Speech*. New York: The Evening Post Publishing Co., 1886.

——. *The Silver Question.* New York: Scribner, Armstrong & Co., 1876.

——. "A Substitute for Silver." *Harper's Weekly* 37 (July 22, 1893): 698.

——. *Surplus and the Tariff.* Boston: Massachusetts Tariff Reform League, 1888.

——. "The Tariff Question." *Galaxy* 24 (October, 1877): 501–511.

——. "The Tariff Question and Its Relations to the Present Commercial Crisis." *Journal of Social Science* 9 (January, 1878) : 117–131.

——. *Third Term Politics.* New York: Independent Republican Association, 1880.

——. *Union Pacific Railroad Discriminations.* House Committee on the Pacific Railroads, 45th Cong. 2d sess.

Whitney, Henry C. *Life of Lincoln.* 2 vols. New York: Baker and Taylor Co., 1908.

Williams, T. Harry. *Lincoln and the Radicals.* Madison, Wisconsin: University of Wisconsin Press, 1941.

Woodman, Harold D. "Chicago Businessmen and the 'Granger' Laws." *Agricultural History* 36 (January, 1962) : 16–24.

Wreszin, Michael. *Osward Garrison Villard, Pacifist at War.* Bloomington, Ind.: Indiana University Press, 1965.

Index

245–246, 252; Democrats endorse, 246, 250–252; post-1872 division of, 262–263, 304, 311; compared with Mugwump success, 317–318

Liberalism: English-American connections, 139, 174, 270–271, 305, 310, 339, 355n73, 357–358; and *Chicago Tribune*, 173–175; business support for, 179; impact of Greeley on, 239–241; crisis of, 267; impact of racism on, 271

Liberty Congress, 369

Lincoln, Abraham: debates with Douglas in 1854, 21–22, 46; influence on White, 21–23, 47–48, 385, 389; 1854 Senate race of, 23–24; 1858 Senate race of, 43–61; House-Divided speech, 44; presidential election of, 59–61; assassination threat to, 66; controversy over Cabinet of, 68–70; and slavery, 65–67, 73–74, 82–83, 86–87, 89–90, 93–94; and the Radical Republicans, 98–99, 112; parentage of, 385, 390n3

Lincoln–Douglas debates, 50–55, 390n1

Lloyd, Henry D., 203, 243, 276n35, 350n9, 387

Logan, John A., 178, 217n66, 316

Lowell, Josephine, 382n69

McClellan, George, 84, 86, 88, 91

McCormick, Cyrus, 251

McCulloch, Hugh, 111, 157

McDonald, John, 181

McDougall, Amelia, 269

McKinley, William, 345–348, 359–360, 361, 366–371 passim

McVeagh, Wayne, 372

Maine, 360

Malthus, Thomas, 328, 329, 340, 349n7

Manning, William, 332–334

Marble, Manton, 135, 188n34, 221, 318, 333, 389

Marx, Karl, 264, 265, 310, 343

Matthews, Stanley, 222–226 passim, 254n15

Medill, Joseph: power within *Chi-*

cago *Tribune*, 39–40, 72, 94, 99, 106, 206, 268–269; on Freeport Question, 51–53; on 1860 compromise, 66; on Cameron, 68–70; investigates Fremont, 74; opposes Johnson, 111–112, 151, 156; disagrees with White, 116, 118, 156, 158, 325n46; on tariff, 118, 123, 126, 127, 152; on carpetbaggers, 186n10; on city taxes, 189n46; and Chicago fire, 197–199; as Chicago mayor, 201; supports Grant, 202, 215n36; opposes Liberal Republicans, 215n49; death of, 357

Medill, Samuel, 197

Merrill, Sereno T., 8

Mill, John Stuart, 174

Monitor, 88

Monopoly, 117, 159n2, 174, 337–339

Moreley, John, 277n46

Morrill, Justin, 78, 119, 132n46

Morton, J. Sterling, 341

Morton, Oliver P., 193, 203, 306

Mulligan letters, 307, 313, 315, 319, 325n46

Nation, 238, 269, 285–286, 291–292

National Kansas Committee, 28–33

Negro suffrage: *Tribune* caution on, 107–109, 112–113, 115, 128; *Tribune* endorses universal application of, 120–126, 137–141; Liberal Republicans on, 193, 241–242, 247–248, 252, 257n57; White questions, 247–248, 267, 273, 275n33, 308, 310, 360, 374–376

New England Anti-Imperialist League, 369

New England Emigrating Company, 3–4

New England Emigrant Aid Company, 28

New York Associated Press, 24, 96, 97–98, 157n2

New York Evening Post: Villard's role in, 282–285, 288–289, 299n39, 365; editorial control of, 284, 289–296, 321, 365–366, 373; financial condition of, 285, 320, 361, 364–365, 380n33; on strikes, 291–294,